D1327089

LANDOR

In the same series:

BELLOC
a biographical anthology
compiled and edited by Herbert van Thal

THE KINGSLEYS
a biographical anthology
compiled and edited by Elspeth Huxley

National Portrait Gallery

LANDOR

A Biographical Anthology

COMPILED AND EDITED BY
HERBERT VAN THAL

WITH AN INTRODUCTION BY
MALCOLM ELWIN

London
GEORGE ALLEN & UNWIN LTD
RUSKIN HOUSE   MUSEUM STREET

FIRST PUBLISHED IN 1973

© *George Allen & Unwin Ltd, 1973*

ISBN 0 04 828006 2

PRINTED IN GREAT BRITAIN
in 11 point Plantin type 1 point leaded
BY W. & J. MACKAY LIMITED, CHATHAM

DEDICATED TO
JAMES HARDING

INTRODUCTION

BY MALCOLM ELWIN

I have written two biographies of Walter Savage Landor—two full-length studies of his life and work. Each occupied three years in its writing. No fool spends on one subject more than six years of his life—more, because many months of preparatory reading were spread over other years—unless the subject is exceptional. Landor was exceptional—as extraordinary in his life as in the quality and quantity of work that he left behind him. Though he lived till his ninetieth year—longer than any English writer between Thomas Hobbes and Bernard Shaw—to be decrepit, deaf, inarticulate, nearly blind, he could still write in indignation against injustice. He died, as he had lived, an unrepentant rebel and pagan.

There is surely something magnificent in a life spent in refusal to compromise with one's sense of rectitude and justice, to conform with the conventions of a materialist society, to condone the cant and servility of expediency. So the great novelist Charles Dickens felt when, himself in the last year of his life, he remembered how as a young man he had known Landor still vigorous at seventy and reflected that his name was 'inseparably associated in the writer's mind with the dignity of generosity: with a noble scorn of all littleness, all cruelty, oppression, fraud, and false pretence'. His writings reflect the man: no writer has written English prose with more lucidity, economy, and force, and melodic eloquence only enhances clarity of meaning in his best poetry.

Hence his writings have always appealed to youth, as his personality in life appealed to the youthful Dickens; for youth has not yet learnt the arts of compromise. Swinburne was barely twenty-seven and not yet author of his sensational *Poems and Ballads*, when a few months before Landor's death in 1864, he 'hunted out the most ancient of the demi-gods' in his Florentine exile; later he wrote that Landor 'had won for himself such a double crown of glory in verse and in prose as has been worn by no other Englishman but Milton'. A generation later George Moore was thirty-three when he wrote in *Confessions of a Young Man* (1886) of how he fell 'to dreaming of the great and beautiful men and women (exalted melodies) that rise out of Landor's pages—a writer as great as

9

Shakespeare, surely? The last heir of a noble family. All that follows Landor is decadent.' In 1902 John Cowper Powys in his thirtieth year was on the threshold of his career as the most popular literary lecturer in the United States when he included Landor as fifth in a course of twelve lectures on *Representative Prose Writers of the Nineteenth Century*, and said of him: 'His character revives and restores in the midst of the nineteenth century the monumental dignity of antiquity. De Quincey and Hazlitt seemed dreamers and ineffectual aesthetes compared with this Master Intellect. Landor does not shrink from the material facts of the world but moulds them to his purpose and stamps them with his tremendous signature.'

When I first stumbled on Landor, I was even younger than these, only just opening puppy's eyes to the splendours of imaginative thought and the power of expressing them. Then fancying myself a student of drama (the subject of my first book), I realized, like Powys, that many of the *Imaginary Conversations* are 'not really dramatic' because so many of their men and women 'speak the language of Landor and utter the sentiments of Landor'. But this made the 'Master Intellect' seem the more fascinating, and I spouted of Landor with the same enthusiasm as of Shelley.

Why was he not rated 'as great as Shakespeare'? At Oxford in the 1920s I talked with only three dons who felt enthusiasm in reading Landor; of the three only one, Walter Raleigh, belonged to the 'Eng. Lit.' faculty, most of the practitioners of which regarded Landor's work as Dr Johnson said of Congreve's novel *Incognita*—they would 'rather praise it than read it.' I recognized—as Landor makes Barrow tell Newton—that 'No very great man ever reached the standard of his greatness in the crowd of his contemporaries,' but not yet that 'little minds in high places are the worst impediments to great' ('Vittoria Colonna and Michel-Angelo').

While still at Oxford I learnt the difference between knowledge and wisdom that Landor draws in 'Aristoteles and Callisthenes': 'We may know many things without an increase of wisdom; but it would be a contradiction to say that we can know anything new without an increase of knowledge.' I learnt, too, that the qualities admired by Dickens in Landor were precisely those that excited hostility against him. His very clearness puzzles and perplexes them, he makes Southey say of Wordsworth to Porson, 'and they

INTRODUCTION

imagine that straightness is distortion, as children on seeing a wand dipped in limpid and still water. Clear writers, like clear fountains, do not seem so deep as they are: the turbid look the most profound.' This explains the obscurity and diffuseness of style in most academic writers of our slipshod age: it is a mask for lack of meaning.

Even as a boy I found that, if you protest against the injustice of any institution, defenders of the Establishment will jeer, 'What would *you* put in its place?' Landor was past eighty when Emerson published *English Traits* in 1856 and reported Carlyle as having said, 'Landor's principle was mere rebellion, and *that* he feared was the American principle'. The old man retorted, 'I would eradicate any species of evil, political, moral, or religious, as soon as it springs up, with no reference to the blockheads who cry out *"What would you substitute in its place?"* When I pluck up a dock or a thistle, do I ask any such question?' He went on to tell Emerson, 'Democracy, such as yours in America, is my abhorrence. Republicanism far from it; but,' he added, as John Stuart Mill was to emphasize only five years later in *Representative Government*, 'there are few nations capable of receiving, fewer of retaining, this pure and efficient form.'

He had always proclaimed the difference between republicanism and democracy. In his first series of *Imaginary Conversations* (1824) he makes Machiavelli tell Michel-Angelo, 'Republican as I have lived, and shall die, I would rather any other state of social life, than naked and rude democracy; because I have always found it more jealous of merit, more suspicious of wisdom, more proud of riding on great minds, more pleased at raising up little ones above them, more fond of loud talking, more impatient of calm reasoning, more unsteady, more ungrateful, and more ferocious.' Who can say that he was not right in the light of history, as he has been proved right by events during the century since his death? But such views could not be popular in English-speaking countries where every politician pays lip-service to illusions of democracy.

In the imaginary conversation between Barrow and Newton, Landor asserts the detachment necessary if you are not to be a party to the world's pollution: 'the best thing is to stand above the world; the next is, to stand apart from it on any side. You *may* attain the first: in trying to attain it, you are certain of the second.'

Worldlings have condemned this attitude as arrogant, but is it arrogance to endure the poverty, persecution, and neglect that society inflicts upon those who stand aside from it?

Inclination rather than Landor's precept induced me at only twenty-three to turn my back on urban life; it seemed common sense that a scholar's life of contemplation should be lived close to Nature, especially after our statesmen's performance in suppressing the General Strike of 1926. 'To fly from, need not be to hate, mankind,' wrote Byron in *Childe Harold* (iii, 69), but, as we are told in *Pericles and Aspasia*, 'it is better to be austere than ambitious: better to live out of society than to court the worst.' I was fumbling my way to such a 'poetic faith' as Llewelyn Powys proclaimed during the 1930s in *Impassioned Clay, Damnable Opinions*, and *Glory of Life*—a creed based on that of Epicurus, so poetically epitomized in Landor's imaginary conversation, 'Epicurus, Leontion, and Ternissa,' where the old philosopher, wandering round his garden, whimsically expounds his opinions to his girl friends.

Epicurus finds 'advantage in a place at some distance from the city', where he can 'assemble and arrange my thoughts with freedom and with pleasure in the fresh air, under the open sky,' where 'the mind is soothed and satisfied', where 'we meet Nature face to face, undisturbed and solitary'. Told that people blame him because 'you live so little in public, and entertain such a contempt for opinion', he replies, 'Prove them to be wiser and more disinterested in their wisdom than I am, and I will then go down to them and listen to them.' He allows that 'what I myself follow and embrace, what I recommend to the studious, to the irritable, to the weak in health, would ill agree with the commonality of citizens', for 'my philosophy is not for the populace nor for the proud: the ferocious will never attain it'. 'Having seen that the most sensible men are the most unhappy', he examined the causes and found 'that the same sensibility to which they are indebted for the activity of their intellect, is also the restless mover of their jealousy and ambition'. Even among 'celebrated philosophers' he found 'a love of domination, a propensity to imposture, a jealousy of renown, and a cold indifference to simple truth'.

So he was moved to ask himself, 'What is the most natural and the most universal of our desires?' The answer was '*to be happy*', and he found it wonderful 'that the gratification of a desire which is at once the most universal and the most natural, should be the seldomest attained'. Landor then puts into his mouth the Epicurean philosophy he so often summarized: 'To be wise indeed and happy and self-possessed, we must often be alone: we must mix as little as we can with what is called society, and abstain rather more than seems desirable even from the better few.'

The story of Landor's life shows that he practised the precepts of his philosophy, but did he attain the happiness that he regarded as the prime object of life? Given his temperament and his philosophy, he could not with integrity have lived otherwise than he did; but in a materialist's view his life was a failure, for he inherited wealth and ended in poverty.

While cutting my biographical teeth on simpler subjects, I recognized that Landor had been unfortunate in his biographers. For both John Forster and Sidney Colvin were materialists.

Of Forster I wrote a study in *Victorian Wallflowers*, treating him more sympathetically than he deserved. A grammar-school boy who depended on an uncle's bounty for the means to study law at London University, he entered literary journalism while still a student and busily cultivated every celebrity with whom he could scrape acquaintance. Many he offended by his blustering self-assertion: 'Heavens preserve us from a monster of the name of Forster,' exclaimed a friend of Charles Lamb's when Lamb died and Forster was considered among his possible biographers. But 'he had a knack of making people do as he liked, whether they liked it or not', said Harrison Ainsworth. His energy, pertinacity, and zeal enabled him to be useful to those who could be useful to him; he showed shrewd judgment in becoming an indispensable friend to three of the most popular contemporary novelists, Dickens, Bulwer Lytton, and Ainsworth, and to the rising poet Browning.

He was equally clever in using his elders. Not long before his death in 1834 Charles Lamb remarked to Forster of Landor's *Citation and Examination of William Shakespeare* that only two men could have written it, 'he who wrote it, and the man it was written on'. Taking the hint, Forster reviewed this minor work of Landor's as 'a book of remarkable genius—an honour to the age'. Landor was then still living in Italy, but soon after leaving his wife and family he settled at Bath and came to London to be lionized at

Lady Blessington's salon in the spring of 1836 on the publication of *Pericles and Aspasia*. This remarkable epistolary novel offered finer material for Forster's applause, and the pushing young man was soon enabled to record his impression on meeting Landor at sixty-one: not above middle height, he 'had a stout stalwart presence' and 'walked without a stoop' with decidedly 'a distinguished bearing'; silvered hair receded from 'the broad white massive head,' with 'strangely-lifted eyebrows' above 'large gray eyes' that reflected the expressions of a mobile mouth—'the lips that seemed compressed with unalterable will would in a moment relax to a softness more than feminine, and a sweeter smile it was impossible to conceive.'

While Landor gave him some useful introductions, notably to Lady Blessington, Forster repaid him amply over twenty years by successfully launching all his books and opening the columns of the weekly *Examiner*, of which he was literary editor, to shrewd and far-sighted comments on contemporary politics that might otherwise have remained unprinted by more timid editors. He also introduced Dickens to Landor, who declared unbounded admiration for the author of *Pickwick Papers* and read all his novels as they came out. This friendship had a dubious effect on Landor's reputation, as Dickens caricatured him as Boythorn in *Bleak House*.

The two young men made a practice of travelling to Bath to dine with Landor and of staying the night near his lodgings. It was on one of the last of these visits, when Dickens and Forster had left him after celebrating his seventy-fourth birthday on 30 January 1849, that Landor wrote one of the best-known quatrains in English poetry, his 'Dying Speech of an Old Philosopher':

> I strove with none, for none was worth my strife:
> Nature I loved, and, next to Nature, Art:
> I warm'd both hands before the fire of Life;
> It sinks; and I am ready to depart.

Less than two years later, when Dickens began to write *Bleak House*, he drew upon his impressions of Landor in his late sixties and early seventies when making Jarndyce describe Boythorn in the novel as 'a tremendous fellow . . . with his head thrown back like an old soldier, his stalwart chest squared, his hands like a clean blacksmith's, and his lungs!—there's no simile for his lungs. Talking, laughing, or snoring, they make the beams of the house shake. . . . But it's the inside of the man, the warm heart of the man, the fresh blood of the man. . . . His language is as sounding as his voice. He is always in extremes; perpetually in the superlative degree.'

Forster acknowledged that Dickens drew in Boythorn only a few of Landor's 'many attractive and original qualities, omitting all the graver', but when he came to write Landor's biography, published in 1869, he saw Landor always in caricature as Boythorn throughout all the sixty years before he knew him. Moreover, the lovableness of Boythorn in *Bleak House* is tainted by the change in Forster himself from the ebullient young careerist to the pompous materialist caricatured by Dickens as Podsnap in *Our Mutual Friend*. Forster could no longer regard Boythorn's eccentricities with tolerant affection, for his own life had become absorbed in that materialism of Podsnappery against which Landor had rebelled and protested throughout his long life.

When Landor's impetuosity involved him in a libel action six years before his death, Forster was concerned primarily with escaping from the embarrassment of his responsibility, his advice betraying the old man into a last exile of poverty and dependence. In the same year as his betrayal of Landor his want of sympathy with Dickens in separating from his wife revealed his insensibility of spiritual and sexual problems. Landor left his wife because she had become a termagant, who regularly abused him in the presence of his children and servants, played upon the children's affections to engage their sympathy for herself, and had already excited their eldest son's antagonism against his father. As he confided to his friend Southey, that his children 'might not hear every day such language as no decent person should ever hear once, nor despise both parents, I left the only delight of my existence'. He also left them with three-quarters of his income.

Forster, like Podsnap, took it upon himself to speak with 'the Voice of Society'. He himself married a rich widow late in life and proved a domineering husband. Disbelieving Landor and disregarding the evidence, he concluded that 'the more he condemns what had become unbearable by himself, the more he condemns himself for having left his children exposed to it'. He could not conceive that a woman might be more tolerant as a mother than as a wife, nor that children might be damaged by an upbringing in the unhappiness of dissension. Accordingly he 'quit the subject' as 'a very disagreeable one', having said enough to show that Landor's domestic tragedy—as Podsnap said of poverty—'will render you cautious how you fly in the face of Providence'.

The effect of Forster's condescension to his subject appeared when Sidney Colvin, commenting on Forster's facts without independent research, published in 1881 his study of Landor in the long popular 'English Men of Letters' series. 'Did Landor then really . . . feel very deeply the breaking up of his beautiful Italian home or not?' he asked: 'A few years before he could not bear his children to be out of his sight even for a day; did he suffer as we should have expected him to suffer at his total separation from them now?' Smugly he concluded, without regard for evidence or even for Landor's own comments, that 'the injury done to his children by leaving them subject to no discipline at such an age and in such surroundings, would appear hardly to have weighed on Landor's mind at all, and that it failed to do so is, I think, the most serious blot upon his character.'

It is not surprising to find that Colvin's own matrimonial experience, like Forster's, came to him late in life. He was fifty-eight when he married the widow who, when separated from her first husband, had encouraged romantic attentions from Robert Louis Stevenson as a young man. As editor of Stevenson's letters, he could not have read those addressed to his wife—as Somerset Maugham said of Mrs Barton Trafford's husband in his satirical novel, *Cakes and Ale*—'with unmixed feelings', and on reading the published letters, Henry James felt uneasily 'the vague sense of omissions and truncations—one *smells* the things unprinted'. How much was left unprinted appeared when I used the original letters in my book, *The Strange Case of Robert Louis Stevenson*, 1950.

Discretion, both as a curator of museums and in his services to literature, earned Colvin a knighthood in his old age. He was too discreet to be honest and therefore ill-equipped to write the biography of a man who always preferred honesty to self-interest. Of the libel case that drove Landor into his last exile, Forster's account inspired from Colvin an interpretation 'which could not but make those who loved and honoured him regret that he had not succumbed earlier to the common lot'—a contemptibly callous comment from a biographer upon his subject's attempt, however ill-considered, to expose the exploitation of a girl by a much older woman. Smugly the future Sir Sidney consoled himself that 'it is the work and not the life of a man like Landor which in reality most concerns us'.

He was refuted by Landor himself. 'With great writers whether in poetry or prose, what falls away is scarcely more or other than a vesture,' he wrote in the imaginary conversation, 'Andrew Marvel and Bishop Parker'; 'The features of the man are imprinted on his works.' A man's work is the outcome of his life and character; as of cause and effect, a study of the one inevitably leads to a study of the other.

Begun in 1937, my first biography of Landor was published in New York in 1941, when the war-time paper shortage prevented publication of such a long book in England. At the end of the war I placed my materials at the disposal of Professor R. H. Super of Michigan, who nine years later published in 1954 his *Walter Savage Landor: A Biography*, a massive work in the manner fashionable among American scholars, with one-fifth of its length devoted to source references, but so far surpassing even Forster in deprecating the eccentricities of Landor's character and conduct as to offer a Boythorn caricature dimmed and darkened by detail. So I spent another three years in absorbing the sixteen volumes of Landor's works in the edition by T. Earle Welby and Stephen Wheeler while writing my second biography, *Landor: A Replevin*, so called because it attempts to recover Landor's character from misrepresentation and his work from neglect.

Perhaps Americans must feel unsympathetic towards a writer who declared that 'Democracy is the blubbery spawn begotten by the drunkenness of aristocracy' ('The Benefits of Parliament'), for they resent criticism of a system devised by Jefferson for government of thirteen pioneering colonies and since applied to administration of one of the three most densely populated federal unions in the world. With almost pained astonishment, Professor Ernest Dilworth in his *Walter Savage Landor* (1971) remarks that Landor's 'was truly a life rather than a career'. The living of life for its own sake is not to be commended in an age when culture passes from O-levels and A-levels, scholarships and grants, to degrees, awards, and doctorates. All his life Landor was a rebel against conformity. At sixteen he was expelled from Rugby for insubordination and

'subversive influence', and so enabled to cultivate his lifelong
appreciation of Latin and Greek under a scholarly tutor in the
beautiful Derbyshire dales. At nineteen he was rusticated from
Oxford for an impetuous prank, refused to return to submit himself
to the examiners, and taking refuge in Wales from his father's
wrath, lost his chance of marrying an heiress by involving himself
with the heroine of the beautiful elegy, beginning, 'And thou too,
Nancy!--why should Heaven remove'.

As he remarks in the imaginary conversation, 'Florentine,
English Visitor, and Landor,' 'Had avarice or ambition guided me,
remember I started with a larger hereditary estate than those of
Pitt, Fox, Canning, and twenty more such. . . . My education, and
that which education works upon or produces, was not below
theirs: yet certain I am that, if I had applied to be made a tide-
waiter on the Thames, the minister would have refused me.' The
reason lay in his revolutionary sympathies. His *Moral Epistle to
Earl Stanhope*, published when he was only twenty, shows that his
attitude to the war against revolutionary France was much the same
as that of Coleridge and Wordsworth, whose opinions were considered so subversive that a government spy was sent down to
Somerset to report on their private lives. With the left-wing Whigs
under Charles James Fox he believed that William Pitt's 'court war'
from 1793 to 1802 was 'necessary to create that danger in the
midst of which all clamours for reform were to be stifled' and
'succeeded in nothing but in preventing the demolition of the
French monarchy', since 'a sense of common danger united all
parties in France' under the 'more formidable dynasty' of
Napoleon.

When the French threatened invasion during the winter of
1796–7, he was inspired to write his epic poem, *Gebir*, to exhibit
'the folly, the injustice, and the punishment of Invasion, with the
calamities which must ever attend the superfluous colonization of a
peopled country'. Before 1802 he resorted to anonymity in ex-
pounding unpopular principles in English and Latin verse, and still
thought of playing a part in politics. But he abandoned thought of a
political future when fear of Napoleon as emperor induced many of
his former sympathizers to unite in support of the war; he despised
Fox for collaborating with Pitt because 'I detested his abandon-
ment of right principles in a coalition with a minister he had just

before denounced'. As he makes Anaxagoras write in *Pericles and Aspasia*, he had to avoid expression of 'perilous doctrines' for which 'the citizens would have poisoned or stoned me'. He had good reason to believe, as he caused Diogenes to tell Plato, that 'Those who are born for the benefit of the human race, go but little into it: those who are born for its curse, are crowded'.

While pursuing his studies in rural seclusion, he often visited such watering places as Bath and Clifton, where he met the heroines of the graceful amatory verse included in his poetry of that period. The Ianthe of his poems is identified as Sophia Jane Swift, who became Countess de Molandé by a second marriage, but he was probably as fastidious in choosing as he was chivalrous in concealing several amours. In 1808 he served briefly in Spain as a volunteer when Napoleon invaded that country, returning home in disgust at the vacillating policy of the governor of Gibraltar eventually resulting in the disaster of Sir John Moore's retreat to Corunna.

Master of his inheritance after his father's death in 1805, he sold his Staffordshire property to purchase the beautiful Vale of Llanthony in Monmouthshire, where he hoped to develop a model estate and to build a house on a site with a superb view. But the Welsh peasantry resented the intrusion of a 'foreigner' and carried on a guerrilla warfare of petty crime against him, while he was subjected to systematic plunder by a cabal of lawyers and land agents. In 1814 he took refuge on the continent to avoid trial for libel brought by an attorney whose conduct he seems to have described justly but injudiciously.

He was not the man to humble himself under reproach, so perhaps that explains why the first of his four children was not born till seven years after his marriage in 1811 to a pretty girl of good birth but no fortune. Having married a reputedly rich landed proprietor, she had reason for disappointment on finding that her home was in lodgings while a half-built house made little progress in the Welsh mists, and that after three years she must share her husband's self-banishment abroad. Discreet about his married life as about his earlier amours, he wrote only enough to explain his decision to leave his wife and children after twenty-four years of married life, apart from some hints on his domesticity in 'Andrew Marvel and Bishop Parker'.

Through twenty years of exile at Florence and Fiesole he wrote incessantly; five volumes of *Imaginary Conversations* were published between 1824 and 1829. Throughout the rest of his long life he continued productive—through twenty years of celibate retirement at Bath and through those last six years of second self-banishment which Colvin impertinently regretted and which I have described in a chapter with a title stolen from Lawrence, 'Twilight in Italy'.

'Poetry was always my amusement, prose my study and business,' he wrote at seventy-eight in the autobiographical conversation, 'Archdeacon Hare and Walter Landor' (1853): 'I have Publisht five volumes of *Imaginary Conversations*: cut the worst of them thro the middle, and there will remain in this decimal fraction quite enough to satisfy my appetite for fame.' This is not enough: it must be remembered that his reputation in early life rested on his poetry, which offers much more of beauty and melody worthy of inclusion in anthologies besides the well-known 'Rose Aylmer' and 'Dirce'. Reviewing the first collected edition of Landor's works in 1846, De Quincey wrote: 'He is a man of great genius, and, as such, he *ought* to interest the public. More than enough appears of his strong, eccentric nature through every page of his now extensive writings to win, amongst those who have read him, a corresponding interest in all that concerns him personally,—in his social relations, in his biography, in his manners, in his appearance. . . . His moral nature, shining with coloured light through the crystal shrine of his thoughts, will not allow of your forgetting it.'

On finishing *Landor: A Replevin*. I proposed to edit a selection of Landor's poetry and prose, arranged chronologically with linking narrative comments, showing the development of the mind and work of 'a writer as great as Shakespeare surely'. Unluckily my publishers were discouraging. Now Herbert van Thal has enjoyed better luck and shown better judgment. An editor of long and varied experience, he was more than forty years ago, like myself, a student of drama, who has grown in appreciation of Landor's greatness and seen for himself the need for a chronological arrangement of a representative anthology.

His choice is not always what mine would have been. I would have liked 'Andrew Marvel and Bishop Parker' for Landor's comments on his own marriage in discussing Milton's *Treatise on*

INTRODUCTION

Divorce, 'Middleton and Magliabechi' for its controversial arguments on religion, the two Ciceros because their dialogue was admired by both Hazlitt and Wordsworth, 'Barrow and Newton' for its many pungent pronouncements, e.g. 'I should entertain a mean opinion of myself, if all men or the most part praised and admired me: it would prove me to be somewhat like them'; 'Never hate, never dislike men, for difference of religion'; 'Money is like muck; not good except it be spread'; 'At every step we take to gain the approbation of the wise, we lose something in the estimation of the vulgar.' Yet I should hesitate to substitute any one of these for 'Southey and Porson', 'Washington and Franklin', 'Diogenes and Plato', or 'Epicurus, Leontion, and Ternissa', all of which are here.

I pleaded for inclusion of 'Pitt and Canning' as peculiarly appropriate to our own times, for Stanley Baldwin might well have advised any one of his ministerial successors as the dying Pitt advised Canning: 'Employ men of less knowledge and perspicacity than yourself, if you can find them. Do not let any stand too close or too much above; because in both positions they may look down into your shallows and see the weeds at the bottom.' Adoption of this advice leads in progression to the outcome, described in 'Marvel and Parker', of 'Little men in lofty places, who throw long shadows because our sun is setting'.

Asked to suggest what could be omitted to admit 'Pitt and Canning', I could suggest only the much shorter 'John of Gaunt and Joanna of Kent' because, as a purely dramatic dialogue, it is inferior to 'Henry VIII and Anne Boleyn', which so dramatically damns the caprice of dictators, to 'Leofric and Godiva', which mingles poetry with its drama, and to 'Lady Lisle and Elizabeth Gaunt', which tragically illustrates how much heroism and martyrdom has resulted from treachery and injustice.

The truth is that Landor is indeed comparable with Shakespeare in his fertility, variety, and excellence, and any anthology must omit much that every reader will regret. Within the limit of its space, Herbert van Thal's selection can hardly be faulted: it presents a splendid anthology of Landor's work against the background of his life and mind's development.

MALCOLM ELWIN

Putsborough Sands
June 1972

EDITOR'S NOTE

It should be made quite clear that this book does not pretend to shed new light on Landor as a person, nor does it contain an evaluation of his work. No great writer of English has suffered so much from critical neglect as has Landor. His works are entirely out of print, and other than Mr Elwin's biography of Landor and that of his predecessor, Robert Super,[1] no major critic has given a thought to Landor.

The purpose of the present volume is to give an outline of Landor's life and works in one volume—an almost impossible task, since he was active until the last months of his eighty-nine years. Therefore, only a tithe from his works could possibly be included, as can be seen from studying the check list of his works included in this volume. Most of the work chosen has been taken from the *Imaginary Conversations* for the simple reason that it has always been recognized as Landor's principal work, as well as the medium in which he best expressed himself and enjoyed working. That many other of his important works are reduced to 'snippets' is much to be regretted. There was little alternative if this book be kept within reasonable length.

I am indebted to my wife for her assidious help in correcting these proofs.

H.V.T.

1972

[1] *Landor*: New York 1954.

'Few men have ever impressed their pen so much, or the general public so little as Walter Savage Landor.'

Sir Sidney Colvin

'Nowhere in the range of the English language are the glory and happiness of moderation of mind more nobly preached and illustrated than in the writings of this most intemperate man; nowhere is the sacredness of the placid life more hallowed and honoured than in the utterances of this tossed and troubled spirit; nowhere are heroism and self-sacrifice and forgiveness more eloquently adored than by this intense and fierce individuality, which seemed unable to forget for an instant its own claims, its own wrongs, its own fancied superiority over all its fellow-men.'

Lord Houghton, *Monographs*, 1873.

'He was one of the most quarrelsome men who ever lived.'

Professor Simmons, *Southey*, p. 134

'As a writer of prose none has surpassed him.'

Ernest de Selincourt

'I thought of you last night, my editor from Harper's was here for dinner, we were going over his story-of-my-life and we came to the story of how I dramatized Landor's "Aesop and Rhodope" for the "Hallmark Hall of Fame". Did I ever tell you that one? Sarah Churchill starred as Landor's dewy-eyed Rhodope. The show was aired on a Sunday afternoon. Two hours before it went on the air, I opened the *New York Times* Sunday book review section, and there on page 3 was a review of a book called *A House is Not a Home* by Polly Adler, all about whorehouses, and under the title was the photo of a sculptured head of a Greek girl with a caption reading: "Rhodope, the most famous prostitute in Greece". Landor had neglected to mention this. Any scholar would have known Landor's Rhodope was the Rhodopis who took Sappho's brother for every dime he had but I'm not a scholar. I memorized Greek endings one stoic winter but they didn't stay with me. So we were going over this anecdote and Gene (my editor) said, "Who is Landor?" and I plunged into an enthusiastic explanation—and Gene shook his head and cut in impatiently: "You and your Olde English books!" '

Helene Hanff, 84 Charing Cross Road, p. 82

LIST OF LANDOR'S PUBLICATIONS

The Poems of Walter Savage Landor, 1795

Moral Epistle, Respectfully Dedicated to Earl Stanhope, 1795

To the Burgesses of Warwick, 1797

Gebir, 1798; 2nd edition, 1803

Poems from the Arabic and Persian, 1800

Iambi (? 1802)

Poetry by the Author of Gebir, 1802

Gebirus, 1803

Simonidea, 1806

Latin Idyls and Alcaics (? 1807)

The Dun Cow, 1808

Hints to a Junta (? 1808)

Three Letters, Written in Spain, to Don Francisco Riquelme, 1809

Ode ad Gustavum Regem, 1810

Letters to Sir Francis Burdett, 1810

Count Julian, 1812

Commentary on Memoirs of Mr. Fox, 1812

Address to the Freeholders of Monmouthshire, 1812

Letters addressed to Lord Liverpool, and The Parliament, on the Preliminaries of Peace, by Calvus, 1814

Letter from Mr. Landor to Mr. Jervis, 1814

Idyllia Nova Quinque Heroum atque Heroidum, 1815

Sponsalia Polyxenae, 1819

Idyllia Heroica Decem, 1820

Poche Osservazioni, 1821

Imaginary Conversations of Literary Men and Statesmen, 2 vols., 1824; 2nd edition, 1826

Imaginary Conversations of Literary Men and Statesmen, vol. 3, 1828

Imaginary Conversations of Literary Men and Statesmen, Second Series, 2 vols., 1829

Gebir, Count Julian, and Other Poems, 1831

Citation and Examination of William Shakespeare, 1834

Pericles and Aspasia, 2 vols., 1836; American edition, 1839.

Letters of a Conservative, 1836

A Satire on Satirists, 1836

Terry Hogan, An Eclogue, 1836

The Pentameron and Pentalogia, 1837

Andrea of Hungary, and *Giovanna of Naples,* 1839

Fra Rupert, 1840

To Robert Browning, 1845

The Works of Walter Savage Landor, 2 vols., 1846

Poemata et Inscriptiones, 1847

The Hellenics of Walter Savage Landor, 1847; new edition, enlarged, 1859

Imaginary Conversation of King Carlo-Alberto and the Duchess Belgioioso, on the Affairs and Prospects of Italy, 1848

The Italics of Walter Savage Landor, 1848

Carmen ad Heroinam, 1848

Savagius Landor Lamartino, 1848

Epistola ad Romanos, 1849

Statement of Occurrences at Llanbedr, 1849

Two Poems, 1850 (attacking J. G. Lockhart, editor of the *Quarterly Review*)

Popery: British and Foreign, 1851

On Kossuth's Voyage to America, 1851

Tyrannicide, 1851

Imaginary Conversations of Greeks and Romans, 1853

Two Poems, 1853

Last Fruit Off an Old Tree, 1853

Letters of an American, mainly on Russia and Revolution, 1854

Antony and Octavius. Scenes for the Study, 1856

Letter from W. S. Landor to R. W. Emerson, 1856

Walter Savage Landor and the Honourable Mrs. Yescombe, 1857

Mr. Landor Threatened, 1857; 2nd edition, 1857

Dry Sticks, Fagoted by Walter Savage Landor, 1858

Mr. Landor's Remarks on a Suit preferred against him, 1859

Savonarola e Il Priore di San Marco, 1860

Letters of a Canadian, 1862

Heroic Idyls, 1863

CONTENTS

CONTENTS

Landor was born at Warwick on 30 January 1775, the eldest son of Dr Walter Landor and his second wife Elizabeth, née Savage, of Tachbrooke. There were three other sons of the marriage, Charles (b. 1777) who became a parson, Henry Eyres (b. 1780), a lawyer and land-agent, and Robert Eyres (b. 1781) who, as well as being Rector of Birlingham, was a distinguished writer, although little remembered today. There were also three daughters, Elizabeth (b. 1776), Mary Anne (b. 1778) and Ellen (b. 1782) none of whom married.

When he was four years old, Landor was sent to school at Knowle, some ten miles from Warwick, remaining there until he was ten, when it was decided to send him to Rugby, where Dr James was then head-master. Forster describes the headmaster as a 'Scholar of fair repute'. He was a hard man, who it was said delighted in caning his pupils, and although James was proud of Landor and appreciated his mind, Landor disliked him. Landor's characteristics were now beginning to assert themselves, among them a dislike of competition. Already he had shown his proficiency in Latin verse, and awards were made on half-days for such verse. Only too well aware of his own qualifications, he was annoyed when he was not chosen and therefore imagined that the headmaster had a grudge against him. Landor took further offence when the headmaster chose some of his verse which Landor thought was his worst, so he added to his 'fair copy' some insulting remarks. Dr James therefore asked for his removal, at which time Landor was sixteen and within five places of head of the school.[1] He then became a pupil with the Reverend William Langley, rector of Fenny Bentley and head-master of Ashbourne Grammar School. He liked him, and in later years recorded his appreciation of him in an 'Imaginary Conversation' between Izaak Walton, Cotton and Oldways, where Langley is remembered as the good parson of Ashbourne.

Landor was soon to become the enfant terrible *at home. When friends of the family were in the house, his father would send him out of*

---

[1] In his *Simonidea*, fifteen years later, Landor published a Latin poem on James's death, a rather uncertain mixture of praise, blame, regret and jest, the Preface to which commemorated his reconciliation with the doctor during one of Landor's frequent visits to the home of Fleetwood Parkhurst. 'I called on [James] while he was living at Upton, and of my own accord offered him my right hand, which he freely accepted.' [Super, *Landor*, p. 10.]

the room because of the violence with which he expressed his opinions. Like De Quincey, he was impatient to grow up, to be rid of pedantic authority and to be independent.[1] He was growing into an extremely handsome young man of fine and imposing physique, as attractive to women as he was attracted to them.

He matriculated and entered Trinity College, Oxford, on 13 November 1792, going into residence the following January. His tutor, Dr Benwell, was delighted with his scholarship. Landor was under no delusion as to his own abilities, considering that he wrote better Latin verse 'than any other undergraduate'. His rebellious attitude, however, continued to assert itself, for he was becoming impatient of academic methods. Sartorially he had no interest in his person and refused to wear his hair powdered.[2] He was such a tremendous individualist that all his life he enjoyed swimming against the tide of accepted opinion, yet cared not at all whether he was successful, as is proved by the fact that none of his published works made him any money.

Oxford lasted precisely a year. It was in the autumn of 1794 that Landor, hearing a good deal of ribaldry coming from the room opposite his own, occupied by a student whom he disliked simply because he was an 'obnoxious Tory', seized his 'fowling piece' and fired several shots at the window. Luckily the shutters of the windows were closed, and no harm was done. An enquiry was made and Landor refused to give any explanation about the affair, with the result that he was rusticated. His father heard of the matter and, not unnaturally, was extremely angry. Landor then took himself off to Tenby for the summer, where he experienced his first love affair with a blonde girl called Nancy Evans, to whom he wrote some of his earliest love poems. He called her 'Ione'. This matter also came to the ears of his father, so Landor took himself off to London, where he lodged at 38 Beaumont Street, Portland Place.

The year 1795 saw Landor's work in print for the first time; it was a volume of poems of which he himself paid the publishing costs. Like so many authors who wish to forget their early ventures, he subsequently

---

[1] Elwin, *Landor*, p. 43.
[2] Southey, who had entered Balliol at the same time as Landor entered Trinity, though they never met while at Oxford, protested at Pitt's powder-tax which had been imposed in 1786, and also wore his hair unpowdered. Southey recorded, 'As our hall is repairing, and in the room appropriated for eating, Liberty and Equality are prevalent.' One is tempted to wonder whether Landor would have taken different steps had he then met Southey and his new friend Coleridge. Would he, too, have been rapt in visions of Pantisocracy?

disowned 'prentice work. In the same year he published anonymously a twenty-page pamphlet, Moral Epistle, *written in heroic verse and addressed to Earl Stanhope.*[1] *It was a satire condemning Pitt's government for trying to suppress liberal influences which favoured the French Revolution.*

[1] Lord Stanhope was an outstanding statesman of his day, and was both politician and scientist. He was elected for Chipping Wycombe through Lord Shelburne's influence in 1780. He advocated the cessation of the American War, and he called for parliamentary reform in 1781. He was against the coalition of Fox and North, and in 1786 he opposed Pitt's proposals for a sinking fund; he also disagreed with Pitt on the French Revolution. He himself published a paper in 1792 on the treatment of negroes in Paris, and in 1794 moved an acknowledgement of the French Republic. He was frequently caricatured by Gillray, and his house was set on fire by rioters in 1794.

From *Moral Epistle*

Respectfully Dedicated to Earl Stanhope, 1795.

Yet O the pleasures! when mid none but friends
The trusty secret where it rises ends:
At which no hireling politician storms.
No scoring rector catches, and *informs*!
Now, even Friendship bursts her golden hand,
Kens one with caution ere she shakes one's hand;
No longer gives she that accustom'd zest
Which made luxurious e'en the frugal feast;
Nor hold we converse, in these fearful days,
More than the horses in your lordship's chaise.
Yet wine was once almighty! silent care
Fill'd high his bowl, and laugh'd at poor Despair;
Wine bade his wand'ring heart with alien warmth expand.
But—honest minister or sound divine—
He lies who tells us now there's truth in wine.
For George's premier, never known to reel,
Drinks his two bottles, Bacchus at a meal.

1798

It was now felt that Landor might settle down with Dorothea Lyttelton, a friend of her sister Elizabeth, and an heiress who lived with two rich bachelor uncles. Landor had been corresponding with her and realized that she was not indifferent to him. It was also thought by the family that he would now take up a profession. This he had no intention of doing, and he announced to Dorothea that he proposed going to Italy to seek a fortune, a plan of which she did not at all approve. When Landor was eighty he told John Forster, his biographer, '. . . if I had been independent I should have married this lovely girl. My future property was equal to hers, my expectations greater. But, having nothing, I would not ask the hand of one to whom something would be given by her Uncle, who loved me heartily.'[1]

Landor left London and went to Wales, where he met the Honourable Rose Whitworth Aylmer, the daughter of Lord Aylmer. His love for her lasted all his life. She, however, sailed with an aunt for India in 1798, where, within two years, she died of cholera. It was, however, through Rose that Landor came to write the first work that was to give him recognition among his contemporaries. She had lent him, from Swansea Public Library, a book of stories by the 'Gothic' novelist Clara Reeve,[2] The Progress of Romance, *which included the story 'The History of Charoba, Queen of Egypt'. It was from this that Landor derived his inspiration for his poem* Gebir. *It was published in 1798. Southey, who was to become one of his greatest admirers, reviewed the work most enthusiastically in the* Critical Review *for September 1799. Southey told Coleridge about the poem. After reading it, Coleridge shared Southey's opinion. There were others who thought just as highly of the work, including Henry Carey, the translator of Dante and a close friend of Landor at Oxford. The plot is a very fanciful one. At first Landor was prepared to write it in Latin (he*

[1] Forster, *Landor*, vol. i, p. 63.
[2] Clara Reeve's [1729–1807] principal work was *The Old English Baron* (1777). The story in question, The History of Charoba, Queen of Egypt, was taken from *L'Egypte de Murtadi*, translated from the Arabic by Pierre Vattier, Paris, 1663; or perhaps she had only seen an English translation of Vattier's book brought out by John Davies of Kidwelly in 1672. Other versions of the legend are given by Ali Abul Hasayn, called Mas'udi, and in a work translated from the Arabic by Baron Carra de Vaux under the title *L'Abrégé des Merveilles*, Paris 1898. [1st edition note to *Gebir*.]

subsequently translated his own English text into Latin, which was published five years later), but, fortunately decided to proceed in English. (He lost the first draft.)

'For loftiness of thought and language together, there are passages in Gebir *that will bear comparison with Milton.'*[1] *wrote Colvin. He also wrote:*

'The Lyrical Ballads, *the joint venture of Coleridge and Wordsworth which appeared in the same year as* Gebir, *began with "The Ancient Mariner", a work of even more vivid and haunting, if also more unearthly, imagery, and ended with the "Lines Written on Revisiting Tintern Abbey", which conveyed the first notes of a far deeper message. But nowhere in the works of Wordsworth or Coleridge do we find anything resembling Landor's peculiar qualities of haughty splendour and massive concentration.'*[2]

Forster commented:

'Style and treatment constitute the charm of it. The vividness with which everything in it is presented to sight as well as though, the wealth of its imagery, its moods of language—these are characteristics preeminent in* Gebir. *In the treatment, never abruptly contrasted, natural and supernatural agencies are employed with excellent art; and everywhere as real to the eye as to the mind are its painted pictures, its sculptured forms, and the profusion of its varied but always thoughtful emotion.'*[3]

Landor sent a copy to Dr Parr, who wrote on the title-page 'The work of a Scholar and a Poet', and Southey wrote to Cottle: 'There is a poem called Gebir *of which I know not whether my review of it in the* Critical *be yet printed; but in that review you will find some of the most exquisite poetry in the language. I would go a hundred miles to see the (Anonymous) author.' And writing to Coleridge on starting for Lisbon, Southey said: 'I take with me for the voyage your poems—the "Lyrics", the "Lyrical Ballads" and "Gebir". These make all my library. I like "Gebir" more and more.'*[4]

But not everybody agreed with Southey. William Taylor observed: 'It wants commonsense, there are exquisitely fine passages; but they

[1] Colvin, *Landor*, p. 27.
[2] *Idem*, p. 28.
[3] Forster, *Landor*, vol. i, p. 82.
[4] Houghton, *Monographs*, p. 81.

succeed each other by such flea-skips of association, that I am unable to track the path of the author's mind, and verily suspect him of insanity.'[1] *Gifford wrote that the poem was 'a jumble of incomprehensible trash ... the most vile and despicable effusion of a mad and muddy brain that ever disgraced, I will not say the press, but the "darkened walls" of Bedlam.'*[2] *Gifford was always to be a harsh critic of Landor, to say the least !*

[1] Robberds, *William Taylor*, 1, 357–8.
[2] W. Gifford, *Examination of the Strictures of the Critical Reviewers on the Translations of Juvenal* (1803), p. 7; quoted in Super's *Landor*, p. 46.

From *Gebir*
1798

THE LOVE; OF GEBIR AND OF TAMAR

*Gebir, a prince of Spain, meets and falls in love with his enemy
Charoba, Queen of Egypt, whose country he has invaded in revenge for
ancestral wrongs. He sets out to confide his passion to his shepherd
brother Tamar. Tamar on his part discloses his own love for a sea-
nymph, who in the guise of a sailor had challenged him to wrestle and
overthrown him.*

GEBIR, at Egypt's youthful queen's approach,
Laid by his orbèd shield; his vizor-helm,
His buckler and his corslet he laid by,
And bade that none attend him; at his side
Two faithful dogs that urge the silent course,
Shaggy, deep-chested, crouch'd; the crocodile,
Crying, oft made them raise their flaccid ears
And push their heads within their master's hand.
There was a brightening paleness in his face,
Such as Diana rising o'er the rocks
Shower'd on the lonely Latmian; on his brow
Sorrow there was, yet nought was there severe.
But when the royal damsel first he saw,
Faint, hanging on her handmaid, and her knees
Tottering as from the motion of the car,
His eyes look'd earnest on her, and those eyes
Show'd, if they had not, that they might have, loved,
For there was pity in them at that hour.
With gentle speech, and more with gentle looks,
He sooth'd her; but lest Pity go beyond
And cross'd Ambition lose her lofty aim,
Bending, he kiss'd her garment, and retired.
He went, nor slumber'd in the sultry noon,

When viands, couches, generous wines, persuade,
And slumber most refreshes; nor at night,
When heavy dews are laden with disease,
And blindness waits not there for lingering age.
　　Ere morning dawn'd behind him, he arrived
At those rich meadows where young Tamar fed
The royal flocks entrusted to his care.
'Now,' said he to himself, 'will I repose
At least this burthen on a brother's breast.'
His brother stood before him: he, amazed,
Rear'd suddenly his head, and thus began.
'Is it thou, brother? Tamar, is it thou?
Why, standing on the valley's utmost verge,
Lookest thou on that dull and dreary shore
Where beyond sight Nile blackens all the sand?
And why that sadness? When I past our sheep
The dew-drops were not shaken off the bar,
Therefore if one be wanting, 'tis untold.'
　　'Yes, one is wanting, nor is that untold,'
Said Tamar; 'and this dull and dreary shore
Is neither dull nor dreary at all hours.'
Whereon the tear stole silent down his cheek,
Silent, but not by Gebir unobserved:
Wondering he gazed awhile, and pitying spake.
'Let me approach thee; does the morning light
Scatter this wan suffusion o'er thy brow,
This faint blue lustre under both thine eyes?'
　　'O brother, is this pity or reproach?'
Cried Tamar, 'cruel if it be reproach,
If pity, O how vain!' 'Whate'er it be
That grieves thee, I will pity, thou but speak,
And I can tell thee, Tamar, pang for pang.'
　　'Gebir! then more than brothers are we now!
Everything (take my hand) will I confess.
I neither feed the flock nor watch the fold;
How can I, lost in love? But, Gebir, why
That anger which has risen to your cheek?
Can other men? could you? what, no reply!
And still more anger, and still worse conceal'd!

Are these your promises? your pity this?'
  'Tamar, I well may pity what I feel—
Mark me aright—I feel for thee—proceed—
Relate me all.' 'Then will I all relate,'
Said the young shepherd, gladden'd from his heart.
' 'Twas evening, though not sunset, and the tide
Level with these green meadows, seem'd yet higher:
Twas pleasant, and I loosen'd from my neck
The pipe you gave me, and began to play.
O that I ne'er had learnt the tuneful art!
It always brings us enemies or love.
Well, I was playing, when above the waves
Some swimmer's head methought I saw ascend;
I, sitting still, survey'd it with my pipe
Awkwardly held before my lips half-closed.
Gebir! it was a Nymph! a Nymph divine!
I cannot wait describing how she came,
How I was sitting, how she first assumed
The Sailor; of what happen'd there remains
Enough to say, and too much to forget.
The sweet deceiver stepp'd upon this bank
Before I was aware; for with surprise
Moments fly rapid as with love itself.
Stooping of tune afresh the hoarsen'd reed,
I heard a rustling, and where that arose
My glance first lighted on her nimble feet.
Her feet resembled those long shells explored
By him who to befriend his steed's dim sight
Would blow the pungent powder in the eye.
Her eyes too! O immortal gods! her eyes
Resembled—what could they resemble? what
Ever resemble those? Even her attire
Was not of wonted woof nor vulgar art:
Her mantle show'd the yellow samphire-pod,
Her girdle the dove-colour'd wave serene.
"Shepherd," said she, "and will you wrestle now,
And with the sailor's hardier race engage?"
I was rejoiced to hear it, and contrived
How to keep up contention: could I fail

By pressing not too strongly, yet to press?
"Whether a shepherd, as indeed you seem,
Or whether of the hardier race you boast,
I am not daunted; no; I will engage."
"But first," said she, "what wager will you lay?"
"A sheep," I answered: "add whate'er you will."
"I cannot," she replied, "make that return:
Our hided vessels in their pitchy round
Seldom, unless from rapine, hold a sheep.
But I have sinuous shells or pearly hue
Within, and they that lustre have imbibed
In the sun's palace-porch, where when unyoked
His chariot-wheel stands midway in the wave:
Shake one and it awakens, then apply
Its polish'd lips to your attentive ear,
And it remembers its august abodes,
And murmurs as the ocean murmurs there.
And I have others given me by the nymphs,
Of sweeter sound than any pipe you have;
But we, by Neptune! for no pipe contend;
This time a sheep I win, a pipe the next."
Now came she forward eager to engage,
But first her dress, her bosom then survey'd,
And heaved it, doubting if she could deceive.
Her bosom seem'd, inclosed in haze like heaven,
To baffle touch, and rose forth undefined:
Above her knee she drew the robe succinct,
Above her breast, and just below her arms.
"This will preserve my breath when tightly bound,
If struggle and equal strength should so constrain."
Thus, pulling hard to fasten it, she spake,
And, rushing at me, closed: I thrill'd throughout
And seem'd to lessen and shrink up with cold.
Again with violent impulse gush'd my blood,
And hearing nought external, thus absorb'd,
I heard it, rushing through each turbid vein,
Shake my unsteady swimming sight in air.
Yet with unyielding though uncertain arms
I clung around her neck; the vest beneath

Rustled against our slipper limbs entwined:
Often mine springing with eluded force
Started aside and trembled till replaced:
And when I most succeeded, as I thought,
My bosom and my throat felt so compress'd
That life was almost quivering on my lips.
Yet nothing was there painful: these are signs
Of secret arts and not of human might;
What arts I cannot tell; I only know
My eyes grew dizzy and my strength decay'd;
I was indeed o'ercome—with what regret,
And more, with what confusion, when I reach'd
The fold, and yielding up the sheep, she cried,
"This pays a shepherd to a conquering maid."
She smiled, and more of pleasure than disdain
Was in her dimpled chin and liberal lip,
And eyes that languish'd, lengthening, just like love.
She went away; I on the wicker gate
Leant, and could follow with my eyes alone.
The sheep she carried easy as a cloak;
But when I heard its bleating, as I did,
And saw, she hastening on, its hinder feet
Struggle, and from her snowy shoulder slip,
One shoulder its poor efforts had unveil'd,
Then all my passions mingling fell in tears;
Restless then ran I to the highest ground
To watch her; she was gone; gone down the tide;
And the long moonbeam on the hard wet sand
Lay like a jasper column half unprear'd.'

[XXIV]
THE MARRIAGE MORNING

Gebir and Charoba are to be united in the presence of their respective hosts. The poet describes the excitement in the camp and in the city, and how the bridegroom and bride severally rise and begin the day.

THE long awaited day at last arrived,
When, link'd together by the seven-arm'd Nile,
Egypt with proud Iberia should unite.

Here the Tartessian, there the Gadite tents
Rang with impatient pleasure: here engaged
Woody Nebrissa's quiver-bearing crew
Contending warm with amicable skill;
While they of Durius raced along the beach
And scatter'd mud and jeers on all behind.
The strength of Bætis too removed the helm
And stripp'd the corslet off, and staunch'd the foot
Against the mossy maple, while they tore
Their quivering lances from the hissing wound.
Others push forth the prows of their compeers,
And the wave, parted by the pouncing beak,
Swells up the sides, and closes far astern:
The silent oars now dip their level wings,
And weary with strong stroke the whitening wave
Others, afraid of tardiness, return:
Now, entering the still harbour, every surge
Runs with a louder murmur up their keel,
And the slack cordage rattles round the mast.
  Sleepless with pleasure and expiring fears
Had Gebir risen ere the break of dawn,
And o'er the plains appointed for the feast
Hurried with ardent step: the swains admired
What so transversely could have swept the dew:
For never long one path had Gebir trod,
Nor long—unheeding man—one pace preserved.
  Not thus Charoba: she despair'd the day:
The day was present; true; yet she despair'd.
In the too tender and once tortured heart
Doubts gather strength from habit, like disease;
Fears, like the needle verging to the pole,
Tremble and tremble into certainty.
How often, when her maids with merry voice
Call'd her and told the sleepless queen 'twas morn,
How often would she feign some fresh delay,
And tell them (though they saw) that she arose.
Next to her chamber, closed by cedar doors,
A bath of purest marble, purest wave
On its fair surface bore its pavement high:

Arabian gold enchased the crystal roof,
With fluttering boys adorn'd and girls unrobed:
These, when you touch the quiet water, start
From their aërial sunny arch, and pant
Entangled mid each other's flowery wreaths,
And each pursuing is in turn pursued.
    Here came at last, as ever wont at morn,
Charoba: long she linger'd at the brink;
Often she sigh'd, and, naked as she was,
Sate down, and leaning on the couche's edge
On the soft inward pillow of her arm
Rested her burning cheek: she moved her eyes:
She blush'd; and blushing plunged into the wave.
    Now brazen chariots thunder through each street
And neighing steeds paw proudly from delay,
While o'er the palace breathes the dulcimer,
Lute, and aspiring harp, and lisping reed;
Loud rush the trumpets bursting through the throng
And urge the high-shoulder'd vulgar; now are heard
Curses and quarrels and constricted blows,
Threats and defiance and suburban war.
Hark! the reiterated clangour sounds!
Now murmurs like the sea or like the storm
Or like the flames on forests, move and mount
From rank to rank, and loud and louder roll,
Till all the people is one vast applause.
Yes, 'tis herself, Charoba—now the strife
To see again a form so often seen!
Feel they some partial pang, some secret void,
Some doubt of feasting those fond eyes again?
Panting imbibe they that refreshing sight
To reproduce in hour of bitterness?
She goes, the king awaits her from the camp:
Him she described, and trembled ere he reach'd
Her car, but shudder'd paler at his voice.
So the pale silver at the festive board
Grows paler fill'd afresh and dew'd with wine;
So seems the tenderest herbage of the spring
To whiten, bending from a balmy gale.

During the next few unsettled years of Landor's life he formed a close friendship with Dr Samuel Parr, who lived at Hatton, four miles from Warwick. Parr, *who was nicknamed 'the Whig Johnson', and who had been an assistant master at Harrow and subsequently a head-master at other schools, now took in private pupils. A great Latin scholar and an arrogant, epigrammatical conversationalist, he was exactly the type of man to appeal to Landor. Indeed, Landor used to boast that 'he was the only man for whom Parr had ever ridden half a dozen miles "with his dinner in his mouth and his pipe out of it".'*[1] *Parr died in 1825, but he had introduced Landor to Daniel Stuart, editor of the* Morning Post, *as well as to Robert Adair, Fox's party organizer. As a result, Landor wrote many articles and letters for them.*

1800–02

Two years were to elapse before Landor published anything else. His volume Poems from the Arabic and Persian *(1800) attracted little attention. He had also privately printed a pamphlet of Latin verses,* Iambi, *which, as Mr Elwin points out,*[2] *'must have pleased Parr, but was probably read by nobody else, except Walter Birch'.*[3]

Among Landor's friends at this period was Isaac Mocatta, who was responsible to quite an extent for Landor's enthusiasm for art. Unfortunately he died in July 1801. On 5 December 1800 he had written to Landor regarding his Postscript to Gebir:

'*Since my last [letter] I have given your work a perusal which I do not intend shall be the last, for like a scientific piece of music, it will probably gain by repetition. It appears to me, however, more likely to please highly some few than to be generally tasted. The typographic errors are at least as numerous as you mention; but I did not include in them* wherefor, *which if you recollect, I stated as a peculiarity. Though I had never thought on the subject before, it immediately struck me as proper, "wherefor" being only by elision "where is the reason or motive for". Most undoubtedly a tragedy replete with sentiments such as you could not help to infuse, would not be received by the manager and sanctioned by the Lord*

[1] Elwin, *Landor*, p. 75.
[2] Elwin, *Landor*, p. 74.
[3] 'My friend at Oxford, whom I fought at Rugby and who thrashed me well. He was a year older, and a better boxer: we were intimate ever afterwards till his death.' [Forster: *Landor*, vol. i, p. 24.]

Chamberlain; So that I much wish you could hit on some other plan more lucid and better thought out than you have hitherto produced. For I honestly think your talents equal to the greatest undertaking, but I dread that impetuosity that disdains those minor niceties of language which are yet necessary to show where the narrative stands, and what is going on. Are you not too profound and classical for most readers? I think I discover that your imagination has been warmed in more than one instant by Painting. By the bye, do not construe my approbation to extend to your encomiums on pride and revenge. Adieu. From Is. Mocatta.'[1]

He spoke the truth and would have continued being an admirable mentor to Landor. Much more important, Landor liked him and listened to him.

Through his friendship with Parr, Landor was introduced to Robert Adair, and it was arranged for him to have a seat in the reporters' gallery. But Landor was not successful as a political journalist.

In March of the year 1802 the Treaty of Amiens was signed. This was an excuse for Landor to go to France. He stayed in Paris in an hotel where there was no fire in any of its sixty rooms, and he had to put on his shirt 'as damp as a newspaper from the press.'[2] On 15 August he wrote to his sister Elizabeth describing his first sight of Napoleon:

'I stood within six or eight yards of him, nearly a quarter of an hour. His countenance is not of that fierce cast which you see in the prints, & which perhaps it may assume in battle. He seems melancholy and reserved, but not morose or proud ... He rode a little white horse, about the size of my father's, and cantered up & down six or eight lines of military drawn out in the Court of the Tuileries, which is about the size of Lincolns-inn-Fields. Each line lowered its colours as he passed and he took off his hat in return. The French are not mightily civil, and one cannot much wonder, but I got an admirable place by a piece of well-timed flattery. After I had seen Buonaparte canter by me, at the distance of about a dozen yards, I left my situation by the window, and went down close to the gate of the palace. Presently came the Chief Consul & half a score generals. The people made room, thro fear of the horses, which indeed were fierce enough, being covered with blue or red velvet, one half of

[1] Forster, *Landor*, vol. i, p. 140.
[2] Elwin, *Landor*, p. 90.

which was hid with gold lace. Instead of going with the crowd, I pushed forward & got by the side of Buonaparte's Mamalouk, in a place where there were none but soldiers. There was a very tall fellow just before me. I begged him to let me see Buonaparte, and observed that probably he *had seen him often and shared his victories. The youth was delighted. Ah! le voila, Monsieur, said he and in a moment there was nothing between me and this terror of Europe, but the backs of two horses over which I could see him as distinctly as I see this paper.*'[1]

During this year Poetry by the Author of Gebir *was published. This volume contained two short narrative poems—the heroic idyll, the* Story of Crysaor *and* The Phocaeans, *together with a few miscellaneous lyrics in Latin and English.* Crysaor *is concerned with war between Gods and Titans, and Colvin considered it Landor's finest piece of narrative writing in blank verse; less monotonous in its movement than* Gebir, *more lofty and impassioned than any of the later* Hellenics *with which it was afterwards incorporated.*[2] The Phocaeans *is a poem, founded on Herodotus, about those Phocaeans who left their cities rather than face the invading terror of the Persians.*

[1] Forster, *Landor*, vol. i, p. 173.
[2] Colvin, *Landor*, p. 37.

Crysaor
Published 1802

Hardly any thing remains that made ancient Iberia classic land. We have little more than the titles of fables—than portals, as it were, covered over with gold and gorgeous figures, that shew us what once must have been the magnificence of the whole interior edifice. Lucan has wandered over Numidia, and Virgil too at the conclusion of his Georgics, has left the indelible mark of his footstep celebrated Pharos of Egypt. But, in general, the poets of Greece and Italy were afraid of moving far from the latest habitations of their tutelar gods and heroes. I am fond of walking by myself; but others, who have gone before me, may have planted trees, or opened vistas, and rendered my walks more amusing. I had begun to write a poem[1] connected in some degree with the early history of Spain; but doubtful whether I should ever continue it, and grown every hour more indifferent, I often sat down and diverted my attention with the remotest views I could find. The present is a sketch.

STORY OF CRYSAOR

COME, I beseech ye, Muses! who, retired
Deep in the shady glens by Helicon,
Yet know the realms of ocean, know the laws
Of his wide empire, and throughout his court
Know every Nymph, and call them each by name;
Who from your sacred mountain see afar
O'er earth and heaven, and hear and memorize
The crimes of men and counsels of the Gods;
Sing of those crimes and of those counsels, sing
Of Gades sever'd from the fruitful main;
And what befel, and from what mighty hand,
Crysäör, sovereign of the golden sword.

[1] *The Phocaeans.*

CRYSAOR

'Twas when the high Olympus shook with fear,
Lest all his temples, all his groves, be crushed
By Pelion piled on Ossa: but the sire
Of mortals and immortals waved his arm
Around, and all below was wild dismay:
Again—'twas agony: again—'twas peace.
Crysäör still in Gades tarrying,
Hurl'd into ether, tinging, as it flew,
With sudden fire the clouds round Saturn's throne,
No pine surrender'd by retreating Pan,
Nor ash, nor poplar pale; but swoln with pride
Stood towering from the citadel; his spear
One hand was rested on, and one with rage
Shut hard, and firmly fixt against his side;
His frowning visage, flusht with insolence,
Rais'd up oblique to heaven. 'O thou,' he cried,
'Whom nations kneel to, not whom nations know,
Hear me, and answer, if indeed thou can'st,
The last appeal I deign thee or allow.
Tell me, and quickly, why should I adore,
Adored myself by millions? why invoke,
Invoked with all thy attributes? men wrong
By their prostrations, prayers, and sacrifice,
Either the gods, their rulers, or themselves:
But flame and thunder fright them from the *Gods
Themselves* they cannot, dare not—they are ours,
Us—dare they, can they, *us*? but triumph, Jove!
Man for one moment hath engaged his lord,
Henceforth let merchants value him, not kings.
No! lower thy sceptre, and hear Atrobal,
And judge aright to whom men sacrifice.
My children, said the sage and pious priest,
Mark there the altar! tho' the fumes aspire
Twelve cubits ere a nostril they regale,
'Tis myrrh for Titans, 'tis but air for Gods.
Time changes, Nature changes, I am changed!
Fronting the furious lustre of the sun,
I yielded to his piercing swift-shot beams
Only when quite meridian, then abased

These orbits to the ground, and there surveyed
My shadow—strange and horrid to relate!
My very shadow almost disappeared!
Restore it, or by earth and hell I swear
With blood enough will I refascinate
The cursed incantation: thou restore,
And largely; or my brethren, all combined,
Shall rouse thee from thy lethargies, and drive
Far from thy cloud-soft pillow, minion-prest,
Those leering lassitudes that follow Love.'

The smile of disappointment and disdain
Sat sallow on his pausing lip half-closed;
But, neither headlong importunity,
Nor gibing threat of reed-propt insolence,
Let loose the blast of vengeance: heaven shone bright,
Still, and Crysäör spurn'd the prostrate land.
But the triumphant Thunderer, now mankind
(Criminal mostly for enduring crimes—)
Provoked his indignation, thus besought
His trident-sceptred brother, triton-borne.
'O Neptune! cease henceforward to repine.
They are not cruel, no—the destinies
Intent upon their loom, unoccupied
With aught beyond it's moody murmuring sound,
Will neither see thee weep nor hear thee sigh:
And wherefor weep, O Neptune, wherefor sigh!
Ambition? 'tis unworthy of a God,
Unworthy of a brother! I am Jove,
Thou, Neptune,—happier in uncitied realms,
In coral hall or grotto samphire-ciel'd,
Amid the song of Nymphs and ring of shells,
Thou smoothest at thy will the pliant wave
Or liftest it to heaven.—I also can
Whatever best beseems me, nor for aid
Unless I loved thee, Neptune, would I call.
Tho' absent, thou hast heard, and hast beheld,
The profanation of that monsterous race,
That race of earth-born giants—one survives—

CRYSAOR

The rapid-footed Rhodan, mountain-rear'd,
Beheld the rest defeated; still remain
Scatter'd throughout interminable fields,
Sandy and sultry, and each hopeless path
Choaked up with crawling briars and bristling thorns,
The flinty trophies of their foul disgrace.
Crysäör, Sovereign of the golden sword,
Still hails as brethren men of stouter heart,
But, wise confederate, shuns Phlegrœan fields.
No warrior he, yet who so fond of war,
Unfeeling, scarce ferocious; flattery's dupe
He fancies that the gods themselves are his;
Impious, but most in prayer:—now re-assert
Thy friendship, raise thy trident, strike the rocks,
Sever him from mankind.' Then thus replied
The Nymph-surrounded monarch of the main.

'Empire bemoan I not, however shared,
Nor Fortune frail, nor stubborn Fate, accuse:
No!—mortals I bemoan! when Avarice,
Plowing these fruitless furrows, shall awake
The basking Demons, and the dormant Crimes,
Horrible, strong, resistless, and transform
Meekness to Madness, Patience to Despair.
What is Ambition? What but Avarice?
But Avarice in richer guize arrayed,
Stalking erect, loud-spoken, lion-mien'd,
Her brow uncrost by care, but deeply markt,
And darting downwards 'twixt her eyes hard-lasht
The wrinkle of command.—could ever I
So foul a fiend, so fondly too, caress?
Judge me not harshly, judge me by my deeds.'

Tho' seated then on Africs further coast,
Yet sudden, at his voice, so long unheard—
For he had grieved, and treasured up his grief—
With short kind greeting, meet from every side
The Triton herds, and warm with melody
The azure concave of their curling shells.

Swift as an arrow, as the wind, as light,
He glided thro' the deep, and now, arrived,
Lept from his pearly beryl-studded car.
Earth trembled—the retreating tide, black-brow'd,
Gather'd new strength, and rushing on, assail'd
The promontory's base: but when the God
Himself, resistless Neptune, struck one blow,
Rent were the rocks asunder, and the sky
Was darkened with their fragments ere they fell.
Lygea vocal, Zantho yellow-hair'd,
Spio with sparkling eyes, and Beroë
Demure, and sweet Iöné, youngest-born,
Of mortal race, but grown divine by song—
Had you seen playing round her placid neck
The sunny circles, braidless and unbound,—
Of who had call'd them boders of a storm!
These, and the many sister Nereïds,
Forgetful of their lays and of their loves,
All, unsuspicious of the dread intent,
Stop suddenly their gambols, and with shrieks
Of terror plunge amid the closing wave:
Still, just above, one moment more, appear
Their darken'd tresses floating in the foam.

Thrown prostrate on the earth, the Sacrilege
Rais'd up his head astounded, and accurs'd
The stars, the destinies, the gods—his breast
Panted from consternation, and dismay,
And pride untoward, on himself o'erthrown.
From his distended nostrils issued gore,
At intervals, with which his wiry locks,
Huge arms, and bulky bosom, shone beslimed:
And thrice he call'd his brethren, with a voice
More dismal than the blasts from Phlegethon
Below, that urge along ten thousand ghosts
Wafted loud-wailing o'er the firey tide.
But answer heard he none—the men of might
Who gather'd round him formerly, the men
Whom frozen at a frown, a smile revived,

Were far—enormous mountains interposed,
Nor ever had the veil-hung pine out-spread
O'er Tethys then her wandering leafless shade:
Nor could he longer under wintry stars
Suspend the watery journey, nor repose
Whole nights on Ocean's billowy restless bed;
No longer, bulging thro' the tempest, rose
That bulky bosom; nor those oarlike hands,
Trusted ere mortal's keenest ken conceived
The bluest shore—threw back opposing tides.
Shrunken mid brutal hair his violent veins
Subsided, yet were hideous to behold
As dragons panting in the noontide brake.
At last, absorbing deep the breath of heaven,
And stifling all within his deadly grasp,
Struggling, and tearing up the glebe, to turn;
And from a throat that, as it throb'd and rose,
Seem'd shaking ponderous links of dusky iron,
Uttering one anguish-forced indignant groan,
Fired with infernal rage, the spirit flew.

Nations of fair Hesperia! lo o'erthrown
Your peace-embracing war-inciting king!
Ah! thrice twelve years, and longer, ye endured
Without one effort to rise higher, one hope
That heaven would wing the secret shaft aright,
The abomination!—hence 'twas Jove's command
That, many hundred, many thousand, more,
Freed from one despot, still from one unfreed,
Ye crouch unblest at Superstition's feet.
Her hath he sent among ye; her, the pest
Of men below, and curse of Gods above:
Hers are the last worst tortures they inflict
On all who bend to any kings but them.
Born of Sicanus, in the vast abyss
Where never light descended, she survived
Her parent; he omnipotence defied,
But thunderstruck fell headlong from the clouds;
She tho' the radiant ether overpower'd

Her eyes, accustom'd to the gloom of night,
And quenched their lurid orbs, Religion's helm
Assuming, vibrated her Stygian torch,
Till thou, Astræa! tho' behind the Sire's
Broad egis, tremblest on thy golden throne.

1803–06

Landor returned to England and abandoned his idea of adopting a political career. He worked on a revised edition of Gebir; *his brother Robert adding notes and elucidating 'difficult pages'. The poem was enlarged by some fifty lines. It was, however, revised again in 1831 when Landor reduced the length of the work. He also published an edition in Latin,* Gebirus, *which hardly increased his readership, though, of course, Dr Parr expressed his pleasure in the work.*

Landor by 1805 was in constant debt. He flitted about the country but mostly lived in Bath, his favourite city. He had met Jane Swift, who was 'the traditional Irish girl, gay, ripe, warm-hearted, impulsive'.[1] She was a daughter of Richard Swifte of Lynn in Ireland. To her, whom he called Ianthé, Landor was to write some of his most beautiful verses.[2]

On 3 November 1805, Landor's father died, and Landor was now able to live on a grand scale. His brother Robert, visiting him at Bath soon after their father's death, found him credited with the 'reputation of very great wealth, and the certainty, at his mother's death, of still greater. A fine carriage, three horses, two men-servants, books, plate, china, pictures, in everything a profuse and wasteful outlay, all confirmed the grandeur'.[3]

Fortunately Landor was not discouraged by the tiny sales his books had. His next publication, Simonidea *(1806), was to fare no better. Most of the verses included in this volume are love-poems addressed to Ianthé as well as the moving elegy quoted here to his earlier love the golden haired Nancy Jones. The volume also included* Gunlaug and Helga, *a narrative poem on an Icelandic work from William Herbert's* Select Icelandic Poems.

[1] Elwin, *Landor*, p. 103.
[2] Jane Swift's children restored the old spelling of the name with the final *e*.
[3] Elwin, *Landor*, p. 103.

From Simonidea
1806

Gone! thou too, Nancy! why should Heaven remove
Each tender object of my early love?
Why was I happy? O ye conscious rocks!
Was I not happy? When Iöne's locks
Claspt round her neck and mine their golden chain,
Ambition, fame, and fortune, smiled in vain.
While warring winds with deafening fury blew,
Near, and more near, our cheeks, our bosoms, grew.
Wave after wave the lashing ocean chased,
She smiled, and prest me closer to her waist.
'Suppose this cave should crush us,' once I cried;
'It cannot fall,' the loving maid replied.
'You, who are shorter, may be safe,' I said;
'O let us fly!' exclaim'd the simple maid.
Springing, she drew me forward by the hand
Upon the sunny and the solid sand,
And then lookt round, with fearful doubt, to see
If what I spoke so seriously, could be.
　　Ah memory, memory! thou alone canst save
Angelic beauty from the grasping grave.
Tho' Nancy's name for ever dwell unknown
Beyond her briar-bound sod and upright stone;
Yet, in the lover's, in the poet's eye,
The young Iöne hath not bloom'd to die.

Darling Shell, where has thou been,
What far regions has thou seen;
From what pastimes art thou come:
Can we make amends at home?

SIMONIDEA

Whether thou has timed the dance
To the maids of ocean,
Know I not—but Ignorance
Never hurts Devotion—

This I know, my darling Shell,
I shall ever love thee well.
Though too little to resound
While the Nereids dance around.

For, of all the shells that are,
Thou art sure the brightest:
Thou, Ianthé's infant care,
Most these eyes delighted—

Earlier to whose aid she owes
Teeth like budding snowdrop rows;
Teeth, whose love-incit'd pow'rs
I have felt in happier hours.

On my shoulder, on my neck,
Still the cherisht mark remains
Well pourtray'd in many a speck
Round thy smooth and quiet veins.

Who can wonder then, if thou
Hearest breathe my tender vow;
If thy lips, so pure, so bright,
Are dim with kisses day and night.[1]

[1] 'Ianthé' married her cousin Godwin Swift, who died in 1814, leaving her
with four sons and three daughters.

In 1807 Landor visited the Lake District, carrying with him an introduction from Dr Parr; but he was unfortunate, for he missed seeing both Wordsworth and Southey. Wordsworth was according to Southey in London, 'he flourishes in London, he powders and goes with a cocked hat under his arm to all great routes. No man is more flattered by the attentions of the great, and no man would be more offended to be told so.'[1]

Southey was on his way back to Greta Hall, but went via Taunton to see his last remaining and eccentric uncle. Southey had always wanted to meet the author of Gebir, a work for which he had the greatest admiration and this was accomplished in April. They were to find much else with which they were in agreement, in particular their hatred for Napoleon.

In June of 1807, Napoleon had conceived his plan to make himself master of the Peninsula. Politically in England the Whigs were rapidly losing favour. Fox had died in September 1806, and before the end of 1807 the Grenville administration collapsed and the Duke of Portland became Prime Minister. In the following year the Spanish rose against the French and demanded help from England, with a result that the Government sent Sir Arthur Wellesley to Portugal.

One evening at Brighton, Landor was preaching 'a crusade' to an audience of two Irishmen; by 8 August he wrote to Southey 'I am going to Spain. In three days I shall have sailed'. While waiting to embark for Spain, Landor employed himself learning Spanish. After Landor had sailed, Southey hailed him as a hero, and wrote to his brother:

'Landor has gone to Spain! to fight as a private in the Spanish army, and he has found two Englishmen to go with him. A noble fellow! This is something like the days of old, as we poets and romancers represent them; something like the best part of chivalry: old honours, old generosity, old heroism, are reviving, and the cancer of that nation is stopped, I believe and fully trust, now and for ever. A man like Landor cannot long remain without command; and, of all things in the world, I should most rejoice to hear that King

---

[1] Simmons, *Southey*, p. 117.

*Joseph had fallen into his hands;—he would infallibly hang him on
the nearest tree, first, as a Buonaparte by blood; secondly as a
Frenchman by adoption; thirdly as a king by trade.'*[1]

Landor landed at Corunna, where he introduced himself to the
British envoy Charles Stuart (later Baron Stuart de Rothesay).
'Landor whereupon offered 10,000 reals for the relief of the unfortunate town of Venturada', which had been sacked by the French;
he also announced his intention of enlisting under the Spanish General
Don Joachim Blake. With Blake's army 'sometimes at Reÿnosa, sometimes at Aguilar', Landor waited fretfully for a decisive action, seeing
little but guerilla skirmishing and no battle fought. He told Southey
that he wished to have seen Madrid, but feared to go lest the long-
expected battle might be fought in his absence. Late in September he
was present at the occupation of Bilbao, where 'I had the satisfaction
of serving three launches with powder and muskets, and of carrying on
my shoulders six or seven miles, a child too heavy for its exhausted
mother'. He 'was near being taken the following day' when the French
re-occupied the town, escaping with the aid of 'Juan Santos de
Murieta, a poor man of Castro'. During September and early October
he beguiled himself in writing three letters to Riquelme, the Brigadier
commanding his division under Blake—the first on a 'means of supply-
ing an adequate force of cavalry', the second 'a view of parties in
England, their errors and designs', the third, dated from Santander on
3 October, a review of 'our conduct at Ferrol, at Buenos Ayres, and at
Cintra'.[2] These letters were published in 1809. The Convention of
Cintra, whereby the French evacuated Portugal, caused tremendous
dissatisfaction in England, and particularly to Landor.

Landor was thanked by the Spanish Government and King
Ferdinand appointed him a Colonel in the Spanish Army. But when
the King restored the detested Jesuits, the disgusted Landor returned
his commission to the Spanish authorities.

Before Landor had set off for Spain an anonymous pamphlet had
been published, called Guy's Porridge Pot, (1806). Satanic in nature,
it attacked Dr Parr. It was thought that Landor was the author. This
he vehemently denied, and indeed he wrote to Parr disclaiming such
rumours. Parr accepted his disclaimer: 'I had not even heard of the

[1] Elwin, *Landor*, p. 116.
[2] Elwin, *Landor*, p. 118.

*poem you mention; and if it contains any abuse of me, I should
instantly have pronounced it impossible for such abuse to flow from
your pen . . .'*[1] *The satire is actually attributed to Landor's younger
brother Robert. A defence of Parr, called* The Dun Cow, *was published
in 1808 by Landor.*[2]

On his return from Spain, Landor wrote to Southey:

'*I believe I should have been a good and happy man if I had married.
My heart is tender. I am fond of children and of talking childishly.
I hate to travel even two stages. Never without a pang do I leave
the house where I was born. Even a short stay attaches me to any
place. But, Southey, I love a woman who will never love me, and
am beloved by one who never ought. I do not say I shall never be
happy. I shall be often so, if I live; but I shall never be at rest.
My evil genius drags me through existence against the current of my
best inclinations. I have practised self-denial, because it gave me a
momentary and false idea that I am firm; and I have done some
other things not amiss, in compliance with my heart; but my most
virtuous hopes and sentiments have uniformly led to misery, and
I never have been happy but in consequence of some weakness or
some vice.*'

*This letter is a true testament of the then Landor and the Landor that
was to be.*

Southey replied to him that he had learnt from Rousseau, *before
he laid Epictetus to his heart . . . and bade him and warning him, of
being poor as he grows old; and of solitariness in old age . . . and that
he should find a woman whom he would esteem . . .*[3]

*On his return to England in 1809, Landor had determined to
become a model landowner. The purchase, however, of his Welsh
estate at Llanthony was to cost him thousands of pounds and to involve
him in countless legal fights. In the end he had to flee the country,
financially ruined. During all this feverish activity, as well as going to
Brighton and Bath, he published his* Three Letters to Don Francisco

---

[1] Forster, *Landor*, p. 322, vol. i.

[2] Super, in his biography *Landor*, dissents: that it was probably not by Landor.
Nonetheless it is included in the Wise–Wheeler bibliography and the Collected
Works edited by Welby and Wheeler.

[3] Forster, *Landor*, vol. i, pp. 237–8. Super in a footnote concerning the two
women mentioned in the letter, queries this, as the original letter has not even
come to light and that Forster may have tampered with it. The present editor
doubts this.

Riquelme. *Meanwhile, the country seethed with discontent at Buonaparte's military aggressions. Cobbett and many others were sent to prison for seditious libel. Landor, who now wished for the termination of the war,[1] wrote an ode in Latin to Gustavus IV of Sweden, whose hatred of the dictator caused him to lose his throne to Bernadotte. He also wrote to the press under various pseudonyms.*

In April 1810, Landor published his 'brave and good' letter to Sir Francis Burdett, who had been imprisoned for his defiance of the Government's restraints upon the freedom of the press. This was followed by a tragedy called Count Julian. *Like all Landor's work in 'dramatic form', it was devoid of dramatic technique; moreover none of the characters had any substance of flesh and blood. Like the dramas of Shelley, Byron, Tennyson and Browning,* Count Julian *is a play for the study, and could never be entertained as a practical stage proposition.*

The play was written with great speed and in one burst of enthusiasm he told Southey that he had written 'a thousand lines in forty minutes'. He was, in fact, always an impulsive writer. He lacked, as Malcolm Elwin reminds us, 'self-discipline'. He never took the trouble to learn the art *of drama or that of the novel; if he had he might well have succeeded, yet Landor never sought techniques that would popularise his work. What he did do was to read deeply. He had a remarkable memory. De Quincey recognized Landor's ability but equally realized his shortcomings. He wrote of* Count Julian *that 'Mr Landor is probably the one man in Europe that has adequately conceived the situation, the stern self-dependency, and the monumental misery of Count Julian'.*

The play is supposed to take place after the defeat of the last Visigothic King of Spain, when Count Julian allies himself with the Moors in order to avenge himself upon the King Roderic, who has done dishonour to his daughter. 'It is the old story of crime propagating crime; of evil failing ever to expiate evil; and of blind necessity, out of one fatal wrong, reproducing wrong in endless forms of retaliatory guilt and suffering,' wrote Forster.[2] Southey was also at work on a similar subject, Roderick.

The usual difficulties beset Landor in his attempts, first of all, to see whether it was possible for Count Julian *to be produced. Nothing came*

[1] Forster, *Landor*, vol. i, p. 305.
[2] Forster, *Landor*, vol. i, p. 270 et seq.

of this. Then he tried to find a publisher. The manuscript was first sent to Longmans, who refused to print it even at the author's expense. This so enraged Landor that he burnt another tragedy that he had been at work on, called Ferranti and Giulio. *'My literary career,' he wrote to Southey, 'has been a very curious one. You cannot imagine how I feel relieved at laying down its burden and abandoning this tissue of humiliations. I fancied I had at last acquired, the right tone of tragedy, and was treading down at heel the shoes of Alfieri.'*[1]

Finally, Southey persuaded John Murray to publish the work at Landor's expense, and an edition of 250 copies was issued. It was never republished as a separate volume.

1811–12

Early in 1811, it is said, Landor went to a ball in Bath, and on seeing there a pretty girl exclaimed, 'That's the nicest girl in the room, I'll marry her.' After four months' courtship he did. Her name was Julia Thuillier. She was the daughter of a small banker at Banbury and she possessed no dowry. Not only did she lack material possessions, but she was obviously unsuited to marry a man like Landor, since she had neither the wit, learning nor qualities to deal with a man of his temperament. They were married at St James's Church, Bath, on 24 May 1811. Few of Landor's friends were present; several heard of the marriage only after the event. He wrote to his friend Walter Birch: 'I often feared I should be tempted to marry a woman of fortune, and particularly as my expenses in plain living and other things have lately been very great.' Walter Birch replied:

> 'You will think me a strange fellow for talking in this coarse and homely way on such an occasion. The air of a college perhaps contributes to chill one's feelings a little prematurely, though indeed it is time they should be pretty well sobered by the age of thirty-seven, at which I am now arrived. Well, then, do not smile at me, but it is my belief that an excellent wife is seldom made perfect to our hands, but is in part the creation of the husband after marriage, the result of his character and behaviour acting upon her own.'[2]

Of women, Landor has been known to remark that they 'pay dearly

---

[1] Forster, *Landor*, vol. i, p. 270 et seq.
[2] *Idem*, vol. i, p. 325.

for expression. English women have no expression; they are therefore so beautiful.'[1]

By the middle of June 1911, Landor and his wife had taken up their abode at Llanthony, and at the end of that month he reminded Southey of his promised visit.

'*After my marriage I stayed at Rodboro' and Petty France for three weeks, intending to spring upon you on your way to London. There was a disinclination in my wife either to remain at Bath or visit Clifton. She wished to escape from visits of ceremony and curiosity, and I would not hint to her any reason why I should be happy to pass a few days at Bath.*'

Telling him then of his correspondence with Longmans about Count Julian, *the ruin of his hopes and the burning of his unfinished tragedies, as already mentioned, he goes on:*

'*I now employ my mornings in cutting off the heads of thistles with my stick, and hoeing my young chestnuts. My house is raised half its height. Do we lie out of your way? I cannot promise you much comfort here, but I should be most heartily glad to see you. I live among ruins and rubbish, and what is infinitely worse, band-boxes and luggage and broken chairs: but I have a spare bed in the same turret where I sleep; and I have made a discovery, which is, that there are both nightingales and glowworms in my valley. I would give two or three thousand pounds less for a place that was without them. I hardly know one flower from another, but it appears to me that here is an infinite variety. The ground is of so various a nature and of such different elevations, that this might be expected. I love these beautiful and peaceful tribes, and wish I was better acquainted with them. They always meet one in the same place, at the same season; and years have no more effect on their placid countenances than on so many of the most favoured gods.*'[2]

Landor now began work on Charles James Fox, a Commentary on His Life and Character. *The 'Commentary' was written after John Bernard Trotter's* Memories of the Later Years of The Right Honourable Charles James Fox *had been published. Trotter was a young Irishman, a nephew of the Bishop of Down, who hero-worshipped*

[1] Houghton, *Monographs*, p. 99.
[2] Forster, *Landor*, vol. i, p. 327.

LANDOR

Fox, and became his secretary; it was said that his 'hero-worship was so great and his sententiousness puts Boswell in the shade.'¹ When in 1802 Fox went to Paris, after having declared his admiration for Napoleon, his remarks enraged public opinion, not to mention that Southey's and Landor's. Trotter accompanied Fox and his wife to Paris, where they stayed for some three months, going everywhere and meeting everyone, including Napoleon. Fox died in 1806, and in 1811 Trotter's memoir was published. It was dedicated to the Prince Regent and was highly successful, running through three editions and being reviewed at great length in the twelfth number of the Quarterly Review.

On 10 February 1812, Southey wrote to Landor to the effect that he had heard from John Murray that he, Murray, had received an unfinished manuscript from Landor—the 'Commentary on Trotter's Fox'. It so happened that Southey had just negotiated with Murray for the publication of Count Julian, *and Landor had not mentioned to Southey that he had of his own volition sent this further manuscript to Murray. Murray told Southey that the 'Commentary' contained libellous passages, and he could not possibly publish it as it stood. Landor replied that he would do what Southey recommended. It had come to be written, Landor explained, in this way. He had been trying to compose an oration which should be more in the Athenian manner, praising the living rather than the dead; he had pronounced a eulogy on Warren Hastings, comparing with him Charles James Fox but admitting that the great Indian ruler might possibly have been deaf to the voice of misery and of justice; and he had compared Lord Peterborough with Wellington, proving to his satisfaction that Wellington was, at any rate, the equal of Peterborough or Hastings.*

> *'But of what avail to write orations in the Athenian or any other style? After all, who will read anything I write? One enemy, an adept in bookery and reviewship, can without talents and without industry, suppress in a great degree all my labours, as easily as a mischievous boy could crush with a roller a whole bed of crocuses. Yet, I would not destroy what I had written. It filled, indeed, but eight or nine sheets; interlined it is true, in a thousand places and everywhere close. I transferred, then, whatever I could conveniently, with some observations I had written on Trotter's silly book, and preserved nearly half, I think, by adopting this plan.'²*

¹ Hobhouse, *Fox*, p. 237.
² Landor, *Charles James Fox*, ed. Stephen Wheeler, 1907, pp. xi–xii.

Landor, moreover, had dedicated the book to Madison, President of the United States. But the Tory Gifford, the editor of the Quarterly, *took great exception to the book, with the result that Murray procrastinated and then suggested to Southey that he would prefer Southey to procure another publisher for it on behalf of Landor. This was hardly surprising, for Canning was also on the editorial board of the* Quarterly, *and was attacked in the book, for Landor had always disliked him. Landor commented to Southey that Murray had been persuaded 'either by Canning or some other scoundrel whom I have piquitted in the work to withdraw from the publication of it; although I have soaped all the bristles that could have been clutched by the foulhand of our Attorney-General'.*[1] *The work was apparently printed but all copies disappeared, except Southey's, which came into the hands of Monckton-Milnes, and was subsequently discovered in Lord Crewe's library, when it was edited by Stephen Wheeler and published in 1907 by none other than John Murray!*

[1] Elwin, *Landor*, p. 145.

From *Count Julian*
1812

Tent of Julian

Roderigo and Julian

JULIAN. The people had deserted thee, and throng'd
My standard, had I raised it, at the first;
But once subsiding, and no voice of mine
Calling by name each grievance to each man,
They, silent and submissive by degrees,
Bore thy hard yoke, and hadst thou but opprest,
Would still have born it: thou hast now deceived;
Thou hast done all a foreign foe could do
And more against them; with ingratitude
Not hell itself could arm the foreign foe;
'Tis forged at home and kills not from afar.
Amid whate'er vain glories fell upon
Thy rainbow span of power, which I dissolve,
Boast not how thou conferredst wealth and rank,
How thou preservedst me, my family,
All my distinctions, all my offices,
When Witiza was murder'd; that I stand
Count Julian at this hour by special grace.
The sword of Julian saved the walls of Ceuta,
And not the shadow that attends his name:
It was no badge, no title, that o'erthrew
Soldier and steed and engine. Don Roderigo!
The truly and the falsely great here differ:
These by dull wealth or daring fraud advance;
Him the Almighty calls amid his people
To sway the wills and passions of mankind.
The weak of heart and intellect beheld

64

Thy splendour, and adored thee lord of Spain:
I rose . . . Roderigo lords o'er Spain no more.
  RODERIGO. Now to a traitor's add a boaster's name.
  JULIAN. Shameless and arrogant, dost thou believe
I boast for pride or pastime? forced to boast,
Truth cost me more than falsehood e'er cost thee.
Divested of that purple of the soul,
That potency, that palm of wise ambition,
Cast headlong by thy madness from that high,
That only eminence 'twixt earth and heaven,
Virtue, which some desert, but none despise,
Whether thou art beheld again on earth,
Whether a captive or a fugitive,
Miner or galley-slave, depends on me;
But he alone who made me what I am
Can make me greater or can make me less.
  RODERIGO. Chance, and chance only, threw me in thy
    power;
Give me my sword again and try my strength.
  JULIAN. I tried it in the front of thousands.
  RODERIGO   Death
At least vouchsafe me from a soldier's hand.
  JULIAN. I love to hear thee ask it: now my own
Would not be bitter; no nor immature.
  RODERIGO. Defy it, say thou rather.
  JULIAN.   Death itself
Shall not be granted thee, unless from God;
A dole from his and from no other hand.
Thou shalt now hear and own thine infamy.
  RODERIGO. Chains, dungeons, tortures . . . but I hear no
    more.
  JULIAN. Silence, thou wretch! live on . . . ay, live . . .
    abhorr'd.
Thou shalt have tortures, dungeons, chains enough;
They naturally rise and grow around
Monsters like thee, everywhere, and for ever.
  RODERIGO. Insulter of the fallen! must I endure
Commands as well as threats? my vassal's too?
Nor breathe from underneath his trampling feet?

JULIAN. Could I speak patiently who speak to thee,
I would say more: part of thy punishment
It should be, to be taught.
RODERIGO.   Reserve thy wisdom
Until thy patience come, its best ally:
I learn no lore, of peace or war, from thee.
    JULIAN. No, thou shalt study soon another tongue,
And suns more ardent shall mature thy mind.
Either the cross thou bearest, and thy knees
Among the silent caves of Palestine
Wear the sharp flints away with midnight prayer,
Or thou shalt keep the fasts of Barbary,
Shalt wait amid the crowds that throng the well
From sultry noon till the skies fade again,
To draw up water and to bring it home
In the crackt gourd of some vile testy knave,
Who spurns thee back with bastinaded foot
For ignorance or delay of his command.
    RODERIGO. Rather the poison or the bowstring.
    JULIAN.   Slaves
To other's passions die such deaths as those:
Slaves to their own should die . . .
    RODERIGO.   What worse?
    JULIAN.   Their own.
    RODERIGO. Is this thy counsel, renegade?
    JULIAN.   Not mine:
I point a better path, nay, force thee on.
I shelter thee from every brave man's sword
While I am near thee: I bestow on thee
Life: if thou die, 'tis when thou sojournest
Protected by this arm and voice no more:
'Tis slavishly, 'tis ignominiously,
'Tis by a villian's knife.
    RODERIGO.   By whose?
    JULIAN.   Roderigo's.
    RODERIGO. O powers of vengeance! must I hear? . . .
        endure? . . .
Live?
    JULIAN. Call thy vassals: no? then wipe the drops

Of froward childhood from thy shameless eyes.
So! thou canst weep for passion; not for pity.
   RODERIGO. One hour ago I ruled all Spain! a camp
Not larger than a sheepfold stood alone
Against me: now, no friend throughout the world
Follows my steps or hearkens to my call.
Behold the turns of fortune, and expect
No better: of all faithless men the Moors
Are the most faithless: from thy own experience
Thou canst not value nor rely on them.
   JULIAN. I value not the mass that makes my sword,
Yet while I use it I rely on it.
   RODERIGO. Julian, thy gloomy soul still meditates . . .
Plainly I see it . . . death to me . . . pursue
The dictates of thy leaders, let revenge
Have its full sway, let Barbary prevail,
And the pure creed her elders have embraced:
Those placid sages hold assassination
A most compendious supplement to law.
   JULIAN. Thou knowest not the one, nor I the other.
Torn hast thou from me all my soul held dear,
Her form, her voice, all, hast thou banisht from me,
Nor dare I, wretched as I am! recall
Those solaces of every grief erewhile.
I stand abased before insulting crime,
I falter like a criminal myself;
The hand that hurl'd thy chariot o'er its wheels,
That held thy steeds erect and motionless
As molten statues on some palace-gate,
Shakes as with palsied age before thee now.
Gone is the treasure of my heart for ever,
Without a father, mother, friend, or name.
Daughter of Julian . . . Such was her delight . . .
Such was mine too! what pride more innocent,
What surely less deserving pangs like these,
Than springs from filial and parental love!
Debarr'd from every hope that issues forth
Will stretch before her their whole weary length
Amid the sameness of obscurity.

She wanted not seclusion to unveil
Her thoughts to heaven, cloister, nor midnight bell;
She found it in all places, at all hours:
While to assuage my labours she indulged
A playfulness that shunn'd a mother's eye,
Still to avert my perils there arose
A piety that even from *me* retired.

RODERIGO. Such was she! what am I! those are the arms
That are triumphant when the battle fails.
O Julian! Julian! all thy former words
Struck but the imbecile plumes of vanity,
These thro' its steely coverings pierce the heart.
I ask not life nor death; but, if I live,
Send my most bitter enemy to watch
My secret paths, send poverty, send pain . . .
I will add more . . . wise as thou art, thou knowest
No foe more furious than forgiven kings.
I ask not then what thou would'st never grant:
May heaven, O Julian, from thy hand receive
A pardon'd man, a chasten'd criminal.

JULIAN. This further curse hast thou inflicted; wretch!
I can not pardon thee.

RODERIGO.   Thy tone, thy mien,
Refute those words.

JULIAN.   No . . . I can *not* forgive.

RODERIGO. Upon my knee, my conqueror, I implore!
Upon the earth, before thy feet . . . hard heart!

JULIAN. Audacious! hast thou never heard that prayer
And scorn'd it? 'tis the last thou shouldst repeat.
Upon the earth! upon her knees, O God?

RODERIGO. Resemble not a wretch so lost as I:
Be better; O! be happier; and pronounce it.

JULIAN. I swerve not from my purpose: thou art mine,
Conquered; and I have sworn to dedicate,
Like a torn banner on my chapel's roof,
Thee to that power from whom thou hast rebell'd.
Expiate thy crimes by prayer, by penances.

RODERIGO. Hasten the hour of trial, speak of peace.
Pardon me not then, but with purer lips

Implore of God, who *would* hear *thee*, to pardon.
   JULIAN. Hope it I may . . . pronounce it . . . O Roderigo!
Ask it of him who can; I too will ask,
And, in my own transgressions, pray for thine.
   RODERIGO. One name I dare not . . .
   JULIAN.   Go; abstain from that;
I do conjure thee, raise not in my soul
Again the tempest that has wreckt my fame;
Thou shalt not breathe in the same clime with her.
Far o'er the unebbing sea thou shalt adore
The eastern star, and may thy end be peace.

Within four years of purchasing his estate at Llanthony, Landor was in the thick of one legal entanglement after another. There was little mirth from 'Boythorn'. He disliked the Welsh, as they him. With all Landor's headstrong impetuosity, his genius for upsetting his neighbours, his pride and his quick rise to anger, one cannot help feeling great sorrow for him, in so much as all the money he had and was to pour into his estate was to be completely wasted, to leave him a poor man for the rest of his life. He had as solicitor one Charles Gabell, who mainly preferred the company of local farmers, as well as fancying himself as something of a dandy with the local females. He thought Landor an easy and 'pluckable' client, while it was undoubtedly bruited about that Landor was an eccentric and impossible man to deal with. Thus, when Landor wrote to the bishop of the diocese asking permission to restore a part of Llanthony priory and received no reply, he naturally wrote again, remarking 'God alone is great enough for to ask anything twice'; to which came the cold answer that an Act of Parliament would be required before it could be carried out. Landor had experience of 'Acts of Parliament'!

More serious to Landor was his brush with the Lord-Lieutenant of the county, the Duke of Beaufort. Landor had wished to become a magistrate (there was not one locally) but Beaufort had heard of a 'row' Landor had had on a recent assize case when he was on the jury; the Duke's brother had sat on that same jury and had reported dissentions caused by Landor, and further added that his reputation was for 'republican' sympathies, which certainly did not please the Duke, who therefore did not deign to reply to Landor. Pursuing the matter further, Landor wrote to the Lord Chancellor, Lord Eldon, well known for his High Tory sympathies; Landor again received no reply, yet in his first letter to the Chancellor he explained how much he 'personally had done for Llanthony', which, indeed, was only too true. Of the Welsh, he wrote to Eldon: 'If drunkenness, idleness, mischief and revenge are the principal characteristics of the savage state, what nation—I will not say in Europe, but in the world—is so singularly tattooed with them as the Welsh?—The earth contains no race of human beings so totally vile and worthless as the Welsh.'[1]

[1] Colvin, *Landor*, p. 73.

The final straw came when the Betham family who had rented lands from him for ludicrously small rentals, repaid him by totally neglecting them. Eventually the estate became bankrupt and legal cases sprang up all over the place, so that Landor fled, leaving his half-built mansion, his untilled farmlands in disarray, and the estate in the hands of a trustee.

Meantime, with all his troubles, Landor wrote a comedy entitled Charitable Dowager. *He pretended that this was a manuscript written in Bath in 1687 by one Hardcastle. He wrote to Southey concerning this play in August, having previously sent it to him.*

'*I wish to improve my comedy, and to have it acted. The acting I never thought of; but Juan Santos de Murieta, a poor man of Castro, who received me hospitably when I found Bilbao in occupation of the French, is perhaps ruined by those barbarians. I see no speedier way, little speed as there is in this, of sending him some money. If some dashing and adventurous bookseller would give me 100£, or 50£, or 30£ for all I can ever get by the comedy and the preface—which is, I think, a humorous specimen of modern editorship—he might recover as much by the mere acting. But not unless you will suggest some improvement in the plan. I never could keep to any plan of my own. I am romantic, and I am in external dread of being absurd. This has often thrown a chill over me, and closed the petals of my fairest flowers. I will add a portion of the preface, in which I defend the character of Hardcastle, my own manner . . .*'

But of this play not even a single copy was printed.

In the middle of May 1814, Landor decided to leave England. So bad had been his financial position that he had had to beg for two or three pounds to keep himself going. But, at length, after the most protracted and complicated negotiations, and finding means to escape his creditors, Landor wrote to Southey:

'*Every hope of meeting you again in England has vanished. Pardon me if this is only the second of my wishes. My first is, that I may become by degrees indifferent to this country. The Court of Exchequer has decided in my favour; but Betham has been able to promise bail and a reprieve, so that the ends of justice are defeated. Nearly three*

*years rent will be due before I can receive one farthing from him;
and all my timber is spoiled. I shall be utterly ruined. Not being
able to pay the interest of 10,000£ debt on the Llanthony estate,
the mortgagee will immediately seize on it until he has paid himself
the whole of the principal. The laws of England are made entirely
for the protection of guilt. A creditor could imprison me for twenty
pounds, while a man who owes me two thousand more, can convert
wealth and affluence into poverty and distress—can, in short, drive
me forever from my native country, and riot with impunity on the
ruins of my estate. I had promised my mother to visit her. I never
can hope to see her again. She is 72, and her sorrow at my
overwhelming and most unmerited misfortunes will too surely shorten
her days. My wife, when she married me, little thought she would
leave all her friends, to live in obscurity, and perhaps in want. For
my sake she refused one of the largest fortunes that any private
gentleman possesses, and another person of distinguished rank.
Whoever comes near me is either unhappy or ungrateful . . .'[1]*

1814–18

*Landor, having arrived in Jersey, was later joined by his wife and one
of her sisters. Julia, who had thought that she was marrying a well-to-
do man with whom she would enjoy a gay life in society in Bath, was
now bitterly disillusioned. A keen argument ensued when they were in
Jersey, with the result that Landor arose at four o'clock in the morning
and left for Tours. On 2 October he informed Southey from Tours that
he had left his wife. But when he heard a few days later that she was
grief-stricken and ill, Landor told Southey that he would fetch her.
'My own fear is, that I shall never be able to keep my promise to its
full extent, to forgive humiliating and insulting language. Certainly I
shall never be so happy as I was before; that is beyond all question.'*

*At least in Tours Landor made a great friendship; he met Francis
Hare, who had arrived to be with his sick father who died there in 1815.
Francis George Hare, the second of that name, had been born in 1786
and died fifty-six years later. He was the father of the famous Augustus
Hare, the youngest of his five children, and was renowned for his
learning. 'At the little court of Weimar,' his son records,[2] 'he was*

[1] Forster, *Landor*, vol. i, pp. 407–8.
[2] Augustus Hare, *The Story of My Life*, abridged and edited by Malcolm Barnes
in two volumes: Vol. 1, *The Years with Mother*, p. 6.

adored.' 'Careful as to his personal appearance, Francis Hare was always dressed in the height of fashion. It is remembered how he would retire and change his dress three times in the course of a single ball! In everything he followed the foibles of the day.'

Meanwhile, Napoleon escaped from Elba, and the English colony at Tours dispersed, though Landor remained, writing to Carnot and declaring he would remain in France. He was assured of protection, but after Waterloo, with the monarchy restored, Landor grew restless, and on the arrival of his brother Robert en route for Italy, he decided to join him.

The journey from Tours to Milan was hardly successful:

'. . . tempers frayed, the brothers fell to antagonism, and Robert became less sympathetically inclined. At least Julia had been badly frightened when Landor had abruptly left her; possibly her mother had shown no taste for the liability of a daughter living apart from her husband and less sympathy with her desolate state than she expected. She had returned full of good resolutions to play the submissive wife, and finding him in real danger of arrest, she felt both anxiety for his sake and sympathy with his troubles.'[1]

Landor and his wife finally settled at Como, where they were to remain for the next three years. But even at Como there was to be trouble, for here resided that very troublesome lady, Caroline of Brunswick. Landor had written to Southey about her. As rumours were rife that the Prince Regent was contemplating getting a divorce from her, and as there were agents everywhere watching her movements, it was assumed that Landor was one of them. It was the last thing that Landor wanted, as he himself was hiding from his creditors. However, he found a pleasant house, where he and Julia were able to settle. 'Landor now cultivated the habit of detachment which he pursued for the rest of his life.'[2] *He remained at Como until September 1818. During these years he published nothing but occasional verse in English or Latin, and could not afford to pay for their publication. In 1817 Southey came to visit him.*

Some of the meetings between Southey and Landor are recorded in subsequent 'Imaginary Conversations': 'Well do I remember our long

[1] Elwin, *Landor*, p. 176.
[2] *Idem.*

conversations in the silent and solitary church of Sant'Abodia (surely the coolest spot in Italy), and how often I turned back my head toward the open door, fearing lest some pious passer-by, or some more distant one in the wood above, pursuing the pathway that leads to the tower of Luitprand, should hear the roof echo with your laughter at the stories you had collected about the brotherhood and sisterhood of the place.'
They also talked much about Wordsworth, and the scandals concerning the Princess of Wales. When Southey returned to England he wrote to Landor warning him not to become involved with her or her entourage. He also told him the tragic news that the Regent's only child, the Princess Charlotte had died.

On 5 March 1818, to Landor's great delight, his first son was born. He was christened Arnold Savage, after Sir Arnold Savage, a speaker of the House of Commons, whom Landor believed to have been of his mother's family.

Later in the year he was forced to leave Como. He had read of an attack on England by a Milanese poet named Vincenzo Monti, who 'wrote a most violent attack invective in the form of a sonnet against England,

'*I answered it in latin, and attempted to print my poem, with an epigram on Voltaire and four others, in which no name whatever was employed. The censor declared that there were six libels I expostulated with him. I informed him, for I had consulted a sensible jurist, that censors never refused their licence in Latin compositions unless sovereigns of their alliances, or religion or morals were attacked. I attributed his proceeding to ignorance of these customs, and not to injustice; and I directed a copy of my letter to Count Strasoldo, principal of the council. Instead of correcting a gross abuse of power, this gentleman wrote a long letter to the regio delegato of the province. The regio delegato sent me information that my Latin Poems were detained* only *because it was customary to send two copies, one of which continued in the archives of the censor, but that if I was desirous of it I might apply to his office. Not caring about the copy, I never went. About a week afterwards he sent a second letter to inform me that he requested my attendance on affairs very interesting to me. I went immediately. He then discovered his first fallacy, and began to read a letter from Count Strasoldo, in which this fellow expressed his surprise that I should use*

74

injurious *expressions towards the royal censor, a person immediately acting under government. He then closed the letter and thought it requisite to make comment upon it. He was astonished that I should write an* insolent *letter. I stopped him quietly, and said, "Sir the word* insolent *is never applied to a gentleman. If you had known the laws of honour or propriety you would not have used it; and if you had dared to utter it in any other place you would not have received a bella bastonata." At this he sprang from his chair and rang the bell. He called the guards and all the officers of the police, who live under the same roof during the daytime, with these reinforcements he pursued: "Prepare instantly to conduct this gentleman to Milan. Sir, unless you immediately retract your words you answer to government." I replied, "I never retract any word of mine; but I tell you in the presence of all these persons that before I leave this room you shall retract yours." He then pretended that he had said* rather *insolent, that insolent meant disrespectful or violent, that if I understood the language that I should not have animadverted on the expression, that he expressed the sentiments of Count Strasoldo. I replied, "I care not a quattrino what are the sentiments of Count Strasoldo; but he would not dare, from me, to use such expressions towards his equal. There is not one among the guards you have called in who would endure it. As for your sending me to Milan under arrest, do it, if you are not afraid of exposing yourself still more than you have done." He then began talking of his honour, that he had been in the service, that a threat of a caning was not to be borne, and that if it was not for his high office he would settle the business with his sword in the square. I laughed in his face; and the rascal had the baseness to offer his hand in token of reconciliation, and to tell me what a friend he had always been of the English. The story was carried all over town the same evening, although it rained heavily; and what surprises me is that it was told correctly. I remained in Como a week longer, rather wishing to be sent for to Milan. My time expired on the 19th of September. I protracted my stay till the 28th, and no attempt was made to assassinate me.'*[1]

This letter is wonderfully typical of Landor's temperament, of his impetuous and quixotic nature.

From Como they went to Genoa and on 1 October 1818 rented the

---

[1] Forster, *Landor*, vol. i, pp. 443-5.

Marchese Pallavicini's palace. Landor describes Genoa as 'the most magnificent city in the world' and 'the most reasonably discontented'. From Genoa he went to Pisa because he heard it was cheaper there, but, having arrived, he found that city dearer than Genoa. There he read Wordsworth's poetry and was tremendously impressed with his work. 'Wordsworth, Southey, Miss Baillie, what a class! Even the breakfast-table poets, Campbell, Ld Biron, Scott, Crabbe, Rogers, put all the continent to shame.'

Landor had heard that the Royal Academy of Stockholm had offered a prize for the best ode on the accession of Bernadotte. He set to work on this and wrote an ode to Gustavum Regem *which he sent to Southey. When he did not hear from Southey, he sent him a further copy. Southey had, however, sent the work to the Swedish Ambassador in London, but like the majority of Landor's works of this nature he heard nothing. He himself published, when in Italy, a Latin idyll entitled* Sponsalia Polyxenae.

1821–24

It was not until 1821 that Landor finally settled down to a period of peace. He found a suite of apartments in the Medici Palace in Florence, where he lived for five years, and for the next three years at the Villa Castiglione just outside Florence. From a literary point of view this period of his life was by far the most important, since he no longer continued to experiment in literary modes. What best suited his genius was the form of writing conversational dialogues in prose. These are the works by which he is now remembered and which made his name famous, though he was never financially enriched.

His choice of figures included Greek classicists, Latin poets, medieval scholars, historical figures, and all who came into his ken. He had no regard for historical accuracy, and allowed fact and fiction to mingle. He was a collector of pictures, not books, and therefore his writing in Florence was accomplished without recourse to the vast reference library he would have needed to achieve historical accuracy. Nevertheless, he possessed a remarkably retentive memory. No man, however, could carry in his head so catholic an array of persons and subjects without using poetic licence. But all the vast number of persons Landor used, enabled his capacious mind to display his theories, his beliefs, and to expound arguments.

'*When I was younger,*' Landor declared, '*I was fond of wandering in solitary places, and was never afraid of slumbering in woods and grottoes. Among the chief pleasures of my life, and among the commonest of my occupations, was the bringing before me such heroes and heroines of antiquity, such poets and sages, such of the prosperous and the unfortunate, as most interested me by their courage, their eloquence and their adventures. Engaging them in conversations best suited to their characters, I knew perfectly their manners, their steps, their voices; and often did I moisten with my tears the models I had been forming of the less happy.*'

The idea of the 'Conversations' was encouraged by his correspondence with Southey, who too had planned a book of 'Colloquies'. It went through their minds to collaborate. By 9 March 1822, Landor had finished fifteen dialogues (having burnt two in a rage); these were sent to Longmans. Landor had no luck with Longmans, so he placed the whole matter in the hands of Julius Hare, the elder brother of his greatest friend Francis. Julius Hare was friendly with John Taylor, the principal of a firm called Taylor & Hessey, and he endeavoured to suggest a contract by which the profits or losses were shared equally by publisher and author. Having favourably considered this suggestion, Taylor then read the manuscripts and began suggesting alterations. Endless arguments ensued. Both Wordsworth and Southey were brought into these discussions. In the end Southey undertook the responsibilities. Not least enviably for Southey, one of the 'Conversations' was between Southey and Porson upon the merits of Wordsworth's poetry. Landor's comments, however, caused no offence to Wordsworth, and the result was that this 'Conversation' was first printed in 1823 in the London Magazine. *Originally, the first volume of the* Conversations *had been dedicated to Wordsworth, but what with the delay of publication, and the contentiousness of some of the arguments and opinions which might have offended Wordsworth, Landor changed his mind and dedicated the volume to his brother-in-law, Colonel Edward Stopford.*

Thirty-six 'Conversations' appeared in the first two volumes— eighteen in each volume. Hazlitt reviewed them in the Edinburgh Review, *in an article which was tempered with both praise and criticism. The* Quarterly Review *was hostile, but Julius Hare countered it with his review in the* London Magazine *just before the appearance of the* Quarterly; *he anticipated all the reprehensions of the Tory oracle, putting them into the mouth of an imaginery interlocutor whom he calls Hargreaves and represents as a cynical, scribbling barrister, and himself traversing and over-riding them.*[1]

[1] Colvin, *Landor*, p. 106.

From *Imaginary Conversations*
Vol. 1, 1824

QUEEN ELIZABETH AND CECIL

ELIZABETH. I advise thee again, churlish Cecil, how that our Edmund Spenser, whom thou callest most uncourteously a whining whelp, hath good and solid reason for his complaint. God's blood! shall the lady that tieth my garter and shuffles the smock over my head, or the lord that steadieth my chair's back while I eat, or the other that looketh to my buck-hounds lest they be mangy, be holden by me in higher esteem and estate than he who hath placed me among the bravest of past times, and will as safely and surely set me down among the loveliest in the future?

CECIL. Your Highness must remember he carouseth fully for such deserts: fifty pounds a-year of unclipped moneys, and a butt of canary wine; not to mention three thousand acres in Ireland, worth fairly another fifty and another butt, in seasonable and quiet years.

ELIZABETH. The moneys are not enough to sustain a pair of grooms and a pair of palfreys, and more wine hath been drunken in my presence at a feast. The moneys are given to such men, that they may not incline nor be obligated to any vile or lowly occupation; and the canary, that they may entertain such promising wits as court their company and converse; and that in such manner there may be alway in our land a succession of these heirs unto fame. He hath written, not indeed with his wonted fancifulness, nor in learned and majestical language, but in homely and rustic wise, some verses which have moved me, and haply the more inasmuch as they demonstrate to me that his genius hath been dampened by his adversities. Read them.

CECIL.
'How much is lost when neither heart nor eye
    Rosewinged Desire or fabling Hope deceives;
When boyhood with quick throb hath ceased to spy

79

The dubious apple in the yellow leaves;
'When, rising from the turf where youth reposed,
We find but deserts in the far-sought shore;
When the huge book of Faery-land lies closed,
And those strong brazen clasps will yield no more.'

ELIZABETH. The said Edmund hath also furnished unto the weaver at Arras, John Blanquieres, on my account, a description for some of his cunningest wenches to work at, supplied by mine own self, indeed, as far as the subject-matter goes, but set forth by him with figures and fancies, and daintily enough bedecked. I could have wished he had thereunto joined a fair comparison between Dian—no matter—he might perhaps have fared the better for it; but poets' wits,—God help them!—when did they ever sit close about them? Read the poesy, not over-rich, and concluding very awkwardly and meanly.

CECIL.
'Where forms the lotus, with its level leaves
And solid blossoms, many floating isles,
What heavenly radiance swift descending cleaves
The darksome wave! Unwonted beauty smiles
'On its pure bosom, on each bright-eyed flower,
On every nymph, and twenty sate around.
Lo! 'twas Diana—from the sultry hour
Hither she fled, nor fear'd she sight or sound.
'Unhappy youth, whom thirst and quiver-reeds
Drew to these haunts, whom awe forbade to fly!
Three faithful dogs before him rais'd their heads,
And watched and wonder'd at that fixèd eye.
'Forth sprang his favourite—with her arrow-hand
Too late the goddess hid what hand may hide,
Of every nymph and every reed complain'd,
And dashed upon the bank the waters wide.
'On the prone head and sandal'd feet they flew—
Lo! slender, hoofs and branching horns appear!
The last marr'd voice not e'en the favourite knew,
But bay'd and fasten'd on the upbraiding deer.
'Far be, chaste goddess, far from me and mine
The stream that tempts thee in the summer noon!
Alas, that vengeance dwells with charms divine—

QUEEN ELIZABETH AND CECIL

ELIZABETH. Pshaw! give me the paper: I forewarned thee how it ended,—pitifully, pitifully.

CECIL. I cannot think otherwise than that the undertaker of the aforecited poesy hath chosen your Highness; for I have seen painted—I know not where, but I think no farther off than Putney —the identically same Dian, with full as many nymphs, as he calls them, and more dogs. So small a matter as a page of poesy shall never stir my choler nor twitch my purse-string.

ELIZABETH. I have read in Plinius and Mela of a runlet near Dodona, which kindled by approximation an unlighted torch, and extinguished a lighted one. Now, Cecil, I desire no such a jetty to be celebrated as the decoration of my court: in simpler words, which your gravity may more easily understand, I would not from the fountain of honour give lustre to the dull and ignorant, deadening and leaving in its tomb the lamp of literature and genius. I ardently wish my reign to be remembered: if my actions were different from what they are, I should as ardently wish it to be forgotten. Those are the worst of suicides, who voluntarily and propensely stab or suffocate their fame, when God hath commanded them to stand on high for an example. We call him parricide who destroys the author of his existence: tell me, what shall we call him who casts forth to the dogs and birds of prey its most faithful propagator and most firm support? Mark me, I do not speak of that existence which the proudest must close in a ditch,—the narrowest, too, of ditches and the soonest filled and fouled, and whereunto a pinch of ratsbane or a poppyhead may bend him; but of that which reposes on our own good deeds, carefully picked up, skilfully put together, and decorously laid out for us by another's kind understanding: I speak of an existence such as no father is author of, or provides for. The parent gives us few days and sorrowful; the poet, many and glorious: the one (supposing him discreet and kindly) best reproves our faults; the other best remunerates our virtues.

A page of poesy is a little matter: be it so; but of a truth I do tell thee, Cecil, it shall master full many a bold heart that the Spaniard cannot trouble; it shall win to it full many a proud and flighty one that even chivalry and manly comeliness cannot touch. I may shake titles and dignities by the dozen from my breakfast-board; but I may not save those upon whose heads I shake them from rottenness and oblivion. This year they and their sovereign dwell together;

next year, they and their beagle. Both have names, but names perishable. The keeper of my privy-seal is an earl: what then? the keeper of my poultry-yard is a Caesar. In honest truth, a name given to a man is no better than a skin given to him: what is not natively his own falls off and comes to nothing.

I desire in future to hear no contempt of penmen, unless a depraved use of the pen shall have so cramped them as to incapacitate them for the sword and for the Council Chamber. If Alexander was the Great, what was Aristotle who made him so, and taught him every art and science he knew, except three,—those of drinking, of blaspheming, and of murdering his bosom friends? Come along: I will bring thee back again nearer home. Thou mightest toss and tumble in thy bed many nights and never eke out the substance of a stanza; but Edmund, if perchance I should call upon him for his counsel, would give me as wholesome and prudent as any of you. We should indemnify such men for the injustice we do unto them in not calling them about us, and for the mortification they must suffer at seeing their inferiors set before them. Edmund is grave and gentle: he complains of fortune, not of Elizabeth; of courts, not of Cecil. I am resolved,—so help me, God!—he shall have no further cause for his repining. Go, convey unto him those twelve silver spoons, with the apostles on them, gloriously gilded; and deliver into his hand these twelve large golden pieces, sufficing for the yearly maintenance of another horse and groom. Beside which, set open before him with due reference this Bible, wherein he may read the mercies of God toward those who waited in patience for His blessing; and this pair of crimson silk hose, which thou knowest I have worn only thirteen months, taking heed that the heel-piece be put into good and sufficient restoration, at my sole charges, by the Italian woman nigh the pollard elm at Charing Cross.

SOUTHEY AND PORSON[1]

PORSON. I suspect, Mr Southey, you are angry with me for the freedom with which I have spoken of your poetry and Wordsworth's.

[1] Richard Porson (1759–1808) was one of the greatest scholars of his age, if not the greatest. Son of a parish clerk of East Ruston, Norfolk, he attracted the attention of the curate of the parish by his astonishing memory. He was able to go to Eton by the help of a patron and then went to Cambridge and became a

SOUTHEY AND PORSON

SOUTHEY. What could have induced you to imagine it, Mr Professor ? You have indeed bent your eyes upon me, since we have been together, with somewhat of fierceness and defiance: I presume you fancied me to be a commentator. You wrong me in your belief that any opinion on my poetical works hath molested me; but you afford me more than compensation in supposing me acutely sensible of injustice done to Wordsworth. If we must converse on these topics, we will converse on him. What man ever existed who spent a more inoffensive life, or adorned it with nobler studies ?

PORSON. I believe so; and they who attack him with virulence are men of as little morality as reflection. I have demonstrated that one of them, he who wrote the *Pursuits of Literature*, could not construe a Greek sentence or scan a verse; and I have fallen on the very *Index* from which he drew out his forlorn hope on the parade. This is incomparably the most impudent fellow I have met with in the course of my reading, which has lain, you know, in a province where impudence is no rarity. . . .

I had visited a friend in *King's Road* when he entered.
'Have you seen the *Review* ?' cried he. 'Worse then ever! I am resolved to insert a paragraph in the papers, declaring that I had no concern in the last number.'
'Is it so very bad ?' said I, quietly.
'Infamous! detestable!' exclaimed he.
'Sit down, then: nobody will believe you,' was my answer.
Since that morning he has discovered that I drink harder than usual, that my faculties are wearing fast away, that once, indeed, I had some Greek in my head, but—he then claps the forefinger to the side of his nose, turns his eye slowly upward, and looks compassionately and calmly.

SOUTHEY. Come, Mr Porson, grant him his merits: no critic is

---

fellow of Trinity College. This position he lost by refusing to take orders. In 1792, however, he was appointed Professor of Greek in the University though he mainly lived in London, where he indulged in drinking heavily. Nevertheless he was sought by fellow scholars. He left, however, very little literary work, though he translated four plays of Euripedes, while his most renowned work was his *Letters* to Archdeacon Travis.

In this 'Imaginary Conversation' Southey and Porson discuss in particular Wordsworth's *Laodamia*.

better contrived to make any work a monthly one, no writer more dexterous in giving a finishing touch.

PORSON. The plagiary has a greater latitude of choice than we; and if he brings home a parsnip or turnip-top, when he could as easily have pocketed a nectarine or a pineapple, he must be a block-head. I never heard the name of the *Pursuer of Literature*, who has little more merit in having stolen than he would have had if he had never stolen at all; and I have forgotten that other man's, who evinced his fitness to be the censor of our age, by a translation of the most naked and impure satires of antiquity—those of Juvenal, which owe their preservation to the partiality of the Friars. I shall entertain an unfavourable opinion of him if he has translated them well: pray, has he?

SOUTHEY. Indeed, I do not know. I read poets for their poetry, and to extract that nutriment of the intellect and of the heart which poetry should contain. I never listen to the swans of the cesspool, and must declare that nothing is heavier to me than rottenness and corruption.

PORSON. You are right, sir, perfectly right. A translator of Juvenal would open a public drain to look for a needle, and may miss it. My nose is not easily offended; but I must have something to fill my belly. Come, we will lay aside the scrip of the transpositor and the pouch of the pursuer, in reserve for the days of unleavened bread; and again, if you please, to the lakes and mountains. Now we are both in better humour, I must bring you to a confession that in your friend Wordsworth there is occasionally a little trash.

SOUTHEY. A haunch of venison would be trash to a Brahmin, a bottle of Burgundy to the xerif of Mecca. We are guided by precept, by habit, by taste, by constitution. Hitherto our sentiments on poetry have been delivered down to us from authority; and if it can be demonstrated, as I think it may be, that the authority is inadequate, and that the dictates are often inapplicable and often misinterpreted, you will allow me to remove the cause out of court. Every man can see what is very bad in a poem; almost every one can see what is very good: but you, Mr Porson, who have turned over all the volumes of all the commentators, will inform me whether I am right or wrong in asserting that no critic hath yet appeared who hath been able to fix or to discern the exact degrees of excellence above a certain point.

SOUTHEY AND PORSON

PORSON. None.

SOUTHEY. The reason is, because the eyes of no one have been upon a level with it. Supposing, for the sake of argument, the contest of Hesiod and Homer to have taken place: the judges who decided in favour of the worse, and he, indeed, in the poetry has little merit, may have been elegant, wise, and conscientious men. Their decision was in favour of that to the species of which they had been the most acustomed. Corinna was preferred to Pindar no fewer than five times, and the best judges in Greece gave her the preference; yet whatever were her powers, and beyond a question they were extraordinary, we may assure ourselves that she stood many degrees below Pindar. Nothing is more absurd than the report that the judges were prepossessed by her beauty. Plutarch tells us that she was much older than her competitor, who consulted her judgment in his earlier odes. Now, granting their first competition to have been when Pindar was twenty years old, and that the others were in the years succeeding, her beauty must have been somewhat on the decline; for in Greece there are few women who retain the graces, none who retain the bloom of youth, beyond the twenty-third year. Her countenance, I doubt not, was expressive: but expression, although it gives beauty to men, makes women pay dearly for its stamp, and pay soon. Nature seems, in protection to their loveliness, to have ordered that they who are our superiors in quickness and sensibility should be little disposed to laborious thought, or to long excursions in the labyrinths of fancy. We may be convinced that the verdict of the judges was biassed by nothing else than the habitudes of thinking; we may be convinced, too, that living in an age when poetry was cultivated highly, and selected from the most acute and the most dispassionate, they were subject to no greater errors of opinion than are the learned messmates of our English colleges.

PORSON. You are more liberal in your largesses to the fair Greeks than a friend of mine was, who resided in Athens to acquire the language. He assured me that beauty there was in bud at thirteen, in full blossom at fifteen, losing a leaf or two every day at seventeen, trembling on the thorn at nineteen, and under the tree at twenty.

SOUTHEY. Mr Porson, it does not appear to me that anything more is necessary, in the first instance, than to interrogate our hearts in what manner they have been affected. If the ear is satisfied;

if at one moment a tumult is aroused in the breast, and tranquillised at another, with a perfect consciousness of equal power exerted in both cases; if we rise up from the perusal of the work with a strong excitement to thought, to imagination, to sensibility; above all, if we sat down with some propensities toward evil, and walk away with much stronger toward good, in the midst of a world which we never had entered and of which we never had dreamed before—shall we perversely put on again the *old man* of criticism, and dissemble that we have been conducted by a most beneficent and most potent genius? Nothing proves to me so manifestly in what a pestiferous condition are its lazarettos, as when I observe how little hath been objected against those who have substituted words for things, and how much against those who have reinstated things for words.

Let Wordsworth prove to the world that there may be animation without blood and broken bones, and tenderness remote from the stews. Some will doubt it; for even things the most evident are often but little perceived and strangely estimated. Swift ridiculed the music of Handel and the generalship of Marlborough; Pope the perspicacity and the scholarship of Bentley; Gray the abilities of Shaftesbury and the eloquence of Rousseau. Shakespeare hardly found those who would collect his tragedies; Milton was read from godliness; Virgil was antiquated and rustic; Cicero, Asiatic. What a rabble has persecuted my friend! An elephant is born to be consumed by ants in the midst of his unapproachable solitudes: Wordsworth is the prey of Jeffrey. Why repine? Let us rather amuse ourselves with allegories, and recollect that God in the creation left his noblest creature at the mercy of a serpent. . . .

PORSON. Wordsworth goes out of his way to be attacked; he picks up a piece of dirt, throws it on the carpet in the midst of the company, and cries, *This is a better man than any of you!* He does indeed mould the base material into what form he chooses; but why not rather invite us to contemplate it than challenge us to condemn it? Here surely is false taste.

SOUTHEY. The principal and the most general accusation against him is, that the vehicle of his thoughts is unequal to them. Now did ever the judges at the Olympic games say, 'We would have awarded to you the meed of victory, if your chariot had been equal

to your horses: it is true they have won; but the people are displeased at a car neither new nor richly gilt, and without a gryphon
or sphinx engraved on the axle?' You admire simplicity in
Euripides; you censure it in Wordsworth: believe me, sir, it arises
in neither from penury of thought—which seldom has produced it
—but from the strength of temperance, and at the suggestion of
principle.

Take up a poem of Wordsworth's and read it—I would rather
say, read them all; and, knowing that a mind like yours must grasp
closely what comes within it, I will then appeal to you whether any
poet of our country, since Milton, hath exerted greater powers with
less of strain and less of ostentation. I would, however, by his permission, lay before you for this purpose a poem which is yet unpublished and incomplete.

PORSON. Pity, with such abilities, he does not imitate the
ancients somewhat more.

SOUTHEY. Whom did they imitate? If his genius is equal to
theirs he has no need of a guide. He also will be an ancient; and the
very counterparts of those who now decry him will extol him a
thousand years hence in malignity to the moderns.

THE ABBÉ DELILLE[1] AND WALTER LANDOR

The Abbé Delille was the happiest of creatures, when he could
weep over the charms of innocence and the country in some
crowded and fashionable circle at Paris. We embraced most
pathetically on our first meeting there, as if the one were condemned to quit the earth, the other to live upon it.

DELILLE. You are reported to have said that descriptive poetry
has all the merits of a handkerchief that smells of roses ?

LANDOR. This, if I said it, is among the things which are neither
false enough nor true enough to be displeasing. But the Abbé

---

[1] *The Abbé Jacques Delille* (1738–1813) was in his day a popular versifier, a
welcome visitor to fashionable salons where his talk was gay and witty. He
translated Virgil (*Georgics*, 1770; the *Aeneid*, 1804); and Milton (*Paradise Lost*,
1805). His own poetry is elegant but mediocre, and he is best known for *Les
Jardins*, 1782. In the best traditions of eighteenth-century literary vendetta, he
was ridiculed by the cruelly witty Rivarol. He was elected to the Académie
Francaise in 1774.

Delille has merits of his own. To translate Milton well is more laudable than originality in trifling matters; just as to transport an obelisk from Egypt, and to erect it in one of the squares, must be considered a greater labour than to build a new chandler's shop.

DELILLE. Milton is indeed extremely difficult to translate; for, however noble and majestic, he is sometimes heavy, and often rough and unequal.

LANDOR. Dear Abbé! porphyry is heavy, gold is heavier; Ossa and Olympus are rough and unequal; the steppes of Tartary, though high, are of uniform elevation: there is not a rock, nor a birch, nor a cytisus, nor an arbutus upon them great enough to shelter a new-dropped lamb. Level the Alps one with another, and where is their sublimity? Raise up the vale of Tempe to the downs above, and where are those sylvan creeks and harbours in which the imagination watches while the soul reposes; those recesses in which the gods partook the weaknesses of mortals, and mortals the enjoyments of the gods?

You have treated our poet with courtesy and distinction; in your trimmed and measured dress, he might be taken for a Frenchman. Do not think me flattering. You have conducted Eve from Paradise to Paris, and she really looks prettier and smarter than before she tripped. With what elegance she rises from a most awful dream! You represent her (I repeat your expression) as springing up *en sursaut*, as if you had caught her asleep and tickled the young creature on that sofa.

Homer and Virgil have been excelled in sublimity by Shakespeare and Milton, as the Caucasus and Atlas of the old world by the Andes and Teneriffe of the new; but you would embellish them all.

DELILLE. I owe to Voltaire my first sentiments of admiration for Milton and Shakespeare.

LANDOR. He stuck to them as a woodpecker to an old forest-tree, only for the purpose of picking out what was rotten: he has made the holes deeper than he found them, and, after all his cries and chatter, has brought home but scanty sustenance to his starveling nest.

DELILLE. You must acknowledge that there are fine verses in his tragedies.

LANDOR. Whenever such is the first observation, be assured,

M. l'Abbé, that the poem, if heroic or dramatic, is bad. Should a work of this kind be excellent, we say, 'How admirably the characters are sustained! What delicacy of discrimination! There is nothing to be taken away or altered without an injury to the part or to the whole.' We may afterward descend on the versification. In poetry, there is a greater difference between the good and the excellent than there is between the bad and the good. Poetry has no golden mean; mediocrity here is of another metal, which Voltaire however had skill enough to encrust and polish. In the least wretched of his tragedies, whatever is tolerable is Shakespeare's; but gracious Heaven! how deteriorated! When he pretends to extol a poet he chooses some defective part, and renders it more so whenever he translates it. I will repeat a few verses from Metastasio in support of my assertion. Metastasio was both a better critic and a better poet, although of the second order in each quality; his tyrants are less philosophical, and his chambermaids less dogmatic. Voltaire was, however, a man of abilities, and author of many passable epigrams, beside those which are contained in his tragedies and heroics; yet it must be confessed that, like your Parisian lackeys, they are usually the smartest when out of place.

DELILLE. What you call epigram gives life and spirit to grave works, and seems principally wanted to relieve a long poem. I do not see why what pleases us in a star should not please us in a constellation.

From *Imaginary Conversations*
Vol. II, 1824

HENRY VIII AND ANNE BOLEYN

HENRY. Dost thou know me, Nanny, in this yeoman's dress? 'S blood! does it require so long and vacant a stare to recollect a husband after a week or two? No tragedy-tricks with me! a scream, a sob, or thy kerchief a trifle the wetter, were enough. Why, verily the little fool faints in earnest. These whey faces, like their kinsfolk the ghosts, give us no warning. Hast had water enough upon thee? Take that, then: art thyself again?

ANNE. Father of mercies! do I meet again my husband, as was my last prayer on earth? Do I behold my beloved lord—in peace—and pardoned, my partner in eternal bliss? it was his voice. I cannot see him: why cannot I? Oh why do these pangs interrupt the transports of the blessed?

HENRY. Thou openest thy arms: faith! I came for that. Nanny, thou art a sweet slut. Thou groanest, wench: art in labour? Faith! among the mistakes of the night, I am ready to think almost that thou hast been drinking, and that I have not.

ANNE. God preserve your Highness: grant me your forgiveness for one slight offence. My eyes were heavy; I fell asleep while I was reading. I did not know of your presence at first; and, when I did, I could not speak. I strove for utterance: I wanted no respect for my liege and husband.

HENRY. My pretty warm nestling, thou wilt then lie! Thou wert reading, and aloud too, with thy saintly cup of water by thee, and—what! thou art still girlishly fond of those dried cherries!

ANNE. I had no other fruit to offer your Highness the first time I saw you, and you were then pleased to invent for me some reason why they should be acceptable. I did not dry these: may I present them, such as they are? We shall have fresh next month.

HENRY. Thou art always driving away from the discourse. One moment it suits thee to know me, another not.

ANNE. Remember, it is hardly three months since I miscarried. I am weak, and liable to swoons.

HENRY. Thou hast, however, thy bridal cheeks, with lustre upon them when there is none elsewhere, and obstinate lips resisting all impression; but, now thou talkest about miscarrying, who is the father of that boy?

ANNE. Yours and mine—He who hath taken him to his own home, before (like me) he could struggle or cry for it.

HENRY. Pagan, or worse, to talk so! He did not come into the world alive: there was no baptism.

ANNE. I thought only of our loss: my senses are confounded. I did not give him my milk, and yet I loved him tenderly; for I often fancied, had he lived, how contented and joyful he would have made you and England.

HENRY. No subterfuges and escapes. I warrant, thou canst not say whether at my entrance thou wert waking or wandering.

ANNE. Faintness and drowsiness came upon me suddenly.

HENRY. Well, since thou really and truly sleepedst, what didst dream of?

ANNE. I begin to doubt whether I did indeed sleep.

HENRY. Ha! false one—never two sentences of truth together! But come, what didst think about, asleep or awake!

ANNE. I thought that God had pardoned me my offences, and had received me unto him.

HENRY. And nothing more?

ANNE. That my prayers had been heard and my wishes were accomplishing: the angels alone can enjoy more beatitude than this.

HENRY. Vexatious little devil! She says nothing now about me, merely from perverseness. Hast thou never thought about me, nor about thy falsehood and adultery?

ANNE. If I had committed any kind of falsehood, in regard to you or not, I should never have rested until I had thrown myself at your feet and obtained your pardon; but, if ever I had been guilty of that other crime, I know not whether I should have dared to implore it, even of God's mercy.

HENRY. Thou hast heretofore cast some soft glances upon Smeaton; hast thou not?

ANNE. He taught me to play on the virginals, as you know, when I was little, and thereby to please your Highness.

HENRY. And Brereton and Norris—what have they taught thee?

ANNE. They are your servants, and trusty ones.

HENRY. Has not Weston told thee plainly that he loved thee?

ANNE. Yes; and—

HENRY. What didst thou?

ANNE. I defied him.

HENRY. Is that all?

ANNE. I could have done no more if he had told me that he hated me. Then, indeed, I should have incurred more justly the reproaches of your Highness: I should have smiled.

HENRY. We have proofs abundant: the fellows shall one and all confront thee. Aye, clap thy hands and kiss thy sleeve, harlot!

ANNE. Oh that so great a favour is vouchsafed me! My honour is secure; my husband will be happy again; he will see my innocence.

HENRY. Give me now an account of the moneys thou hast

received from me within these nine months. I want them not back: they are letters of gold in record of thy guilt. Thou has had no fewer than fifteen thousand pounds in that period, without even thy asking; what hast done with it, wanton?

ANNE. I have regularly placed it out to interest.

HENRY. Where? I demand of thee.

ANNE. Among the needy and ailing. My Lord Archbishop has the account of it, sealed by him weekly. I also had a copy myself; those who took away my papers may easily find it; for there are few others, and they lie open.

HENRY. Think on my munificence to thee; recollect who made thee. Dost sigh for what thou hast lost?

ANNE. I do, indeed.

HENRY. I never thought thee ambitious; but thy vices creep out one by one.

ANNE. I do not regret that I have been a queen and am no longer one; nor that my innocence is called in question by those who never knew me; but I lament that the good people who loved me so cordially, hate and curse me; that those who pointed me out to their daughters for imitation check them when they speak about me; and that he whom next to God I have served with most devotion is my accuser.

HENRY. Wast thou conning over something in that dingy book for thy defence? Come, tell me, what wast thou reading?

ANNE. This ancient chronicle. I was looking for some one in my own condition, and must have missed the page. Surely in so many hundred years there shall have been other young maidens, first too happy for exaltation, and after too exalted for happiness—not, perchance, doomed to die upon a scaffold, by those they ever honoured and served faithfully; that, indeed, I did not look for nor think of; but my heart was bounding for any one I could love and pity. She would be unto me as a sister dead and gone; but hearing me, seeing me, consoling me, and being consoled. O my husband! it is so heavenly a thing—

HENRY. To whine and whimper, no doubt, is vastly heavenly.

ANNE. I said not so; but those, if there be any such, who never weep, have nothing in them of heavenly or of earthly. The plants, the trees, the very rocks and unsunned clouds, show us at least the semblances of weeping; and there is not an aspect of the globe we live on, nor of the waters and skies around it, without a reference and a similitude to our joys or sorrows.

HENRY. I do not remember that notion anywhere. Take care no enemy rake out of it something of materialism. Guard well thy empty hot brain; it may hatch more evil. As for those odd words, I myself would fain see no great harm in them, knowing that grief and frenzy strike out many things which would else lie still, and neither spirt nor sparkle. I also know that thou hast never read any thing but Bible and history—the two worst books in the world for young people, and the most certain to lead astray both prince and subject. For which reason I have interdicted and entirely put down the one, and will (by the blessing of the Virgin and of holy Paul) commit the other to a rigid censor. If it behooves us kings to enact what our people shall eat and drink—of which the most unruly and rebellious spirit can entertain no doubt—greatly more doth it behoove us to examine what they read and think. The body is moved according to the mind and will; we must take care that the movement be a right one, on pain of God's anger in this life and the next.

ANNE. O my dear husband! it must be a naughty thing, indeed, that makes him angry beyond remission. Did you ever try how pleasant it is to forgive any one? There is nothing else wherein we can resemble God perfectly and easily.

HENRY. Resemble God perfectly and easily! Do vile creatures talk thus of the Creator?

ANNE. No, Henry, when his creatures talk thus of him, they are no longer vile creatures! When they know that he is good, they love him; and, when they love him, they are good themselves. O Henry! my husband and King! the judgments of our Heavenly Father are righteous; on this, surely, we must think alike.

HENRY. And what, then? Speak out; again I command thee, speak plainly! thy tongue was not so torpid but this moment. Art ready? Must I wait?

ANNE. If any doubt remains upon your royal mind of your equity in this business; should it haply seem possible to you that passion or prejudice, in yourself or another, may have warped so strong an understanding—do but suplicate the Almighty to strengthen and enlighten it, and he will hear you.

HENRY. What! thou wouldst fain change thy quarters, ay?

ANNE. My spirit is detached and ready, and I shall change them shortly, whatever your Highness may determine.

HENRY. Yet thou appearest hale and resolute, and (they tell me) smirkest and smilest to everybody.

ANNE. The withered leaf catches the sun sometimes, little as it can profit by it; and I have heard stories of the breeze in other climates that sets in when daylight is about to close, and how constant it is, and how refreshing. My heart, indeed, is now sustained strangely; it became the more sensibly so from that time forward, when power and grandeur and all things terrestrial were sunk from sight. Every act of kindness in those about me gives me satisfaction and pleasure, such as I did not feel formerly. I was worse before God chastened me; yet I was never an ingrate. What pains have I taken to find out the village-girls who placed their posies in my chamber ere I arose in the morning! How gladly would I have recompensed the forester who lit up a brake on my birth-night, which else had warmed him half the winter! But these are times past: I was not Queen of England.

HENRY. Nor adulterous, nor heretical.

ANNE. God be praised!

HENRY. Learned saint! thou knowest nothing of the lighter, but perhaps canst inform me about the graver, of them.

ANNE. Which may it be, my liege?

HENRY. Which may it be? Pestilence! I marvel that the walls of this tower do not crack around thee at such impiety.

ANNE. I would be instructed by the wisest of theologians: such is your Highness.

HENRY. Are the sins of the body, foul as they are, comparable to those of the soul?

ANNE. When they are united, they must be worse.

HENRY. Go on, go on: thou pushest thy own breast against the sword. God hath deprived thee of thy reason for thy punishment. I must hear more: proceed, I charge thee.

ANNE. An aptitude to believe one thing rather than another, from ignorance or weakness, or from the more persuasive manner of the teacher, or from his purity of life, or from the strong impression of a particular text at a particular time, and various things beside, may influence and decide our opinion; and the hand of the Almighty, let us hope, will fall gently on human fallibility.

HENRY. Opinion in matters of faith! rare wisdom! rare religion! Troth, Anne! thou hast well sobered me. I came rather warmly and lovingly; but these light ringlets, by the holy rood, shall not shade this shoulder much longer. Nay, do not start; I tap it for the last time, my sweetest. If the Church permitted it, thou shouldst set forth on thy long journey with the eucharist between thy teeth, however loath.

ANNE. Love your Elizabeth, my honoured lord, and God bless you! She will soon forget to call me. Do not chide her: think how young she is.

Could I, could I kiss her, but once again! it would comfort my heart,—or break it.

WASHINGTON AND FRANKLIN

WASHINGTON. Well met again, my friend Benjamin! Never did I see you, I think, in better health: Paris does not appear to have added a single day to your age. I hope the two years you have spent there for us, were spent as pleasantly to yourself as they have been advantageously to your country.

FRANKLIN. Pleasantly they were spent indeed, but, you may well suppose, not entirely without anxiety. I thank God, however, that all this is over.

WASHINGTON. Yes, Benjamin, let us render thanks to the Disposer of events, under whom, by the fortitude, the wisdom, and the endurance of our Congress, the affairs of America are brought at last to a triumphant issue.

FRANKLIN. Do not refuse the share of merit due to yourself, which is perhaps the largest.

WASHINGTON. I am not of that opinion: if I were, I might acknowledge it to you, although not to others. Suppose me to have made a judicious choice in my measures, the Congress then made a judicious choice in me: so that whatever praise may be allowed me, is at best but secondary.

FRANKLIN. I do not believe that the remainder of the world contains so many men who reason rightly as New England. Serious, religious, peaceable, inflexibly just and courageous, their stores of intellect are not squandered in the regions of fancy, nor in the desperate ventures of new-found and foggy metaphysics, but warehoused and kept sound at home, and ready to be brought forth in good and wholesome condition at the first demand. Their ancestors had abandoned their estates, their families, and their country, for the attainment of peace and freedom; and they themselves were ready to traverse the vast wildernesses of an unexplored continent, rather than submit to that moral degradation which alone can satisfy the capriciousness of despotism. Their gravity is converted into enthusiasm: even those among them who never in childhood itself expressed by speech or countenance a sign of admiration, express it strongly in their old age at your exploits.

WASHINGTON. Benjamin, one would imagine that we both had been educated in courts, and that I were a man who could give, and you a man who could ask. Prythee, my friend, be a philosopher in somewhat more than books and bottles, and, as you have learned to manage the clouds and lightnings, try an experiment on the management of your fancies. I declare on my conscience I do not know what I have done extraordinary, unless we are forced to acknowledge, from the examples to which we have been accustomed, that it is extraordinary to possess power and remain honest. I believe it may be: but this was a matter of reflection with me: by serving my country I gratified my heart and all its wants. Perhaps I am not so happy a creature as he who smokes his pipe on the bench at the tavern-door; yet I am as happy as my slow blood allows; and I keep my store of happiness in the same temperature the whole year round, by the double casement of activity and integrity.

FRANKLIN. I do not assert that there never was a general who disposed his army in the day of battle with skill equal to yours: which, in many instances, must depend almost as much on his adversary as on himself: but I assert that no man ever displayed such intimate knowledge of his whole business, guarded so frequently and so effectually against the impending ruin of his forces, and showed himself at once so circumspect and so daring. To have inoculated one half of your troops under the eye of the enemy—

WASHINGTON. Those actions are great, which require great calculation, and succeed in consequence of its correctness: those alone, or nearly alone, are called so, which succeed without any. I knew the supineness of the British general, his utter ignorance of his profession, his propensity to gaming, to drinking, in short to all the camp vices. I took especial care that he should be informed of my intention to attack him, on the very day when my army was, from the nature of its distemper, the most disabled. Instead of anticipating me, which this intelligence, credited as it was, would have induced a more skilful man to do, he kept his troops unremittingly on the alert, and he himself is reported to have been sober three days together. The money which he ought to have employed in obtaining just and necessary information, he lost at cards; and when he heard that I had ventured to inoculate my army, and that the soldiers had recovered, he little imagined that half the number was at that moment under the full influence of the disease.

Attribute no small portion of our success to the only invariable policy of England, which is, to sweep forward to the head of her armaments the grubs of rotten boroughs and the droppings of the gaming-table; and, Benjamin, be assured that, although men of eminent genius have been guilty of all other vices, none worthy of more than a secondary name has ever been a gamester. Either an excess of avarice, or a deficiency of what in physics is called excitability, is the cause of it: neither of which can exist in the same bosom with genius, with patriotism, or with virtue. Clive, the best English general since Marlborough and Peterborough, was apparently an exception: but he fell not into this degrading vice until he was removed from the sphere of exertion, until his abilities had begun to decay, and his intellect in some measure to be deranged.

FRANKLIN. I quite agree with you in your main proposition, and see no exception to it in Clive, who was more capable of ruining a country than of raising one. Those who record that chess was invented in the Trojan war, would have informed us if Ulysses, Agamemnon, or Diomedes ever played at it: which however is usually done without a stake, nor can it be called in any way a game of chance. Gustavus Adolphus, and Eugene of Savoy, and Marlborough, and Frederick of Prussia, and Charles XII of Sweden, and William III of England, had springs and movements within themselves, which did not require to be wound up every night. They deemed it indecorous to be selvages to an ell of green cloth, and scandalous to cast upon a card what would cover a whole country with plenteousness.

Gaming is the vice of those nations which are too effeminate to be

97

barbarous, and too depraved to be civilized, and which unite the worst qualities of both conditions; as for example, the rags and lace of Naples, its lazzaroni and other titulars. The Malays, I acknowledge, are less effeminate, and in all respects less degraded, and still are gamesters: but gaming with the Malays is a substitute for betel; the Neapolitan games on a full snuff-box. Monarchs should encourage the practice, as the Capets have done constantly: for it brings the idle and rich into their capitals, holds them from other intrigues and from more active parties, makes many powerful families dependent, and satisfies young officers who would otherwise want employment. Republics, on the contrary, should punish the first offence with fine and imprisonment, the second with a public whipping and a year's hard labour, the third with deportation.

WASHINGTON. As you please in monarchies and republics: but prythee say nothing of them in mixed governments: do not affront the earliest coadjutors and surest reliances of our commonwealth. The leaders of party in England are inclined to play; and what was a cartouche but yesterday will make a rouleau to-morrow.

FRANKLIN. Fill it then with base money, or you will be over-reached, little as is the danger to be apprehended from them in any higher species of calculation. They are persons of some repute for eloquence; but if I conducted a newspaper in that country, I should think it a wild speculation to pay the wiser of them half-a-crown a-day for his most elaborate composition. When either shall venture to publish a history, or even a speech of his own, his talents will then be appreciated justly. God grant (for our differences have not yet annihilated the remembrance of our relationship) that England may never have any more painful proofs, any more lasting documents, of their incapacity. Since we Americans can suffer no farther from them, I speak of them with the same indifference and equanimity as if they were among the dead.

WASHINGTON. But come, come: the war is ended: God be praised! Objections have been made against our form of government, and assertions have been added that the republican is ill-adapted to a flourishing or an extensive country. We know from the experience of Holland that it not only can preserve but can make a country flourishing, when Nature herself has multiplied the impediments, and when the earth and all the elements have conspired against it. Demonstration is indeed yet wanting that a very extensive territory is best governed by its people: reason and sound common-sense are the only vouchers. Many may fancy they have an interest in seizing what is another's; but surely no man can suppose that he has any in ruining or alienating his own.

FRANKLIN. Confederate states, under one President, will never be all at once, or indeed in great part, deprived of their freedom.

WASHINGTON. Adventurers may aspire to the supreme power illegally; but none can expect that the majority will sacrifice their present interests to his ambition, in confidence or hope of greater. He never will raise a standing army who can not point out the probable means of paying it, which no one can do here; nor will a usurper rise up anywhere, unless there are mines to tempt the adventurous and avaricious, or estates to parcel out with labourers to cultivate them, or slaves to seduce and embody, or treasures to confiscate.

FRANKLIN. The objections bear much more weightily against monarchal and mixed governments: because these, in wide dominions, are always composed of parts at variance in privileges and interests, in manners and opinions, and the inhabitants of which are not unreluctant to be employed one against the other. Hence, while we Americans leave our few soldiers to the states where they were levied, the kings of Europe will cautiously change the quarters of theirs, and send them into provinces as remote as possible. When they have ceased to have a home, they have ceased to have a country: for all affinities are destroyed by breaking the nearest. Thrones are constructed on the petrifaction of the human heart.

WASHINGTON. Lawless ambition has no chance whatever of success where there are neither great standing armies nor great national debts. Where either of those exist, freedom must waste away and perish. We are as far from the one as from the other.

FRANKLIN. Dangers grow familiar and unsuspected: slight causes may produce them, even names. Suppose a man calling another his subject, and having first received from him marks of deference, and relying on his good-temper and passiveness, and exerting by degrees more and more authority over him, and leaving him at last to the care and protection of his son or grandson. We are well acquainted with the designation; but we are ignorant how deeply it cuts into the metal. After a time a shrewd jurist will instruct the subject in his duties, and give him arguments and proofs out of the name itself. What so irrefragable!

The Latin language, which answers so nearly all our demands upon it from its own resources, or, not having quite wherewithal, borrows for us a trifle from the Greek, neither can give us nor help us to find, directly or circuitously, a word for *subject*. *Subditus*, the term in use, is not Latin in that sense, whether of the golden, the silver, or the brazen age: it means *substitute* primarily, and then *subdued* or *subjected*. Yet people own themselves to be subjects who would be outrageous if you called them vassals; an appellation quite as noble.

Poetry, closing her eyes, has sung until people slept over it, that liberty is never more perfect or more safe than under a mild monarch: history teaches us the contrary. Where princes are absolute, more tyranny is committed under the mild than under the austere: for the latter are jealous of power and entrust it to few. The mild delegate it inconsiderately to many: and the same easiness of temper which allows them to do so, permits their ministers and those under them to abuse the trust with impunity. It has been said that in a democracy there are many despots, and that in a kingdom there can be one only. This is false: in a republic the tyrannical temper creates a check to itself in the very person next it: but in a monarchy all entrusted with power become tyrannical by a nod from above, whether the nod be of approbation or of drowsiness. Royalty not only is a monster of more heads, but also of more claws, and sharper.

It is amusing to find us treated as visionaries. All the gravest nations have been republics, both in ancient times and in modern. I shall believe that a king is better than a republic, when I find that a single tooth in a head is better than a set, and that in its solitariness there is a warrant for its strength and soundness.

WASHINGTON. Many have begun to predict our *future* greatness:[1] in fact, no nation is ever greater than at the time when it recovers its freedom from under one apparently more powerful. America

[1] Of the Americans in late years Madame de Staël says, *There is a people which will one day be very great*, placing her fine impressive pen on the broad rude mark of the vulgar, who measure greatness by the standard of aggression. America was never so great as on the day when she declared her independence, and never will be greater; although she will constitute *two* great empires, more powerful and more unassailable than any now existing.—W. S. L.

will never have to make again such a struggle as she made in 1775, and never can make one so glorious. A wide territory does not constitute a great people, nor does enormous wealth, nor does excessive population. The Americans are at present as great a people as we can expect them to be in future. Can we hope that they will be more virtuous, more unanimous, more courageous, more patriotic? They may become more learned and more elegant in their manners: but these advantages are only to be purchased by paying down others equivalent.

FRANKLIN. All acquisitions, to be advantageous, must have some mart and vent. Elegance grows familiar with venality. Learning may perhaps be succeeded by a Church Establishment; an institution perversive of those on which the government of America is constructed. Erudition (as we use the word) begins with societies, and ends with professions and orders. Priests and lawyers, the flies and wasps of ripe and ripening communities, may darken and disturb America. A few of these (we will allow) are necessary; many are, of all the curses that the world is subject to, the most pernicious. These guardians have been proved in every country the poisoners of their wards, Law and Religion. They never let us exist long together in an equable and genial temperature: it is either at fever heat or at zero.

WASHINGTON. The solid sense of our people, their speculative habits, their room for enterprise around home, and their distance from Europe, ensure to them, if not a long continuance of peace, exemption from such wars as can affect in a material degree their character or their prosperity. We might have continued the hostilities, until a part or even the whole of Canada had been ceded to us. The Congress has done what, if my opinion had been asked, I should have urgently recommended. Let Canada be ours when she is cultivated and enriched; let not the fruit be gathered prematurely; indeed let it never be plucked; let it fall when our bosom can hold it. This must happen within the century to come: for no nation is, or ever has been, so intolerably vexatious to its colonies, its dependencies, and its conquests, as the British. I have known personally several Governors, many of them honest and sensible men, many of them of mild and easy character; but I never knew one, nor ever heard of any from older officers, who attempted to conciliate the affections, or systematically to promote the interests, of the governed. Liberality has been occasionally extended to them; the liberality of a master toward a slave, and only after grievous sufferings. Services have then been exacted, not hard perhaps in themselves, but in manner to cancel all recollection and deaden all sense of kindness. The French and Spaniards act differently: they extract advantage from their undisturbed possessions, appealing to the generosity of their children, and softening their commands by kind offices and constant attentions. Wherever a French regiment is quartered, there are balls and comedies: wherever an English, there are disturbances in the street, and duels. Give the Spaniard a bull-fight, and you may burn his father at the stake, commending him to the God of Mercy in a cassock painted with the flames of hell. The English (and we their descendants are most deserving of the name) require but justice; whatever comes as a favour comes as an affront. To what a pitch then must our indignation be excited, when we are not permitted even to pay that which is required of us, unless we present it with the left hand, or upon the nose, or from our knees amid the mire! The orators of the British parliament, while they are colouring this insolence and injustice, keep the understanding of the people at tongue's length.

FRANKLIN. In good truth then the separation is now narrow one. I have been present while some of them have thrown up the most chaffy stuff two hours together, and have never called for a glass of water. This is thought the summit of ability, and he who is capable of performing it, is deemed capable of ruling the east and west.[1] The rich families that govern this assembly have made us independent; they have given us thirteen provinces, and they will people them all for us in less than fifty years. Religious and grave men, for none are graver or more religious than the beaten, are praising the loving-mercies of God, in loosening from their necks the mill-stone of America. What a blessing to throw aside such an extent of coast, which of itself would have required an immense navy for its defence! No one dreams that England, in confederacy with America, would have been so strong in sailors, in ports, in naval stores, as to have become (I do not say with good management, I say in spite of bad) not invincible only, but invulnerable.

[1] Pitt may be complimented on his oratory in the words wherewith Anacreon congratulates the tettinx, ἀπαθὴς, ἄναιμ᾽, ἄσαρκε.—W. S. L.

WASHINGTON. If she turns her attention to the defects of her administration in all its branches, she may recover not much less than she has lost. Look at the nations of Europe, and point out one, despotic or free, of which so large a portion is so barbarous and wretched as the Irish. The country is more fertile than Britain; the inhabitants are healthy, strong, courageous, faithful, patriotic, and quick of apprehension. No quality is wanting which constitutes the respectability of a state; yet, from centuries of misrule, they are in a condition more hopeless than any other nation or tribe upon the globe, civilized or savage.

FRANKLIN. There is only one direct way to bring them into order, and that appears so rough it never will be trodden. The chief misery arises from the rapacity of the gentry, as they are styled, and the nobility, who, to avoid the trouble of collecting their rents from many poor tenants, and the greater of hearing their complaints, have leased their properties to what are called *middle-men*. These harass their inferiors in the exact ratio of their industry, and drive them into desperation. Hence slovenliness and drunkenness; for the appearance of ease and comfort is an allurement to avarice. To pacify and reclaim the people, leases to middle-men must be annulled: every cultivator must have a lease for life, and (at the option of his successor) valid for as many years afterward as will amount in the whole to twenty-one. The extent of ground should be proportionate to his family and his means. To underlet land should be punished by law as *regrating*.

WASHINGTON. Authority would here be strongly exercised, not tyrannically, which never can be asserted of plans sanctioned by the representatives of a people, for the great and perpetual benefit of the many, to the small and transient inconvenience of the few.

FRANKLIN. Auxiliary to this reform should be one in church-livings. They should all embrace as nearly as possible the same number of communicants. Suppose three thousand souls under each cure: a fourth part would consist of the infirm, and of children not yet prepared for the reception of doctrine. The service, as formerly, should be shorter, and performed thrice each Sunday: so that all might in turn be present, and that great concourse would be avoided, which frequently is the prelude to licentiousness and brutality. Abolishing tithes, selling the property of the crown, of the church, and of corporations, I would establish a fund sufficient to allow each clergyman, in addition to his house, one hundred and forty pounds annually. Each would be remunerated, not for his profession, but for services done toward the state by his attention to the morals of his communicants. If the people pay forty pounds for taking up a felon, would they not willingly pay four times as much for reclaiming a dozen?

WASHINGTON. I do not know: for we must never argue that men or their rulers are the likelier to do a thing because it is rational or useful. If ever the poorer clergy are rendered more comfortable, it will be only when the richer are afraid of losing a part of their usurped dominions. English and Irish bishops, who possess ten and twelve thousand a year, will be the last to relieve the necessities of their brethren: and their selfishness will not alienate from them those who are habituated to long abuses. The fine linen of popery sticks close to the skin: and there is much of it in the wardrobe of the English church.

On all subjects I can talk dispassionately, and perhaps the most so on that topic which renders the great body of mankind the most furious and insane. Never would I animadvert on the tenets of the Catholic or any other church, apart from civil polity. But I am suspicious, if not inquisitive, when I see questionable articles day after day smuggled in, and when I am pushed aside if I venture to read the direction or lift up the wrapping. Articles of faith are innocent in themselves: but upon articles of faith what incontrollable domination, what insupportable prerogatives, what insolent frauds, what incessant tyranny, have been asserted and enforced.

FRANKLIN. I am ready to be of that church, if you will tell me which it is, in which there are the fewest of them. Show me that a single pope in one country tells fewer lies and sits quieter than twenty in another, and he is the pope for my money, when I lay it out on such a commodity. The abuses of the clergy were first exposed by the clergy, the lower assailing the higher. If something more like equality, something more near moderation, had pervaded all, fewer sects would have arisen, and those fewer less acrimonious. Dogmas turn sour upon too full stomachs, and empty ones rattle against them. Envy, which the wolves and bears are without, and the generous dog alone seems by his proximity to have caught from us, Envy, accompanying Religion, swells amid her genuflexions to the episcopal canopy, at seeing so much wealth so ill distributed.

The low cannot be leaders without a change nor without a party. Some unintelligible syllable is seized; and the vulgar are taught to believe that salvation rests upon it. Even this were little: they are instructed that salvation may be yet perhaps insecure, unless they drag others to it by the throat, and quicken their paces at the dagger's point. Popery first laid down this doctrine; the most abominable and monstrous of her tenets, and the only one that all establishments, splitting off from her, are unanimous in retaining.

WASHINGTON. The reductions you propose would bring about another: they would remove the necessity of a standing army in that unfortunate country, and would enable the government to establish three companies for fisheries, the herring, the cod, and the whale, and to enrich her remote dominions with the superabundance of a discontented peasantry. The western part of Ireland in another century may derive as great advantages from her relative position with America, as the eastern from hers with the mercantile and manufacturing towns of Lancashire. The population is already too numerous, and is increasing, which of itself is the worst of curses, unless when high civilization regulates it; and the superflux must be diverted by colonization, or occupied on the seas by commerce. Manufactures tend to deteriorate the species, but begin by humanizing it. Happy those countries which have occasion for little more of them than may supply the home consumption! National debts are evils, not so much because they take away from useful and honest gains, as because they create superfluous and dishonest ones; and because, when carried as far as England would carry hers, they occasion half the children of the land to be cooped up in buildings which open into the brothel and the hospital.

In assenting to you, I interrupted your propositions; pray go on.

FRANKLIN. I would permit no Englishman to hold in Ireland a place of trust or profit, whether in church or state. I would confer titles and offices on those Irish gentlemen who reside in the country; and surely they would in time become habituated to a regular and decorous mode of life. The landlord and clergyman might in the beginning lose something of current coin; but if you consider that their lives, houses, and effects would be safe, that provisions would be plentiful in proportion to the concessions they make, and that in no year would their rents and incomes fail, as they now do at least thirty in each century, you will find that their situation, like the situation of their inferiors, must be improved.

WASHINGTON. Many will exclaim against the injustice of taking from one class alone a portion of its property as insurance-money.

FRANKLIN. Not from one alone: property should be protected at its own cost: this is the right and the object of governments. The insurance is two-fold; that of the private man and that of the community; the latter is the main consideration. I perceive nothing arbitrary, nothing novel, in its principle.[1] The King of England and Ireland, as head of the church, succeeds by consent of Parliament to the disposal of benefices. He surely can do in his own kingdom what the pope can do in another's, where ecclesiastical property (if any can be called so) is concerned. The religion of a state is established for the correction of its morals, and its morals are requisite to the maintenance of the laws. Religion then, in the view of a statesman, is only a thing that aids and assests the laws, removing from before them much of their painful duties, and lessening (if good and effectual) the number of their officers and executioners. So that in political economy there is between them a close and intimate connection, and both alike are subject to regulations in them from the same authority. Where there is a state religion the salary of a clergyman should be as much subject to the state as the stipend of a custom-house officer and exciseman. If a government exerts the power of taxing one trade or profession, it does the same thing or more. Suppose it should levy a tax of a hundred pounds on every man who begins the business of an apothecary or lawyer, is not the grievance even heavier, as pressing on those whose gains are yet uncertain and to be derived from others, than it would be if bearing upon those whose emoluments are fixed, and proceed from the government which regulates and circumscribes them? But they have been accustomed, you will say, to the enjoyment of more. So much clear gain for them; and I hope they may have made a liberal and prudent use of the superfluity. Those who have done so, will possess minds ready to calculate justly

[1] There is an argument which could not be attributed to Franklin, because it is derived from an authority to which he never appealed, and the words containing it are unlikely to have lain within the range of his reading:—

'Le Pape peut révoquer la loi établie par lui ou par prédécesseur, et oster *mesme sans occasion* les effects procédens d'icelle, et le bénéfice valide à un chacun: car il a entière disposition sur les bénéfices.' *Em. Sa.* p. 528.—W. S. L.

their own lasting interests, and the interests of the community for whose benefit they have been appointed. If there is anything the existence of which produces great and general evil, and the abolition of which will produce great and general good, in perpetuity, the government is not only authorized by right, but bound by duty, to remove it. Compensation should be made to the middle-men for all losses; it should be made even to the worst; these losses may as easily be ascertained, as those occasioned to proprietors and tenants through whose lands we open a road or a canal.

WASHINGTON. Methods, far short of what you indicate, will be adopted, and will fail. Constitutional lawyers will assent that Ireland be subject to martial law for thirty years in the century, and to little or none for the remainder, but will not assent that everything unlawful be unnecessary and unprovoked. In consequence of which, within the lifetime of some in existence we shall have two millions of Irishmen in America, reclaimed from their ferocity by assuaging their physical and moral wants, and addicted to industry by the undisturbed enjoyment of its reward. Experience seems to have given no sort of instruction to their rulers: they profit by nothing old, they venture on nothing new.

FRANKLIN. We are informed by the scientific in chemistry, that a diamond and a stick of charcoal on the hearth are essentially of the same materials. In like manner those among men who to the vulgar eye are the most dissimilar in externals, are nearly the same in mind and intellect; and their difference is the effect of accident and fortune, of position and combination. Those who, governing the political, influence in a high degree the moral world, can perform at once what Nature is myriads of years in accomplishing: they can convert the stick of charcoal into a diamond by the aliment and situation they allow to it. Our government will find its interest in doing so: others will pursue their old occupation in reducing the diamond to its dark original, and exercise their divine right to keeping it unextracted.

If I were a member of the British Ministry, I should think I acted wisely, not in attempting to prove that the constitution is the best in the world, but in demonstrating, if I could, the reverse. For in proportion as they labour to extol it, in the same proportion do they oblige us to suppose them its most impudent and outrageous violators, or, at the least, ignorant of its spirit and incapable of its application. Otherwise how could this excellent form be the parent of deformity? How could the population, where the country is so fertile and the race so industrious, contain a larger number of indigent families, and those among the most laborious and the most virtuous, than any other upon earth?

WASHINGTON. If the constitution were what it is represented, its agents could not abuse it; and if its agents could not abuse it, America would not have been at this time separated from England; nor would Ireland have been condemned to a massacre once at furthest in two generations; nor would the British people be more heavily taxed in its comforts and its necessaries than the Algerines and Turks, when its industry is so much greater, and when its territory has not been occupied nor invaded nor endangered by an enemy.

FRANKLIN. The Persian despots never debased the souls of the nations they had conquered, and do not appear to have coveted their purses. Herodotus calls the taxation of the Ionian states a tranquillising and pacificatory measure. No portion of the globe was more advantageously situated for commerce than the Greek republics in Asia; no soil richer, no climate healthier, no people more industrious. Æolians, Ionians, and Dorians, together with Pamphylia, Lycia, the islands of Rhodes, Cos, Samos, Chios, and Sestos, on the whole exceeding four hundred miles by forty, were taxed unalterably at four hundred talents (about £105,000), by Darius, according to a scale *submitted to their deputies* by his father Artaxerxes. Italy in the time of Nero contained at the lowest computation twenty-six millions of inhabitants, and paid less in taxes than the City of London with its appurtenances. Appian states that Pompey imposed on the Tyrians and Cilicians a hundredth of their income. Hadrian was accused of great severity toward the Jews, in having somewhat augmented the rate which Vespasian had decreed, and which, according to Zonaras and Xiphilinus, was about sixteen pence on each. Strabo remarks that Egypt brought a revenue of about £180,000 to the father of Cleopatra, which was doubled by Augustus. When he was declared Imperator against M. Antonius, the Senate decreed a temporary property-tax of a twentieth. Plutarch in his *Life of Pompey* informs us that he levied on Asia £192,000. M. Antonius had exacted in advance at one time the tribute of ten years.

WASHINGTON. The possibility of levying in a single year the ordinary taxes of ten, is a proof how extremely light were the impositions on the richest subjects of the Roman empire. Labouring under the enormous debt of £200,000,000, the English could not in any emergency pay the rate of three years anticipated.

FRANKLIN. The nations of Asia had recently paid more heavily: for it was objected to them as a reproach, and as a cause for this exaction, that they had raised for Cassius and Brutus in the one preceding year what was now demanded for ten.

WASHINGTON. So long as the English tolerate the absorption of their wealth under the patronage of their Peerage, wars and taxation will severely scourge them. Wars, the origin of taxation, are systematical in their periods, however little so in their conduct, and must recur about every twenty years, as a new generation springs up from the aristocracy, for which all the great civil employments, however multiplied, are insufficient, and which disdains all other professions than the military and the naval. But when this devourer hath exhausted and concentrated in itself nearly all the land and riches of the nation, then it will begin to discuss the question, whether it can gain most by suppressing the church establishment, or by maintaining it in its rankness.

FRANKLIN. May it not happen that the question be tried before a session of other jurors; and that the benches of the Lords Spiritual have nothing else upon them than the benches of the Lords Temporal with the legs uppermost? If state religions were abolished, the world would be quieter and better: in England the national debt would be liquidated in a century, and in Ireland the public tranquillity would be established in a year. Among our own injuries on the part of England, this never bore upon us, namely, to pay for hearing what we knew or for what we disbelieved. If there existed no establishment in England, fear would be entertained of puritanism.

WASHINGTON. Against what could puritanism act? It overthrew the established church in her state of inebriety: it kicked into the street her crosiers and mitres, and other such ensigns of barbarism and paganism and despotism. When it finds nothing to quarrel with out of doors, it will quarrel at home.

FRANKLIN. It grows strong by being kept in the cool, and bunged up by the ecclesiastical excise.

WASHINGTON. Benjamin, I do not like to meddle with religions, nor indeed to speak about them. All of them appear to me inoffensive, excepting the Popish, which not only would have a hand in every man's pocket, but an ear on every man's pillow.

FRANKLIN. I know not whether the Irish are very fervent in their devotion to the Bishops of Rome. Probably they are unaware of some among the benefits they have heretofore received from them. Few, I dare say, have ever heard that their Holy Father, Hadrian the Fourth, solemnly gave his sanction to Henry the Second to invade and subjugate their country. This, I dare likewise say, would be loudly contradicted by the few who know it. Indeed I must correct my words before I go farther. Hadrian did not give his sanction; he sold it. A tax was to be paid the Holy See on every Irish family. So that the Holy See was as much interested as Henry himself that the conquest should be effectual and complete. The Holy Father chose rather a tax on families than a capitation: for, although many thousands of men would be exterminated, few whole families would.

WASHINGTON. We may talk together in private of these historical facts; but if we mention them to people whose eyes might be opened by them, we shall render them in the same degree our enemies as we are their true friends.

FRANKLIN. I knew a certain man who would take the most nauseous medicine in health, because he had paid money for it at the apothecary's when he was ill; at the same time he would not eat a fresh salad at the next door. Things are valued by the places they come from. If a reasoner were to say what a Saint hath said about the Blessed Trinity, in most countries he would be called an infidel, and even in some of the most tolerant he would be subject to fine and imprisonment.

WASHINGTON. How is that?

FRANKLIN. St Augustine says, 'We talk of Three Persons merely for the sake of talking.'

WASHINGTON. O the knave!

FRANKLIN. And scholars do say that the Latin expression is an ugly one: 'Dictum est Tres *Personæ*, non ut aliquid diceretur, sed ne taceretur.'

WASHINGTON. Instead of sending to a rotten old city, the most profligate and the most venal on earth, for spiritual advice and counsel, which always comes to you in the form of a command, and enclosing an order to pay a pretty round sum to the bearer, could not every city and every hamlet find some worthy inhabitant, capable of giving his opinion upon those matters, if indeed there be any such, which the Disciples of Christ were unable or inattentive or indifferent to elucidate and explain? I see nothing worth a quarrel in them; and certainly there is nothing which the blessed Author of our religion would recommend us to fight about. If there were no hierarchy in England and Ireland, the people of both countries would be brotherly and contented. They would mind their own business, and not the business of those who fare sumptuously on their credulity, and ride in rich housings on their fiery animosities. The revenues of ecclesiastics would overpay the just demands of a protecting and frugal government. Let the Protestant Church be no longer a hireling; and the Popish will drop away rag after rag, image after image, to the great emolument of the barber's shop. The poor people of that persuasion would not long be so foolish and besotted as to pay tithes where the heretic pays none. Inequality would shake their creed, extortion would open their eyes, and they would feel on that occasion what they now feel on another, that they were not, as they ought to be, in the same condition as the Protestant. The parties will never be peaceable until the banners are thrown into the dust between them, and each tramples upon his own. Absurdities in worship would soon cease if nobody gained by them. Within half a century, the whole people would find in their hands and hearts nothing else than the unencumbering and unexhausting page, which, if its spirit were received in its purity, might well be denominated the Book of Life. So mischievous a use however has been made of it for above a thousand years, that, if you take, as churches would force you, their glosses and interpretations for part of it, then indeed may it be called more properly the book of imposture and extortion, of darkness and destruction.

FRANKLIN. We may become so habituated to tyranny as neither to feel nor see it. The part on which its poison has been perpetually dropping, is deadened; else would it be possible that throughout a whole nation, incomparably the most enlightened of any upon earth, young men should be sent from a distance, quite unknown to the parishioners, and often of a vicious or loose character, and for the greater part of a light one, to teach the experienced as well as the inexperienced their duties, and to be paid for a lesson which has been already taught by others!

WASHINGTON. Supposing an establishment to exist at all, the uttermost that a grave and reflecting people could reasonably be expected to endure is, that the bishop or presbyter, chosen by the clergy of the diocese, should nominate at least three natives of it, in order for the parishioners to appoint one of them to the vacant benefice. They should agree with him upon the stipend, which they would do amicably, just as they agree with an apothecary for his attendance on the paupers. He should be removable for any offence against the laws, or for any habits which they and the bishop should declare to be inconsistent with his office.

FRANKLIN. These remarks of yours are reasonable. In regard to the appointment of clergymen, the Roman Church is more observant of propriety than the English. It rarely if ever happens that a parish-priest is sent from a distance to his cure: he almost always is chosen from among his townsmen or provincials. This difference would be a subject of wonder to me, if I did not likewise see the representatives of boroughs, not selected as they were formerly from among the most respectable of the burgesses, but invited for the greater part from a distance, and utterly unknown both morally and politically by those who depute them to parliament. Can anything be more disgraceful to the inhabitants of a city, than to declare by their actions that none of them is worthy of confidence, or capable of transacting their affairs? And either this must be the inference, or we must attribute their conduct to the most scandalous venality.

WASHINGTON. I would obviate present evils by present remedies, as in the case of Ireland. Many good things can not be done, many indifferent ones may be: if indeed those are to be called indifferent which are only so at the time, and very far from it in the consequences. Religion, I agree with you, is too pure for corporations: it is best meditated on in our privacy, and best acted on in our ordinary intercourse with mankind. If we believe in Revelation, we must believe that God wishes us to converse with him but little, since the only form of address he has prescribed to us is an extremely short one. He has placed us where our time may be more beneficially employed in mutually kind offices, and he does not desire us to tell him hour after hour how dearly we love him, or how much we want from him: he knows these things exactly.

FRANKLIN. These however are the things which occupy the pulpit: and the ceremonies attending them and the modes of doing them, together with disquisitions on his body and parentage, have cost the lives of millions. In money too and lands I have calculated what Europe has paid for them; but the sum total, if I could repeat it, would confound the head of any arithmetician; nor was there ever a man in the world who could remember the figures, if he had heard them but once or twice read to him. The despots of France never exacted by their detested *corvée* so large a portion as the pastors claim in England; a tenth forsooth of every man's industry; and this tenth is taken off the ground untaxed, while the other nine parts are liable to new deductions. If truths are plain, they ought not to cost so much; if not plain, still less are they worth it. The tyrants of Sicily demanded a tenth of the corn, but not a tenth of oil or wine or hay or legumes, or fruits of any kind, in which the island was equally abundant. This satisfied them, and sufficed to keep the bodies and minds of their subjects in order and subjection.

WASHINGTON. We never had to complain of England for persecuting us by her fox-hunters in the Church; nor indeed, to speak honestly and freely, so much of any persecution, as of idle and unprofitable vexation.

FRANKLIN. The conduct of England toward us resembles that of Ebenezer Bullock toward his eldest son Jonas.

WASHINGTON. I remember old Ebenezer; and I believe it was Jonas who, when another youth, after giving him much offence and seeing him unresisting, would fain fight him, replied, 'Nay, I will not fight thee, friend! but if thou dost with that fist what thou threatenest, by the Lord's help I will smite thee sore, marking thee for one of an ill unprofitable flock; and thou shalt walk home in heaviness, like a wether the first morning he was made one.' Whereat he took off his coat, folded it up, and laid it on the ground, saying, 'This at least hath done no harm, and deserveth good treatment.' The adversary, not admiring such an object of contemplation, went away, muttering more reasonable threats, conditional and subjunctive. Ebenezer, I guess, aggravated and wore out his son's patience; for the old man was rich and testy, and would have his comforts neither encroached upon nor much partaken.

FRANKLIN. My story is this. Jonas had been hunting in the woods, and had contracted a rheumatism in the face which drew it awry, and, either from the pain it occasioned or from the medicines he took to cure it, rotted one of his grinders. Old Ebenezer was wealthy, had little to do or to care about, made few observations on his family, sick or sound, and saw nothing particular in his son's countenance. However, one day after dinner, when he had eaten heartily, he said, 'Son Jonas, methinks thy appetite is not over-keen: pick (and welcome) the other half of that hog's foot.'

'Father,' answered he, 'I have had a pain in my tooth the last fortnight; the northerly wind does it no good to-day: I would rather, if so be that you approve of it, eat a slice of yon fair cheese-cake in the closet.'

'Why, what ails the tooth?' said Ebenezer. 'Nothing more,' replied Jones, 'than that I can not chew with it what I used to chew.' 'Drive a nail in the wall,' quoth stoutly and courageously Ebenezer, 'tie a string to one end and lace the other round thy tooth.'

The son performed a part of the injunction, but could not very dexterously twist the string around the grinder, for his teeth were close and the cord not over-fine. Then said the father kindly, 'Open thy mouth, lad! give me the twine: back thy head: back it, I tell thee, over the chair.'

'Not that, father, not that; the next'; cried Jonas. 'What dost mean?' proudly and impatiently said Ebenezer. 'Is not the string about it? dost hold my hand too, scape-grace? dost give me this trouble for nought?' 'Patience now, father!' meekly said Jonas with the cord across his tongue; 'let me draw my tooth my own way.'

'Follow thine own courses, serpent!' indignantly exclaimed Ebenezer. 'As God's in Boston, thou art a most wilful and un-dutiful child.' 'I hope not, father.' 'Hope not! rebel! Did not I beget thee and thy teeth one and all? have not I lodged thee, clothed thee, and fed thee, these forty years? and now, I warrant ye, all this bustle and backwardness about a rotten tooth! should I be a groat the richer for it, out or in!'

WASHINGTON. Dignity in private men and in governments has been little else than a stately and stiff perseverance in oppression; and spirit, as it is called, little else than the foam of hard-mouthed insolence. Such at last is become the audacity of Power, from a century or more of holidays and riot, it now complains that you deprive it of its prerogative if you limit the exercise of its malignity.

I lament that there are those who can learn no lesson of humanity, unless we write it broadly with the point of the sword.

FRANKLIN. Let us hope, however, that we may see the day when these scholars shall be turned out of school.

WASHINGTON. The object of our cares and solicitudes, at present, is the stability of the blessings we have obtained. No attempt against them is dangerous from without, nor immediately from within; but the seeds of corruption are inherent, however latent, in all bodies, physical and political; guards therefore should be stationed, and laws enacted, to deter adventurers from attempts at despotism.

FRANKLIN. Other offences, even the greatest, are the violation of one law: despotism is the violation of all. The despot then should be punished, not only by loss of life, which the violation of only one law may incur, and which leaves no pain, no repentance, no example, but also with exposure and scourges, as among the Romans. Conspiracies are weak and frivolous: the hand of every man should be directed against him whose hand is directed against every man. Societies, on the contrary, should be instituted to recompense the avenger of humanity: every land should be his country, ever free citizen his brother. The greatest men, according to what is taught in schools and colleges, are those who have offered the greatest violence to reason and humanity. Destroyers of freedom are more celebrated than its founders; Pompey than Pelopidas, Cæsar than Timoleon; just as we hear more of him who burns a house than of him who builds one.

WASHINGTON. In the proper choice of teachers, and in the right course of education, are to be found the best preventive laws against despotism. Wherever there is a political church, of whatever creed, supported by the shoulders of the people, whether against their will or partially with it, there will be much dissatisfaction and much intolerance. Unhappily most of Christ's doctrines are superseded or explained away. There is one indeed which was never in fashion, and which, where all are good, is among the best. *Commune with thine own heart in thy chamber and be still.* This, if attended to in England and Ireland, would speedily send episcopal thrones into the lumber-room.

FRANKLIN. When certain men cry loudest they feel least. Indeed there is a great deal less of bigotry in the world than is usually supposed, and a great deal more insincerity. Our faith is of little moment or concern to those who declaim against it. They are angry, not at our blindness, but that the blind will trust his own dog and staff rather than theirs; and, what is worse, that he will carry the scrip. This is wilfulness: they would fain open his eyes to save him from the sin of it: and they break one or two bones because he will not take them for his oculists.

WASHINGTON. Love of power resides in the breast of every man, and is well regulated and discreet in few. Accompanied by genius, it is likewise too frequently accompanied by pride and arrogance. Although it assumes to itself the highest character, it is really among the weakest of our affections. Christianity, in its unadulterated form, is perfectly adapted to control it: in its adulterated, it has been the main support of aggression and iniquity. If ever we reduce it in America to an *Establishment* (as people call it) its spirit flies, and its body so weighs upon us, that we cast it down, or let it slip quietly from our arms. For Christianity is in itself of such simplicity, that, whoever would make an establishment of it, must add imposture; and from imposture grows usurpation.

FRANKLIN. Every mother, if left to herself, would teach her child what that child during the whole of his lifetime pays dearly for being taught, and what from such payment makes often an unkindly and unjust impression on him. He is obliged to purchase a commodity he does not require, and one which, sometimes it may happen, he has a larger store of then the patentee and vender. The most pious and moral men upon earth are the inhabitants of New England; and they are so because their consciences have never been drilled nor swathed, and because they never have been taught to divide their offering, the prayer and psalm on this side, the bag of wheat and truss of clover on that, between God and the ministers of the church.

WASHINGTON. While such men as the New England men are existing, our independence and liberty are secure. Governments, in which there are establishments, will, without great prudence, fall into danger from sects: every new one gives a fresh security and an additional stability to ours.

FRANKLIN. A mixture of sects is as advantageous to a political system as a mixture of blood is to the strength and perpetuity of the human race. Everything wants gentle, insensible, unrestricted, renovation; air, fire, earth, water, the vegetables, the animals, man, states. To you, fellow-citizen and defender, the most beneficent on record is principally owing. If America had been conquered, the breath of Freedom had been stifled in every region of the world, and we should have lamented the fate even of the people who in their blindness had enslaved us.

Looking to what may happen in future, on the ground you have marked out to me, I recollect an admirable law of Solon, which enacts that in case of usurpation the magistrates should resign their offices; and that he who continued his functions after the extinction of the popular power, should, together with the subverter of it, be punished with death by any private citizen. Let jurists decide whether it be not right and expedient to punish not usurpers only, but (if in compliance with the vulgar use of language we must distinguish them) conquerors too, in this manner; on the principle that every individual may recover his own property, and slay the spoiler who detains it aggressively. And let moralists judge, whether a few of such chastisements, on choice subjects, would not cool in a great degree the lust of spoliation and conquest. We will not be morose and captious with the lovers of peace and order: we will concede to them that it is a dangerous question to agitate, whether an arbitrary but salutary imprisonment now and then, with now and then an unlucky but well-meant torture, should be resisted or endured: for such things (they will tell us) happen occasionally in the most flourishing and best-regulated governments. But when constitutions are destroyed and legal magistrates are displaced, every man may pick up the broken laws; and it is a virtue to exercise the most solemn and the most imperative of them gratuitously. That of Solon, moderate as he was, goes farther. A similar law was enacted at Rome on the abolition of the decemvirate.[1]

WASHINGTON. Our constitution is flexible and yielding, by reason of its homogeneousness and its purity. Like the surface of our country, it may in some measure be changed by improvements and still preserve its character and features. The better part of what we have imported from England is retained for the present; because it is difficult to introduce new regulations in times of trouble; and that the mischievous should not burst in between the old paling

---

[1] Ne quis ullum magistratum sine provocatione crearet: qui creasset, eum jus fasque esset occidi, neve ea cædes capitalis noxæ haberetur. *Liv.* iii. 55.—W. S. L.

and the new. Several of these must be repealed, but gradually and occasionally.

FRANKLIN. In England more have been made and repealed again within one century than in all the rest of the universe within three; not reckoning, as would be unfair, what has been effected by revolutions. The worst have lasted the longest.[1] Barrenness is perennial; fertility is the produce of a season.

WASHINGTON. The whole system of representation, on which everything depends of law and liberty, has been changed within our memory.

FRANKLIN. Except the Chancery-court.

Sedet æternumque sedebit.

It has carried more ruin and desolation into innocent families than all the gaming-houses and other haunts of vice in the three kingdoms. Orphans, charities, schools, hospitals, are absorbed by the hundred, and swallowed up in this inland Maëlstrom.

WASHINGTON. The English talk of other grievances, and hardly notice this: we may be so near an object as not to see it in its full extent nor clearly.

FRANKLIN. A sailor condemned to be hanged, was thus admonished; 'Prepare yourself to appear before your eternal judge.' 'What does his lordship mean?' said he to the gaoler who was conducting him away. 'Sure, I can have nothing to do with my Lord Chancellor! I have neither land nor tenement; and he would turn up his nose at my jacket and trousers.'

There is no country where laws are so disproportionate to offences, so sanguinary, so disputable, so contradictory, so tardy, so

[1] Nevertheless it is proved and declared from the Bench that the mass of the people lives in comfort, not to say in affluence; for Mr Justice Best informs us that *most of the industrious part of the community live upon nothing else than bread and water*. That the laws are liberal is proved also and declared from the Bench by the same high authority. He tells us that writers of newspapers ought to report *nothing* of the King but what has been communicated by the Ministry. Mr Justice Best being raised to the Peerage, said, '*I bullied them into it.*' At a public dinner he proposed the health of George IV, enumerated his manifold virtues, and stated the benefits he had conferred on the nation. Upon which Mr T. Erskine begged to remind him of one omission, and to suggest that the national thanks should be humbly offered to his Majesty for the late abundant harvest. We may hope that ere long allied kings, instead of sending each other stars, snuff-boxes, and crosses, will amicably exchange ministers, jurists, and judges; all good and useful for all.—W. S. L.

expensive. Now these are the six principal defects of law, and to which it would be difficult to add a seventh of weight: for laxity can not co-exist with them. More fortunes have been wrecked upon the quicksands of British jurisprudence than ever have been engulfed by any one despotism: and more crimes are capital in England than were even known by name among the Jews in the time of Moses, or among the Athenians in the time of Draco.

WASHINGTON. Sometimes it is not the ignorant who act the most absurdly. Our late enemies are now just as angry with us as if they fancied we were mocking their mutability; some of them are more alarmed at the form of government we have chosen than at any other consequence of our liberation; I think, without reason. Republicanism is fit only for nations grown up, and is equally ill adapted to those in decay and to those in infancy. Europeans do indeed call ours an infant state.

FRANKLIN. Ay indeed? I never heard of an infant who kicked its mother down-stairs.

WASHINGTON. Be graver, Benjamin, and inform me whether, in your opinion, states do not reasonably date from their instruction and experience, and not from this or from that effect of vicissitude; and whether any nation in the world was ever better informed than ours, in its duties and interests.

FRANKLIN. None on record: and God grant that every novelty in our country may be as just and reasonable as that contained in your observation with regard to dates. We are as old a nation as the English, although we are not so old in America as they in England. Crossing the ocean does not make a man younger, neither does it a people.

WASHINGTON. Other accusations than those of juvenility are brought against us, and in appearance weightier. We are accused of the worst ingratitude, in having turned our strength and prosperity against the authors of it. Prosperity and strength never have excited a colony to rebellion, nor is wealth a whisperer to independence. But when arrogance and injustice stride forth into a colony strong and prosperous, it takes the advantage of its strength and prosperity; and then indeed wealth which has not been the mover, becomes the supporter, of emancipation. Every colony of England hath evinced a desire of quitting her when it could; not a single one of ancient Rome. Under the government of Hadrian, Utica,

Italica, and Gades, enjoying the privileges of municipal towns, entreated and obtained the title of colonies; though in the former condition they might exercise all the magistracies, and enjoy all the dignities of the republic. Yet Rome, we are informed, was the subjugator of mankind, and England the protector.

FRANKLIN. God protect the wretchedest of his creatures from such protection.

WASHINGTON. We have spoken of the danger to which every state, sooner or later, is subject from arbitrary power, and on the principles which ought to be instilled into every young citizen, first to guard against it, and then, if unsuccessful in his precautions, to exterminate it. Aristocracy, in the eyes of many, is as great an evil, and more imminent. Hence we have a party in force against the institution of a senate; and indeed if I could consider it as anything like an aristocracy or oligarchy in its gait or tendency, I should disapprove of it openly and loudly. But in fact ours is the only intermediate body which can do good; and I think it capable of this to a great extent. Hereditary Senates, under whatever name, are eternally tearing and consuming the vitals of their country. Our senate brings no such evil with it: on the contrary, everything about it is conservative and prospective. Its beneficent effects go beyond itself, and exceed its attributions: for, as none can be elected into it whose fortunes do not show him to have been prudent, and whose demeanour has not been regular and decorous, many spirits which from their nature, from youth, from zeal, from ambition, would be clamorous and unruly among our representatives, are controlled and guided by the hope of rising thence into this venerable assembly.

FRANKLIN. Tiberius, the wisest of despots, to increase his own power, increased that of the senate, and transferred to it the business of the *comitia*. In more barbarous times the king and aristocracy will contend for power, and the people will lift up its head between them: in more civilized, when abundance of wealth produces abundance of offices, the two will unite, and the people sink imperceptibly under them. For it is requisite in such a state to the existence of both that the mass do not become rich or instructed; against which evils, wars and lucrative places are devised, and elections are so managed as to occasion a vast expenditure, and to be accompanied by as many vices as can find room. Where senates have not been the executive power or the appointers of it, they have been instruments, but never intermediaries. That of papal Rome is in nothing less respectable than that of imperial. The venerable body, consisting of one man, a robe, and a periwig, went this year before the 'Holiness of our Lord,' requesting his permission to wear masks the last[1] week of the carnival. Who can doubt the utility and dignity of such institutions, or that something of such gravity and decorum ought always to stand between the prince and the people?

WASHINGTON. Other nations seem to entertain more fears for us, in the abundance of their benevolence, than we entertain for ourselves. They acknowledge you and some few more among us to be honest and well-meaning persons, and, pressing them hardly, do not deny altogether that you are moderate, reasonable, capable of instruction, nay indeed wise: yet the merest youths, whist-players and jockeys, turn their heads across their shoulders to give you a word of advice. When the popular part, the senatorial part, the executive part, are summarily discussed, the whole together is taken up as lightly and as easily disposed of. 'Republics can not stand' is the exclamation of council-board and sounding-board; the echo of Church and Chamber.

FRANKLIN. I would reduce the question to as few words as they would. A single argument is enough for a single truth: whatever comes after, is in part illustration, in part confusion.

When the advantages of kingship and republicanism are opposed, the main inquiry is, not about forms or families, not about the government of the fewer or the more; but whether the good shall control the bad or the bad control the good. A whole people can not long err in its choice. One man or two may agree with a groom that an unsound horse is a sound one; but twenty will not, take the twenty even at hazard. The great advantage is, however, when you can send back the horse after trying him, or change him on discovering his infirmity.

WASHINGTON. There are certain parts of our constitution which are capable of improvement. In my situation it would be imprudent and indecorous to point them out. But it is better in its present condition than if it were more centralized and compact. It is like those bridges which are overlaid with loose planks, and of which,

---

[1] This was likewise done in 1824.—W. S. L.

when the tide is rising rapidly, the platform would be heaved up and broken if it were more strained into apparent solidity.

FRANKLIN. In government, as in other things, we, and not only we, but even those wiser and greater men, the ministers of kings, may profit by reading the first half-page in the *Elements of Geometry*, in which we find that 'the right line is the shortest way from one point to another,' and, I would add, *cæteris paribus*, the easiest and surest.

We were called, a little while ago, the partisans of anarchy. At that time we could not argue with our opponents, they being in a state of frenzy, and running loose; but now that their arms are tied behind them, and that they are at home and abed, we may reason calmly with them, and tell them that no number is so near to nothing as one, and no government so near to anarchy as monarchy. There is more than one kind of anarchy, though there is only one known by name; as there are plants and metals under our feet, unclassed and undescribed. We are in the habit of calling those bodies of men anarchal which are in a state of effervescence; but the most anarchal of all are those which surrender self-rule to the caprice of the worst informed and least tractable members of society. Anarchy, like other things, has its certain state and season of quiescence; and its features are only the more flushed and discomposed by the somnolence of repletion and supineness.

WASHINGTON. A third question, of less intense anxiety, is raised by those who read our fortunes, not in the palms of our hands, but in the clouds. At some future day, they portend to us that every province will be an independent state.

FRANKLIN. Horrible prediction! We shall experience the misfortune then to have cultivated our wilds; to have subdivided and peopled hill, forest, and savannah; to have excavated quarries, mines, canals; to have erected arsenals, to have constructed navies; to be so rich in short and so powerful as to fear no enemy and to need no alliance. The time undoubtedly will come when each province will produce as much as all do now: so that as easily and safely as all now stand together, each will then stand alone. A long experience of their true interests, a certainty that they depend upon peace and concord, will render wars impossible among them; and if any European power should have the temerity to attack the weakest, not only will our other states chastise that power, but its own subjects will abandon or subvert it. Repose from oppression, refuge from persecution, respect for honesty, and reward for industry, are found here. A labourer gains more in this country than a 'professor of humanity' in some of the most civilized on the other continent. Resolute to defend these advantages, the children of America are for ever free: those of Europe, many years yet, must thread the labyrinth and face the Minotaur.

Meantime, quite a number of celebrities had arrived in Florence. Leigh Hunt and his family had settled at the village of Maiano, together with Charles Brown, a close friend of Keats in his last days, Seymour Kirkup the English painter, and Lord Dillon.[1]

In February 1825, Hazlitt called on Landor, and it was Hazlitt who introduced Landor to Leigh Hunt and Brown, while Brown introduced him to Kirkup. All of them became considerable friends. Hunt describes Landor as '. . . like a strong mountain pine, that should produce lilies. He was a man of vehement nature, with great delicacy of imagination—his temperament perhaps rather than a mind poetical.'[2] *At least Landor had some friends around him with whom he could discuss the arrangements for the publication of his work. All through his life Landor never cared a scrap about the financial side of his efforts. Indeed he was (and is) unique in that respect; in fact he was totally indifferent about* Imaginery Conversations. *His publishers completely sold the first edition; Hare therefore arranged for a second edition of a thousand copies. For the first edition Landor received £80.*

In September 1825, Landor had, as previously mentioned, taken a three years' lease of the Villa Castiglione, two miles outside Florence from the Porta San Niccolo. His wife's health was poor. Landor himself was in a melancholy frame of mind and battling over the publication of his next volume of Imaginary Conversations. *He wrote to his favourite sister Ellen:*

> 'To relieve this, and to improve the health of Julia, I have taken a
> country house for three years. Of which 2 months only are expired . . .
> I wish Julia would consent to live entirely in the country, but she
> cannot live without some company in the evening, one or two, old
> or young. For my part, I could live and even enjoy life, if I never
> were to see any other face, or hear any other voice, than those of
> my children.'[3]

After the birth of Arnold, Julia was born on 6 March 1820, his

---

[1] See Leigh Hunt, *Lord Byron and Some of His Contemporaries*, 1828, pp. 492, et seq.
[2] Super, *Landor*, p. 178.
[3] Elwin, *Landor*, pp. 214-15.

*second son Walter in 1822 and his third son Charles in 1825. None of
his children were to reciprocate the great love he had for them. His
mode of bringing up his children was a characteristic mixture of
wisdom and unpracticality.*[1]

He had written to Birch in 1819:

'. . . *There are three places where my son shall never have the consent
to enter—gaming houses, brothels and colleges. I hope he will be
habitually fond of gardening,—a great preventation from mischief
and conductor to health. I shall repress too evident a desire for
study, if he should have it. Health, good humour and the habitude
of pleasing are the only objects I keep constantly in view.*'[2]

*In 1826, Landor accompanied Francis Hare to Rome, where he
spent his time being the thorough tourist, and here he also met, through
Hare, many of the leaders of British Society. Back in Florence, he was
introduced to William Bewick, who drew his portrait, the likeness of
which was praised by Sir David Wilkie.*

The second edition of his first two volumes of Imaginary Conversa-
tions, *after being withdrawn from Taylor & Hessey, was published by
Henry Colburn in May 1826, but the third volume, although set up in
type, waited two years before publication by Colburn in May 1828.*[3]
*Landor was now urged by Hare to bring his number of dialogues to a
hundred—certainly he had enough material for two further volumes,
'Whether they be printed I know not, and never will inquire,' he told
Southey, 'this is left with Julius Hare.'*[4]

*Exasperated by Colburn's delay, Julius Hare took Landor's fourth
and fifth volumes to young Harrison Ainsworth, who was making a
short-lived venture into publishing.*[5]

*Landor was not unnaturally equally furious at the delay: he wrote
to his sister Ellen on 18 November 1827:*

'*I heard yesterday, for the first time, that the three last volumes of
my Conversations are printed or printing, and will come out early
in the ensuing year. The third vol. has indeed been printed these
ten or eleven months, but Colburn has been* pursuaded *to delay, and*

---

[1] *Idem,* p. 219.
[2] *Idem,* p. 220.
[3] *Idem,* p. 233.
[4] *Idem,* p. 235.
[5] *Idem,* p. 236.

*if possible to prevent, its publication. Another publisher has
undertaken the fourth and fifth. I am sick of writing, Never will I
write anything more. I have burnt all the things I had begun and
many that I had nearly completed.' Hare frankly told Landor at
the end of July 1829, 'The* Conversations *are too classical and
substantial for the morbid and frivolous taste of the English public.'*[1]

*Nevertheless, a publisher was found in James Duncan, who undertook
to issue the fourth and fifth volumes which appeared in the spring of
1829 under the title of* Imaginary Conversations of Literary Men
and Statesmen, Second Series.

[1] Forster, *Landor*, vol. ii, p. 166.

From *Imaginary Conversations*
Vol. III, 1829

EPICTETUS[1] AND SENECA

SENECA. Epictetus, I desired your master, Epaphroditus, to send you hither, having been much pleased with his report of your conduct, and much surprised at the ingenuity of your writings.

EPICTETUS. Then I am afraid, my friend—

SENECA. *My friend!* are these the expressions—Well, let it pass. Philosophers must bear bravely. The people expect it.

EPICTETUS. Are philosophers, then, only philosophers for the people; and, instead of instructing them, must they play tricks before them? Give me rather the gravity of dancing dogs. Their motions are for the rabble; their reverential eyes and pendant paws are under the pressure of awe at a master; but they are dogs, and not below their destinies.

SENECA. Epectetus? I will give you three talents to let me take that sentiment for my own.

EPICTETUS. I would give thee twenty, if I had them, to make it thine.

SENECA. You mean, by lending to it the graces of my language?

EPICTETUS. I mean, by lending it to thy conduct. And now let me console and comfort thee, under the calamity I brought on thee

---

[1] Epictetus was born in AD 50?/60? at Hierapolis in south-west Phrygia. His name means 'acquired'—his original name is said to be unknown for, as a boy, he was a slave in the house of Epaphroditus, a courtier of the Emperor Nero. He attended the lectures of the Stoic Musonius Rufus, but was expelled with others by Domitian, who was irritated by the support and encouragement which the opposition to his tyrany found amongst the adherents of Stoicism. He then went to Nicopolis where he remained for the rest of his life, and taught. He never married, nor did he write anything, but much of his learning was preserved from his pupil Flavius Arrianus, who became the historian of Alexander the Great. Arrianus' work was called Discourses of Epictetus and was followed by the *Encheiridion*.

The philosophy of Epictetus is practical and is of a high idealistic type of morality. He is concerned solely on the proper behaviour of a balanced life, to see things as they are, and that will and purpose are the integral parts of a personal life.

by calling thee *my friend*. If thou art not my friend, why send for me? Enemy I can have none: being a slave, Fortune has now done with me.

SENECA. Continue, then, your former observations. What were you saying?

EPICTETUS. That which thou interruptedst.

SENECA. What was it?

EPICTETUS. I should have remarked that, if thou foundest ingenuity in my writings, thou must have discovered in them some deviation from the plain, homely truths of Zeno[1] and Cleanthes.[2]

SENECA. We all swerve a little from them.

EPICTETUS. In practice too?

SENECA. Yes, even in practice, I am afraid.

EPICTETUS. Often?

SENECA. Too often.

EPICTETUS. Strange! I have been attentive, and yet have remarked but one difference among you great personages at Rome.

SENECA. What difference fell under your observation?

EPICTETUS. Crates and Zeno and Cleanthes taught us that our desires were to be subdued by philosophy alone. In this city, their acute and inventive scholars take us aside, and show us that there is not only one way, but two.

SENECA. Two ways?

EPICTETUS. They whisper in our ear, 'These two ways are philosophy and enjoyment: the wiser man will take the readier, or, not finding it, the alternative.' Thou reddenest.

SENECA. Monstrous degeneracy.

EPICTETUS. What magnificent rings! I did not notice them until thou liftedst up thy hands to heaven, in detestation of such effeminacy and impudence.

SENECA. The rings are not amiss; my rank rivets them upon my fingers: I am forced to wear them. Our emperor gave me one,

[1] Zeno of Citium in Cyprus, famous philosopher and founder of the Stoic School, was born about 335 BC, d. 263 BC. Came to Athens when he was about twenty, and attached himself to the Cynic Crates. He studied under Stilipo, Diodorus Cronus, and Plulo. He established his own school in the Stoa Poikile, whence his pupil were known as Stoics.

[2] Cleanthes (301 BC–232 BC). Stoic philosopher who studied under Zeno, whom he succeeded as head of the Stoa in 263 BC. He died of voluntary starvation.

Epaphroditus another, Tigellinus the third. I cannot lay them aside, a single day, for fear of offending the gods, and those whom they love the most worthily.

EPICTETUS. Although they make thee stretch out thy fingers, like the arms and legs of one of us slaves upon a cross.

SENECA. Oh horrible! Find some other resemblance.

EPICTETUS. The extremities of a fig-leaf.

SENECA. Ignoble!

EPICTETUS. The claws of a toad, trodden on or stoned.

SENECA. You have great need, Epictetus of an instructor in eloquence and rhetoric: you want topics, and tropes, and figures.

EPICTETUS. I have no room for them. They make such a buzz in the house, a man's own wife cannot understand what he says to her.

SENECA. Let us reason a little upon style. I would set you right, and remove from before you the prejudice of a somewhat rustic education. We may adorn the simplicity of the wisest.

EPICTETUS. Thou canst not adorn simplicity. What is naked and defective is susceptible of decoration: what is decorated is simplicity no longer. Thou mayest give another thing in exchange for it; but if thou wert master of it, thou wouldst preserve it inviolate. It is no wonder that we mortals, little able as we are to see truth, should be less able to express it.

SENECA. You have formed at present no idea of style.

EPICTETUS. I never think about it. First, I consider whether what I am about to say is true; then, whether I can say it with brevity, in such a manner as that others shall see it as clearly as I do in the light of truth; for, if they survey it as an ingenuity, my desire is ungratified, my duty unfulfilled. I go not with those who dance round the image of Truth, less out of honour to her than to display their agility and address.

SENECA. We must attract the attention of readers by novelty, and force, and grandeur of expression.

EPICTETUS. We must. Nothing is so grand as truth, nothing so forcible, nothing so novel.

SENECA. Sonorous sentences are wanted to awaken the lethargy of indolence.

EPICTETUS. Awaken it to what? Here lies the question; and a weighty one it is. If thou awakenest men where they can see nothing and do no work, it is better to let them rest: but will not they, thinkest thou, look up at a rainbow, unless they are called to it by a clap of thunder?

SENECA. Your early youth, Epictetus, has been, I will not say neglected, but cultivated with rude instruments and unskilful hands.

EPICTETUS. I thank God for it. Those rude instruments have left the turf lying yet toward the sun; and those unskilful hands have plucked out the docks.

SENECA. We hope and believe that we have attained a vein of eloquence, brighter and more varied than has been hitherto laid open to the world.

EPICTETUS. Than any in the Greek?

SENECA. We trust so.

EPICTETUS. Than your Cicero's?

SENECA. If the declaration may be made without an offence to modesty. Surely, you cannot estimate or value the eloquence of that noble pleader?

EPICTETUS. Imperfectly, not being born in Italy; and the noble pleader is a much less man with me than the noble philosopher. I regret that, having farms and villas, he would not keep his distance from the pumping up of foul words against thieves, cut-throats, and other rogues; and that he lied, sweated, and thumped his head and thighs, in behalf of those who were no better.

SENECA. Senators must have clients, and must protect them.

EPICTETUS. Innocent or guilty?

SENECA. Doubtless.

EPICTETUS. If I regret what is and might not be, I may regret more what both is and must be. However, it is an amiable thing, and no small merit in the wealthy, even to trifle and play at their leisure hours with philosophy. It cannot be expected that such a personage should espouse her, or should recommend her as an inseparable mate to his heir.

SENECA. I would.

EPICTETUS. Yes, Seneca, but thou hast no son to make the match for; and thy recommendation, I suspect, would be given him before he could consummate the marriage. Every man wishes his sons to be philosophers while they are young; but takes especial care, as they grow older, to teach them its insufficiency and unfitness for their intercourse with mankind. The paternal voice says, 'You must not be particular; you are about to have a profession to live by; follow those who have thriven the best in it.' Now, among these, whatever be the profession, canst thou point out to me one single philosopher?

SENECA. Not just now; nor, upon reflection, do I think it feasible.

EPICTETUS. Thou, indeed, mayest live much to thy ease and satisfaction with philosophy, having (they say) two thousand talents.

SENECA. And a trifle to spare—pressed upon me by that godlike youth, my pupil Nero.

EPICTETUS. Seneca! where God hath placed a mine, he hath placed the materials of an earthquake.

SENECA. A true philosopher is beyond the reach of Fortune.

EPICTETUS. The false one thinks himself so. Fortune cares little about philosophers; but she remembers where she hath set a rich man, and she laughs to see the Destinies at his door.

MARCELLUS AND HANNIBAL

Marcellus, the Commander of the Roman army, lies before Hannibal, mortally wounded.

HANNIBAL. Could a Numidian horseman ride no faster? Marcellus! ho! Marcellus! He moves not—he is dead. Did he not stir his fingers? Stand wide, soldiers—wide, forty paces—give him air—bring water—halt! Gather those broad leaves, and all the rest, growing under the brushwood—unbrace his armour. Loose the helmet first—his breast rises. I fancied his eyes were fixed on me—they have rolled back again. Who presumed to touch my shoulder? This horse? It was surely the horse of Marcellus! Let no man mount him. Ha! ha! the Romans, too, sink into luxury: here is gold about the charger.

GAULISH CHIEFTAIN. Execrable thief! The golden chain of our king under a beast's grinders! The vengeance of the gods hath overtaken the impure—

HANNIBAL. We will talk about vengeance when we have entered

Rome, and about purity among the priests, if they will hear us. Sound for the surgeon. That arrow may be extracted from the side. deep as it is.—The conqueror of Syracuse lies before me.—Send a vessel off to Carthage. Say Hannibal is at the gates of Rome.— Marcellus, who stood alone between us, fallen. Brave man! I would rejoice and cannot.—How awfully serene a countenance! Such as we hear are in the islands of the Blessed. And how glorious a form and stature! Such too was theirs! They also once lay thus upon the earth wet with their blood—few other enter there. And what plain armour!

GAULISH CHIEFTAIN. My party slew him—indeed I think I slew him myself. I claim the chain: it belongs to my king; the glory of Gaul requires it. Never will she endure to see another take it.

HANNIBAL. My friend, the glory of Marcellus did not require him to wear it. When he suspended the arms of your brave king in the temple, he thought such a trinket unworthy of himself and of Jupiter. The shield he battered down, the breast-plate he pierced with his sword—these he showed to the people and to the gods; hardly his wife and little children saw this, ere his horse wore it.

GAULISH CHIEFTAIN. Hear me, O Hannibal!

HANNIBAL. What! when Marcellus lies before me? when his life may perhaps be recalled? when I may lead him in triumph to Carthage? when Italy, Sicily, Greece, Asia, wait to obey me? Content thee! I will give thee mine own bridle, worth ten such.

GAULISH CHIEFTAIN. For myself?

HANNIBAL. For thyself.

GAULISH CHIEFTAIN. And these rubies and emeralds, and that scarlet—

HANNIBAL. Yes, yes.

GAULISH CHIEFTAIN. O glorious Hannibal! unconquerable hero! O my happy country! to have such an ally and defender. I swear eternal gratitude—yes, gratitude, love, devotion, beyond eternity.

HANNIBAL. In all treaties we fix the time: I could hardly ask a longer. Go back to thy station.—I would see what the surgeon is about, and hear what he thinks. The life of Marcellus! the triumph of Hannibal! what else has the world in it? Only Rome and Carthage: these follow.

MARCELLUS. I must die then? The gods be praised! The commander of a Roman army is no captive.

HANNIBAL (*to the Surgeon*). Could not he bear a sea-voyage? Extract the arrow.

SURGEON. He expires that moment.

MARCELLUS. It pains me: extract it.

HANNIBAL. Marcellus I see no expression of pain on your countenance, and never will I consent to hasten the death of an enemy in my power. Since your recovery is hopeless, you say truly you are no captive.

(*To the Surgeon.*) Is there nothing, man, that can assuage the mortal pain? for, suppress the signs of it as he may, he must feel it. Is there nothing to alleviate and allay it?

MARCELLUS. Hannibal, give me thy hand—thou hast found it and brought it me, compassion.

(*To the Surgeon.*) Go, friend; others want thy aid; several fell around me.

HANNIBAL. Recommend to your country, O Marcellus, while time permits it, reconciliation and peace with me, informing the Senate of my superiority in force, and the impossibility of resistance. The tablet is ready: let me take off this ring—try to write, to sign it, at least. Oh, what satisfaction I feel at seeing you able to rest upon the elbow, and even to smile!

MARCELLUS. Within an hour or less, with how severe a brow would Minos say to me, 'Marcellus, is this thy writing?'

Rome loses one man: she hath lost many such, and she still hath many left.

HANNIBAL. Afraid as you are of falsehood, say you this? I confess in shame the ferocity of my countrymen. Unfortunately, too, the nearer posts are occupied by Gauls, infinitely more cruel. The Numidians are so in revenge: the Gauls both in revenge and in sport. My presence is required at a distance, and I apprehend the barbarity of one or other, learning, as they must do, your refusal to execute my wishes for the common good, and feeling that by this refusal you deprive them of their country, after so long an absence.

MARCELLUS. Hannibal, thou art not dying.

HANNIBAL. What then? What mean you?

MARCELLUS. That thou mayest, and very justly, have many things yet to apprehend: I can have none. The barbarity of thy soldiers is nothing to me: mine would not dare be cruel. Hannibal is forced to be absent; and his authority goes away with his horse. On this turf lies defaced the semblance of a general; but Marcellus is yet the regulator of his army. Dost thou abdicate a power conferred on thee by thy nation? Or wouldst thou acknowledge it to have become, by thy own sole fault, less plenary than thy adversary's?

I have spoken too much: let me rest; this mantle oppresses me.

HANNIBAL. I placed my mantle on your head when the helmet was first removed, and while you were lying in the sun. Let me fold it under, and then replace the ring.

MARCELLUS. Take it, Hannibal. It was given me by a poor woman who flew to me at Syracuse, and who covered it with her hair, torn off in desperation that she had no other gift to offer. Little thought I that her gift and her words should be mine. How suddenly may the most powerful be in the situation of the most helpless! Let that ring and the mantle under my head be the exchange of guests at parting. The time may come, Hannibal, when thou (and the gods alone know whether as conqueror or conquered) mayest sit under the roof of my children, and in either case it shall serve thee. In thy adverse fortune, they will remember on whose pillow their father breathed his last; in thy prosperous (Heaven grant it may shine upon thee in some other country!) it will rejoice thee to protect them. We feel ourselves the most exempt from affliction when we relieve it, although we are then the most conscious that it may befall us.

There is one thing here which is not at the disposal of either.

HANNIBAL. What?

MARCELLUS. This body.

HANNIBAL. Whither would you be lifted? Men are ready.

MARCELLUS. I meant not so. My strength is failing. I seem to hear rather what is within than what is without. My sight and my other senses are in confusion. I would have said—This body, when a few bubbles of air shall have left it, is no more worthy of thy notice than of mine; but thy glory will not let thee refuse it to the piety of my family.

HANNIBAL. You would ask something else. I perceive an inquietude not visible till now.

MARCELLUS. Duty and Death make us think of home sometimes.

HANNIBAL. Thitherward the thoughts of the conqueror and of the conquered fly together.

MARCELLUS. Hast thou any prisoners from my escort?

HANNIBAL. A few dying lie about—and let them lie—they are Tuscans. The remainder I saw at a distance, flying, and but one brave man among them—he appeared a Roman—a youth who turned back, though wounded. They surrounded and dragged him away, spurring his horse with their sword. These Etrurians measure their courage carefully, and tack it well together before they put it on, but throw it off again with lordly ease.

Marcellus, why think about them? or does aught else disquiet your thoughts?

MARCELLUS. I have suppressed it long enough. My son,—my beloved son!

HANNIBAL. Where is he? Can it be? Was he with you?

MARCELLUS. He would have shared my fate—and has not. Gods of my country! beneficent throughout life to me, in death surpassingly beneficent: I render you, for the last time, thanks.

1829

Meanwhile life in Florence was not to run without mishap. There was the theft of silver which Landor reported to the police, reminding them at the same time of the picture stolen the previous year and not recovered. The police in their turn questioned servants and tradesmen, who affirmed that Landor was a 'dangerous' man. Landor thereupon appealed to the Grand Duke himself and it was decreed he should be banished from Florentine society. His friends thereupon persuaded him to retire to Lucca for a month. Meanwhile the Grand Duke was appealed to again. He then took the view that it was all a 'storm in a tea-cup', and Landor was allowed to return.

Francis Hare, hearing of these troubles, wrote to Landor, begging him to avoid further scrapes that might drive him out of the city, which he believed to be 'the best and fittest above' for him. Landor needed no such persuasion and wrote to Southey:

'. . . *Such being the case, I resolved to pitch my tent in the midst of them; and have now bought a villa, belonging to the Count Gheradescha of the family of C. Ugolino, and upon the spot where Boccaccio led his women to bathe when they had left the first scene of their story-telling. Here I shall pass my life; long or short, no matter; but God grant without pain and sickness, and with only such friends and such enemies as I enjoy at present. Pray come and pass the vintage and winter with me—this year if possible; if not the next. I will give you a cool and beautiful chapel to write and read in, and then be sure it is consecrated. Bring your son.*'[1]

With the financial help of his close friend Joseph Ablett, he moved to the Villa Gheradescha in the autumn of 1829.
Landor then heard of his mother's death. He wrote to Southey:

'*At eighty-five such a loss might have been expected: and, after not seeing her for fifteen years, I fancied I should have been less affected by it. But it is only by the blow itself that early remembrances are awakened to the uttermost. She had always been kind to me.—You do not give me any fresh hopes of seeing you in Italy. I am making a fresh garden, and doing other more foolish things. Such as*

---

[1] Forster, *Landor*, vol. ii, p. 220.

building: but this is as much for the convenience of my labourers as for mine. I am removing all their offices from my own residence. The Italian gentlemen are fond of pigging with them. I cannot bear anyone near me, particularly those who leave traces of their proximity unquestionable to eyes or nose. Whenever you come I can give you two bedrooms and two below; so you may arrange with Mrs Southey, and bring such of your family as are most inclined for Italy. I shall consider this the most delightful event that has occurred since my residence abroad. To-day I shall have (they tell me) about fifteen barrells of wine, fifty-five quarts to the barrell. They rob a tenth of it for themselves, and a tenth for the priest. Since Peter Leopold[1] abolished the tithes the priests tell the contadini they will go to the devil if they assist in such impiety; and, from the robbery of the master, the tithes are as regularly paid as ever. The pious rob both for priest and themselves, being absolved in the default, and placing the theft on the opposite page to the duty. This fact was told me by Piamonte, formerly presidente del "buon governo".[2]

Landor was made happy, however, by the arrival of his 'dearest Ianthé' (Jane Swift), who had married, as her second husband, the Count de Molandé after the death of Godwin Swift, her first husband, in 1814. Molandé also had died two years previous to her arrival in Florence, and she had received proposals of marriage from the Earl of Bective and the Duke of Luxembourg. She had rejected the former, feeling he was too young, while the Duke, an eminently suitable husband, was not a Catholic. 'Ianthé' was now in her late forties, and with her reappearance in his life, Landor took to writing verse again.

1 The Grand Duke.
2 Forster, *Landor*, vol. ii, p. 221.

From *Imaginary Conversations*
Vol. IV, 1829

DIOGENES AND PLATO[1]

(This is throughout a criticism of Plato, Diogenes gaining an easy victory at every point. Landor, who loved concrete thought and hated all forms of mysticism, had formed a very unfavourable opinion of Plato, and often goes out of his way to attack him. He frequently defends the character and philosophy of Diogenes, and speaks of him elsewhere as the wisest man of his time.—Ed.)

DIOGENES. Stop! stop! come hither! Why lookest thou so scornfully and askance upon me?

PLATO. Let me go! loose me! I am resolved to pass.

DIOGENES. Nay, then, by Jupiter and this tub! thou leavest three good ells of Milesian cloth behind thee. Whither wouldst thou amble?

PLATO. I am not obliged in courtesy to tell you.

DIOGENES. Upon whose errand? Answer me directly.

PLATO. Upon my own.

DIOGENES. Oh, then I will hold thee yet awhile. If it were upon another's, it might be a hardship to a good citizen, though not to a good philosopher.

---

[1] When Crabb Robinson read this *Imaginary Conversation* he commented, 'I suspect, a just attack on the famous philosopher. Landor [on Sunday evening] expressed his contempt of Plato in unmeasured language, and he said what I had half thought when a young man, but did not dare to think fully. By the bye, a word which incidentally fell from Landor has rendered the famous beginning of St John's gospel very clear and very harmless. Λόγος, he said, means in Plato *thought* or *idea*, and in that sense words are realities. If so, then this famous text is but an assertion that God is essentially an active or thinking being—that thought was with Him from the beginning and He had been eternally thought. Such verbose and tautological assertions are common to Oriental and Greek writers. Diogenes in this dialogue says many acute and striking things, but Plato is too insignificant by far. He is a feeble and inane objector without any power of reply. Landor would say: Such I believe (him) to have been in his famous dialogues, and I could not give him a *sense* which I meant by my dialogue to prove he *never had*...' (Henry Crabb Robinson: *Books and Their Writers*, ed. Edith Morley, vol. i, pp. 384–5.)

PLATO. That can be no impediment to my release: you do not think me one.

DIOGENES. No, by my Father Jove!

PLATO. Your father!

DIOGENES. Why not? Thou shouldst be the last man to doubt it. Hast not thou declared it irrational to refuse our belief to those who assert that they are begotten by the gods, though the assertion (these are thy words) be unfounded on reason or probability? In me there is a chance of it: whereas in the generation of such people as thou art fondest of frequenting who claim it loudly, there are always too many competitors to leave it probable.

PLATO. Those who speak against the great do not usually speak from morality, but from envy.

DIOGENES. Thou hast a glimpse of the truth in this place, but as thou hast already shown thy ignorance in attempting to prove to me what a *man* is, ill can I expect to learn from thee what is a *great man*.

PLATO. No doubt your experience and intercourse will afford me the information.

DIOGENES. Attend, and take it. The great man is he who hath nothing to fear and nothing to hope from another. It is he who, while he demonstrates the iniquity of the laws, and is able to correct them, obeys them peaceably. It is he who looks on the ambitious both as weak and fraudulent. It is he who hath no disposition or occasion for any kind of deceit, no reason for being or for appearing different from what he is. It is he who can call together the most select company when it pleases him.

PLATO. Excuse my interruption. In the beginning of your definition I fancied that you were designating your own person, as most people do in describing what is admirable; now I find that you have some other in contemplation.

DIOGENES. I thank thee for allowing me what perhaps I *do* possess, but what I was not then thinking of; as is often the case with rich possessors: in fact, the latter part of the description suits me as well as any portion of the former.

PLATO. You may call together the best company, by using your hands in the call, as you did with me; otherwise I am not sure that you would succeed in it.

DIOGENES. My thoughts are my company; I can bring them

together, select them, detain them, dismiss them. Imbecile and vicious men cannot do any of these things. Their thoughts are scattered, vague, uncertain, cumbersome: and the worst stick to them the longest; many indeed by choice, the greater part by necessity, and accompanied, some by weak wishes, others by vain remorse.

PLATO. Is there nothing of greatness, O Diogenes! in exhibiting how cities and communities may be governed best, how morals may be kept the purest, and power become the most stable?

DIOGENES. *Something* of greatness does not constitute the great man. Let me however see him who hath done what thou sayest: he must be the most universal and the most indefatigable traveller, he must also be the oldest creature, upon earth.

PLATO. How so?

DIOGENES. Because he must know perfectly the climate, the soil, the situation, the peculiarities, of the races, of their allies, of their enemies; he must have sounded their harbours, he must have measured the quantity of their arable land and pasture, of their woods and mountains; he must have ascertained whether there are fisheries on their coasts, and even what winds are prevalent. On these causes, with some others, depend the bodily strength, the number, the wealth, the wants, the capacities of the people.

PLATO. Such are low thoughts.

DIOGENES. The bird of wisdom flies low, and seeks her food under hedges: the eagle himself would be starved if he always soared aloft and against the sun. The sweetest fruit grows near the ground, and the plants that bear it require ventilation and lopping. Were this not to be done in thy garden, every walk and alley, every plot and border, would be covered with runners and roots, with boughs and suckers. We want no poets or logicians or metaphysicians to govern us: we want practical men, honest men, continent men, unambitious men, fearful to solicit a trust, slow to accept, and resolute never to betray one. Experimentalists may be the best philosophers: they are always the worst politicians. Teach people their duties, and they will know their interests. Change as little as possible, and correct as much.

Philosophers are absurd from many causes, but principally from laying out unthriftily their distinctions. They set up four virtues: fortitude, prudence, temperance, and justice. Now a man may be a very bad one, and yet possess three out of the four. Every cut-throat must, if he has been a cut-throat on many occasions, have more fortitude and more prudence than the greater part of those whom we consider as the best men. And what cruel wretches, both executioners and judges, have been strictly just! how little have they cared what gentleness, what generosity, what genius, their sentence hath removed from the earth! Temperance and beneficence contain all other virtues. Take them home, Plato; split them, expound them; do what thou wilt with them, if thou but use them.

Before I gave thee this lesson, which is a better than thou ever gavest any one, and easier to remember, thou wert accusing me of invidiousness and malice against those whom thou callest the great, meaning to say the powerful. Thy imagination, I am well aware, had taken its flight toward Sicily, where thou seekest thy great man, as earnestly and undoubtingly as Ceres sought her Persephonè, Faith! honest Plato, I have no reason to envy thy worthy friend Dionysius. Look at my nose! A lad seven or eight years old threw an apple at me yesterday, while I was gazing at the clouds, and gave me nose enough for two moderate men. Instead of such a godsend, what should I have thought of my fortune if, after living all my lifetime among golden vases, rougher than my hand with their emeralds and rubies, their engravings and emboss-ments; among Parian caryatides and porphyry sphinxes; among philosophers with rings upon their fingers and linen next their skin; and among singing-boys and dancing-girls, to whom alone thou speakest intelligibly—I ask thee again, what should I in reason have thought of my fortune, if, after these facilities and superfluities, I had at last been pelted out of my house, not by one young rogue, but by thousands of all ages, and not with an apple (I wish I could say a rotten one), but with pebbles and broken pots; and, to crown my deserts, had been compelled to become the teacher of so promising a generation? Great men, forsooth! thou knowest at last who they are.

PLATO. There are great men of various kinds.

DIOGENES. No, by my beard, are there not!

PLATO. What! are there not great captains, great geometricians, great dialectitians?

DIOGENES. Who denied it? A great man was the postulate. Try thy hand now at the powerful one.

PLATO. On seeing the exercise of power, a child cannot doubt who is powerful, more or less; for power is relative. All men are weak, not only if compared to the Demiurgos, but if compared to the sea or the earth, or certain things upon each of them, such as elephants and whales. So placid and tranquil is the scene around us, we can hardly bring to mind the images of strength and force, the precipices, the abysses—

DIOGENES. Prythee hold thy loose tongue, twinkling and glittering like a serpent's in the midst of luxuriance and rankness! Did never this reflection of thine warn thee that, in human life, the precipices and abysses would be much farther from our admiration if we were less inconsiderate, selfish, and vile? I will not however stop thee long, for thou wert going on quite consistently. As thy great men are fighters and wranglers, so thy mighty things upon the earth and sea are troublesome and intractable encumbrances. Thou perceivedst not what was greater in the former case, neither art thou aware what is greater in this. Didst thou feel the gentle air that passed us?

PLATO. I did not, just then.

DIOGENES. That air, so gentle, so imperceptible to thee, is more powerful not only than all the creatures that breathe and live by it; not only than all the oaks of the forest, which it rears in an age and shatters in a moment; not only than all the monsters of the sea, but than the sea itself, which it tosses up into foam, and breaks against every rock in its vast circumference; for it carries in its bosom, with perfect calm and composure, the incontrollable ocean and the peopled earth, like an atom of a feather.

To the world's turmoils and pageantries is attracted, not only the admiration of the populace, but the zeal of the orator, the enthusiasm of the poet, the investigation of the historian, and the contemplation of the philosopher: yet how silent and invisible are they in the depths of air! Do I say in those depths and deserts? No; I say in the distance of a swallow's flight,—at the distance she rises above us, ere a sentence brief as this could be uttered.

What are its mines and mountains? Fragments welded up and dislocated by the expansion of water from below; the most part reduced to mud, the rest to splinters. Afterwards sprang up fire in many places, and again tore and mangled the mutilated carcass, and still growls over it.

What are its cities and ramparts, and moles and monuments? Segments of a fragment, which one man puts together and another throws down. Here we stumble upon thy great ones at their work. Show me now, if thou canst, in history, three great warriors, or three great statesmen, who have acted otherwise than spiteful children.

PLATO. I will begin to look for them in history when I have discovered the same number in the philosophers or the poets. A prudent man searches in his own garden after the plant he wants, before he casts his eyes over the stalls in Kenkrea or Keramicos.

Returning to your observation on the potency of the air, I am not ignorant or unmindful of it. May I venture to express my opinion to you, Diogenes, that the earlier discoverers and distributors of wisdom (which wisdom lies among us in ruins and remnants, partly distorted and partly concealed by theological allegory) meant by Jupiter the air in its agitated state; by Juno the air in its quiescent. These are the great agents, and therefore called the king and queen of the gods. Jupiter is denominated by Homer the *compeller of clouds*: Juno receives them, and remits them in showers to plants and animals.

I may trust you, I hope, O Diogenes?

DIOGENES. Thou mayest lower the gods in my presence, as safely as men in the presence of Timon.

PLATO. I would not lower them: I would exalt them.

DIOGENES. More foolish and presumptuous still!

PLATO. Fair words, O Sinopean! I protest to you my aim is truth.

DIOGENES. I cannot lead thee where of a certainty thou mayest always find it; but I will tell thee what it is. Truth is a point; the subtilest and finest; harder than adamant; never to be broken, worn away, or blunted. Its only bad quality is, that it is sure to hurt those who touch it; and likely to draw blood, perhaps the life-blood, of those who press earnestly upon it. Let us away from this narrow lane skirted with hemlock, and pursue our road again through the wind and dust, toward the *great* man and the *powerful*. Him I would call the powerful one who controls the storms of his mind, and turns to good account the worst accidents of his fortune. The great man, I was going on to demonstrate, is somewhat more. He must be able to do this, and he must have an intellect which puts into motion the intellect of others.

PLATO. Socrates, then, was your great man.

DIOGENES. He was indeed; nor can all thou hast attributed to him ever make me think the contrary. I wish he could have kept a little more at home, and have thought it as well worth his while to converse with his own children as with others.

PLATO. He knew himself born for the benefit of the human race.

DIOGENES. Those who are born for the benefit of the human race go but little into it: those who are born for its curse are crowded.

PLATO. It was requisite to dispel the mists of ignorance and error.

DIOGENES. Has he done it? What doubt has he elucidated, or what fact has he established? Although I was but twelve years old and resident in another city when he died, I have taken some pains in my inquiries about him from persons of less vanity and less perverseness than his disciples. He did not leave behind him any true philosopher among them; any who followed his mode of argumentation, his subjects of disquisition, or his course of life; any who would subdue the malignant passions or coerce the looser; any who would abstain from calumny or from cavil; any who would devote his days to the glory of his country, or, what is easier and perhaps wiser, to his own well-founded contentment and well-merited repose. Xenophon, the best of them, offered up sacrifices, believed in oracles, consulted soothsayers, turned pale at a jay, and was dysenteric at a magpie.

PLATO. He had courage at least.

DIOGENES. His courage was of so strange a quality, that he was ready, if jay or magpie did not cross him, to fight for Spartan or Persian. Plato, whom thou esteemest much more, and knowest somewhat less, careth as little for portent and omen as doth Diogenes. What he would have done for a Persian I cannot say; certain I am that he would have no more fought for a Spartan than he would for his own father: yet he mortally hates the man who hath a kinder muse or a better milliner, or a seat nearer the minion of a king. So much for the two disciples of Socrates who have acquired the greatest celebrity!

PLATO. Diogenes! If you must argue or discourse with me, I will endure your asperity for the sake of your acuteness; but it appears to me a more philosophical thing to avoid what is insulting and vexatious, than to breast and brave it.

DIOGENES. Thou hast spoken well.

PLATO. It belongs to the vulgar, not to us, to fly from a man's opinions to his actions, and to stab him in his own house for having received no wound in the school. One merit you will allow me: I always keep my temper; which you seldom do.

DIOGENES. Is mine a good or a bad one?

PLATO. Now, must I speak sincerely?

DIOGENES. Dost thou, a philosopher, ask such a question of me, a philosopher? Ay, sincerely or not at all.

PLATO. Sincerely as you could wish, I must declare, then, your temper is the worst in the world.

DIOGENES. I am much in the right, therefore, not to keep it. Embrace me: I have spoken now in thy own manner. Because thou sayest the most malicious things the most placidly, thou thinkest or pretendest thou art sincere.

PLATO. Certainly those who are most the masters of their resentments are likely to speak less erroneously than the passionate and morose.

DIOGENES. If they would, they might; but the moderate are not usually the most sincere, for the same circumspection which makes them moderate makes them likewise retentive of what could give offence: they are also timid in regard to fortune and favour, and hazard little. There is no mass of sincerity in any place. What there is must be picked up patiently, a grain or two at a time; and the season for it is after a storm, after the overflowing of banks, and bursting of mounds, and sweeping away of landmarks. Men will always hold something back; they must be shaken and loosened a little, to make them let go what is deepest in them, and weightiest and purest.

PLATO. Shaking and loosening as much about you as was requisite for the occasion, it became you to demonstrate where and in what manner I had made Socrates appear less sagacious and less eloquent than he was; it became you likewise to consider the great difficulty of finding new thoughts and new expressions for those who had more of them than any other men, and to represent them in all the brilliancy of their wit and in all the majesty of their genius. I do not assert that I have done it; but if I have not, what man has? what man has come so nigh to it? He who could bring Socrates, or Solon, or Diogenes through a dialogue, without disparagement, is much nearer in his intellectual powers to them, than any other is near to him.

DIOGENES. Let Diogenes alone, and Socrates, and Solon. None of the three ever occupied his hours in tingeing and curling the tarnished plumes of prostitute Philosophy, or deemed anything worth his attention, care, or notice, that did not make men brave and independent. As thou callest on me to show thee where and in what manner thou hast misrepresented thy teacher, and as thou seemest to set an equal value on eloquence and on reasoning, I shall attend to thee awhile on each of these matters, first inquiring of thee whether the axiom is Socratic, that it is never becoming to get drunk, *unless* in the solemnities of Bacchus?

PLATO. This god was the discoverer of the vine and of its uses.

DIOGENES. Is drunkenness one of its uses, or the discovery of a god? If Pallas or Jupiter hath given us reason, we should sacrifice our reason with more propriety to Jupiter or Pallas. To Bacchus is due a libation of wine; the same being his gift, as thou preachest.

Another and a graver question.

Did Socrates teach thee that 'slaves are to be scourged, and by no means admonished as though they were the children of the master?'

PLATO. He did not argue upon government.

DIOGENES. He argued upon humanity, whereon all government is founded: whatever is beside it is usurpation.

PLATO. Are slaves then never to be scourged, whatever be their transgressions and enormities?

DIOGENES. Whatever they be, they are less than his who reduced them to their condition.

PLATO. What! though they murder his whole family?

DIOGENES. Ay, and poison the public fountain of the city. What am I saying? and to whom? Horrible as is this crime, and next in atrocity to parricide, thou deemest it a lighter one than stealing a fig or grape. The stealer of these is scourged by thee; the sentence on the poisoner is to cleanse out the receptacle. There is, however, a kind of poisoning which, to do thee justice, comes before thee with all its horrors, and which thou wouldst punish capitally, even in such a sacred personage as an aruspex or diviner:

I mean the poisoning by incantation. I, and my whole family, my whole race, my whole city, may bite the dust in agony from a truss of henbane in the well; and little harm done forsooth! Let an idle fool set an image of me in wax before the fire, and whistle and caper to it, and purr and pray, and chant a hymn to Hecate while it melts, entreating and imploring her that I may melt as easily,— and thou wouldst, in thy equity and holiness, strangle him at the first stave of his psalmody.

PLATO. If this is an absurdity, can you find another?

DIOGENES. Truly, in reading thy book, I doubted at first, and for a long continuance, whether thou couldst have been serious; and whether it were not rather a satire on those busy-bodies who are incessantly intermeddling in other people's affairs. It was only on the protestation of thy intimate friends that I believed thee to have written it in earnest. As for thy question, it is idle to stoop and pick out absurdities from a mass of inconsistency and injustice; but another and another I could throw in, and another and another afterward, from any page in the volume. Two bare, staring false-hoods lift their beaks one upon the other, like spring frogs. Thou sayest that no punishment decreed by the laws tendeth to evil. What! not if immoderate? not if partial? Why then repeal any penal statute while the subject of its animadversion exists? In prisons the less criminal are placed among the more criminal, the inexperienced in vice together with the hardened in it. This is part of the punishment, though it precedes the sentence; nay, it is often inflicted on those whom the judges acquit: the law, by allowing it, does it.

The next is, that he who is punished by the laws is the better for it, however the less depraved. What! if anteriorly to the sentence he lives and converses with worse men, some of whom console him by deadening the sense of shame, others by removing the apprehension of punishment? Many laws as certainly make men bad, as bad men make many laws; yet under thy regimen they take us from the bosom of the nurse, turn the meat about upon the platter, pull the bed-clothes off, make us sleep when we would wake, and wake when we would sleep, and never cease to rummage and twitch us, until they see us safe landed at the grave. We can do nothing (but be poisoned) with impunity. What is worst of all, we must marry certain relatives and connections, be they distorted,

147

blear-eyed, toothless, carbuncled, with hair (if any) eclipsing the reddest torch of Hymen, and with a hide outrivalling in colour and plaits his trimmest saffron robe. At the mention of this indeed, friend Plato, even thou, although resolved to stand out of harm's way, beginnest to make a wry mouth, and findest it difficult to pucker and purse it up again, without an astringent store of moral sentences. Hymen is truly no acquaintance of thine. We know the delicacies of love which thou wouldst reserve for the gluttony of heroes and the fastidiousness of philosophers. Heroes, like gods, must have their own way; but against thee and thy confraternity of elders I would turn the closet-key, and your mouths might water over, but your tongues should never enter those little pots of comfiture. Seriously, you who wear embroidered slippers ought to be very cautious of treading in the mire. Philosophers should not only live the simplest lives, but should also use the plainest language. Poets, in employing magnificent and sonorous words, teach philosophy the better by thus disarming suspicion that the finest poetry contains and conveys the finest philosophy. You will never let any man hold his right station: you would rank Solon with Homer for poetry. This is absurd. The only resemblance is in both being eminently wise. Pindar, too, makes even the cadences of his dithyrambics keep time to the flute of Reason. My tub, which holds fifty-fold thy wisdom, would crack at the reverberation of thy voice.

PLATO. Farewell ...

DIOGENES. I mean that every one of thy whimsies hath been picked up somewhere by thee in thy travels; and each of them hath been rendered more weak and puny by its place of concealment in thy closet. What thou hast written on the immortality of the soul goes rather to prove the immortality of the body; and applies as well to the body of a weasel or an eel as to the fairer one of Agathon or of Aster. Why not at once introduce a new religion, since religions keep and are relished in proportion as they are salted with absurdity, inside and out? and all of them must have one great crystal of it for the centre; but Philosophy pines and dies unless she drinks limpid water. When Pherecydes and Pythagoras felt in themselves the majesty of contemplation, they spurned the idea that flesh and bones and arteries should confer it; and that what comprehends the past and the future should sink in a moment and be annihilated for ever. 'No,' cried they, 'the power of thinking is no more in the brain than in the hair, although the brain may be the instrument on which it plays. It is not corporeal, it is not of this world; its existence is eternity, its residence is infinity.' I forbear to discuss the rationality of their belief, and pass on straightway to thine; if, indeed, I am to consider as one, belief and doctrine.

PLATO. As you will.

DIOGENES. I should rather, then, regard these things as mere ornaments; just as many decorate their apartments with lyres and harps, which they themselves look at from the couch, supinely complacent, and leave for visitors to admire and play on.

PLATO. I foresee not how you can disprove my argument on the immortality of the soul, which, being contained in the best of my dialogues, and being often asked for among my friends, I carry with me.

DIOGENES. At this time?

PLATO. Even so.

DIOGENES. Give me then a certain part of it for my perusal.

PLATO. Willingly.

DIOGENES. Hermes and Pallas! I wanted but a cubit of it, or at most a fathom, and thou art pulling it out by the plethron.

PLATO. This is the place in question.

DIOGENES. Read it.

PLATO (reads). 'Sayest thou not that death is the opposite of life, and that they spring the one from the other?' 'Yes.' 'What springs then from the living?' '*The dead.*' 'And what from the dead?' '*The living.*' 'Then all things alive spring from the dead.'

DIOGENES. Why thy repetition? but go on.

PLATO. (reads). 'Souls therefore exist after death in the infernal regions.'

DIOGENES. Where is the *therefore*? where is it even as to *existence*? As to the *infernal regions*, there is nothing that points toward a proof, or promises an indication. Death neither springs from life, nor life from death. Although death is the inevitable consequence of life, if the observation and experience of ages go for anything, yet nothing shows us, or ever hath signified, that life comes from death. Thou mightest as well say that a barley-corn dies before the germ of another barley-corn grows up from it, than which nothing is more untrue; for it is only the protecting parts of the germ that perishes, when its protection is no longer necessary. The consequence, that souls exist after death, cannot be drawn from the corruption of the body, even if it were demonstrable that out of this corruption a live one could rise up. Thou hast not said that the soul is among those dead things which living things must spring from; thou hast not said that a living soul produces a dead soul, or that a dead soul produces a living one.

PLATO. No, indeed.

DIOGENES. On my faith, thou hast said, however, things no less inconsiderate, no less inconsequent, no less unwise; and this very thing must be said and proved, to make thy argument of any value. Do dead men beget children?

PLATO. I have not said it.

DIOGENES. Thy argument implies it.

PLATO. These are high mysteries, and to be approached with reverence.

DIOGENES. Whatever we cannot account for is in the same predicament. We may be gainers by being ignorant if we can be thought mysterious. It is better to shake our heads and to let nothing out of them, than to be plain and explicit in matters of difficulty. I do not mean in confessing our ignorance or our imperfect knowledge of them, but in clearing them up perspicuously: for, if we answer with ease, we may haply be thought good-natured, quick, communicative; never deep, never sagacious; not very defective possibly in our intellectual faculties, yet unequal and chinky, and liable to the probation of every clown's knuckle.

PLATO. The brightest of stars appear the most unsteady and tremulous in their light; not from any quality inherent in themselves, but from the vapours that float below, and from the imperfection of vision in the surveyor.

DIOGENES. Draw thy robe round thee; let the folds fall gracefully, and look majestic. That sentence is an admirable one; but not for me. I want sense, not stars. What then? Do no vapours float below the others? and is there no imperfection in the vision of those who look at *them*, if they are the same men, and look the next moment? We must move on: I shall follow the dead bodies, and the benighted driver of their fantastic bier, close and keen as any hyena.

JOHN OF GAUNT AND JOANNA OF KENT

PLATO. Certainly, O Diogenes, you excel me in elucidations and similes: mine was less obvious.

DIOGENES. I know the respect thou bearest to the dogly character, and can attribute to nothing else the complacency with which thou hast listened to me since I released thy cloak. If ever the Athenians, in their inconstancy, should issue a decree to deprive me of the appelation they have conferred on me, rise up, I pray thee, in my defence, and protest that I have not merited so severe a mulct. Something I do deserve at thy hands; having supplied thee, first with a store of patience, when thou wert going without any about thee, although it is the readiest viaticum and the heartiest sustenance of human life; and then with weapons from this tub, wherewith to drive the importunate cock before thee out of doors again.

JOHN OF GAUNT AND JOANNA OF KENT

[The people have risen against John's suspected intention of seizing his nephew's crown; when he is saved only by the intervention of the popular idol, his brother's widow, the mother of the child he would have wronged; the stronghold which missiles had well-nigh shaken down is in almost greater danger of being rent asunder by wild acclamations of joy.]

JOANNA. How is this, my cousin, that you are besieged in your own house, by the citizens of London? I thought you were their idol.

GAUNT. If their idol, madam, I am one which they may tread on as they list when down; but which, by my soul and knighthood! the ten best battle-axes among them shall find it hard work to unshrine.

Pardon me: I have no right perhaps to take or touch this hand; yet, my sister, bricks and stones and arrows are not presents fit for you. Let me conduct you some paces hence.

JOANNA. I will speak to those below in the street. Quit my hand: they shall obey me.

GAUNT. If you intend to order my death, madam, your guards who have entered my court, and whose spurs and halberts I hear upon the staircase, may overpower my domestics; and, seeing no such escape as becomes my dignity, I submit to you. Behold my sword and gauntlet at your feet! Some formalities, I trust, will be used in the proceedings against me. Entitle me, in my attainder, not John of Gaunt, not Duke of Lancaster, not King of Castile; nor commemorate my father, the most glorious of princes, the vanquisher and pardoner of the most powerful; nor style me, what those who loved or who flattered me did when I was happier, cousin to the Fair Maid of Kent. Joanna, those days are over! But no enemy, no law, no eternity can take away from me, or move further off, my affinity in blood to the conqueror in the field of Crecy, of Poitiers, and Najora. Edward was my brother when he was but your cousin; and the edge of my shield has clinked on his in many a battle. Yes, we were ever near—if not in worth, in danger. She weeps.

JOANNA. Attainder! God avert it! Duke of Lancaster, what dark thought—alas! that the Regency should have known it! I came hither, sir, for no such purpose as to ensnare or incriminate or alarm you.

These weeds might surely have protected me from the fresh tears you have drawn forth.

GAUNT. Sister, be comforted! this visor, too, has felt them.

JOANNA. O my Edward! my own so lately! Thy memory—thy beloved image—which never hath abandoned me, makes me bold: I dare not say 'generous;' for in saying it I should cease to be so— and who could be called generous by the side of thee? I will rescue from perdition the enemy of my son.

Cousin, you loved your brother. Love, then, what was dearer to him than his life: protect what he, valiant as you have seen him, cannot! The father, who foiled so many, hath left no enemies; the innocent child, who can injure no one, finds them!

Why have you unlaced and laid aside your visor? Do not expose your body to those missiles. Hold your shield before yourself, and step aside. I need it not. I am resolved—

GAUNT. On what, my cousin? Speak, and, by the saints! it shall be done. This breast is your shield; this arm is mine.

JOANNA. Heavens! who could have hurled those masses of stone from below? they stunned me. Did they descend all of them together; or did they split into fragments on hitting the pavement?

GAUNT. Truly, I was not looking that way: they came, I must believe, while you were speaking.

JOANNA. Aside, aside! further back! disregard *me*! Look! that last arrow sticks half its head deep in the wainscot. It shook so violently I did not see the feather at first.

No, no, Lancaster! I will not permit it. Take your shield up again; and keep it all before you. Now step aside: I am resolved to prove whether the people will hear me.

GAUNT. Then, madam, by your leave—

JOANNA. Hold!

GAUNT. Villains! take back to your kitchens those spits and skewers that you, forsooth, would fain call swords and arrows; and keep your bricks and stones for your graves!

JOANNA. Imprudent man! who can save you? I shall be frightened: I must speak at once.

O good kind people! ye who so greatly loved me, when I am sure I had done nothing to deserve it, have I (unhappy me!) no merit with you now, when I would assuage your anger, protect your fair fame, and send you home contented with yourselves and me? Who is he, worthy citizens, whom ye would drag to slaughter?

True, indeed, he did revile some one. Neither I nor you can say whom—some feaster and rioter, it seems, who had little right (he thought) to carry sword or bow, and who, to show it, hath slunk away. And then another raised his anger: he was indignant that, under his roof, a woman should be exposed to stoning. Which of you would not be as choleric in a like affront? In the house of which among you should I not be protected as resolutely?

No, no: I never can believe those angry cries. Let none ever tell me again he is the enemy of my son, of his king, your darling child, Richard. Are your fears more lively than a poor weak female's? than a mother's? yours, whom he hath so often led to victory, and praised to his father, naming each—he, John of Gaunt, the defender of the helpless, the comforter of the desolate, the rallying signal of the desperately brave!

Retire, Duke of Lancaster! This is no time—

GAUNT. Madam, I obey; but not through terror of that puddle at the house-door, which my handful of dust would dry up. Deign to command me!

JOANNA. In the name of my son, then, retire!

GAUNT. Angelic goodness! I must fairly win it.

JOANNA. I think I know his voice that crieth out, 'Who will answer for him?' An honest and loyal man's, one who would counsel and save me in any difficulty and danger. With what pleasure and satisfaction, with what perfect joy and confidence, do I answer our right-trusty and well-judging friend!

'Let Lancaster bring his sureties,' say you, 'and we separate.' A moment yet before we separate; if I might delay you so long, to receive your sanction of those securities: for, in such grave matters, it would ill become us to be over-hasty. I could bring fifty, I could bring a hundred, not from among soldiers, not from among courtiers; but selected from yourselves, were it equitable and fair to show such partialities, or decorous in the parent and guardian of a king to offer any other than herself.

Raised by the hand of the Almighty from amidst you, but still one of you, if the mother of a family is a part of it, here I stand surety for John of Gaunt, Duke of Lancaster, for his loyalty and allegiance.

GAUNT (*running back toward Joanna*). Are the rioters, then, bursting into the chamber through the windows?

JOANNA. The windows and doors of this solid edifice rattled and shook at the people's acclamation. My word is given for you: this was theirs in return. Lancaster! what a voice have the people when they speak out! It shakes me with astonishment, almost with consternation, while it establishes the throne: what must it be when it is lifted up in vengeance!

GAUNT. Wind; vapour—

JOANNA. Which none can wield nor hold. Need I say this to my cousin of Lancaster?

GAUNT. Rather say, madam, that there is always one star above which can tranquilize and control them.

JOANNA. Go, cousin! another time more sincerity!

GAUNT. You have this day saved my life from the people; for I now see my danger better, when it is no longer close before me. My Christ! if ever I forget—

JOANNA. Swear not: every man in England hath sworn what you would swear. But if you abandon my Richard, my brave and beautiful child, may—Oh! I could never curse, nor wish an evil; but, if you desert him in the hour of need, you will think of those who have not deserted you, and your own great heart will lie heavy on you, Lancaster.

Am I graver than I ought to be, that you look dejected? Come, then, gentle cousin, lead me to my horse, and accompany me home. Richard will embrace us tenderly. Every one is dear to every other upon rising out fresh from peril; affectionately then will he look, sweet boy, upon his mother and his uncle! Never mind how many questions he may ask you, nor how strange ones. His only displeasure, if he has any, will be that he stood not against the rioters or among them.

GAUNT. Older than he have been as fond of mischief, and as fickle in the choice of a party.

I shall tell him that, coming to blows, the assailant is often in the right; that the assailed is always.

LADY LISLE AND ELIZABETH GAUNT

[*Burnet related from William Penn, who was present, that Elizabeth Gaunt placed the faggots round her body with her own hands. Lady Lisle was not burned, though sentenced to it, but hanged and beheaded. Moreover, these two noble ladies never met. Crabb Robinson,*[1] *when he read this 'conversation', commented, 'Never was greater justice done to the pious character than in this beautiful composition'.*—Ed.]

LADY LISLE. Madam, I am confident you will pardon me; for affliction teaches forgiveness.

ELIZABETH GAUNT. From the cell of the condemned we are going, unless my hopes mislead me, where alone we can receive it.

Tell me, I beseech you, lady! in what matter or manner do you think you can have offended a poor sinner such as I am. Surely we come into this dismal place for our offences; and it is not here that any can be given or taken.

LADY LISLE. Just now, when I entered the prison, I saw your countenance serene and cheerful; you looked upon me for a time with an unaltered eye; you turned away from me, as I fancied, only to utter some expressions of devotion; and again you looked upon me, and tears rolled down your face. Alas that I should, by

[1] Crabb Robinson *Books and Their Writers*. Ed. Edith Morley, vol. i, p. 385.

any circumstance, any action, or recollection, make another unhappy! Alas that I should deepen the gloom in the very shadow of death!

ELIZABETH GAUNT. Be comforted: you have not done it. Grief softens and melts and flows away with tears.

I wept because another was greatly more wretched than myself. I wept at that black attire—at that attire of modesty and of widowhood.

LADY LISLE. It covers a wounded, almost a broken heart—an unworthy offering to our blessed Redeemer.

ELIZABETH GAUNT. In his name let us now rejoice! Let us offer our prayers and our thanks at once together! We may yield up our souls, perhaps, at the same hour.

LADY LISLE. Is mine so pure? Have I bemoaned, as I should have done, the faults I have committed? Have my sighs arisen for the unmerited mercies of my God; and not rather for him, the beloved of my heart, the adviser and sustainer I have lost?

Open, O gates of Death!

Smile on me, approve my last action in this world, O virtuous husband! O saint and martyr! my brave, compassionate, and loving Lisle!

ELIZABETH GAUNT. And cannot you, too, smile, sweet lady? Are not you with him even now? Doth body, doth clay, doth air, separate and estrange free spirits? Bethink you of his gladness, of his glory; and begin to partake them.

Oh! how could an Englishman, how could twelve, condemn to death—condemn to so great an evil as they thought it and may find it—this innocent and helpless widow?

LADY LISLE. Blame not *that* jury!—blame not the jury which brought against me the verdict of guilty. I was so: I received in my house a wanderer who had fought under the rash and giddy Monmouth. He was hungry and thirsty, and I took him in. My Saviour had commanded, my King had forbidden it.

Yet the twelve would not have delivered me over to death, unless the judge had threatened them with an accusation of treason in default of it. Terror made them unanimous: they redeemed their properties and lives at the stated price.

ELIZABETH GAUNT. I hope, at least, the unfortunate man whom you received in the hour of danger may avoid his penalty.

LADY LISLE AND ELIZABETH GAUNT

LADY LISLE. Let us hope it.

ELIZABETH GAUNT. I, too, am imprisoned for the same offence; and I have little expectation that he who was concealed by me hath any chance of happiness, although he hath escaped. Could I find the means of conveying to him a small pittance, I should leave the world the more comfortably.

LADY LISLE. Trust in God; not in one thing or another, but in all. Resign the care of this wanderer to *his* guidance.

ELIZABETH GAUNT. He abandoned that guidance.

LADY LISLE. Unfortunate! How can money then avail him?

ELIZABETH GAUNT. It might save him from distress and from despair, from the taunts of the hard-hearted, and from the inclemency of the godly.

LADY LISLE. In godliness, O my friend! there cannot be inclemency.

ELIZABETH GAUNT. You are thinking of perfection, my dear lady; and I marvel not at it, for what else hath ever occupied your thoughts! But godliness, in almost the best of us, often is austere, often uncompliant and rigid—proner to reprove than to pardon, to drag back or thrust aside than to invite and help onward.

Poor man! I never knew him before; I cannot tell how he shall endure his self-reproach, or whether it will bring him to calmer thoughts hereafter.

LADY LISLE. I am not a busy idler in curiosity; nor, if I were, is there time enough left me for indulging in it; yet gladly would I learn the history of events, at the first appearance so resembling those in mine.

ELIZABETH GAUNT. The person's name I never may disclose; which would be the worst thing I could betray of the trust he placed in me. He took refuge in my humble dwelling, imploring me in the name of Christ to harbour him for a season. Food and raiment were afforded him unsparingly; yet his fears made him shiver through them. Whatever I could urge of prayer and exhortation was not wanting; still, although he prayed, he was disquieted. Soon came to my ears the declaration of the King, that his Majesty would rather pardon a rebel than the concealer of a rebel. The hope was a faint one; but it *was* a hope, and I gave it him. His thanksgivings were now more ardent, his prayers more humble, and oftener repeated. They did not strengthen his heart:

it was unpurified and unprepared for them. Poor creature! he consented with it to betray me; and I am condemned to be burned alive. Can we believe, can we encourage the hope, that in his weary way through life he will find those only who will conceal from him the knowledge of this execution? Heavily, too heavily, must it weigh on so irresolute and infirm a breast.

Let it not move you to weeping.

LADY LISLE. It does not; oh! it does not.

ELIZABETH GAUNT. What, then?

LADY LISLE. Your saintly tenderness, your heavenly tranquility.

ELIZABETH GAUNT. No, no: abstain! abstain! It was I who grieved; it was I who doubted. Let us now be firmer: we have both the same rock to rest upon. See! I shed no tears.

I saved his life, an unprofitable and (I fear) a joyless one; he, by God's grace, has thrown open to me, and at an earlier hour than ever I ventured to expect it, the avenue to eternal bliss.

LADY LISLE. O my angel! that strewest with fresh flowers a path already smooth and pleasant to me, may those timorous men who have betrayed, and those misguided ones who have prosecuted us, be conscious on their death-beds that we have entered it! and they too will at last find rest.

LEOFRIC AND GODIVA[1]

GODIVA. There is a dearth in the land, my sweet Leofric! Remember how many weeks of drought we have had, even in the deep pastures of Leicestershire; and how many Sundays we have heard the same prayers for rain, and supplications that it would please the Lord in his mercy to turn aside his anger from the poor, pining cattle. You, my dear husband, have imprisoned more than one malefactor for leaving his dead ox in the public way; and other hinds have fled before you out of the traces, in which they, and their sons and their daughters, and haply their old fathers and mothers, were dragging the abandoned wain homeward. Although we were accompanied by many brave spearmen and skilful

---

[1] Godiva was a favourite heroine of Landor's. In his boyhood he used to steal away from Warwick to attend her fairs and festivals. This conversation is said to have been Landor's favourite (Forster, *Landor*, vol. ii, p. 181.)

archers, it was perilous to pass the creatures which the farm-yard dogs, driven from the hearth by the poverty of their masters, were tearing and devouring; while others, bitten and lamed, filled the air either with long and deep howls or sharp and quick barkings, as they struggled with hunger and feebleness, or were exasperated by heat and pain. Nor could the thyme from the heath, nor the bruised branches of the fir-tree, extinguish or abate the foul odour.

LEOFRIC. And now, Godiva, my darling, thou art afraid we should be eaten up before we enter the gates of Coventry; or perchance that in the gardens there are no roses to greet thee, no sweet herbs for thy mat and pillow.

GODIVA. Leofric, I have no such fears. This is the month of roses: I find them everywhere since my blessed marriage. They, and all other sweet herbs, I know not why, seem to greet me wherever I look at them, as though they knew and expected me. Surely they cannot feel that I am fond of them.

LEOFRIC. O light, laughing simpleton! But what wouldst thou? I came not hither to pray; and yet if praying would satisfy thee, or remove the drought, I would ride up straightway to Saint Michael's and pray until morning.

GODIVA. I would do the same, O Leofric! but God hath turned away his ear from holier lips than mine. Would my own dear husband hear me, if I implored him for what is easier to accomplish,—what he can do like God?

LEOFRIC. How! what is it?

GODIVA. I would not, in the first hurry of your wrath, appeal to you, my loving lord, in behalf of these unhappy men who have offended you.

LEOFRIC. Unhappy! is that all?

GODIVA. Unhappy they must surely be, to have offended you so grievously. What a soft air breathes over us! how quiet and serene and still an evening! how calm are the heavens and the earth!— Shall none enjoy them; not even we, my Leofric? The sun is ready to set; let it never set, O Leofric, on your anger. These are not my words: they are better than mine. Should they lose their virtue from my unworthiness in uttering them?

LEOFRIC. Godiva, wouldst thou plead to me for rebels?

GODIVA. They have, then, drawn the sword against you? Indeed, I knew it not.

LEOFRIC. They have omitted to send me my dues, established by my ancestors, well knowing of our nuptials, and of the charges and festivities they require, and that in a season of such scarcity my own lands are insufficient.

GODIVA. If they were starving, as they said they were—

LEOFRIC. Must I starve too? Is it not enough to lose my vassals?

GODIVA. Enough! O God! too much! too much! May you never lose them! Give them life, peace, comfort, contentment. There are those among them who kissed me in my infancy, and who blessed me at the baptismal font. Leofric, Leofric! the first old man I meet I shall think is one of those; and I shall think on the blessing he gave, and (ah me!) on the blessing I bring back to him. My heart will bleed, will burst; and he will weep at it! he will weep, poor soul, for the wife of a cruel lord who denounces vengeance on him, who carries death into his family!

LEOFRIC. We must hold solemn festivals.

GODIVA. We must, indeed.

LEOFRIC. Well, then?

GODIVA. Is the clamorousness that succeeds the death of God's dumb creatures, are crowded halls, are slaughtered cattle, festivals?—are maddening songs, and giddy dances, and hireling praises from parti-coloured coats? Can the voice of a minstrel tell us better things of ourselves than our own internal one might tell us; or can his breath make our breath softer in sleep? O my beloved! let everything be a joyance to us: it will, if we will. Sad is the day, and worse must follow, when we hear the blackbird in the garden, and do not throb with joy. But, Leofric, the high festival is strown by the servant of God upon the heart of man. It is gladness, it is thanksgiving; it is the orphan, the starveling, pressed to the bosom, and bidden as its first commandment to remember its benefactor. We will hold this festival; the guests are ready: we may keep it up for weeks, and months, and years together, and always be the happier and the richer for it. The beverage of this feast, O Leofric, is sweeter than bee or flower or vine can give us: it flows from heaven; and in heaven will it abundantly be poured out again to him who pours it out here abundantly.

LEOFRIC. Thou art wild.

GODIVA. I have, indeed, lost myself. Some Power, some good

kind Power, melts me (body and soul and voice) into tenderness and love. O my husband, we must obey it. Look upon me! look upon me! lift your sweet eyes from the ground! I will not cease to supplicate; I dare not.

LEOFRIC. We may think upon it.

GODIVA. O never say that! What! think upon goodness when you can be good? Let not the infants cry for sustenance! The mother of our blessed Lord will hear them; us never, never afterward.

LEOFRIC. Here comes the Bishop: we are but one mile from the walls. Why dismountest thou? no bishop can expect it. Godiva! my honour and rank among men are humbled by this. Earl Godwin will hear of it. Up! up! the Bishop hath seen it: he urgeth his horse onward. Dost thou not hear him now upon the solid turf behind thee?

GODIVA. Never, no, never will I rise, O Leofric, until you remit this most impious task—this tax on hard labour, on hard life.

LEOFRIC. Turn round: look how the fat nag canters, as to the tune of a sinner's psalm, slow and hard-breathing. What reason or right can the people have to complain, while their bishop's steed is so sleek and well caparisoned? Inclination to change, desire to abolish old usages.—Up! up! for shame! They shall smart for it, idlers! Sir Bishop, I must blush for my young bride.

GODIVA. My husband, my husband! will you pardon the city?

LEOFRIC. Sir Bishop! I could not think you would have seen her in this plight. Will I pardon? Yes, Godiva, by the holy rood, will I pardon the city, when thou ridest naked at noontide through the streets!

GODIVA. O my dear, cruel Leofric, where is the heart you gave me? It was not so: can mine have hardened it?

BISHOP. Earl, thou abashest thy spouse; she turneth pale, and weepeth. Lady Godiva, peace be with thee.

GODIVA. Thanks, holy man! peace will be with me when peace is with your city. Did you hear my Lord's cruel word?

BISHOP. I did, lady.

GODIVA. Will you remember it, and pray against it.

BISHOP. Wilt *thou* forget it, daughter?

GODIVA. I am not offended.

BISHOP. Angel of peace and purity!

GODIVA. But treasure it up in your heart: deem it an incense, good only when it is consumed and spent, ascending with prayer and sacrifice. And, now, what was it?

BISHOP. Christ save us! that he will pardon the city when thou ridest naked through the streets at noon.

GODIVA. Did he swear an oath?

BISHOP. He sware by the holy rood.

GODIVA. My Redeemer, thou hast heard it! save the city!

LEOFRIC. We are now upon the beginning of the pavement: these are the suburbs. Let us think of feasting: we may pray afterward; to-morrow we shall rest.

GODIVA. No judgments, then, to-morrow, Leofric?

LEOFRIC. None: we will carouse.

GODIVA. The saints of heaven have given me strength and confidence; my prayers are heard; the heart of my beloved is now softened.

LEOFRIC. Ay, ay.

GODIVA. Say, dearest Leofric, is there indeed no other hope, no other mediation?

LEOFRIC. I have sworn. Beside, thou hast made me redden and turn my face away from thee, and all the knaves have seen it; this adds to the city's crime.

GODIVA. I have blushed too, Leofric, and was not rash nor obdurate.

LEOFRIC. But thou, my sweetest, art given to blushing: there is no conquering it in thee. I wish thou hadst not alighted so hastily and roughly: it hath shaken down a sheaf of thy hair. Take heed thou sit not upon it, lest it anguish thee. Well done! it mingleth now sweetly with the cloth of gold upon the saddle, running here and there, as if it had life and faculties and business, and were working thereupon some newer and cunninger device. O my beauteous Eve! there is a Paradise about thee! the world is refreshed as thou movest and breathest on it. I cannot see or think of evil where thou art. I could throw my arms even here about thee. No signs for me! no shaking of sunbeams! no reproof or frown of wonderment.—I *will* say it —now, then, for worse—I could close with my kisses thy half-open lips, ay, and those lovely and loving eyes, before the people.

GODIVA. To-morrow you shall kiss me, and they shall bless you for it. I shall be very pale, for to-night I must fast and pray.

LEOFRIC. I do not hear thee; the voices of the folk are so loud under this archway.

GODIVA (*to herself*). God help them! good kind souls! I hope they will not crowd about me so to-morrow. O Leofric! Could my name be forgotten, and yours alone remembered! But perhaps my innocence may save me from reproach; and how many as innocent are in fear and famine! No eye will open on me but fresh from tears. What a young mother for so large a family! Shall my youth harm me? Under God's hand it gives me courage. Ah! when will the morning come? Ah! when will the noon be over?

MR PITT AND MR CANNING

PITT. Dear Canning, my constitution is falling to pieces, as fast as, your old friend Sheridan would tell you, the constitution of the country is, under my management. Of all men living, you are the person I am most desirous to appoint my successor. My ambition is unsatisfied, while any doubt of my ability to accomplish it remains upon my mind. Nature has withholden from me the faculty of propagating my species: nor do I at all repine at it, as many would do: since every great man must have some imbecile one very near him, if not next to him, in descent.

CANNING. I am much flattered, sir, by your choice of me, there being so many among your relatives who might expect it for themselves. However, this is only another instance of your great disinterestedness.

PITT. You may consider it in that light if you will: but you must remember that those who have exercised power long together, and without control, seldom care much about affinities. The Mamelukes do not look out for brothers and cousins: they have favourite slaves who leap into their saddles when vacant.

CANNING. Among the rich families, or the ancient aristocracy of the kingdom—

PITT. Hold your tongue! prythee hold your tongue! I hate and always hated these. I do not mean the rich: they served me. I mean the old houses: they overshadowed me. There is hardly one however that I have not disgraced or degraded; and I have filled them with smoke and sore eyes by raising a vassal's hut over them.

I desire to be remembered as the founder of a new system in England: I desire to bequeath my office by will, a verbal one: and I intend that you, and those who come after you, shall do the same!

As you are rather more rash than I could wish, and allow your words to betray your intentions; and as sometimes you run counter to them in your hurry to escape from them, having thrown them out foolishly where there was no occasion nor room; I would advise you never to speak until you have thoroughly learnt your sentences. Do not imagine that, because I have the gift of extemporary eloquence, you have the same. No man ever possessed it in the same degree, excepting the two fanatics, Wesley and Whitfield.

CANNING. In the same degree certainly not; but many in some measure.

PITT. Some measure is not enough.

CANNING. Excuse me: Mr Fox possessed it greatly, though not equally with you, and found it enough for his purpose.

PITT. Fox foresaw, as any man of acuteness may do, the weaker parts of the argument that would be opposed to him, and he always learnt his replies: I had not time for it. I owe everything to the facility and fluency of my speech, excepting the name bequeathed me by my father: and, although I have failed in everything I undertook, and have cast in solid gold the clay colossus of France, people will consider me after my death as the most extraordinary man of my age.

CANNING. Do you groan at this? or does the pain in your bowels grow worse? Shall I lift up the cushion of your other chair yonder?

PITT. Oh! oh!

CANNING. I will make haste, and then soften by manipulation those two or three letters of condolence.

PITT. Oh! oh!—next to that cursed fellow who foiled me with his broken weapon, and befooled me with his half-wit, Bonaparte.

CANNING. Be calmer, sir! be calmer.

PITT. The gout and stone be in him! Port wine and Cheltenham-water! An Australian wife, Italian jealousy, his country's ingratitude, and his own ambition, dwell with him everlastingly.

CANNING. Amen! let us pray!

PITT. Upon my soul, we have little else to do. I hardly know where we can turn ourselves.

CANNING. Hard indeed! when we can not do that!

Be comforted, sir! The worse the condition of the country, the greater is the want of us; the more power we shall possess, the more places we shall occupy and distribute.

PITT. Statesmanlike reflection.

CANNING. Those who have brought us into danger can alone bring us out, has become a maxim of the English people.

PITT. If they should ever be strong again, they would crush us.

CANNING. We have lightened them; and, having less ballast, they sail before the wind at the good pleasure of the pilot.

PITT. A little while ago I would have made you Chancellor or Speaker, for composing and singing that capital song of the *Pilot*: so I thought it: at present I never hear the word but it gives me the sea-sickness, as surely as would a fishing-boat in the Channel. It sounds like ridicule.

CANNING. *We* have weathered the storm.

PITT. I have not. I never believed in any future state; but I have made a very damnable one of the present, both for myself and others. We never were in such danger from without or from within. Money-lenders and money-voters are satisfied: the devil must be in them if they are not: but we have taken the younger children's fortunes from every private gentleman in Great Britain.

CANNING. Never think about it.

PITT. I have formerly been in their houses: I have relatives and connections among them: if you had, you would sympathize. I feel as little as any man can feel for others, you excepted. And this utter indifference, this concentration, which inelegant men call selfishness, is among the reasons why I am disposed to appoint you my successor. You are aware that, should the people recover their senses, they would drive us in a dung-cart to the scaffold: *me* they can not: I shall be gone.

CANNING. We must prevent the possibility: we must go on weakening them. The viper that has bitten escapes: the viper that lies quiet in the road, is cut asunder.

PITT. Why! Canning! I find in you both more reasoning and more poetry than I ever found before. Go on in this manner, and your glory as a poet will not rest on *pilots* and *pebbles*, nor on a ditchside nettle or two of neglected satire. If you exhibit too much reflection, I may change my mind. You will do for my successor: you must not more than do.

CANNING. On the contrary, sir, I feel in your presence my deep inferiority.

PITT. That of course.

CANNING. Condescend to give me some precepts, which, if your disease should continue, it might be painfuller to deliver at any other time. Do not, however, think that your life is at all in danger, or that the supreme power can remain long together in any hands but yours.

PITT. Attempt not to flatter me, Canning, with the prospect of much longer life. The doctors of physic have hinted that it is time I should divert my attention from the affairs of Europe to my own: and the doctors of divinity drive oftener to the Chancellor's door than to mine. The flight of these sable birds portends a change of season and a fall of bones.

I have warned you against some imprudences of yours: now let me warn you against some of mine. You are soberer than I am: but when you are rather warm over claret, you prattle childishly. For a successful Minister three things are requisite on occasion; to speak like an honest man, to act like a dishonest one, and to be indifferent which you are called. Talk of God as gravely as if you believed in him. Unless you do this, I will not say what our Church does, you will be damned; but, what indeed is a politician's true damnation, you will be dismissed. Most very good men are stout partisans of some religion, and nearly all very bad ones. The old women about the prince are as notorious for praying as for prostitution; and if you lose the old women, you lose him. He is their prophet, he is their champion, and they are his Houris.

CANNING. I shall experience no difficulty in observing this commandment. In our days, only men who have some unsoundness of conscience and some latent fear, reason against religion; and those only scoff at it who are pushed back and hurt by it.

PITT. Canning! you must have brought this with you from Oxford: the sentiment is not yours even by adoption: it is too profound for you, and too well expressed. You are brilliant by the multitude of flaws, and not by the clearness or the quantity of light.

CANNING. On second thoughts, I am not quite sure, not perfectly satisfied, that it is, as one may say, altogether mine.

PITT. This avowal suggests another counsel.

Prevaricate as often as you can defend the prevarication, being close pressed: but, my dear Canning! never—I would say—come, come, let me speak it plainly: my dear fellow, never lie.

CANNING. How, sir! what, sir! pardon me, sir! But, sir! do you imagine I ever lied in my lifetime?

PITT. The certainty that you never did, makes me apprehensive that you would do it awkwardly, if the salvation of the country (the only case in question) should require it.

CANNING. I ought to be satisfied: and yet my feelings—If you profess that you believe me incapable—

PITT. What is my profession? what is my belief? If a man believes a thing of me, how can I prevent or alter his belief? or what right have I to be angry at it? Do not play the fool before me. I sent for you to give you good advice. If you apprehend any danger of being thought, what it is impossible any man alive should ever think you, I am ready to swear in your favour as solemnly as I swore at Tooke's trial. I am presuming that you will become Prime Minister; you will then have plenty of folks ready to lie for you; and it would be as ungentlemanly to lie yourself as to powder your own hair or tie your own shoe-string. I usually had Dundas at my elbow, who never lied but upon his honour, or supported the lie but upon his God. As for the more delicate duty of prevarication, take up those letters of inquiry and condolence, whether you have rubbed the seals off or not in your promptitude to serve me, and lay them carefully by; and some years hence, when anyone exclaims, 'What would Mr Pitt have said!' bring out one from your pocket, and cry, 'This is the last letter his hand, stricken by death, could trace.' Another time you may open one from Burke, some thirty years after the supposed receipt of it, and say modestly, 'Never but on this momentous occasion did that great man write to me. He foretold, in the true spirit of prophecy, all our difficulties.' But remember; do not quote him upon finance; else the House will laugh at you. For Burke was as unable to cast up a tailor's bill, as Sheridan is to pay it.

I was about to give you another piece of advice, which on recollection I find to be superfluous. Surely my head sympathizes very powerfully with my stomach, which the physicans tell me is always the case, though not so much with us in office as with the honourable gentlemen out. I was on the point of advising you never to neglect the delivery of long speeches: the Minister who makes short speeches enjoys short power. Now, although I have constantly been in the habit of saying a great deal more than was requisite to the elucidation of my subject, for the same reason as hares, when pursued, run over more ground than would bring them into their thickets, I would have avoided it with you, principally to save my breath. You can no more stop when you are speaking, than a ball can stop on an inclined plane. You bounce at every impediment, and run on; often with the very thing in your mouth that the most malicious of your adversaries would cast against you; and showing what you would conceal, and concealing what you would show. This is of no ill consequence to a Minister: it goes for sincerity and plain dealing. It would never have done at Christ-Church or Eton: for boys dare detect anything, and laugh with all their hearts. I think it was my father who told me (if it was not my father I forget who it was) that a Minister must have two gifts; the gift of places and the gift of the gab. Perfectly well do I remember his defence of this last expression, which somebody at table, on another occasion, called a vulgarism. At the end of the debate on it, he asked the gentleman whether all things ought not to have names; whether there was any better for this; and whether the learning and ingenuity of the company could invent one. The importance of the faculty was admirably exhibited, he remarked, by the word *gift*: he then added, with a smile, 'The alliteration itself has its merit: these short sayings are always the better for it: a pop-gun must have a pellet at both ends.'

Ah, Canning! why have I not remembered my father as perfectly in better things? I have none of his wit, little of his wisdom: but all his experience, all his conduct, were before me and within my reach. I will not think about him now, when it would vex and plague me.

CANNING. It is better to think of ourselves than of others; to consider the present as everything, the past and future as nothing.

PITT. In fact, they are nothing: they do not exist: what does not exist, is nothing.

CANNING. Supposing me to be Prime Minister—I am delighted at finding that the very idea has given a fresh serenity to your countenance.

PITT. Because it makes me feel my power more intensely than ever; or at least makes me fancy I feel it. By my means, by my authority, you are to become the successor of a Shelburne, of a Rockingham, and a Chatham.

CANNING. Sir, I request you to consider—

PITT. Whether I have the right of alluding to what all have the right of recollecting, and which right all will exercise. I wish you as well as if, by some miracle in my favour, I had been enabled to beget you: that which I hope to do is hardly less miraculous; and, if I did not bring to my mind what you are, I should not feel what I am. Do not you partake of the sentiment? Would it be any great marvel or great matter, if the descendant of some ancient family stepped up to the summit of power; even with clean boots on? You must take many steps, and some very indirect ones; all which will only raise you in your own esteem, if you think like a politician.

You are prone to be confident and overweening. Be cautious not to treat Parliament as you may fancy it deserves, and not to believe that you have bought votes when you have paid the money for them.

CANNING. Why, sir?

PITT. Because it will be expected of you in addition to speak for a given space of time. The people must be made to believe that their representatives are *persuaded*: and a few plain words are never thought capable of effecting this. Your zeal and anxiety to leave no scruple on the mind of any reasonable man, must be demonstrated by protestations and explanations; and your hatred of those who obscure the glory of England, in their attempts to throw impediments in your way, must burst forth vehemently, and stalk abroad, and now and then put on a suit that smells of gunpowder.

CANNING. I have no objection to that.

PITT. It saves many arguments, and stops more; and in short is the only comprehensible kind of *political economy*.

Whenever the liberty or restriction of the Press is in debate, you will do wisely to sport a few touches of wit, or to draw out a few sentences of declamation on blasphemy and blasphemers. I have observed by the countenances of country gentlemen, that there is something horrifying in the sound of the word, something that commands silence.

CANNING. I do not well understand the meaning of it.

PITT. Why should you? Are you to understand the meaning of everything you talk about? If you do, you will not be thought deep.

Be fluent, and your audience will be over head and ears in love with you. Never stop short, and you will never be doubted. To be out of breath is the only sign of weakness that is generally understood in a Chancellor of the Exchequer. The bets, in that case, are instantly against him, and the sounder in wind carries off the King's plate.

CANNING. I am aware that to talk solemnly of blasphemy, gives a man great weight at the time, and leaves it with him. But if a dissenter or a lawyer should ask me for a definition of a blasphemer?

PITT. Wish the lawyer more prudence, and the dissenter more grace. Appeal to our forefathers.

CANNING. To which of them? The elder would call the younger so, and the younger the elder.

PITT. Idiots! but go on.

CANNING. In our own days the Lutheran denounces the Unitarian for it: *he* retorts the denunciation. The Catholic comes between, to reconcile and reclaim them. At first he simmers; then he bubbles and boils; at last, inflamed with charity, he damns them both. 'To you, adopted heir of the Devil and Perdition,' says he to the believer in God's unity, 'it would be folly and impiety to listen a moment longer. And you, idle hair-splitter, are ignorant, or pretend to be, that transubstantiation rests upon the same authority as trinitarianism. The one doctrine shocks the senses, the other shocks the reason: both require to be shocked, that faith may be settled.'

'Very like your Saint Augustin,' interposes the Unitarian: 'he should have written this. When Faith enters the school-room, Reason must not whisper: if she might, she would say perhaps, the question is, whether the senses or arithmetic be the most liable to error.'

'Sir! sir!' cries again the Catholic, 'you have no right to bring any question into the house of God without his leave, nor to push your sharp stick against the bellies of his sheep, making them shove one another and break the fold.'

PITT. Do not run wild in this way, retailing the merriment of your Oxford doctors in their snug parties. Such, I am sure, it must be: for you have not had time to read anything since you left Eton: you think but little, and that little but upon yourself: nor has indeed the wing of your wit either such a strength of bone in it or such a vividness of plumage.

CANNING. I don't know that. I must confess, however, I drew a good deal both of my wit and my divinity from our doctors, when they had risen twice or thrice from the bottle, and turned their backs on us from the corner of the room.

PITT. I hope you will be rather more retentive; and remember at what time you are to lament, as well as at what time you are to joke and banter. On these occasions, lower your voice, assume an air of disdain or pity, bless God that such is the peculiar happiness of our most favoured country, every man may enjoy his opinion in security and peace.

CANNING. But some, I shall be reminded, have been forced to enjoy it in solitude and prison.

PITT. Never push an argument or a remark too far: and take care to have a fellow behind you who knows when to cry *question! question!* As for reminding, those only whom you forget will remind you of anything. Others will give you full credit for the wisdom of all your plans, the aptness of all your replies, the vivacity of all your witticisms, and the rectitude of all your intentions.

CANNING. Unless it should fatigue you, sir, will you open your views of domestic polity a little wider before me?

PITT. Willingly. Never choose colleagues for friendship or wisdom. If friends, they will be importunate: if wise, they may be rivals. Choose them for two other things quite different; for tractability and connexions. A few men of business, quite enough for you, may be picked up anywhere on the road-side. Be particular in selecting for all places and employments the handsomest young men, and those who have the handsomest wives, mothers, and sisters. Every one of these brings a large party with him; and it rarely happens that any such is formidable for mental prowess. The man who can bring you three votes, is preferable to him who can bring you thrice your own quantity of wisdom. For, although in private life we may profit much by the acquisition of so much more of it than we had ourselves, yet in public we know not what to do with it. Often it stands in our way; often it hides us; sometimes we are oppressed by it. Oppose in all elections the man, whatever may be his party or principles, who is superior to yourself in attainments, particularly in ratiocination and eloquence. Bring forward, when places are found for all the men of rank who present themselves, those who believe they resemble you; young declaimers, young poets, young critics, young satirists, young journalists, young magazine-men, and young lampooners and libellers: that is, those among them who have never been more than ducked and cudgelled. Every soul of them will hope to succeed you by adoption.

My father made this remark, in his florid way. When an insect dips into the surface of a stream, it forms a circle round it, which catches a quick radiance from the sun or moon, while the stiller water on every side flows without any; in like manner a small politician may attract the notice of the King or people, by putting into motion the pliant element about him; while quieter men pass utterly away, leaving not even this weak impression, this momentary sparkle. On which principle Dundas used to say, 'Keep shoving, keep shoving!' I do not know whether the injunction was taken by all his acquaintance in the manner and in the direction he intended.

A great deal has been spoken, in the House and out of the House, on Parliamentary reform.

CANNING. I have repeatedly said that without it there is no salvation for the country: this is embarrassing.

PITT. Not at all: oppose it: say you have changed your mind: let that serve for your reason; and do not stumble upon worse by running against an adversary. You will find the country going on just as it has gone on.

CANNING. Bad enough; God knows!

PITT. But only for the country. People will see that the fields and the cattle, the streets and the inhabitants, look as usual. The houses stand, the chimneys smoke, the pavements hold together: this will make them wonder at your genius in keeping them up, after all the prophecies they have heard about their going down. Men draw their ideas from sight and hearing. They do not know that the ruin of a nation is in its probity, its confidence, its comforts. While they see every day the magnificent equipages of contractors and brokers, read of sumptuous dinners given by cabinet-ministers and army agents, and are invited to golden speculations in the East and in the West, they fancy there is an abundance of prosperity and wealth; whereas, in fact, it is in these very places that wealth and prosperity are shut up, accumulated, and devoured.

I deferred from session to session a reform in Parliament; because having sworn to promote it by all the means in my power, I did not wish to seem perjured to the people. In the affair of Maidstone nobody could prove me so: I only swore I had forgotten what nobody but myself could swear that I remembered. It was evident to the whole world that I was a perjured man; it was equally that I was a powerful one: and the same nation which would have sent another to the pillory, sent me to the Privy Council. It is inconceivable to you what pleasure I felt in committing it, when I reflected on the difference it proved between me and people in general. But beware of fancying you resemble me. My father's crutch was my sceptre, and it will fall into the grave with me. There is no bequeathing or devising this part of the inheritance. I improved it not a little. My adherents at Maidstone thought my father would have hesitated to forget so bravely. Appearances were against me. The main object of my early life what I had repeated every day, what brought me into credit and into power, was unlikely to escape my memory in an instant; and in the midst of those who at that time had surrounded me, applauded me, and followed me. Yet Bishops and Chancellors will drink to me after my death, as the most honest man that ever lived.

CANNING. What! even when they can get nothing and want nothing from you?

PITT. They want from me more than you are aware of: they want my example to stand upon. They will take their aim against our country from behind my statue.

CANNING. She has fleshier parts about her than the heel, and their old snags will stick tight in them till they rattle in the coffin.

PITT. Do not disturb them. You may give over your dalliance with reform whenever you are tired of it. You did not begin as a states-*man* but as a states-*boy*: you were under me: and you can not act more wisely than by telling folks that I had seen my error in the latter part of my life.

CANNING. Perhaps they will not believe me.

PITT. Likely enough! but courtesy and interest will require their acquiescence, and they will act as if they did. The noisiest of the opposition are the lawyers; partly from rudeness, partly from rapacity. Lay it down as a rule for your conduct, that the most honest one in Parliament is as indifferent about his party as about his brief: whoever offers him his fee has him. Of these there is hardly an individual who had any more of a qualification than you or I had: yet they assume it, as well as we. Is there in this no fallacy, no fraud? Some of them were so wretchedly poor, that a borrowed watch-key hung from a broken shoe-string at their tattered fob; and when they could obtain on credit a yard of damaged muslin for their noses, they begged a pinch of snuff at the next box they saw open, and sneezed that they might reasonably display their acquisition.

CANNING. I wonder that these people should cry out so loudly for a fairer representation.

PITT. Some have really the vanity to believe that they would be chosen, and might choose their colleagues; others follow orders; the greater part wish no such thing; and, if they thought it likely to succeed, would never call for it. The fact is this: the most honest and independent members of Parliament are elected by the rotten boroughs. They pay down their own money, and give their own votes: they are not subservient to the aristocracy nor to the treasury. The same can not be said on any other description of members. I never ventured to make such a remark in Parliament. The people would be alarmed and struck with horror, if you clearly showed that the very best part of their representation is founded on nothing sounder than on rank corruption. Perhaps I am imprudent in suggesting the fact to you, knowing your *diabetes* of mind, and having found that your tongue is as easily set in motion, and as unconsciously, as the head of a mandarin on the chimney-piece at an inn.

Cease to be speculative.

CANNING. We cease to be speculative when we touch the object.

PITT. It is then unnecessary to remind you that you want only a numerical majority. Talents count for talents; respectability for respectability. The veriest fag that Dundas ever breeched for the South gives as efficient a vote as a Romilly or a Newport.

In the beginning of my career as Minister, I sometimes wished that I could have become so and have been consistent. I have since found that inconsistency is taken for a proof of greatness in a politician. "He knows how to manage men; he sees what the times require: his great mind bends majestically to the impulse of the world.' These things are said, or will be. Certain it is, when a robe is blown out by the wind, showing now the outer side, now the inner, then one colour, then another, it seems the more capacious, and the richer.

If at any time you are induced by policy, or impelled by nature, to commit an action more ungenerous or more dishonest than usual; if at any time you shall have brought the country into worse disgrace or under more imminent danger; talk and look bravely: swear, threaten, bluster: be witty, be pious: sneer, scoff: look infirm, look gouty: appeal to immortal God that you desire to remain in office so long only as you can be beneficial to your King and country: that however, at such a time as the present, you should be reluctant to leave the most flourishing of nations a prey to the wild passions of insatiate demagogues: and that nothing but the commands of your venerable sovereign, and the unequivocal voice of the people that recommended you to his notice, shall ever make you desert the station to which the hand of Providence conducted you. They have keen eyes who can see through all these words: I have never found any such, and have tried thousands. The man who possesses them may read Swedenborg and Kant while he is being tossed in a blanket.

Above all things keep your friends and dependants in good humour and good condition. If they lose flesh, you lose people's confidence. My cook, two summers ago, led me to this reflection at Walmer. Finding him in the court-yard, and observing that, however round and rosy, he looked melancholy, and struck his hips with his fists very frequently as he walked along, I called to him, and when he turned round, inquired of him what had happened to discompose him. He answered that Sam Spack the butcher had failed.

'Well, what then?' said I, 'unless you mean that his creditors may come upon me for the last two years' bill?' He shook his head, and told me that he had lent Sam Spack all he was worth, a good five hundred pounds. 'The greater fool you!' replied I. 'Why, sir!' said he, opening his hand to show the clearness of his demonstration, 'who would not have lent him anything, when he swore and ate like the devil, and drank as if he was in hell, and his dog was fatter than the best calf in Kent?'

It occurs to me that I owe this unfortunate cook several years' wages. Write down his name, William Ruffhead. You must do something to help him: a diversion on the coast of France would be sufficient: order one for him: in six months he may fairly pocket his quiet twenty thousands, and have his paltry three guineas a day for life. Write above the name, 'deputy commissary.' Ruffhead is so honest a creature, he will only be a dogfish in a shoal of sharks.

Never consent to any reduction in the national expenditure. Consider what is voted by Parliament for public services as your own property. The largest estate in England would go but a little way in procuring you partisans and adherents: these loosely counted millions purchase them. I have smiled when people in the simplicity of their hearts applauded me for neglecting the aggrandizement of my fortune. Every rood of land in the British dominions has a mine beneath it, out of which, by a vote of Parliament, I oblige the proprietor to extract as much as I want, as often as I will. From every tobacco-pipe in England a dependant of mine takes a whiff; from every salt-vase a spoonful. I have given more to my family than is possessed by those of Tamerlane and Aurungzebe; and I distribute to the amount of fifty millions a-year in the manner I deem convenient. What is any man's private purse other than that into which he can put his hand at his option? Neither my pocket nor my house, neither the bank nor the treasury, neither London nor Westminister, neither England nor Europe, are capacious enough for mine: it swings between the Indies, and sweeps the whole ocean.

CANNING. I am aware of it. You spend only what you have time and opportunity for spending. No man gives better dinners: few better wine—

PITT. Canning! Canning! Canning! always blundering into some coarse compliment!

Reminding me of wine, you remind me of my death, and the cause of it. To spite the French and Bonaparte, I would not drink claret: Madeira was too heating: hock was too light and acid for me.

CANNING. Seltzer water takes off this effect, the Dean of Christchurch tells me.

PITT. It might have made my speeches windier than was expedient; and I declined to bring into action a steam-engine of such power, with Mr Speaker in front and the treasury-bench in rear of me. The detestable beverage of Oporto is now burning my entrails.

CANNING. Beverage fit for the condemned.

PITT. If condemned for poisoning.

As you must return to London in the morning, and as I may not be disposed or able to talk much at another time, what remains to be said I will say now.

Never be persuaded to compose a mixed administration of whigs and tories: for, as you can not please them equally, each will plot eternally to supplant you by some leader of its party.

Employ men of less knowledge and perspicacity than yourself, if you can find them. Do not let any stand too close or too much above; because in both positions they may look down into your shallows and see the weeds at the bottom. Authors may be engaged by you; but never pamper them; keep them in wind and tractability by hard work. Many of them are trusty while they are needy: enrich them only with promised lands, enjoying the most extensive prospect and most favourable exposure. For my part, I little respect any living author. The only one, ancient or modern, I ever read with attention is Bolingbroke, who was recommended to me for a model. His principles, his heart, his style, have formed mine exclusively: everything sits easy upon him: mostly I like him because he supersedes inquiry: the thing best to do and to inculcate. We should have been exterminated long ago, if the House of Commons had not thought so, and had not voted us a Bill of Indemnity: which I was certain I could obtain as often as I should find it necessary, be the occasion what it might. Neither free governments nor arbitrary have such security: ours is constituted for evasion. I hope nobody may ever call me the *Pilot of the Escape-boat*. In Turkey I should have been strangled; in Algiers I should have been impaled; in America I should have mounted the gallows in the market-place; in Sweden I should have been pistolled at a public dinner or court-ball: in England I am extolled above my father.

Ah Canning! how delighted, how exultant was I, when I first heard this acclamation! When I last heard it, how sorrowful! how depressed! He was always thwarted, and always succeeded: I was always seconded, and always failed. He left the country flourishing: I leave it impoverished, exhausted, ruined. He left many able statesmen; I leave *you*.

Excuse me: dying men are destined to feel and privileged to say unpleasant things.

Good night! I retire to rest.

From *Imaginary Conversations*
Vol. V, 1829

EPICURUS[1], LEONTION, AND TERNISSA

LEONTION. Your situation for a garden, Epicurus, is, I think, very badly chosen.

EPICURUS. Why do you think so, my Leontion?

LEONTION. First, because it is more than twenty stadia from the city.

EPICURUS. Certainly the distance is inconvenient, my charming friend! it is rather too far off for us to be seen, and rather too near for us to be regretted. Here however I shall build no villa, nor anything else, and the longest time we can be detained, is from the rising to the setting sun. Now, pray, your other reason why the spot is so ineligible.

LEONTION. Because it commands no view of the town or of the harbour, unless we mount upon that knoll, where we could scarcely

---

[1] Cicero was an opponent of Epicurus, yet in his treatise *On Friendship* he says, 'De quâ Epicurus quidem ita dicit; omnium rerum quas ad *beate vivendum* sapientia comparaverit, nihil esse majus amicitiâ; nihil uberius, nihil jucundius.' This is oratorical and sententious: he goes on, praising the founder and the foundation. 'Neque verò hoc oratione solùm sed *multo magis vitâ et moribus* comprobavit. Quod quàm magnum sit, fictæ veterum fabulæ declarant, in quibus tam multis tamque variis ab ultimâ antiquitate repetitis, tria vix amicorum paria reperiuntur, ut ad Orestem pervenias profectus a Theseo. At verò Epicurus unâ in domo, et eâ quidem angustâ, quàm magnos quantâque amoris conspiratione consentientes tenuit amicorum greges. *Quod fit etiam nunc ab Epicureis.*' Certain it is, that moderation, forbearance, and what St Paul calls *charity*, never flourished in any sect of philosophy or religion, so perfectly and so long as among the disciples of Epicurus.

Cicero adds in another work, 'De sanctitate, de pietate adversus Deos libros scripsit Epicurus: at quomodo in his loquitur? ut Coruncanium aut Scævolam Pontifices Maximos te audire dicas.'

Seneca, whose sect was more adverse, thus expresses his opinion: 'Mea quidem ista sententia (et hoc nostris invitis popularibus dicam) sancta Epicurum et recta præcipere, et, si propius accesseris, tristia.'—W. S. L.

stand together, for the greater part is occupied by those three
pinasters, old and horrible as the three Furies. Surely you will cut
them down.

EPICURUS. Whatever Leontion commands. To me there is this
advantage in a place at some distance from the city. Having by no
means the full possession of my faculties, where I hear unwelcome
and intrusive voices, or unexpected and irregular sounds that
excite me involuntarily to listen, I assemble and arrange my
thoughts with freedom and with pleasure in the fresh air, under the
open sky: and they are more lively and vigorous and exuberant
when I catch them as I walk about, and commune with them in
silence and seclusion.

LEONTION. It always has appeared to me that conversation
brings them forth more readily and plenteously: and that the ideas
of one person no sooner come out than another's follow them,
whether from the same side or from the opposite.

EPICURUS. They do: but these are not the thoughts we keep for
seed: they come up weak by coming up close together. In the
country the mind is soothed and satisfied: here is no restraint of
motion or of posture. These things, little and indifferent as they
may seem, are not so: for the best tempers have need of ease and
liberty, to keep them in right order long enough for the purposes of
composition: and many a froward axiom, many an inhumane
thought, hath arisen from sitting inconveniently, from hearing a
few unpleasant sounds, from the confinement of a gloomy chamber,
or from the want of symmetry in it. We are not aware of this, until
we find an exemption from it in groves, on promontories, or along
the sea-shore, or wherever else we meet Nature face to face,
undisturbed and solitary.

TERNISSA. You would wish us then away?

EPICURUS. I speak of solitude: you of desolation.

TERNISSA. O flatterer! is this philosophy?

EPICURUS. Yes; if you are a thought the richer or a moment the
happier for it.

TERNISSA. Write it down then in the next volume you intend to
publish.

LEONTION. I interpose and controvert it. That is not philosophy
which serves only for one.

EPICURUS. Just criterion! I will write down your sentence

instead, and leave mine at the discretion of Ternissa. And now, my beautiful Ternissa, let me hear *your* opinion of the situation I have chosen. I perceive that you too have fixed your eyes on the pinasters.

TERNISSA. I will tell you in verses; for I do think these are verses, or nearly:

> I hate those trees that never lose their foliage:
> They seem to have no sympathy with Nature:
> Winter and Summer are alike to them.

The broad and billowy summits of yon monstrous trees, one would imagine, were made for the storms to rest upon when they are tired of raving. And what bark! It occurs to me, Epicurus, that I have rarely seen climbing plants attach themselves to these trees, as they do to the oak, the maple, the beech, and others.

LEONTION. If your remark be true, perhaps the resinous are not embraced by them so frequently because they dislike the odour of the resin, or some other property of the juices; for they too have their affections and antipathies, no less than countries and their climes.

TERNISSA. For shame! what would you with me?

EPICURUS. I would not interrupt you while you were speaking, nor while Leontion was replying; this is against my rules and practice; having now ended, kiss me, Ternissa!

TERNISSA. Impudent man! in the name of Pallas, why should I kiss you?

EPICURUS. Because you expressed hatred.

TERNISSA. Do we kiss when we hate?

EPICURUS. There is no better end of hating. The sentiment should not exist one moment; and if the hater gives a kiss on being ordered to do it, even to a tree or a stone, that tree or stone becomes the monument of a fault extinct.

TERNISSA. I promise you I never will hate a tree again.

EPICURUS. I told you so.

LEONTION. Nevertheless I suspect, my Ternissa, you will often be surprised into it. I was very near saying, 'I hate these rude square stones!' Why did you leave them here, Epicurus?

EPICURUS. It is true, they are the greater part square, and seem to have been cut out in ancient times from plinths and columns: they are also rude. Removing the smaller, that I might plant violets and cyclamens and convolvuluses and strawberries, and such other herbs as grow willingly in dry places, I left a few of these for seats, a few for tables and for couches.

LEONTION. Delectable couches!

EPICURUS. Laugh as you may, they will become so when they are covered with moss and ivy, and those other two sweet plants, whose names I do not remember to have found in any ancient treatise, but which I fancy I have heard Theophrastus call 'Leontion' and 'Ternissa.'

TERNISSA. The bold insidious false creature!

EPICURUS. What is that volume? may I venture to ask, Leontion? Why do you blush?

LEONTION. I do not blush about it.

EPICURUS. You are offended then, my dear girl.

LEONTION. No, not offended. I will tell you presently what it contains. Account to me first for your choice of so strange a place to walk in: a broad ridge, the summit and one side barren, the other a wood of rose-laurels impossible to penetrate. The worst of all is, we can see nothing of the city or the Parthenon, unless from the very top.

EPICURUS. The place commands, in my opinion, a most perfect view.

LEONTION. Of what, pray?

EPICURUS. Of itself; seeming to indicate that we, Leontion, who philosophize, should do the same.

LEONTION. Go on, go on! say what you please: I will not hate anything yet. Why have you torn up by the root all these little mountain-ash trees? This is the season of their beauty: come, Ternissa, let us make ourselves necklaces and armlets, such as may captivate old Sylvanus and Pan: you shall have your choice. But why have you torn them up?

EPICURUS. On the contrary, they were brought hither this morning. Sosimenes is spending large sums of money on an olive-ground, and has uprooted some hundreds of them, of all ages and sizes. I shall cover the rougher part of the hill with them, setting the clematis and vine and honey-suckle against them, to unite them.

TERNISSA. O what a pleasant thing it is to walk in the green light of the vine-leaves, and to breathe the sweet odour of their invisible flowers!

EPICURUS. The scent of them is so delicate that it requires a sigh to inhale it; and this, being accompanied and followed by enjoyment, renders the fragrance so exquisite. Ternissa, it is this, my sweet friend, that made you remember the green light of the foliage, and think of the invisible flowers as you would of some blessing from heaven.

TERNISSA. I see feathers flying at certain distances just above the middle of the promontory: what can they mean?

EPICURUS. Can not you imagine them to be feathers from the wings of Zethes and Caläis, who came hither out of Thrace to behold the favourite haunts of their mother Oreithyia? From the precipice that hangs over the sea a few paces from the pinasters, she is reported to have been carried off by Boreas; and these remains of the primeval forest have always been held sacred on that belief.

LEONTION. The story is an idle one.

TERNISSA. O no, Leontion! the story is very true.

LEONTION. Indeed?

TERNISSA. I have heard not only odes, but sacred and most ancient hymns upon it; and the voice of Boreas is often audible here, and the screams of Oreithyia.

LEONTION. The feathers then really may belong to Caläis and Zethes.

TERNISSA. I don't believe it: the winds would have carried them away.

LEONTION. The Gods, to manifest their power, as they often do by miracles, could as easily fix a feather eternally on the most tempestuous promontory, as the mark of their feet upon the flint.

TERNISSA. They could indeed: but we know the one to a certainty, and have no such authority for the other. I have seen these pinasters from the extremity of the Piræus, and have heard mention of the altar raised to Boreas: where is it?

EPICURUS. As it stands in the centre of the platform, we can not see it from hence: there is the only piece of level ground in the place.

LEONTION. Ternissa intends the altar to prove the truth of the story.

EPICURUS. Ternissa is slow to admit that even the young can deceive, much less the old: the gay, much less the serious.

LEONTION. It is as wise to moderate our belief as our desires.

EPICURUS. Some minds require much belief, some thrive on little. Rather an exuberance of it is feminine and beautiful. It acts differently on different hearts: it troubles some, it consoles others: in the generous it is the nurse of tenderness and kindness, of heroism and self-devotion: in the ungenerous it fosters pride, impatience of contradiction and appeal, and, like some waters, what it finds a dry stick or hollow straw, it leaves a stone.

TERNISSA. We want it chiefly to make the way of death an easy one.

EPICURUS. There is no easy path leading out of life, and few are the easy ones that lie within it. I would adorn and smoothen the declivity, and make my residence as commodious as its situation and dimensions may allow: but principally I would cast underfoot the empty fear of death.

TERNISSA. O! how can you?

EPICURUS. By many arguments already laid down: then by thinking that some perhaps, in almost every age, have been timid and delicate as Ternissa; and yet have slept soundly, have felt no parent's or friend's tear upon their faces, no throb against their breasts: in short, have been in the calmest of all possible conditions, while those around were in the most deplorable and desperate.

TERNISSA. It would pain me to die, if it were only at the idea that anyone I love would grieve too much for me.

EPICURUS. Let the loss of our friends be our only grief, and the apprehension of displeasing them our only fear.

LEONTION. No apostrophes! no interjections! Your argument was unsound; your means futile.

EPICURUS. Tell me then, whether the horse of a rider on the road should not be spurred forward if he started at a shadow.

LEONTION. Yes.

EPICURUS. I thought so: it would however be better to guide him quietly up to it, and to show him that it was one. Death is less than a shadow: it represents nothing, even imperfectly.

LEONTION. Then at the best what is it? why care about it, think about it, or remind us that it must befall us? Would you take the same trouble, when you see my hair entwined with ivy, to make me remember that, although the leaves are green and pliable, the stem is fragile and rough, and that before I go to bed I shall have many knots and intanglements to extricate? Let me have them; but let me not hear of them until the time is come.

EPICURUS. I would never think of death as an embarrassment, but as a blessing.

TERNISSA. How! a blessing?

EPICURUS. What, if it makes our enemies cease to hate us? what, if it makes our friends love us the more?

LEONTION. Us? According to your doctrine, we shall not exist at all.

EPICURUS. I spoke of that which is consolatory while we are here, and of that which in plain reason ought to render us contented to stay no longer. You, Leontion, would make others better: and better they certainly will be, when their hostilities languish in an empty field and their rancour is tired with treading upon dust. The generous affections stir about us at the dreary hour of death as the blossoms of the Median apple swell and diffuse their fragrance in the cold.

TERNISSA. I can not bear to think of passing the Styx, lest Charon should touch me: he is so old and wilful, so cross and ugly.

EPICURUS. Ternissa! Ternissa! I would accompany you thither, and stand between. Would not you too Leontion?

LEONTION. I don't know.

TERNISSA. O! that we could go together!

LEONTION. Indeed!

TERNISSA. All three, I mean—I said—or was going to say it. How ill-natured you are, Leontion! to misinterpret me; I could almost cry.

LEONTION. Do not, do not, Ternissa! Should that tear drop from your eyelash you would look less beautiful.

EPICURUS. Whenever I see a tear on a beautiful young face, twenty of mine run to meet it. If it is well to conquer a world, it is better to conquer two.

TERNISSA. That is what Alexander of Macedon wept because he could not accomplish.

EPICURUS. Ternissa! we three can accomplish it; or any one of us.

TERNISSA. How? pray!

EPICURUS. We can conquer this world and the next: for you will have another, and nothing should be refused you.

TERNISSA. The next by piety: but this, in what manner?

EPICURUS. By indifference to all who are indifferent to us; by taking joyfully the benefit that comes spontaneously; by wishing no more intensely for what is a hair's breadth beyond our reach than for a draught of water from the Ganges; and by fearing nothing in another life.

TERNISSA. This, O Epicurus! is the grand impossibility.

EPICURUS. Do you believe the Gods to be as benevolent and good as you are? or do you not?

TERNISSA. Much kinder, much better in every way.

EPICURUS. Would you kill or hurt the sparrow that you keep in your little dressing-room with a string around the leg, because he hath flown where you did not wish him to fly?

TERNISSA. No: it would be cruel: the string about the leg of so little and weak a creature is enough.

EPICURUS. You think so; I think so; God thinks so. This I may say confidently: for whenever there is a sentiment in which strict justice and pure benevolence unite, it must be his.

TERNISSA. O Epicurus! when you speak thus—

LEONTION. Well, Ternissa! what then?

TERNISSA. When Epicurus teaches us such sentiments as this, I am grieved that he has not so great an authority with the Athenians as some others have.

LEONTION. You will grieve more, I suspect, my Ternissa, when he possesses that authority.

TERNISSA. What will he do?

LEONTION. Why turn pale? I am not about to answer that he will forget or leave you. No; but the voice comes deepest from the sepulchre, and a great name hath its root in the dead body. If you invited a company to a feast, you might as well place round the table live sheep and oxen, and vases of fish and cages of quails, as you would invite a company of friendly hearers to the philosopher who is yet living.[1] One would imagine that the iris of our intellectual eye were lessened by the glory of his presence, and that, like eastern kings, he could be looked at near only when his limbs are stiff, by waxlight, in closed curtains.

---

[1] Seneca quotes a letter of Epicurus, in which his friendship with Metrodorus is mentioned, with a remark that the obscurity in which they had lived, so great indeed as to let them rest almost unheard of, in the midst of Greece, was by no means to be considered as an abatement of their good fortune.—W. S. L.

EPICURUS. One of whom we know little leaves us a ring or other token of remembrance, and we express a sense of pleasure and of gratitude; one of whom we know nothing writes a book, the contents of which might (if we would let them) have done us more good and might have given us more pleasure, and we revile him for it. The book may do what the legacy can not; it may be pleasurable and serviceable to others as well as ourselves: we would hinder this too. In fact, all other love is extinguished by self-love: beneficence, humanity, justice, philosophy, sink under it. While we insist that we are looking for Truth, we commit a falsehood. It never was the first object with anyone, and with few the second.

Feed unto replenishment your quieter fancies, my sweetest little Ternissa! and let the Gods, both youthful and aged, both gentle and boisterous, administer to them hourly on these sunny downs: what can they do better?

LEONTION. But those feathers, Ternissa, what God's may they be? since you will not pick them up, nor restore them to Caläis nor to Zethes.

TERNISSA. I do not think they belong to any God whatever; and shall never be persuaded of it unless Epicurus says it is so.

LEONTION. O unbelieving creature! do you reason against the immortals.

TERNISSA. It was yourself who doubted, or appeared to doubt, the flight of Oreithyia. By admitting too much we endanger our religion. Beside, I think I discern some upright stakes at equal distances, and am pretty sure the feathers are tied to them by long strings.

EPICURUS. You have guessed the truth.

TERNISSA. Of what use are they there?

EPICURUS. If you have ever seen the foot of a statue broken off just below the ankle, you have then, Leontion and Ternissa, seen the form of the ground about us. The lower extremities of it are divided into small ridges, as you will perceive if you look round; and these are covered with corn, olives, and vines. At the upper part, where cultivation ceases, and where those sheep and goats are grazing, begins my purchase. The ground rises gradually unto near the summit, where it grows somewhat steep, and terminates in a precipice. Across the middle I have traced a line, denoted by those feathers, from one dingle to the other; the two terminations of my intended garden. The distance is nearly a thousand paces, and the path, perfectly on a level, will be two paces broad, so that I may walk between you; but another could not join us conveniently. From this there will be several circuitous and spiral, leading by the easiest ascent to the summit; and several more, to the road along the cultivation underneath: here will however be but one entrance. Among the projecting fragments and the massive stones yet standing of the boundary-wall, which old pomegranates imperfectly defend, and which my neighbour has guarded more effectively against invasion, there are hillocks of crumbling mould, covered in some places with a variety of moss; in others are elevated tufts, or dim labyrinths, of eglantine.

TERNISSA. Where will you place the statues? for undoubtedly you must have some.

EPICURUS. I will have some models for statues. Pygmalion prayed the Gods to give life to the image he adored: I will not pray them to give marble to mine. Never may I lay my wet cheek upon the foot under which is incribed the name of Leontion or Ternissa!

LEONTION. Do not make us melancholy: never let us think that the time can come when we shall lose our friends. Glory, literature, philosophy, have this advantage over friendship: remove one object from them, and others fill the void; remove one from friendship, one only, and not the earth, nor the universality of worlds, no, nor the intellect that soars above and comprehends them, can replace it.

EPICURUS. Dear Leontion! always amiable, always graceful! how lovely do you now appear to me! what beauteous action accompanied your words!

LEONTION. I used none whatever.

EPICURUS. That white arm was then, as it is now, over the shoulder of Ternissa; and her breath imparted a fresh bloom to your cheek, a new music to your voice. No friendship is so cordial or so delicious as that of girl for girl; no hatred so intense and immovable as that of woman for woman. In youth you love one above the others of your sex: in riper age you hate all, more or less, in proportion to similarity of accomplishments and pursuits; which sometimes (I wish it were oftener) are bonds of union to men. In us you more easily pardon faults than excellences in each other. *Your* tempers are such, my beloved scholars, that even this truth does not ruffle them; and such is your affection, that I look with confidence to its unabated ardour at twenty.

LEONTION. O then I am to love Ternissa almost fifteen months!

TERNISSA. And I am destined to survive the loss of it three months above four years!

EPICURUS. Incomparable creatures! may it be eternal! In loving ye shall follow no example: ye shall step securely over the iron rule laid down for others by the destinies, and *you* for ever be Leontion, and *you* Ternissa.

LEONTION. Then indeed we should not want statues.

TERNISSA. But men, who are vainer creatures, would be good for nothing without them: they must be flattered, even by the stones.

EPICURUS. Very true. Neither the higher arts nor the civic virtues can flourish extensively without the statues of illustrious men. But gardens are not the places for them. Sparrows wooing on the general's truncheon (unless he be such a general as one of ours in the last war), and snails besliming the emblems of the poet, do not remind us worthily of their characters. Porticoes are their proper situations, and those the most frequented. Even there they may lose all honour and distinction, whether from the thoughtlessness of magistrates or from the malignity of rivals. Our own city, the least exposed of any to the effects of either, presents us a disheartening example. When the Thebans in their jealousy condemned Pindar to the payment of a fine, for having praised the Athenians too highly, our citizens erected a statue of bronze to him.

LEONTION. Jealousy of Athens made the Thebans fine him; and jealousy of Thebes made the Athenians thus record it.

EPICURUS. And jealousy of Pindar, I suspect, made some poet persuade the arcons to render the distinction a vile and worthless one, by placing his effigy near a king's, one Evagoras of Cyprus.

TERNISSA. Evagoras, I think I remember to have read in the inscription, was rewarded in this manner for his reception of Conon, defeated by the Lacedemonians.

EPICURUS. Gratitude was due to him, and some such memorial record it. External reverence should be paid unsparingly to the higher magistrates of every country who perform their offices exemplarily: yet they are not on this account to be placed in the same degree with men of primary genius. They never exalt the human race, and rarely benefit it; and their benefits are local and transitory, while those of a great writer are universal and eternal.

If the Gods did indeed bestow on us a portion of their fire, they seem to have lighted it in sport and left it: the harder task and the nobler is performed by that genius who raises it clear and glowing from its embers, and makes it applicable to the purposes that dignify or delight our nature. I have ever said, 'Reverence the rulers.' Let them his image stand; but stand apart from Pindar's. Pallas and Jove! defend me from being carried down the stream of time among a shoal of royalets, and the rootless weeds they are hatched on.

TERNISSA. So much pity would deserve the exemption, even though your writings did not hold out the decree.

LEONTION. Child, the compliment is ill turned: if you are ironical, as you must be on the piety of Epicurus, Atticism requires that you should continue to be so, at least to the end of the sentence.

TERNISSA. Irony is my abhorrence. Epicurus may appear less pious than some others; but I am certain he is more; otherwise the Gods would never have given him—

LEONTION. What? what? let us hear!

TERNISSA. Leontion!

LEONTION. Silly girl! Were there any hibiscus or broom growing near at hand, I would send him away and whip you.

EPICURUS. There is fern, which is better.

LEONTION. I was not speaking to you: but now you shall have something to answer for yourself. Although you admit to statues in the country, you might at least methinks have discovered a retirement with a fountain in it: here I see not even a spring.

EPICURUS. Fountain I can hardly say there is; but on the left there is a long crevice or chasm, which we have never yet visited, and which we can not discern until we reach it. This is full of soft mould, very moist; and many high reeds and canes are growing there; and the rock itself too drips with humidity along it, and is covered with more tufted moss and more variegated lichens. This crevice, with its windings and sinuosities, is about four hundred paces long, and in many parts eleven, twelve, thirteen feet wide, but generally six or seven. I shall plant it wholly with lilies of the valley: leaving the irises which occupy the sides as well as the clefts, and also those other flowers of paler purple, from the autumnal cups of which we collect the saffron; and forming a narrow path of such turf as I can find there, or rather following it as it creeps among the bays and hazels and sweet-briar, which have fallen at different times from the summit, and are now grown old, with an infinity of primroses at the roots. There are nowhere twenty steps without a projection and a turn, nor in any ten together is the chasm of the same width or figure. Hence the ascent in its windings is easy and imperceptible quite to the termination, where the rocks are somewhat high and precipitous: at the entrance they lose themselves in privet and elder, and you must make your way between them through the canes. Do not you remember where I carried you both across the muddy hollow in the foot-path?

TERNISSA. Leontion does.

EPICURUS. That place is always wet; not only in this month of Puanepsion,[1] which we are beginning to-day, but in midsummer. The water that causes it, comes out a little way above it, but originates from the crevice, which I will cover at top with rose-laurel and mountain-ash, with clematis and vine; and I will intercept the little rill in its wandering, draw it from its concealment, and place it like Bacchus under the protection of the nymphs, who will smile upon it in its marble cradle, which at present I keep at home.

TERNISSA. Leontion! why do you turn away your face? have the nymphs smiled upon you in it?

LEONTION. I bathed in it once, if you must know, Ternissa! Why now, Ternissa, why do you turn away yours? have the nymphs frowned upon you for invading their secrets?

TERNISSA. Epicurus, you are in the right to bring it away from Athens; from under the eye of Pallas: she might be angry.

EPICURUS. You approve of its removal then, my lovely friend?

TERNISSA. Mightily.

(*Aside.*) I wish it may break in pieces on the road.

EPICURUS. What did you say?

TERNISSA. I wish it were now on the road—that I might try whether it would hold me—I mean with my clothes on.

EPICURUS. It would hold you, and one a span longer. I have

---

[1] The Attic month of Puanepsion had its commencement in the latter days of October: its name is derived from πύανα, the legumes which were offered in sacrifice to Apollo at that season.—W. S. L.

another in the house; but it is not decorated with fauns and satyrs and foliage, like this.

LEONTION. I remember putting my hand upon the frightful satyr's head, to leap in: it seems made for the purpose. But the sculptor needed not to place the naiad quite so near—he must have been a very impudent man; it is impossible to look for a moment at such a piece of workmanship.

TERNISSA. For shame! Leontion!—why, what was it? I do not desire to know.

EPICURUS. I don't remember it.

LEONTION. Nor I neither; only the head.

EPICURUS. I shall place the satyr toward the rock, that you may never see him, Ternissa.

TERNISSA. Very right; he cannot turn round.

LEONTION. The poor naiad had done it, in vain.

TERNISSA. All these labourers will soon finish the plantation, if you superintend them, and are not appointed to some magistrature.

EPICURUS. Those who govern us are pleased at seeing a philosopher out of the city, and more still at finding in a season of scarcity forty poor citizens, who might become seditious, made happy and quiet by such employment.

Two evils, of almost equal weight, may befall the man of erudition: never to be listened to, and to be listened to always. Aware of these, I devote a large portion of my time and labours to the cultivation of such minds as flourish best in cities, where my garden at the gate although smaller than this, we find sufficient capacious. There I secure my listeners: here my thoughts and imaginations have their free natural current, and tarry or wander as the will invites: may it ever be among those dearest to me! those whose hearts possess the rarest and divinest faculty, of retaining or forgetting at option what ought to be forgotten or retained.

LEONTION. The whole ground then will be covered with trees and shrubs?

EPICURUS. There are some protuberances in various parts of the eminence, which you do not perceive till you are upon them or above them. They are almost level at the top, and overgrown with fine grass; for they catch the better soil, brought down in small quantities by the rains. These are to be left unplanted; so is the platform under the pinasters, whence there is a prospect of the city, the harbour, the isle of Salamis, and the territory of Megara. 'What then,' cried Sosimenes, 'you would hide from your view my young olives, and the whole length of the new wall I have been building at my own expense between us! and, when you might see at once the whole of Attica, you will hardly see more of it than I could buy.'

LEONTION. I do not perceive the new wall, for which Sosimenes, no doubt, thinks himself another Pericles.

EPICURUS. Those old junipers quite conceal it.

TERNISSA. They look warm and sheltering: but I like the rose-laurels much better; and what a thicket of them there is!

EPICURUS. Leaving all the larger, I shall remove many thousands of them; enough to border the greater part of the walk, intermixed with roses.

TERNISSA. Do, pray, leave that taller plant yonder, of which I see there are several springing in several places out of the rock: it appears to have produced on a single stem a long succession of yellow flowers; some darkening and fading, others running up and leaving them behind, others showing their little faces imperfectly through their light green veils.

LEONTION. Childish girl! she means the mullen; and she talks about it as she would have talked about a doll, attributing to it feelings and aims and designs. I saw her stay behind to kiss it; no doubt, for being so nearly of her own highth.

TERNISSA. No indeed, not for that; but because I had broken off one of its blossoms unheedingly, perhaps the last it may bear, and because its leaves are so downy and pliant; and because nearer the earth some droop and are decaying, and remind me of a parent who must die before the tenderest of her children can do without her.

EPICURUS. I will preserve the whole species; but you must point out to me the particular one as we return. There is an infinity of other plants and flowers, or weeds as Sosimenes calls them, of which he has cleared his olive-yard, and which I shall adopt. Twenty of his slaves came in yesterday, laden with hyacinths and narcissuses, anemones and jonquils. 'The curses of our vineyards,' cried he, 'and good neither for man nor beast. I have another estate infested with lilies of the valley: I should not wonder if you accepted these too.'

'And with thanks,' answered I.

The whole of his remark I could not collect: he turned aside, and (I believe) prayed. I only heard 'Pallas'—'father'—'sound mind'—'inoffensive man'—'good neighbour.' As we walked together I perceived him looking grave, and I could not resist my inclination to smile as I turned my eyes toward him. He observed it, at first with unconcern, but by degrees some doubts arose within him, and he said, 'Epicurus, you have been throwing away no less than half a talent on this sorry piece of mountain, and I fear you are about to waste as much in labour: for nothing was ever so terrible as the price we are obliged to pay the workman, since the conquest of Persia, and the increase of luxury in our city. Under three obols none will do his day's work. But what, in the name of all the deities, could induce you to plant those roots, which other people dig up and throw away?'

'I have been doing,' said I, 'the same thing my whole life through, Sosimenes!'

'How!' cried he: 'I never knew that.'

'Those very doctrines,' added I, 'which others hate and extirpate, I inculcate and cherish. They bring no riches, and therefore are thought to bring no advantage: to me they appear the more advantageous for that reason. They give us immediately what we solicit through the means of wealth. We toil for the wealth first; and then it remains to be proved whether we can purchase with it what we look for. Now, to carry our money to the market, and not to find in the market our money's worth, is great vexation: yet much greater has already preceded, in running up and down for it among so many competitors, and through so many thieves.'

After a while he rejoined, 'You really then have not over-reached me?'

'In what? my friend!' said I.

'These roots,' he answered, 'may perhaps be good and saleable for some purpose. Shall you send them into Persia? or whither?'

'Sosimenes! I shall make love-portions of the flowers.'

LEONTION. O Epicurus! should it ever be known in Athens that they are good for this, you will not have, with all your fences of prunes and pomegranates, and precipices with briar upon them, a single root left under ground after the month of Elaphebolion.[1]

[1] The thirtieth of Elaphebolion was the tenth of April.—W.S.L.

EPICURUS. It is not everyone that knows the preparation.

LEONTION. Everybody will try it.

EPICURUS. And you too, Ternissa?

TERNISSA. Will you teach me?

EPICURUS. This, and anything else I know. We must walk together when they are in flower.

TERNISSA. And can you teach me then?

EPICURUS. I teach by degrees.

LEONTION. By very slow ones, Epicurus! I have no patience with you: tell us directly.

EPICURUS. It is very material what kind of recipient you bring with you. Enchantresses use a brazen one: silver and gold are employed in other arts.

LEONTION. I will bring any.

TERNISSA. My mother has a fine golden one: she will lend it me: she allows me everything.

EPICURUS. Leontion and Ternissa! those eyes of yours brighten at inquiry, as if they carried a light within them for a guidance.

LEONTION. No flattery!

TERNISSA. No flattery! come, teach us.

EPICURUS. Will you hear me through in silence?

LEONTION. We promise.

EPICURUS. Sweet girls! the calm pleasures, such as I hope you will ever find in your walks among these gardens, will improve your beauty, animate your discourse, and correct the little that may hereafter rise up for correction in your dispositions. The smiling ideas left in our bosoms from our infancy, that many plants are the favourites of the Gods, and that others were even the objects of their love, having once been invested with the human form, beautiful and lively and happy as yourselves, give them an interest beyond the vision; yes, and a station, let me say it, on the vestibule of our affections. Resign your ingenuous hearts to simple pleasures; and there is none in man where men are Attic that will not follow and outstrip their movements.

TERNISSA. O Epicurus!

EPICURUS. What said Ternissa?

LEONTION. Some of those anemones, I do think, must be still in blossom. Ternissa's golden cup is at home; but she has brought with her a little vase for the filter—and has filled it to the brim.—

Do not hide your head behind my shoulder, Ternissa! no, nor in my lap.

EPICURUS. Yes, there let it lie, the lovelier for that tendril of sunny brown hair upon it. How it falls and rises! Which is the hair? which the shadow?

LEONTION. Let the hair rest.

EPICURUS. I must not perhaps clasp the shadow!

LEONTION. You philosophers are fond of such unsubstantial things. O! you have taken my volume. This is deceit.

You live so little in public, and entertain such a contempt for opinion, as to be both indifferent and ignorant what it is that people blame you for.

EPICURUS. I know what it is I should blame myself for, if I attended to them. Prove them to be wiser and more disinterested in their wisdom than I am, and I will then go down to them and listen to them. When I have well considered a thing, I deliver it, regardless of what those think who neither take the time nor possess the faculty of considering anything well, and who have always lived far remote from the scope of our speculations.

LEONTION. In the volume you snatched away from me so slily, I have defended a position of yours which many philosophers turn into ridicule; namely, that politeness is among the virtues. I wish you yourself had spoken more at large upon the subject.

EPICURUS. It is one upon which a lady is likely to display more ingenuity and discernment. If philosophers have ridiculed my sentiment, the reason is, it is among those virtues which in general they find most difficult to assume or counterfeit.

LEONTION. Surely life runs on the smoother for this equability and polish; and the gratification it affords is more extensive than is afforded even by the highest virtue. Courage, on nearly all occasions, inflicts as much of evil as it imparts of good. It may be exerted in defence of our country, in defence of those who love us, in defence of the harmless and the helpless: but those against whom it is thus exerted may possess an equal share of it. If they succeed, then manifestly the ill it produces is greater than the benefit: if they succumb, it is nearly as great. For, many of their adversaries are first killed and maimed, and many of their own kindred are left to lament the consequences of the aggression.

EPICURUS. You have spoken first of courage, as that virtue which attracts your sex principally.

TERNISSA. Not me; I am always afraid of it. I love those best who can tell me the most things I never knew before, and who have patience with me, and look kindly while they teach me, and almost as if they were waiting for fresh questions. Now let me hear directly what you were about to say to Leontion.

EPICURUS. I was proceeding to remark that temperance comes next; and temperance has then its highest merit when it is the support of civility and politeness. So that I think I am right and equitable in attributing to politeness a distinguished rank, not among the ornaments of life, but among the virtues. And you, Leontion and Ternissa, will have leaned the more propensely toward this opinion, if you considered, as I am sure you did, that the peace and concord of families, friends, and cities, are preserved by it: in other terms, the harmony of the world.

TERNISSA. Leontion spoke of courage, you of temperance: the next great virtue, in the division made by the philosophers, is justice.

EPICURUS. Temperance includes it: for temperance is imperfect if it is only an abstinence from too much food, too much wine, too much conviviality, or other luxury. It indicates every kind of forbearance. Justice is forbearance from what belongs to another. Giving to this one rightly what that one would hold wrongfully, is justice in magistrature, not in the abstract, and is only a part of its office. The perfectly temperate man is also the perfectly just man: but the perfectly just man (as philosophers now define him) may not be the perfectly temperate one: I include the less in the greater.

LEONTION. We hear of judges, and upright ones too, being immoderate eaters and drinkers.

EPICURUS. The Lacedemonians are temperate in food and courageous in battle: but men like these, if they existed in sufficient numbers, would devastate the universe. We alone, we Athenians, with less military skill perhaps, and certainly less rigid abstinence from voluptuousness and luxury, have set before it the only grand example of social government and of polished life. From us the seed is scattered: from us flow the streams that irrigate it: and ours are the hands, O Leontion, that collect it, cleanse it, deposit it, and convey and distribute it sound and weighty through every race and age. Exhausted as we are by war, we can do nothing better than lie down and doze while the weather is fine overhead, and dream (if we can) that we are affluent and free.

O sweet sea-air! how bland art thou and refreshing! Breathe spirits and serenity, many springs and many summers, and when the vine-leaves have reddened and rustle under their feet.

These, my beloved girls, are the children of Eternity: they played around Theseus and the beauteous Amazon, they gave to Pallas the bloom of Venus, and to Venus the animation of Pallas. Is it not better to enjoy by the hour their soft salubrious influence, than to catch by fits the rancid breath of demagogues: than to swell and move under it without or against our will; than to acquire the semblance of eloquence by the bitterness of passion, the tone of philosophy by disappointment, or the credit of prudence by distrust? Can fortune, can industry, can desert itself, bestow on us anything we have not here?

LEONTION. And when shall those three meet? The Gods have never united them, knowing that men would put them asunder at their first appearance.

EPICURUS. I am glad to leave the city as often as possible, full as it is of high and glorious reminiscences, and am inclined much rather to indulge in quieter scenes, whither the Graces and Friendship lead me. I would not contend even with men able to contend with me. You, Leontion, I see, think differently, and have composed at last your long-meditated work against the philosophy of Theophrastus.

LEONTION. Why not? he has been praised above his merits.

EPICURUS. My Leontion! you have inadvertently given me the reason and origin of all controversial writings. They flow not from a love of truth or a regard for science, but from envy and ill-will. Setting aside the evil of malignity, always hurtful to ourselves, not always to others, there is weakness in the argument you have adduced. When a writer is praised above his merits in his own times, he is certain of being estimated below them in the times succeeding. Paradox is dear to most people: it bears the appearance of originality, but is usually the talent of the superficial, the perverse, and the obstinate.

Nothing is more gratifying than the attention you are bestowing on me, which you always apportion to the seriousness of my observations. But, Leontion! Leontion! you defend me too earnestly. The roses on your cheeks should derive their bloom from a cooler and sweeter and more salubrious fountain. In what mythology (can you tell me, Ternissa ?) is Friendship the mother of Anger ?

TERNISSA. I can only tell you that Love lights Anger's torch very often.

LEONTION. I dislike Theophrastus for his affected contempt of your doctrines.

EPICURUS. Unreasonably, for the contempt of them; reasonably, if affected. Good men may differ widely from me, and wise ones misunderstand me; for, their wisdom having raised up to them schools of their own, they have not found leisure to converse with me; and from others they have received a partial and inexact report. My opinion is, that certain things are indifferent, and unworthy of pursuit or attention, as lying beyond our research and almost our conjecture; which things the generality of philosophers (for the generality are speculative) deem of the first importance. Questions relating to them I answer evasively, or altogether decline. Again, there are modes of living which are suitable to some and unsuitable to others. What I myself follow and embrace, what I recommend to the studious, to the irritable, to the weak in health, would ill agree with the commonality of citizens. Yet my adversaries cry out, 'Such is the opinion and practice of Epicurus.' For instance, I have never taken a wife, and never will take one: but he from among the mass who should avow his imitation of my example, would act as wisely and more religiously in saying that he chose celibacy because Pallas had done the same.

LEONTION. If Pallas had many such votaries she would soon have few citizens to supply them.

EPICURUS. And extremely bad ones if all followed me in retiring from the offices of magistracy and of war. Having seen that the most sensible men are the most unhappy, I could not but examine the causes of it: and finding that the same sensibility to which they are indebted for the activity of their intellect, is also the restless mover of their jealousy and ambition, I would lead them aside from whatever operates upon these, and throw under their feet the terrors their imagination has created. My philosophy is not for the populace nor for the proud: the ferocious will never attain it: the gentle will embrace it, but will not call it mine. I do not desire that they should:

let them rest their heads upon that part of the pillow which they find the softest, and enjoy their own dreams unbroken.

LEONTION. The old are all against you: for the name of pleasure is an affront to them: they know no other kind of it than that which has flowered and seeded, and of which the withered stems have indeed a rueful look. What we call dry they call sound: nothing must retain any juice in it: their pleasure is in chewing what is hard, not in tasting what is savoury.

EPICURUS. Unhappily the aged are retentive of long-acquired maxims, and insensible to new impressions, whether from fancy or from truth: in fact, their eyes blend the two together. Well might the poet tell us,

> Fewer the gifts that gnarled Age presents
> To elegantly-handed Infancy,
> Than elegantly-handed Infancy
> Presents to gnarled Age. From both they drop;
> The middle course of life receives them all,
> Save the light few that laughing Youth runs off with,
> Unvalued as a mistress or a flower.

LEONTION. It is reported by the experienced that our last loves and our first are of equal interest to us.

TERNISSA. Surely they are. What is the difference? Can you really mean to say, O Leontion, that there are any intermediate? Why do you look aside? And you too refuse to answer me so easy and plain a question?

LEONTION (*to Epicurus*). Although you teach us the necessity of laying a strong hand on the strong affections, you never pull one feather from the wing of Love.

EPICURUS. I am not so irreligious.

TERNISSA. I think he could only twitch it just enough to make the gentle God turn round, and smile on him.

LEONTION. You know little about the matter, but may live to know all. Whatever we may talk of torments, as some do, there must surely be more pleasure in desiring and not possessing, than in possessing and not desiring.

EPICURUS. Perhaps so: but consult the intelligent. Certainly there is a middle state between love and friendship, more delightful than either, but more difficult to remain in.

LANDOR

LEONTION. To be preferred to all others is the supremacy of bliss. Do not you think so, Ternissa?

TERNISSA. It is indeed what the wise and the powerful and the beautiful chiefly aim at: Leontion has attained it.

EPICURUS. Delightful, no doubt, is such supremacy: but far more delightful is the certainty that there never was any one quite near enough to be given up for us. To be preferred is hardly a compensation for having been long compared. The breath of another's sigh bedims and hangs pertinaciously about the image we adore.

LEONTION. When Friendship has taken the place of Love, she ought to make his absence as little a cause of regret as possible, and it is gracious in her to imitate his demeanour and his words.

EPICURUS. I can repeat them more easily than imitate them.

TERNISSA. Both of you, until this moment, were looking grave; but Leontion has resumed her smiles again on hearing what Epicurus can do. I wish you would repeat to me, O Epicurus, any words so benign a God hath vouchsafed to teach you; for it would be a convincing proof of your piety, and I could silence the noisiest tongue in Athens with it.

LEONTION. Simpleton! we were speaking allegorically.

TERNISSA. Never say that: I do believe the God himself hath conversed with Epicurus. Tell me now, Epicurus, tell me yourself, has not he?

EPICURUS. Yes.

TERNISSA. In his own form?

EPICURUS. Very nearly: it was in Ternissa's.

TERNISSA. Impious man! I am ashamed of you.

LEONTION. Never did shame burn brighter.

TERNISSA. Mind Theophrastus, not me.

LEONTION. Since, in obedience to your institutions, O Epicurus, I must not say I am angry, I am offended at least with Theophrastus, for having so misrepresented your opinions, on the necessity of keeping the mind composed and tranquil, and remote from every object and every sentiment by which a painful sympathy may be excited. In order to display his elegance of language, he runs wherever he can lay a censure on you, whether he believes in its equity or not.

EPICURUS. This is the case with all eloquent men and all disputants. Truth neither warms nor elevates them, neither obtains for them profit nor applause.

TERNISSA. I have heard wise remarks very often and very warmly praised.

EPICURUS. Not for the truth in them, but for the grace, or because they touched the spring of some preconception or some passion. Man is a hater of truth, a lover of fiction.

LEONTION. How then happens it that children, when you have related to them any story which has greatly interested them, ask immediately and impatiently, *is it true?*

EPICURUS. Children are not men nor women: they are almost as different creatures, in many respects, as if they never were to be the one or the other: they are as unlike as buds are unlike flowers, and almost as blossoms are unlike fruits. Greatly are they better than they are about to be, unless Philosophy raises her hand above them when the noon is coming on, and shelters them at one season from the heats that would scorch and wither, and at another from the storms that would shatter and subvert them. There are nations, it is reported, which aim their arrows and javelins at the sun and moon, on occasions of eclipse, or any other offence: but I never have heard that the sun and moon abated their course through the heavens for it, or looked more angrily when they issued forth again to shed light on their antagonists. They went onward all the while in their own serenity and clearness, through unobstructed paths, without diminution and without delay: it was only the little world below that was in darkness. Philosophy lets her light descend and enter wherever there is a passage for it: she takes advantage of the smallest crevice, but the rays are rebutted by the smallest obstruction. Polemics can never be philosophers or philotheists: they serve men ill, and their Gods no better: they mar what is solid in earthly bliss by animosities and dissensions, and intercept the span of azure at which the weary and the sorrowful would look up.

Theophrastus is a writer of many acquirements and some shrewness, usually judicious, often somewhat witty, always elegant: his thoughts are never confused, his sentences are never incomprehensible. If Aristoteles thought more highly of him than his due, surely you ought not to censure Theophrastus with severity on the supposition of his rating me below mine; unless you argue that a slight error in a short sum is less pardonable than in a longer.

Had Aristoteles been living, and had he given the same opinion of me, your friendship and perhaps my self-love might have been wounded; for, if on one occasion he spoke too favourably, he never spoke unfavourably but with justice. This is among the indications of orderly and elevated minds; and here stands the barrier that separates them from the common and the waste. Is a man to be angry because an infant is fretful? Is a philosopher to unpack and throw away his philosophy, because an idiot has tried to overturn it on the road, and has pursued it with jibes and ribaldry?

LEONTION. Theophrastus would persuade us that, according to your system, we not only should decline the succour of the wretched, but avoid the sympathies that poets and historians would awaken in us. Probably for the sake of introducing some idle verses, written by a friend of his, he says that, following the guidance of Epicurus, we should altogether shun the theatre, and not only when *Prometheus* and *Œdipus* and *Philoctetes* are introduced, but even where generous and kindly sentiments are predominant, if they partake of that tenderness which belongs to pity. I know not what Thracian lord recovers his daughter from her ravisher: such are among the words they exchange.

> *Father*. Insects, that dwell in rotten reeds, inert
> Upon the surface of a stream or pool,
> Then rush into the air on meshy vans,
> Are not so different in their varying lives
> As we are. . . . O! what father on this earth,
> Holding his child's cool cheek within his palms
> And kissing his fair front, would wish him man?
> Inheritor of wants and jealousies,
> Of labour, of ambition, of distress,
> And, cruellest of all the passions, lust.
> Who that beholds me, persecuted, scorned,
> A wanderer, e'er could think what friends were mine,
> How numerous, how devoted? with what glee
> Smiled my old house, with what acclaim my courts
> Rang from without whene'er my war-horse neighed.
>
> *Daughter*. Thy fortieth birthday is not shouted yet
> By the young peasantry, with rural gifts

And nightly fires along the pointed hills,
Yet do thy temples glitter with grey hair
Scattered not thinly: ah, what sudden change!
Only thy voice and heart remain the same:
No, that voice trembles, and that heart (I feel)
While it would comfort and console me, breaks.

EPICURUS. I would never close my bosom against the feelings of
humanity: but I would calmly and well consider by what conduct
of life they may enter it with the least importunity and violence.
A consciousness that we have promoted the happiness of others,
to the uttermost of our power, is certain not only to meet them at
the threshold, but to bring them along with us, and to render them
accurate and faithful prompters, when we bend perplexedly over
the problem of evil figured by the tragedians. If indeed there
were more of pain than of pleasure in the exhibitions of the
dramatist, no man in his senses would attend them twice. All the
imitative arts have delight for the principal object: the first of these
is poetry: the highest of poetry is tragic.

LEONTION. The epic has been called so.

EPICURUS. Improperly; for the epic has much more in it of what
is prosaic. Its magnitude is no argument. An Egyptian pyramid
contains more materials than an Ionic temple, but requires less
contrivance, and exhibits less beauty of design. My simile is yet a
defective one; for, a tragedy must be carried on with an unbroken
interest; and, undecorated by loose foliage or fantastic branches,
it must rise, like the palm-tree, with a lofty unity. On these matters
I am unable to argue at large, or perhaps correctly: on those however which I have studied and treated, my terms are so explicit and
clear, that Theophrastus can never have misunderstood them. Let
me recall to your attention but two axioms.

Abstinence from low pleasures is the only means of meriting or
of obtaining the higher.

Kindness in ourselves is the honey that blunts the sting of
unkindness in another.

LEONTION. Explain to me then, O Epicurus, why we suffer so
much from ingratitude.

EPICURUS. We fancy we suffer from ingratitude, while in reality
we suffer from self-love. Passion weeps while she says, 'I did not

deserve this from him': Reason, while she says it, smoothens her brow at the clear fountain of the heart. Permit me also, like Theophrastus, to borrow a few words from a poet.

TERNISSA. Borrow as many such as anyone will entrust to you: and may Hermes prosper your commerce! Leontion may go to the theatre then; for she loves it.

EPICURUS. Girls! be the bosom friends of *Antigone* and *Ismene;* and you shall enter the wood of the Eumenides without shuddering, and leave it without the trace of a tear. Never did you appear so graceful to me, O Ternissa; no, not even after this walk do you; as when I saw you blow a fly from the forehead of *Philoctetes* in the propylëa. The wind, with which Sophocles and the statuary represent him, to drive away the summer insects in his agony, had wearied his flaccid arm, hanging down beside him.

TERNISSA. Do you imagine then I thought him a living man?

EPICURUS. The sentiment was both more delicate and more august from being indistinct. You would have done it, even if he *had* been a living man: even if he could have clasped you in his arms, imploring the deities to resemble you in gentleness, you would have done it.

TERNISSA. He looked so abandoned by all, and so heroic, yet so feeble and so helpless; I did not think of turning round to see if any one was near me; or else perhaps—

EPICURUS. If you could have thought of looking round, you would no longer have been Ternissa. The Gods would have transformed you for it into some tree.

LEONTION. And Epicurus had been walking under it this day perhaps.

EPICURUS. With Leontion, the partner of his sentiments. But the walk would have been earlier or later than the present hour: since the middle of the day, like the middle of certain fruits, is good for nothing.

LEONTION. For dinner surely.

EPICURUS. Dinner is a less gratification to me than to many: I dine alone.

TERNISSA. Why?

EPICURUS. To avoid the noise, the heat, and the intermixture both of odours and of occupations. I can not bear the indecency of speaking with a mouth in which there is food. I careen my body (since it is always in want of repair) in as unobstructed a space as I can, and I lie down and sleep awhile when the work is over.

LEONTION. Epicurus! although it would be very interesting, no doubt, to hear more of what you do after dinner—(*aside to him*) now don't smile: I shall never forgive you if you say a single word —yet I would rather hear a little about the theatre, and whether you think at last that women should frequent it; for you have often said the contrary.

EPICURUS. I think they should visit it rarely; not because it excites their affections, but because it deadens them. To me nothing is so odious as to be at once among the rabble and among the heroes, and, while I am receiving into my heart the most exquisite of human sensations, to feel upon my shoulder the hand of some inattentive and insensible young officer.

LEONTION. O very bad indeed! horrible!

TERNISSA. You quite fire at the idea.

LEONTION. Not I: I don't care about it.

TERNISSA. Not about what is very bad indeed? quite horrible?

LEONTION. I seldom go thither.

EPICURUS. The theatre is delightful when we erect it in our own house or arbour, and when there is but one spectator.

LEONTION. You must lose the illusion in great part, if you only read the tragedy, which I fancy to be your meaning.

EPICURUS. I lose the less of it. Do not imagine that the illusion is, or can be, or ought to be, complete. If it were possible, no Phalaris or Perillus could devise a crueller torture. Here are two imitations: first, the poet's of the sufferer; secondly, the actor's of both: poetry is superinduced. No man in pain ever uttered the better part of the language used by Sophocles. We admit it, and willingly, and are at least as much illuded by it as by anything else we hear or see upon the stage. Poets and statuaries and painters give us an adorned imitation of the object, so skilfully treated that we receive it for a correct one. This is the only illusion they aim at: this is the perfection of their arts.

LEONTION. Do you derive no pleasure from the representation of a consummate actor?

EPICURUS. High pleasure; but liable to be overturned in an instant; pleasure at the mercy of any one who sits beside me. Rarely does it happen that an Athenian utters a syllable in the midst of it: but our city is open to the inhabitants of all the world, and all the world that is yet humanized a woman might walk across in sixty hours. There are even in Greece a few remaining still so barbarous, that I have heard them whisper in the midst of the finest scenes of our greatest poets.

LEONTION. Acord-fed Chaonians!

EPICURUS. I esteem all the wise; but I entertain no wish to imitate all of them in everything. What was convenient and befitting in one or other of them, might be inconvenient and unbefitting in me. Great names ought to bear us up and carry us through, but never to run away with us. Peculiarity and solitariness give an idea to weak minds of something grand, authoritative, and God-like. To be wise indeed and happy and self-possessed, we must often be alone: we must mix as little as we can with what is called society, and abstain rather more than seems desirable even from the better few.

TERNISSA. You have commanded us at all times to ask you anything we do not understand: why then use the phrase 'what is called society'? as if there could be a doubt whether we are in society when we converse with many.

EPICURUS. We may meet and converse with thousands: you and Leontion and myself could associate with few. *Society*, in the philosophical sense of the word, is almost the contrary of what it is in the common acceptation.

LEONTION. Now go on with your discourse.

EPICURUS. When we have once acquired that intelligence of which we have been in pursuit, we may relax our minds, and lay the produce of our chase at the feet of those we love.

LEONTION. Philosophers seem to imagine that they can be visible and invisiable at will; that they can be admired for the display of their tenets, and unobserved in the workings of their spleen. None of those whom I remember, or whose writings I have perused, was quite exempt from it. Among the least malicious is Theophrastus: could he find no other for so little malice but you?

EPICURUS. The origin of his dislike to me, was my opinion that perspicuity is the prime excellence of composition. He and Aristoteles and Plato talk diffusely of attending to harmony, and clap rhetorical rules before our mouths in order to produce it. Natural sequences and right subordination of thoughts, and that just proportion of numbers in the sentences which follows a strong conception, are the constituents of true harmony. You are satisfied with it and dwell upon it; which you would vainly hope to do when you are forced to turn back again to seize an idea or to comprehend a period. Let us believe that opposition, and even hard words, are (at least in the beginning) no certain proofs of hatred; although, by requiring defence, they soon produce heat and animosity in him who hath engaged in so unwise a warfare. On the other hand, praises are not always the unfailing signs of liberality or of justice. Many are extolled out of enmity to others, and perhaps would have been decried had those others not existed. Among the causes of my happiness, this is one: I never have been stimulated to hostility by any in the crowd that has assailed me. If in my youth I had been hurried into this weakness, I should have regretted it as lost time, lost pleasure, lost humanity.

LEONTION. We may expose what is violent or false in anyone; and chiefly in anyone who injures us or our friends.

EPICURUS. We may.

LEONTION. How then?

EPICURUS. By exhibiting in ourselves the contrary. Such vengeance is legitimate and complete. I found in my early days, among the celebrated philosophers of Greece, a love of domination, a propensity to imposture, a jealousy of renown, and a cold indifference to simple truth. None of these qualities lead to happiness; none of them stand within the precincts of Virtue. I asked myself, 'What is the most natural and the most universal of our desires': I found it was, *to be happy*. Wonderful I thought it, that the gratification of a desire which is at once the most universal and the most natural, should be the seldomest attained. I then conjectured the means; and I found that they vary, as vary the minds and capacities of men; that, however, the principal one lay in the avoidance of those very things which had hitherto been taken up as the instruments of enjoyment and content; such as military commands, political offices, clients, hazardous ventures in commerce, and extensive property in land.

LEONTION. And yet offices, both political and military, must be undertaken; and clients will throng about those who exercise them. Commerce too will dilate with Prosperity, and Frugality will square her farm by lopping off the angles of the next.

EPICURUS. True, Leontion! nor is there a probability that my opinions will pervade the heart of Avarice or Ambition: they will influence only the unoccupied. Philosophy hath led scarcely a single man away from commands or magistracies, until he hath first tried them. Weariness is the repose of the politician, and apathy his wisdom. He fancies that nations are contemplating the great man in his retirement, while what began in ignorance of himself is ending in forgetfulness on the part of others. This truth at last appears to him: he detests the ingratitude of mankind: he declares his resolution to carry the earth no longer on his shoulders: he is taken at his word: and the shock of it breaks his heart.

TERNISSA. Epicurus, I have been listening to you with even more pleasure than usual, for you often talk of love, and such other things as you can know nothing about: but now you have gone out of your way to defend an enemy, and to lead aside Leontion from her severity toward Theophrastus.

EPICURUS. Believe me, my lovely friends, he is no ordinary man who hath said one wise thing gracefully in the whole of his existence: now several such are recorded of him whom Leontion hath singled out from my assailants. His style is excellent.

LEONTION. The excellence of it hath been exaggerated by Aristoteles, to lower our opinion of Plato's.

EPICURUS. It may be: I can not prove it, and never heard it.

LEONTION. So blinded indeed is this great master of rhetoric—

EPICURUS. Pardon the rudeness of my interruption, dear Leontion. Do not designate so great a man by a title so contemptible. You are nearly as humiliating to his genius as those who call him the Stagyrite: and those are ignorant of the wrong they do him: many of them are his disciples and admirers, and call him by that name in quoting his authority. Philosophy, until he came among us, was like the habitations of the Troglodytes; vast indeed and wonderful, but without construction, without arrangement: he first gave it order and system. I do not rank him with Democritus, who has been to philosophers what Homer has been to poets, and who is equally great in imagination and in reflection: but no other has left behind him so many just remarks on such a variety of subjects.

Within one olympiad three men have departed from the world, who carried farther than any other three that ever dwelt upon it, reason, eloquence, and martial glory; Aristoteles, Demosthenes, and Alexander. Now tell me which of these qualities do you admire the most?

LEONTION. Reason.

EPICURUS. And rightly. Among the three characters, the vulgar and ignorant will prefer Alexander; the less vulgar and ignorant will prefer Demosthenes; and they who are removed to the greatest distance from ignorance and vulgarity, Aristoteles. Yet, although he has written on some occasions with as much purity and precision as we find in the *Orations* of Pericles, many things are expressed obscurely; which is by much the greatest fault in composition.

LEONTION. Surely you do not say that an obscurity is worse than a defect in grammar.

EPICURUS. I do say it: for we may discover a truth through such a defect, which we can not through an obscurity. It is better to find the object of our researches in ill condition than not to find it at all. We may purify the idea in our own bath, and adorn it with our own habiliments, if we can but find it, though among the slaves or clowns: whereas, if it is locked up from us in a dark chamber at the top of the house, we have only to walk down-stairs again, disappointed, tired, and out of humour.

But you were saying that something had blinded the philosopher.

LEONTION. His zeal and partiality. Not only did he prefer Theophrastus to everyone who taught at Athens; not only did he change his original name, for one of so high an import as to signify that he would elevate his language to the language of the Gods; but he fancied and insisted that the very sound of *Theophrastus* is sweet, of *Tyrtamus* harsh and inelegant.

EPICURUS. Your ear, Leontion, is the better arbitress of musical sounds, in which (I speak of words) hardly any two agree. But a box on the ear does not improve the organ; and I would advise you to leave inviolate and untouched all those peculiarities which rest on friendship. The jealous, if we suffered them in the least to move us, would deserve our commiseration rather than our resentment: but the best thing we can do with them is to make them the comedians of our privacy. Some have recently started up among us, who, when they have published to the world their systems of philosophy, or their axioms, or their paradoxes, and find nevertheless that others are preferred to them, persuade their friends and scholars that enormous and horrible injustice hath been done toward them. By degrees they cool, however, and become more reasonable: they resign the honour of invention, which always may be contested or ascertained, and invest themselves with what they style much greater, that of learning. What constitutes this glory, on which they plume themselves so joyously and gaudily? Nothing else than the reading of those volumes which we have taken the trouble to write. A multitude of authors, the greater part of them inferior in abilities to you who hear me, are the slow constructors of reputations which they would persuade us are the solidest and the highest. We teach them all they know: and they are as proud as if they had taught us. There are not indeed many of these parasitical plants at present, sucking us, and resting their leafy slenderness upon us: but whenever books become more numerous, a new species will arise from them, to which philosophers and historians and poets must give way, for, intercepting all above, it will approximate much nearer to the manners and intellects of the people. At last what is most Attic in Athens will be canvassed and discussed in their booth; and he who now exercised a sound and strong judgment of his own, will indifferently borrow theirs, and become so corrupted with it, as ever afterward to be gratified to his heart's content by the impudent laconism of their oracular decisions. These people are the natural enemies of greater: they can not sell their platters of offal while a richer feast is open to the public, and while lamps of profuser light announce the invitation. I would not augur the decay of philosophy and literature: it was retarded by the good example of our ancestors. The seven wise men, as they are called, lived amicably, and, where it was possible, in intercourse. Our seventy wiser (for we may reckon at least that number of those who proclaim themselves so) stand at the distance of a porcupine's shot, and, like that animal, scatter their shafts in every direction, with more profusion than force, and with more anger than aim.

Hither, to these banks of serpolet; to these strawberries, whose dying leaves breathe a most refreshing fragrance; to this ivy, from which Bacchus may have crowned himself; let us retire at the voice of Discord. Whom should we contend with? the less? it were inglorious: the greater? it were vain. Do we look for Truth? she is not the inhabitant of cities nor delights in clamour: she steals upon the calm and meditative as Diana upon Endymion, indulgent in her chastity, encouraging a modest, and requiting a faithful love.

LEONTION. How Ternissa sighs after Truth!

EPICURUS. If Truth appeared in daylight among mortals, she would surely resemble Ternissa. Those white and lucid cheeks, that youth which appears more youthful (for unless we are near her we think her yet a child), and that calm open forehead—

LEONTION. Malicious girl! she conceals it!

EPICURUS. Ingenious girl! the resemblance was, until now, imperfect. We must remove the veil ourselves; for Truth, whatever the poets may tell us, never comes without one, diaphanous or opaque.

If those who differ on speculative points, would walk together now and then in the country, they might find many objects that must unite them. The same bodily feeling is productive in some degree of the same mental one. Enjoyment from sun and air, from exercise and odours, brings hearts together that schools and council-chambers and popular assemblies have stood between for years.

I hope Theophrastus may live, to walk with us among these bushes when they are shadier, and to perceive that all questions, but those about the way to happiness, are illiberal or mechanical or infantine or idle.

TERNISSA. Are geometry and astronomy idle?

EPICURUS. Such idleness as theirs a wise man may indulge in, when he has found what he was seeking: and, as they abstract the mind from what would prey upon it, there are many to whom I would recommend them earlier, as their principal and most serious studies.

We will return to Theophrastus. He has one great merit in style; he is select and sparing in the use of metaphors: that man sees badly who sees everything double. He wants novelty and vigour in his remarks both on men and things: neither his subject nor his mind is elevated: here however let me observe, my fair disciples, that he and some others, of whom we speak in common conversation with little deference or reserve, may perhaps attract the notice and attention of the remotest nations in the remotest times. Suppose him to have his defects (all that you or anyone has ever supposed in him), yet how much greater is his intellect than the intellect of any among those who govern the world! If these appeared in the streets of Athens, you would run to look at them, and ask your friends whether they had seen them pass. If you can not show as much reverence to Theophrastus, the defect is yours. He may not be what his friends have fancied him: but how great must he be to have obtained the partiality of such friends! how few are greater! how many millions less!

LEONTION. A slender tree, with scarcely any heart or pith in it, ought at least to have some play of boughs and branches: he, poor man, is inert. The leaves just twinkle, and nothing more.

EPICURUS. He writes correctly and observantly. Even bad writers are blamed unjustly when they are blamed much. In comparison with many good and sensible men, they have evinced no slight degree of intelligence: yet we go frequently to those good and sensible men, and engage them to join us in our contempt and ridicule, of one who not only is wiser than they are, but who has made an effort to entertain or to instruct us, which they never did.

TERNISSA. This is inconsiderate and ungrateful.

EPICURUS. Truly and humanely have you spoken. Is it not remarkable that we are the fondest of acknowledging the least favourable and the least pleasurable of our partialities? Whether in hatred or love, men are disposed to bring their conversation very near the object, yet shrink at touching the fairer. In hatred their sensibility is less delicate, and the inference comes closer: in love they readily give an arm to a confidant, almost to the upper step of their treasury.

LEONTION. How unworthy of trust do you represent your fellow men! But you began by censuring *me*. In my Treatise I have only defended your tenets against Theophrastus.

EPICURUS. I am certain you have done it with spirit and eloquence, dear Leontion; and there are but two words in it I would wish you to erase.

LEONTION. Which are they?

EPICURUS. Theophrastus and Epicurus. If you love me, you will do nothing that may make you uneasy when you grow older; nothing that may allow my adversary to say, 'Leontion soon forgot her Epicurus.' My maxim is, never to defend my systems or paradoxes: if you undertake it, the Athenians will insist that I impelled you secretly, or that my philosophy and my friendship were ineffectual on you.

LEONTION. They shall never say that.

EPICURUS. I would entreat you to dismiss altogether things quite unworthy of your notice, if your observations could fall on any subject without embellishing it. You do not want these thorns to light your fire with.

LEONTION. Pardon the weak arm that would have defended what none can reach.

EPICURUS. I am not unmoved by the kindness of your intentions. Most people, and philosophers too, among the rest, when their own conduct or opinions are questioned, are admirably prompt and dexterous in the science of defence; but when another's are assailed, they parry with as ill a grace and faltering a hand as if they never had taken a lesson in it at home. Seldom will they see what they profess to look for; and, finding it, they pick up with it a thorn under the nail. They canter over the solid turf, and complain that there is no corn upon it: they canter over the corn, and curse the ridges and furrows. All schools of philosophy, and almost all authors, are rather to be frequented for exercise than for freight: but this exercise ought to acquire us health and strength, spirits and good-humour. There is none of them that does not supply some truth useful to every man, and some untruth equally so to the few that are able to wrestle with it. If there were no falsehood in the world, there would be no doubt; if there were no doubt, there would be no inquiry; if no inquiry, no wisdom, no knowledge, no genius; and Fancy herself would lie muffled up in her robe, inactive, pale, and bloated. I wish we could demonstrate the existence of utility in some other evils as easily as in this.

LEONTION. My remarks on the conduct and on the style of Theophrastus are not confined to him solely. I have taken at last a general view of our literature, and traced as far as I am able its deviation and decline. In ancient works we sometimes see the mark of the chisel; in modern we might almost suppose that no chisel was employed at all, and that everything was done by grinding and rubbing. There is an ordinariness, an indistinctness, a generalization, not even to be found in a flock of sheep. As most reduce what is sand into dust, the few that avoid it run to a contrary extreme, and would force us to believe that what is original must be unpolished and uncouth.

EPICURUS. There have been in all ages, and in all there will be, sharp and slender heads, made purposely and peculiarly for creeping into the crevices of our nature. While we contemplate the magnificence of the universe, and mensurate the fitness and adaptation of one part to another, the small philosopher hangs upon a hair or creeps within a wrinkle, and cries out shrilly from his elevation that we are blind and superficial. He discovers a wart, he prys into a pore, and he calls it knowledge of man. Poetry and criticism, and all the fine arts, have generated such living things, which not only will be co-existent with them, but will (I fear) survive them. Hence history takes alternately the form of reproval and of panegyric; and science in its pulverized state, in its shapeless and colourless atoms, assumes the name of metaphysics. We find no longer the rich succulence of Herodotus, no longer the strong filament of Thucydides, but thoughts fit only for the slave, and language for the rustic and the robber. These writings can never reach posterity, nor serve better authors near us: for who would receive as documents the perversions of venality and party? Alexander we know was intemperate, and Philip both intemperate and perfidious: we require not a volume of dissertation on the thread of history, to demonstrate that one or other left a tailor's bill unpaid, and the immorality of doing so; nor a supplement to ascertain on the best authorities which of the two it was. History should explain to us how nations rose and fell, what nurtured them in their growth, what sustained them in their maturity; not which orator ran swiftest through the crowd from the right hand to the left, which assassin was too strong for manacles, or which felon too opulent for crucifixion.

LEONTION. It is better, I own it, that such writers should amuse our idleness than excite our spleen.

TERNISSA. What is spleen?

EPICURUS. Do not ask her; she can not tell you. The spleen, Ternissa, is to the heart what Arimanes is to Oromazes.

TERNISSA. I am little the wiser yet. Does he ever use such hard words with you?

LEONTION. He means the evil Genius and the good Genius, in the theogony of the Persians; and would perhaps tell you, as he hath told me, that the heart in itself is free from evil, but very capable of receiving and too tenacious of holding it.

EPICURUS. In our moral system, the spleen hangs about the heart and renders it sad and sorrowful, unless we continually keep it in exercise by kind offices, or in its proper place by serious investigation and solitary questionings. Otherwise it is apt to adhere and to accumulate, until it deadens the principles of sound action, and obscures the sight.

TERNISSA. It must make us very ugly when we grow old.

LEONTION. In youth it makes us uglier, as not appertaining to it: a little more or less ugliness in decrepitude is hardly worth considering, there being quite enough of it from other quarters: I would stop it here, however.

TERNISSA. O what a thing is age!

LEONTION. Death without death's quiet. But we will converse upon it when we know it better.

EPICURUS. My beloved! we will converse upon it at the present hour, while the harshness of its features is indiscernible, not only to you, but even to me, who am much nearer to it. Disagreeable things, like disagreeable men, are never to be spoken of when they are present. Do we think, as we may do in such a morning as this, that the air awakens the leaves around us only to fade and perish? Do we, what is certain, think that every note of music we ever heard, every voice that ever breathed into our bosoms, and played upon its instrument the heart, only wafted us on a little nearer to the tomb? Let the idea not sadden but compose us. Let us yield to it, just as season yields to season, hour to hour, and with a bright serenity, such as Evening is invested with by the departing Sun.

What! are the dews falling, Ternissa? Let them not yet, my lovely one!

TERNISSA. You soothe me, but to afflict me after; you teach me, but to grieve.

EPICURUS. And what just now?

TERNISSA. You are many years in advance of us, and may leave us both behind.

EPICURUS. Let not the fault be yours.

LEONTION. How can it?

EPICURUS. The heart, O Leontion, reflects a fuller and a fairer image of us than the eye can.

TERNISSA. True, true, true!

LEONTION. Yes; the heart recomposes the dust within the sepulchre, and evokes it; the eye too, even when it has lost its brightness, loses not the power of reproducing the object it delighted in. It sees amid the shades of night, like the Gods.

EPICURUS. Sobs, too! Ah, these can only be suppressed by force.

LEONTION. By such! She will sob all day before she is corrected.

TERNISSA. Loose me. Leontion makes me blush.

LEONTION. I?

TERNISSA. It was you then, false Epicurus! Why are you not discreeter? I wonder at you. If I could find my way home alone, I would go directly.

LEONTION. Take breath first.

TERNISSA. O how spiteful! Go away, tormenting girl, you shall not kiss me.

LEONTION. Why? did *he?*

TERNISSA. No indeed; as you saw. What a question! Kiss me? for shame; he only held me in his arms a little. Do not make him worse than he is.

LEONTION. I wonder he ventured. These little barks are very dangerous. Did you find it an easy matter to keep on your feet, Epicurus?

EPICURUS. We may venture, in such parties of pleasure, on waves which the sun shines on; we may venture on affections which, if not quite tranquil, are genial to the soul. Age alone interposes its chain of icy mountains, and the star above their summit soon droops behind. Heroes and demigods have acknowledged it. Recite to me, O Ternissa, in proof of this, the scene of *Peleus and Thetis.*

TERNISSA. You do not believe in Goddesses; and I do not believe in age.

LEONTION. Whosoever fears neither, can repeat it.

EPICURUS. Draw, each of you, one of these blades of grass I am holding, and the drawer of the shortest shall repeat it.

TERNISSA. O Epicurus! have you been quite fair?

EPICURUS. Why doubt me?

TERNISSA. Mine, I see, is the shortest. I drew out from your closed hand the blade which stood above the other.

EPICURUS. Such grasses, like such men, may deceive us.

TERNISSA. Must I begin? You both nod. Leontion, you are poetical: I can only feel poetry. I can not read it tolerably; and I am sure to forget it if I trust to memory. Beside, there is something in the melody of this in particular which I sadly fear will render me inarticulate.

EPICURUS. I will relieve you from half your labour, by representing the character of *Peleus*.

TERNISSA. Let me down.

EPICURUS. The part will never permit it.

TERNISSA. I continue mute then. Be quiet. I can not speak a syllable unless I am on my feet again.

LEONTION. She will be mute a long while, like the Pythoness, and speak at last.

TERNISSA. Mischievous creature! as if you could possibly tell what is passing in my mind. But will not you, Epicurus, let me fall, since it must (I see) be repeated so? Shall I begin? for I am anxious to have it over.

LEONTION. Why don't you? we are as anxious as you are.

TERNISSA (*as Thetis*). 'O Peleus! O thou whom the Gods conferred on me for all my portion of happiness—and it was (I thought) too great—

EPICURUS (*as Peleus*). 'Goddess! to me, to thy Peleus, O how far more than Goddess! why then this sudden silence? why these tears? The last we shed were when the Fates divided us, saying the Earth was not thine, and the brother of Zeus, he the ruler of the waters, had called thee. Those that fall between the beloved at parting, are bitter, and ought to be: woe to him who wishes they were not! but those that flow again at the returning light of the blessed feet, should be refreshing and divine as morn.

TERNISSA (*as Thetis*). 'Support me, support me in thy arms, once more, once only. Lower not thy shoulder from my cheek, to gaze at those features that (in times past) so pleased thee. The sky is serene; the heavens frown not on us: do they then prepare for us fresh sorrow? Prepare for us! ah me! the word of Zeus is spoken: our Achilles is discovered: he is borne away in the black hollow ships of Aulis, and would have flown faster than they sail, to Troy.

'Surely there are those among the Gods, or among the Goddesses, who might have forewarned me: and they did not! Were there no omens, no auguries, no dreams, to shake thee from thy security? no priest to prophesy? And what pastures are more beautiful than Larissa's? what victims more stately? Could the soothsayers turn aside their eyes from these?

EPICURUS (*as Peleus*). 'Approach with me and touch the altar, O

217

my beloved! Doth not thy finger now impress the soft embers of incense? how often hath it burned, for him, for thee! And the lowings of the herds are audible for their leaders, from the sources of Apidanus and Enipeus to the sea-beach. They may yet prevail.

TERNISSA (*as Thetis*). 'Alas! alas! Priests can foretell but not avert the future; and all they can give us are vain promises and abiding fears.

EPICURUS (*as Peleus*). 'Despond not, my long-lost Thetis! Hath not a God led thee back to me? why not hope then he will restore our son? Which of them all hath such a boy offended?

TERNISSA (*as Thetis*). 'Uncertainties . . . worse than uncertainties . . . overthrow and overwhelm me.

EPICURUS (*as Peleus*). 'There is a comfort in the midst of every uncertainty, saving those which perplex the Gods and confound the godlike, Love's. Be comforted! not by my kisses, but by my words. Achilles may live till our old age. *Ours!* Had I forgotten thy divinity? forgotten it in thy beauty? Other mortals think their beloved partake of it then mostly when they are gazing on their charms; but thy tenderness is more than godlike; and never have I known, never have I wished to know, whether aught in our inferior nature may resemble it.

TERNISSA (*as Thetis*). 'A mortal so immutable! the Powers above are less.

EPICURUS (*as Peleus*). 'Time without grief would not have greatly changed me.

TERNISSA (*as Thetis*). 'There is a loveliness which youth may be without, and which the Gods want. To the voice of compassion not a shell in all the ocean is attuned; and no tear ever dropped upon Olympus. Thou lookest as fondly as ever, and more pensively. Have time and grief done this? and they alone? my Peleus! Tell me again, have no freshly fond anxieties—?

EPICURUS (*as Peleus*). 'Smile thus! O smile anew and forget thy sorrows. Ages shall fly over my tomb, while thou art flourishing in imperishable youth, the desire of Gods, the light of the depths of Ocean, the inspirer and sustainer of ever-flowing song.

TERNISSA (*as Thetis*). 'I receive thy words, I deposit them in my bosom, and bless them. Gods *may* desire me: I have loved Peleus. Our union had many obstacles; the envy of mortals, the jealousy of immortals, hostility and persecution from around, from below, and from above. When we were happy they parted us: and again they unite us in eternal grief.

EPICURUS (*as Peleus*). 'The wish of a divinity is powerfuller than the elements, and swifter than the light. Hence thou (what to me is impossible) mayst see the sweet Achilles every day, every hour.

TERNISSA (*as Thetis*). 'How few! alas how few! I see him in the dust, in agony, in death: I see his blood on the flints, his yellow hair flapping in its current, his hand unable to remove it from his eyes. I hear his voice; and it calls not upon me! Mothers are soon forgotten! It is weakness to love the weak! I could not save him! He would have left the caverns of Ocean, and the groves and meadows of Elysium, though resounding with the songs of love and heroism, for a field of battle.

EPICURUS (*as Peleus*). 'He may yet live many years. Troy hath been taken once already.

TERNISSA (*as Thetis*). 'He must perish; and at Troy; and now.

EPICURUS (*as Peleus*). 'The *now* of the Gods is more than life's duration: other Gods and other worlds are formed within it. If indeed he must perish at Troy, his ashes will lie softly on hers. Thus fall our beauteous son! thus rest Achilles!

TERNISSA (*as Thetis*). 'Twice nine years have scarcely yet passed over his head, since "O the youth of Æmathia! O the swift, the golden-haired Peleus!" were the only words sounded in the halls of Tethys. How many shells were broken for their hoarseness! how many reproofs were heard by the Tritons for interrupting the slumbers—of those who never slept! But they feigned sound sleep: and joy and kindness left the hearts of sisters. We loved too well for others to love *us*.

'Why do I remember the day? why do I remind thee of it?— my Achilles dies! it was the day that gave me my Achilles! Dearer he was to me than the light of heaven, before he ever saw it: and how much dearer now! when, bursting forth on earth like its first dayspring, all the loveliness of Nature stands back, and grows pale and faint before his. He is what thou wert when I first beheld thee. How can I bear again so great a deprivation?

EPICURUS (*as Peleus*). 'O, thou art fallen! thou art fallen through my embrace, when I thought on him more than on thee. Look up again; look, and forgive me. No: thy forgiveness I deserve not—but did I deserve thy love? Thy solitude, thy abasement, thy parental tears, and thy fall to the earth, are from me! Why doth aught of youth linger with me? why not come age and death? The monster of Calydon made (as thou knowest) his first and most violent rush against this arm; no longer fit for war, no longer a defence to the people. And is the day too come when it no longer can sustain my Thetis?

TERNISSA (*as Thetis*). 'Protend it not to the skies! invoke not, name not, any deity! I fear them all. Nay, lift me not thus above thy head, O Peleus! reproaching the Gods with such an awful look; with a look of beauty which they will not pity, with a look of defiance which they may not brook.

EPICURUS (*as Peleus*). 'Doth not my hand enclasp that slender foot, at which the waves of Ocean cease to be tumultuous, and the children of Æolus to disturb their peace? O, if in the celestial coolness of thy cheek, now resting on my head, there be not the breath and gift of immortality; O, if Zeus hath any thunder-bolt in reserve for me; let this, my beloved Thetis, be the hour!'

LEONTION. You have repeated it admirably; and you well deserve to be seated as you are, on the only bank of violets in this solitary place. Indeed you must want repose. Why do you continue to look sad? It is all over. Ah my silly comfort! That may be the reason.

TERNISSA. I shall be very angry with him for the way (if you saw it) in which he made me slip down: and I should have been so at the time, if it would not have hurt the representation.

Yes, indeed, you may expect it, sir!

EPICURUS. I shall always say, 'at any hour but this.'

TERNISSA. Talk reasonably; and return to your discourse on age. I wish you had a little more of its prudence and propriety.

EPICURUS. And what else?

TERNISSA. O! those are quite enough.

EPICURUS. There we agree. And no for obedience to your wishes. Peleus, you observe, makes no complaint that age is advancing on him: death itself is not unwelcome: for he had been happier than he could ever hope to be again. They who have long been wretched wish for death: they who have long been fortunate, may with equal reason: but it is wiser in each condition to await it than to desire it.

TERNISSA. I love to hear stories of heroic men, in whose bosoms there is left a place for tenderness.

Leontion said that even bad writers may amuse our idle hours: alas! even good one do not much amuse mine, unless they record an action of love or generosity. As for the graver, why can not they come among us and teach us, just as you do?

EPICURUS. Would you wish it?

TERNISSA. No, no; I do not want them: only I was imagining how pleasant it is to converse as we are doing, and how sorry I should be to pore over a book instead of it. Books always make me sigh, and think about other things. Why do you laugh, Leontion.

EPICURUS. She was mistaken in saying bad authors may amuse our idleness. Leontion knows not then how sweet and sacred idleness is.

LEONTION. To render it sweet and sacred, the heart must have a little garden of its own, with its umbrage and fountains and perennial flowers; a careless company! Sleep is called sacred as well as sweet by Homer: and idleness is but a step from it. The idleness of the wise and virtuous should be both, it being the repose and refreshment necessary for past exertions and for future: it punishes the bad man, it rewards the good: the deities enjoy it, and Epicurus praises it. I was indeed wrong in my remark: for we should never seek amusement in the foibles of another, never in coarse language, never in low thoughts. When the mind loses its feeling for elegance, it grows corrupt and grovelling, and seeks in the crowd what ought to be found at home.

EPICURUS. Aspasia believed so, and bequeathed to Leontion, with every other gift that Nature had bestowed upon her, the power of delivering her oracles from diviner lips.

LEONTION. Fie! Epicurus! It is well you hide my face for me with your hand. Now take it away: we can not walk in this manner.

EPICURUS. No word could ever fall from you without its weight; no breath from you ought to lose itself in the common air.

LEONTION. For shame! What would you have?

TERNISSA. He knows not what he would have nor what he would say. I must sit down again. I declare I scarcely understand a single syllable. Well, he is very good, to tease you no longer. Epicurus has an excellent heart; he would give pain to no one; least of all to you.

LEONTION. I have pained him by this foolish book, and he would only assure me that he does not for a moment bear me malice. Take the volume: take it, Epicurus! tear it in pieces.

EPICURUS. No, Leontion! I shall often look with pleasure on this trophy of brave humanity: let me kiss the hand that raises it!

TERNISSA. I am tired of sitting: I am quite stiff: when shall we walk homeward?

EPICURUS. Take my arm, Ternissa!

TERNISSA. O! I had forgotten that I proposed to myself a trip as far up as the pinasters, to look at the precipice of Oreithyia. Come along! come along! how alert does the sea-air make us! I seem to feel growing at my feet and shoulders the wings of Zethas or Calaïs.

EPICURUS. Leontion walks the nimblest to-day.

TERNISSA. To display her activity and strength, she runs before us. Sweet Leontion, how good she is! but she should have stayed for us: it would be in vain to try to overtake her.

No, Epicurus! Mind! take care! you are crushing these little oleanders—and now the strawberry plants—the whole heap—Not I, indeed. What would my mother say, if she knew it? And Leontion? she will certainly look back.

EPICURUS. The fairest of the Eudaimones never look back: such are the Hours and Love, Opportunity and Leontion.

TERNISSA. How could you dare to treat me in this manner? I did not say again I hated anything.

EPICURUS. Forgive me!

TERNISSA. Violent creature!

EPICURUS. If tenderness is violence. Forgive me; and say you love me.

TERNISSA. All at once? could you endure such boldness?

EPICURUS. Pronounce it! whisper it!

TERNISSA. Go, go. Would it be proper?

EPICURUS. Is that sweet voice asking its heart or me? let the worthier give the answer.

TERNISSA. O Epicurus! you are very, very dear to me—and are the last in the world that would ever tell you were called so.

1830–31

In July 1830 the renowned Crabb Robinson[1] arrived in Florence. He met Landor on the 16 August.

'*Landor is altogether different from what I had imagined him to be. He is a florid man with large eyes, an animated air, having the look of a country man and an officer. He talks decisively and freely, even cynically. He is said to be a man whom it is difficult to keep on good terms with, being apt to take offence. In our first conversation we went over much ground. He spoke of Southey in terms of the warmest affection, as one of the best of men—hostile as he is to his politics . . . Of poetry we also spoke. He incidentally said the greater part of Homer is trash—and so of Dante. This led me to explain Schlegel's theory of epic poetry, which Landor seemed both to comprehend and like. I also explained the first elements of Kantian philosophy. He was a good listener, and I tried him somewhat severely. . . . He was when we parted very civil indeed.*'

Four days later Crabb Robinson walked round in the afternoon to Landor's villa.

'*I found him at home with his family—his wife a beautiful woman still, though the mother of four very fine children. Landor seemed attached to his family and I left him with a favourable opinion of his heart and moral character. He told me something of his life. He was at Oxford. His father wished him to follow a profession and said: "If you will go to London and study the law, I will give you £350, perhaps £400. If not, you shall have £120 and no more, and I do not wish to see your face again." "I thanked my father for his offer, saying: I could take your £350 and deceive you by never studying, but I never did deceive you and never will. I will thank you for the £120." Landor then lived with great economy, refusing to dine out that he might not lose his independence. He was very young when he wrote* Gebir *both in English and Latin (twenty-one). He has probably now inherited his paternal estate.*

[1] Robinson, Henry Crabb (1775–1867) diarist, trained for the law, travelled extensively, met Goethe, studied at Jena University. Foreign editor of *The Times*.

*His establishment seems that of a man of fortune . . . His villa has a
hundred acres of land and lies most delightfully. It grows olives and
grapes. The house too, is large and handsome—just two miles from
the Porta San Gallo. We had a long and desultry chat* de omni
scribili et quibusdam aliis. *And on all, Landor talks like a man
of feeling rather than study. He seems to have of late even left off
reading. He has long seen very few people. He says he shall never
leave Italy, and does not wish to go north of Florence, yet he is not
fond of the Italian character. He speaks ill even of the liberals here,
with the exception of Niccolini*[1] *who, he says, is an honourable man.
They want courage to assert their opinions: they might without
exposing themselves to any resentment, demand a representative
government, but dare not. Not one of them, will subscribe a shilling
for the Parisians*[2] *. . . Landor spoke of Lord Byron as utterly
heartless: he loved no one. . . '*.[3]

The next day Landor called on Crabb Robinson to continue the
conversation, and among the topics they discussed was poetry. *'of
Dante, he [Landor] said there is only about a seventieth part good; of
Ariosto a sixth. "But little of Tasso," I interposed "Not a line worth
anything—yes, one line," which he repeated. Of Wordsworth, however,
he thought very nearly all good. . . .'* Eight days later Landor showed
Crabb Robinson his pictures.

*'Of pictures he speaks as dogmatically as of poets. He considers
Fra Bartolommeo as equal, or, at least second, to Raphael. Were he
a very rich man he would not give £1,000 for the "Transfiguration".
But he would give ten times that sum for the "St Mark". Michael
Angelo he thinks nothing of as a painter. Had he gone on in heaven
improving as he did on earth, he could not now equal "St Mark" by
Fra Bartolommeo. He also spoke slighteningly of Leonardo da Vinci.
Next to Raphael and Fra Bartolommeo, Perugino is his great
favourite. In expression, even Raphael did not equal him'.*[4]

Taking a walk with Landor on *17 September, Crabb Robinson
records:*

---

[1] Niccolini was a constant visitor to Crabb Robinson.
[2] The revolution of 1830 was then in progress.
[3] Robinson, *Books and Their Writers*, vol. i, p. 380.
[4] Robinson, *Books and Their Writers*, vol. i, p. 381.

'*There is but one thing in Landor that disturbs me—his vehement abuse of almost everyone, Englishmen in particular. Yet he says he is glad to see anyone who calls on him who knew his friends in England. Nothing can be more kind than his conduct to me. Yet he talks of hating all society. I told him that he reminded me of what I used to say—that I hated all Frenchwomen except all I had ever seen. . .*[1]

In 1831 Landor published Gebir, Count Julian, and Other Poems. *This volume contained revised versions of* Gebir *and* Count Julian, *which had been published in 1812. The poems included were* Ines de Castro, Ines de Castro at Coimbra, Ipolito di Este, *a re-written version of a tragedy* Ferrante and Giulio, *which Landor had previously burnt, and* Gunlang, *which had been included in his* Simonidea *(1806). The volume also included thirty-one poems to Ianthé, thirty-six miscellaneous poems and some poems on the dead. It was published on commission by Edward Moxon, whose imprint was then new to the publishing trade. Hare told Robinson that after nine months only forty copies had been sold, a sad reflection considering what was included. Landor appeared unconcerned, for he was busying himself with gardening and writing* High and Low Life in Italy. *He completed it that year and sent it to Crabb Robinson, hoping he would be able to find a publisher. Robinson consulted Julius Hare, only to hear the usual sad story about Landor's books—that they did not sell. Robinson tried Baldwin,*[2] *who declined it, and then John Murray, who kept it for three months without reaching a decision.*[3] *When Landor came to England, Robinson gave it back to him and, finally, Leigh Hunt was prevailed upon to publish it in his magazine the* Monthly Repository, *where it appeared during 1837–8.*

[1] *Idem*, p. 385.
[2] Baldwin, Cradock & Joy was the full name of the firm.
[3] Super, *Landor*, p. 225.

From *Gebir, Count Julian, and Other Poems*
1831

When Helen first saw wrinkles in her face
('Twas when some fifty long had settled there
And intermarried and brancht off awide)
She threw herself upon her couch and wept:
On this side hung her head, and over that
Listlessly she let fall the faithless brass
That made the men as faithless.

                      But when you
Found them, or fancied them, and would not hear
That they were only vestiges of smiles,
Or the impression of some amorous hair
Astray from cloistered curls and roseate band,
Which had been lying there all night perhaps
Upon a skin so soft, 'No, no,' you said,
'Sure, they are coming, yes, are come, are here:
Well, and what matters it, while thou art too!'

          *   *   *

I held her hand, the pledge of bliss,
    Her hand that trembled and withdrew;
She bent her head before my kiss . . .
    My heart was sure that hers was true.

          *   *   *

So late removed from him she swore,
    With clasping arms and vows and tears,
In life and death she would adore,
    While memory, fondness, bliss, endears.
Can she forswear? can she forget?
Strike, mighty Love! strike, Vengeance! soft!
Conscience must come and bring Regret . . .
    These let her feel! nor these too oft!

IPPOLITO DI ESTE [FIRST PART][1]
Scene Ferara, 1505-6

IPPOLITO. Now all the people follow the procession
Here may I walk alone, and let my spirits
Enjoy the coolness of these quiet ailes.
Surely no air is stirring; every step
Tires me; the columns shake, the cieling fleets,
The floor beneath me slopes, the altar rises.
Stay! . . . here she stept . . . what grace! what harmony!
It seemed that every accent, every note
Of all the choral music, breathed from her:
From her celestial airiness of form
I could have fancied purer light descended.
Between the pillars, close and wearying,
I watcht her as she went: I had rusht on . . .
It was too late; yet, when I stopt, I thought
I stopt full soon: I cried, *is she not there?*
She had been: I had seen her shadow burst
The sunbeam as she parted: a strange sound,
A sound that stupefied and not aroused me,
Filled all my senses; such was never felt
Save when the sword-girt Angel struck the gate,
And Paradise wail'd loud and closed for ever.
She should return; the hour is past away.
How can I bear to see her (yet I will)
Springing, she fondly thinks, to meet the man
I most abhorr, my father's base-born son,
Ferrante!
    ROSALBA (*entering*). What! I called him! in my haste
To languish at his beauty, to weigh down
His eyelids with my lips for gazing on me:
Surely I spoke the name, and knew it not
Until it bounded back and smote me so!
    IPPOLITO. Curses upon them both!
                Advancing toward her. Welcome, sweet lady!

[1] Ferrante and Guilio were brothers, by the father's side, to the Duke Alfonso and the Cardinal Ippolito di Este. The cardinal deprived Ferrante of his eyes for loving the same object as his Eminence, and because she had praised the beauty of them.—W. S. L.

ROSALBA. Lord Cardinal! you here! and unattended!

IPPOLITO. We wait the happy lover! do we not?

ROSALBA. Ferrante then betrayed the secret to you!
And are you come to honour with your presence . . .

IPPOLITO. Has the Duke signed the contract?

ROSALBA.   For what bride?
Ferrante writes *Ferrante* plain enough;
And I do think, altho I once or twice
Have written it instead of mine, at last
I am grown steddier, and could write *Rosalba*.

IPPOLITO. Sport not with one your charms have cast too low.

ROSALBA. Sport not with one your hand would raise too high.

IPPOLITO. Again that taunt! the time may come, Rosalba,
When I could sanctify the blissful state
I have aspired to.

ROSALBA.   Am not I mere ice?
Shew not I girlish frowardness, the fears
Of infancy, the scruples of old age?
Have not you said so? and said more . . . you hate them?
How could you bear me, or what wish from me?

IPPOLITO. That which another will not long retain.

ROSALBA. You know him little, and me less.

IPPOLITO.   I know
Inconstancy in him.

ROSALBA.   And what in me?

IPPOLITO. Intolerance for his betters.

ROSALBA.   Ignorance,
But not intolerance of them, is my fault.

IPPOLITO. No?

ROSALBA.   Call it thus, and cast it on the rest.

IPPOLITO. Some are there whose close vision sees but one
In the whole world, and would not see another
For the whole world, were that one out of it.

ROSALBA. Are there some such? O may they be my friends!
O how, before I know them, I do love them!

IPPOLITO. After no strife, no censure, no complaint,
Have not your tears been seen, when you have left him,
Thro tediousness, distaste, dislike, and grief,
(Ingenuous minds must feel it, and may own it)

228

That love, so rashly promist, would retire,
Hating exaction, circumvention, bonds?

ROSALBA. Such grief is yet unknown to me; I know
All tears are not for sorrow: many swell
In the warm depths of gratitude and bliss;
But precious over all are those that hang
And tremble at the tale of generous deeds.
These he relates when he might talk as you do
Of passion: but he sees my heart, he finds
What fragrance most refreshes it.
                                        How high,
O Heaven! must that man be, who loves and who
Would stil raise others higher than himself
To interest his beloved!
                              All my soul
Is but one drop from his, and into his
Falls, as Earth's dew falls into Earth again.

IPPOLITO. Yet would it not be wise to trust a friend
Able to counsel in extremes and straits?

ROSALBA. Is it not wise in darkness and in storm
To trust the wave that lashes us and pray
Its guidance on the rocks whereto it tends?
I have my guide, Lord Cardinal! he alone
Is ship and pilot to me, sea and star:
Counsel from others, knowing him, would be
Like worship of false gods; in me no less
Than profanation and apostasy.

IPPOLITO. We may retire; he comes not here to day.

ROSALBA. Then will I not retire, but lay my head
Upon the feet of any pitying saint
Until he comes, altho it be tomorrow?

IPPOLITO. Tomorrow he may fail: the sovran will
By rescript has detained and must delay him.

ROSALBA. Lead, lead me to Ferrante.

IPPOLITO.   Were I worthy.

ROSALBA. Proud cruel man! that bitter sneer bodes ill.
May not I see him?

IPPOLITO.   He may not see you.

ROSALBA. O let him! well my memory can supply

His beauteous image. I can live on love
Saturates, like bees with honey, long drear days.
He must see me, or cannot rest: I can.

[SECOND PART]
IPPOLITO, FERRANTE, *and* GIULIO, *in prison.*

IPPOLITO. Reasons of state, I fear, have dictated
This something like severity; God grant
Here be no heresy: do both avow it,
Staring in silence at discovery?
   GUILIO. No order forced me hither; I am come
To share my brother's fate, whate'er it be,
And mitigate his sufferings.
   IPPOLITO.   May they cease!
   GIULIO. Those words would have dissolved them into air,
Spoken but twenty furlongs from these bars.
   IPPOLITO. I would do much to serve you; but my faith
And my allegiance have two other lords,
The duke my brother, and the pope my God.
Ferrante then says nothing?
   FERRANTE.   He well knows
Thy hatred and its cause.
   IPPOLITO.   Why should I hate you,
My father's son, they say?
   FERRANTE.   *They say!* His blood
Runs in these veins, pure; for pure blood was hers
Who loved the youthful lover, and who died
When falser vows estranged the matchless prince.
   IPPOLITO. He saw his error.
   FERRANTE.   All men do when age
Bends down their heads, or gold shines in their way.
   IPPOLITO. Altho I would have helpt you in distress,
And just removed you from the court awhile,
You called me tyrant.
   FERRANTE.   Called thee tyrant? I?
By heaven! in tyrant there is something great
That never was in thee. I would be killed
Rather by any monster of the wild

Than choaked by weeds and quicksands, rather crusht
By maddest rage than clay-cold apathy.
Those who act well the tyrant, neither seek
Nor shun the name; and yet I wonder not
That thou repeatest it, and wishest me;
It sounds like power, like policy, like courage,
And none that calls thee tyrant can despise thee.
Go, issue orders for imprisonment,
Warrants for death: the gibbet and the wheel,
Lo! the grand boundaries of thy dominion!
O what a mighty office for a minister!
(And such Alfonso's brother calls himself),
To be the scribe of hawkers! Man of genius!
The lanes and allies echo with thy works.

GIULIO. Ah! do not urge him; he may ruin you;
He may pursue you to the grave.

FERRANTE.   He dares not:
Look at his collar! see the saint he wears!
The amber saint may ask too much for that.

IPPOLITO. Atheist! thy scoffs encourage every crime,
And strip thee, like a pestilence, of friends:
Theirs is the guilt to march against the law,
They mount the scaffold, and the blow is thine.

FERRANTE. How venom burnishes his adder's crest!
How eloquent on scaffolds and on laws!
If such a noisome weed as falsehood is
Give frothy vigour to a worm like thee,
Crawl, eat, drink, sleep upon it, and farewell.

IPPOLITO (*to Giulio*). Take you the sentence, and God be with
    both!   *Goes.*

GIULIO. What sentence have we here?

FERRANTE.   Unseal and read it.

GIULIO (*reading*). Of sight! of sight! of sight!

FERRANTE.   Would you escape,
My gentle Giulio? Run not thus around
The wide light chamber, press not thus your brow
Against the walls, with your two palms above.
Seek you the door then? you are uncondemned
To lose the sight of one who is the bloom

And breath of life to you: the bolts are drawn
On me alone. You carry in your breast
Most carefully our brother's precious gift:
Well, take it anywhere, but do not hope
Too much from any one. Time softens rocks,
And hardens men!

  GIULIO.   Pray then our God for help.

  FERRANTE. O my true brother, Giulio, why thus hang
Around my neck and pour forth prayers for me!
Where there are priests and kinsmen such as ours,
God hears not, nor is heard. I am prepared
For death.

  GIULIO. Ah! worse than death may come upon you,
Unless Heaven interpose.

  FERRANTE.   I know the worst,
And bear one comfort in my breast that fire
And steel can ne'er force from it: she I love
Will not be his, but die as she hath lived.
Doubt you? that thus you shake the head, and sigh.

  GIULIO. Far other doubt was mine: even this shall cease.

  FERRANTE. Speak it.

  GIULIO.   I must: God pardon me!

  FERRANTE.   Speak on.

  GIULIO. Have we not dwelt in friendship from our birth,
Told the same courtier the same tale of joy,
And pointed where life's earliest thorn had pierced
Amid the sports of boyhood, ere the heart
Hath aught of bitter or unsound within?

  FERRANTE. We have indeed.

  GIULIO.   Has my advice been ill?

  FERRANTE. Too often ill-observed, but always good.

  GIULIO. Brother, my words are not what better men
Would speak to you; and yet my love, I think,
Must be more warm than theirs can ever be . . .

  FERRANTE. Brother's, friend's, father's, when was it like yours!

  GIULIO. Which of them ever said what I shall say!

  FERRANTE. Speak; my desires are kindled, my fears quencht.

  GIULIO. Do not delay to die, lest crueller
Than common death befall you.

FERRANTE.   Then the wheel
Is ordered in that schedule! Must she too
Have her chaste limbs laid bare? Here lies the rack;
Here she would suffer ere it touch the skin . . .
No, I will break it with the thread of life
Ere the sound reach her. Talk no more of Heaven,
Of Providence, of Justice . . . Look on her!
Why should she suffer? what hath she from Heaven
Of comfort, or protection?
    GIULIO.   Talk not so!
Pity comes down when Hope hath flown away.
    FERRANTE. Illusion!
    GIULIO.   If it were, which it is not,
Why break with vehement words such sweet illusion?
For were there nought above but empty air,
Nought but the clear blue sky where birds delight,
Soaring o'er myriads worlds of living dust
That roll in columns round the noontide ray,
Your heart would faint amid such solitude,
Would shrink in such vacuity: that heart
(Ferrante! can you hide its wants from me?)
Rises and looks around and calls aloud
For some kind Being, some consoling bosom,
Whereon to place its sorrows, and to rest.
    FERRANTE. Oh! that was here . . . I cannot look beyond.
    GIULIO. Hark! hear you not the people? to the window!
They shout and clap their hands when they first meet you
After short absence; what shall they now do?
Up! seize the moment; shew yourself.
    FERRANTE.   Stay, Giulio!
Draw me not thither! speak not of my wrongs . . .
I would await but not arouse their vengeance,
And would deserve but court not their applause.
Little of good shall good men hope from them,
Nothing shall wiser.
                Aside. O were he away!
But if I fail, he must die too, being here.
    GIULIO. Let me call out: they are below the grate.
They would deliver you: try this one chance.

Obdurate! would you hold me down! They're gone!

FERRANTE. Giulio! for shame! weep not, or here I stay
And let vile hands deform me.

GIULIO. They shall never.

FERRANTE. What smoke arises? Are there torches under?
Surely the crowd has passed . . . 'tis from the stairs.

GIULIO. Anticipate the blow.

FERRANTE. One more must grieve!

Landor proposed to visit England. It had been almost exactly eighteen years since he had left his country, and he looked forward to meeting his friends. He returned to this country in an auspicious year—the year of the Reform Bill. He was to observe many changes. He first went to Brighton, where he stayed two days with 'Ianthé' and her family. He met his old friend Lord Wenlock; then his closest friend Joseph Ablett invited him to Cambridge. On returning to London he went to a soirée given by that leftish Whig, the Duke of Sussex, and he was also to pay visits to Enfield to see Charles Lamb, and to Highgate to see Coleridge. Landor was most anxious to meet Wordsworth, so he and Ablett decided to take the steamer from Liverpool to Whitehaven, where they learnt the poet was on a visit to his son at Moreby. There they met. Certainly Wordsworth was taken by Landor, in particular by his infectious laugh, and considered him to be 'warm-hearted'. Landor also took the opportunity of seeing Southey and commented:

> Alas! that snows are shed
> Upon thy Laurell'd head,
> Hunted by many cares and many wrongs!
> Malignity lets none
> Reach safe the Delphic throne;
> A hundred kennel curs bark down Fame's
> hundred tongues.

On his return south Landor visited his cousin Walter Savage at Rugeley. They discussed his disastrous estate at Llanthony. Landor declared that he did not even wish to see the place, and that the best thing to be done was to pull it down and sell any building materials there were. As to the rest of his family, he saw his brother Robert at Evesham on his way to Bath, a city that was to become dear to him. Returning, eventually, to London, he stayed in Upper Brook Street, where one of his first visits was to see Flaxman's drawings for which he had unbounded admiration. On 28 September he accompanied Crabb Robinson to Enfield to meet Charles and Mary Lamb.

'We had scarcely an hour to chat with them, but it was enough to make both Landor and Worsley express themselves afterwards

*delighted with the person of Mary Lamb and pleased with the
conversation of Lamb, though I thought Lamb by no means at his
ease, Miss Lamb quite silent—nothing in the conversation
recollectable.'*[1]

*Once, and once only, have I seen thy face,
Elia! once only has thy tripping tongue
Run o'er my heart, yet never has been left
Impression on it stronger or more sweet
Cordial old man! what youth was in thy years,
What wisdom in thy levity, what soul
In every utterance of that purest breast!
Of all that ever wore man's form, 'tis thee
I first would spring to at the gate of heaven.*

The following day Landor and Crabb Robinson visited Coleridge.

*'We sat not much more than an hour with him; he was horribly bent
and looked seventy years of age—nor did he talk with his usual fire
but quite in his usual style. A great part of his conversation was a
repetition of what I had heard him say before—an abuse of the
Ministry for taking away his pension, speaking of having devoted
himself not to writing for the people, whom the public could reward,
but for the nation, of which the King is the representative. The stay
was too short to allow of our entering upon literary matters. He
spoke only of Oriental poetry with contempt, and he showed his
memory by alluding to Landor's juvenile poems. . . . Landor and he
seemed to like each other. Landor spoke in his dashing way, which
Coleridge could understand and he concurred with him'.*[2]

*Landor left England for Fiesole in October, accompanied by Julius
Hare and Thomas Worsley (later to become Master of Downing), by
way of Belgium, Bonn and Frankfürt, where he lifted his hat in passing
the house where Goethe was born.*[3] *By 30 November he was back home.*

*On his arrival Landor found his children were out of hand and he
came to the decision it was time they had a governess. A German lady,
the Countess von Schaffgotsch, was selected. By the sound of her*

[1] Robinson, *Books and Their Writers*, ed. Morley, vol. i, p. 410.
[2] Robinson, *Books and Their Writers*, ed. Morley, vol. i, pp. 413–14.
[3] Elwin, *Landor*, p. 250.

Dickensian name it would seem she instilled some discipline into the unruly offspring. While Landor had been away he was delighted to learn that his enemy, Lord Burghersh, the British Minister in Florence, had been succeeded by George Hamilton Seymour,[1] and with him and his wife Landor became very friendly.

Among his principal visitors that year was Ralph Waldo Emerson. Emerson was to write of Landor:

'*Mr Landor carries to its height the love of freak which the English delight to indulge, as if to signalize their commanding freedom. He has a wonderful brain, despotic, violent and inexhaustible, meant for a soldier, by what chance converted to letters, in which there is not a style, nor a tint not known to him, yet with an English appetite for action and heroes. The thing done avails and not what is said about it. An original sentence, a step forward, is worth more than all the censures. Landor is strangely undervalued in England; usually ignored, and sometimes savagely attacked in the Reviews. The criticism may be right or wrong, and is quickly forgotten; but year after year the scholar must still go back to Landor for a multitude of elegant sentences—for wisdom, wit, and indignation that are unforgettable*'.[2]

As well as Emerson, Landor met the young Richard Monkton-Milnes; they both took to one another. The future Lord Houghton was to write of Landor in his Monographs: Personal and Social (*1873*)*. Landor introduced him to Charles Brown and persuaded him to present Brown with material for his life of Keats.*

In the autumn of this year he received Captain Basil Hall, a writer of travel books, as well as Bulwer-Lytton and Augustus William Hare, who was a close friend and the uncle of the diarist Augustus. This was the last time Landor saw him, for he died the following year. Among other friends there was the historical novelist G. P. R. James.[3] '*You*

---

[1] Seymour, George Hamilton (1797–1880), diplomat; ed. Eton and Merton College, Oxford, Private Secretary to Lord Castlereagh in 1822 and appointed Minister resident at Florence 1830.

[2] Elwin, *Landor*, p. 263.

[3] James's work is mainly forgotten today. He was the grandson of a Doctor James whose fever powders had been taken by Oliver Goldsmith, Horace Walpole and the Young Pretender among others. His father, too, was a doctor, and one of his aunts, an upholder of the French Revolution, was proposed to by Robespierre. James's knowledge of history was considerable, as can be deduced from his novels.

cannot overvalue James', Landor wrote to Mary Boyle. 'There is not on God's earth (I like this expression, vulgar or not) any better creature of his hand'.[1]

On 8 April 1834 Landor wrote to Lady Blessington:

'*For some time I have been composing* Citation and Examination of Wil. Shakespeare, Euseby Treen, Joseph Carneby, and Silas Gough, *before the Worshipful Sir Thomas Lacy, Knight, touching deer-stalking, on the 19th day of September in the year of grace 1582, now first published from the original papers. . . . This is full of fun, I know not whether of wit. It is the only thing I ever wrote that is likely to sell. . . .*'[2]

She sold it for him to Saunders & Otley.

The examination of Shakespeare is overlong; but it is one of the most amusing and sprightliest of his works. It is especially concerned with Shakespeare's trial at Charlecote for deer-stalking. Sir Thomas Lacy is the examining magistrate and the account of the examination is supposedly written by a clerk, Ephraim Barnett. Shakespeare's accusers are two of Sir Thomas's keepers, and a witness is a malicious chaplain, Silas Gough. Sir Thomas is a kindly, witty magistrate who is amusingly concerned over the matter, which is only terminated by Shakespeare's escape from the great hall at Charlecote before anyone can seize him.

[1] Elwin, *Landor*, p. 268.
[2] Forster, *Landor*, vol. ii, p. 272.

From *Citation of William Shakespeare*
1834

THE MAID'S LAMENT

[*Found in Willy's pockets and read out in the Justice-room*]

I loved him not; and yet now he is gone
    I feel I am alone.
I check'd him while he spoke; yet could he speak,
    Alas, I would not check.
For reasons not to love him once I sought,
    And wearied all my thought
To vex myself and him: I now would give
    My love, could he but live
Who lately lived for me, and when he found
    'Twas vain, in holy ground
He hid his face amid the shades of death.
    I waste for him my breath
Who wasted his for me: but mine returns,
    And this lorn bosum burns
With stifling heat, heaving it up in sleep,
    And waking me to weep
Tears that had melted his soft heart: for years
    Wept he as bitter tears.
'Merciful God!' such was his latest prayer,
    'These may she never spare!'
Quick in his breath, his breast more cold,
    Than daisies in the mould,
Where children spell athwart the dundig and gate,
    His name and life's brief date,
Pray for him, gentle souls, who'er you be,
    And, O, pray too for me.

1835

Further disagreeable differences now enveloped Landor. What affection there had been between him and his wife had faded. This distressing state of marital affairs had been witnessed by his friend Charles Armitage Brown.[1] It would appear that Mrs Landor had publicly denounced her husband in the presence of his children. Brown recalls that Landor behaved with perfect calmness and courtesy, but the unpleasant incident drove him away. Before leaving Italy he wrote to Southey:

> 'It was not willingly that I left Tuscany and my children. There was but one spot upon earth on which I had fixed my heart, and four objects on which my affection rested. That they might not hear every day such language as no decent person should even hear once, nor despise both parents, I left the light of my existence'.[2]

Landor was sixty and his wife forty-two when the break took place. Mrs Landor was (and had been for some years) suffering from such nervous tension as to make her at times hysterical. On occasion she became physically ill and in need of a doctor.[3] This may well have been the case; somehow one cannot imagine that Landor was particularly attentive to his wife's physical desires. On the face of all the evidence, he loved only two women all his life—Ianthé (Jane Swift) and Rose Aylmer. He was devoted to Eliza Lynn Linton and enormously enjoyed the company of Lady Blessington. But apart from his youthful escapades, and the fact that he was attractive to women, Landor probably had little desire in his later life for affaires. When someone once

[1] Brown, Charles Armitage (1786–1842), son of a Scottish stock-broker who as a young man went to St Petersburg to act as agent for his elder brother's business. He returned to England in 1810 when the business failed, and for some time struggled on the verge of destitution until another of his brothers came to the rescue. From this brother he derived a sufficient income to live comfortably and pursue a taste for letters. He wrote a libretto for an opera, which was sufficiently successful to be produced at Drury Lane. In 1817 he met Keats and he went to Italy in 1822. He published a work on the personal interpretation of Shakespeare's sonnets (1838) and gave all his papers and notes on Keats to Lord Houghton. He met Landor in Florence and the two became close friends.

[2] Forster, *Landor*, vol. ii, p. 310.

[3] Super, *Landor*, p. 255.

described his wife as charming and agreeable, Landor replied: 'Why, so she is—to everyone but me!'[1]

Landor made over to his wife £400 a year and, to his son his house and farms at Fiesole. His own income was reduced to no more than £200 per annum, but he was able to double it through the monies invested in a reserve fund.

He arrived in England in September and stayed with his friend Joseph Ablett at Llanbedr for a while, returning to him in the spring of 1836. Ablett encouraged Landor to edit a symposium of prose and verse entitled Literary Hours, which was published privately in 1837 by various friends. He also brought with him his latest manuscript, Pericles and Aspasia, and he asked G. P. R. James to act as his literary agent; this work was eventually published in two volumes by Saunders & Otley after Landor had agreed to lengthen it.

Meanwhile friends endeavoured to persuade him to return to his family, especially as Mrs Landor was unable to exercise proper control over his children. Later in 1837 Crabb Robinson was to write to him, '. . . that your presence might have the happiest effect on the character of your children.' But it was all to no avail.

---

[1] Dickens, 'Landor's Life', *All the Year Round*, 24 July 1869, p. 185.

To Mary Lamb on the Death of her Brother
1835

[*Included in a letter to Lady Blessington, and in a letter to Southey—* Ed.]

Comfort thee, O thou mourner, yet awhile!
    Again shall Elia's smile
Refresh thy heart, where heart can ache no more.
    What is it we deplore?
He leaves behind him, freed from griefs and years,
    Far worthier things than tears.
The love of friends without a single foe:
    Unequall'd lot below!
His gentle soul, his genius, these are thine;
    For these dost thou repine?
He may have left the lowly walks of men;
    Left them he has; what then?
Are not his footsteps followed by the eyes
    Of all the good and wise?
Tho' the warm day is over, yet they seek
    Upon the lofty peak.
Of his pure mind the roseate light that glows
    O'er death's perennial snows,
Behold him! from the region of the blest
    He speaks: he bids thee rest.

1836

On 1 February 1836 Landor set out for Clifton. He travelled incognito. According to John Sterling, who was in the coach, however, Landor 'made himself known by the strange paradoxical style of conversation in which he indulged'. 'Why', said Sterling to Landor, 'this sounds amazingly like an Imaginary Conversation'. Landor was startled by this remark, 'and covered his retreat'. Subsequently, Sterling met Landor at one of Julius Hare's breakfasts and dispute on the Evangelicals became fairly violent; they were censured in particular by a Frenchman present, until the conversation turned to Lamb. Landor had now finished The Letters of a Conservative *which were published in March.*

It was in 1836 that Landor met his future biographer John Forster. Forster at that time was in his early twenties and enjoyed writing literary and dramatic criticism for The Examiner. *He was 'a serious, rather pedantic young man, whose face of character and remarkable political abilities were destined so to impose themselves on more than talented friend, that he became in time a sort of organiser of literary genius and a dominant factor in the lives of Dickens, Bulwer and Ainsworth'.[1] Landor was to be added to Forster's circle; he was naturally flattered by the young man's attention. Forster described Landor at that time:*

'He was not above the middle stature, but had a stout, stalwart presence, walked without a stoop, and in his general aspect, particularly the set and carriage of his head, was decidedly of what is called distinguished bearing. His hair was already silvered gray, and had retired far upward from his forehead, which, wide and full but retreating, could never in the earlier time have been to such advantage. What at first was noticeable, however, in the broad white massive head, were the full yet strangely-lifted eyebrows. . . In the large gray eyes there was a depth of composed expression that even startled by its contrast to the eager restlessness looking out from the surface of them; and in the same variety and quickness of transition the mouth was extremely striking. The lips that seemed compressed with malleable will would in a moment relax to a softness more than

---

[1] Sadleir, *Blessington D'Orsay*, p. 237.

feminine; and a sweeter smile it was impossible to conceive. . . It was altogether a face on which power was visibly impressed, but without the resolution and purpose that generally accompany it'.

In June Landor heard from Florence to the effect that his wife had dismissed the then tutor to his children, Mr MacCarthy, and he complained to his brother Henry that his family had always disregarded his authority:

. . . '*I never can in future live under the same roof with my wife. She knows that it was out of consideration for my children, Julia in particular, that I endured her conduct so long, and might (she thought) do so longer. However, it suited her purpose to render my home intolerable, and she fancied my extreme love of the children would bring me back again at any convenient season!*'[1]

In July, Landor decided to go to Heidelburg and asked Crabb Robinson to accompany him, but Robinson decided otherwise. He was not prepared to risk Landor's capricious moods, so Landor went on his own where he enjoyed the stay in that city, being well-pleased with the civilities he received. But he had heard nothing from his family. Lady Blessington, however, published an Imaginary Conversation, that between 'Colonel Walker and the Hindu woman Hattaji,' and Forster published 'Eldon and Encombe' in the Examiner. Landor meanwhile revised the 'conversation' between Andrew Marvel and Bishop Parker. Anna Maria Dashwood, daughter of Dean Shipley and a cousin of the Hare's, rebuked him for writing 'Eldon and Encombe,' reminding him that the Earl was now eighty years old. Landor remained untouched and replied: 'the devil is older'.

His published output that year was tremendous. Apart from Pericles and Aspasia *and* Letter from a Conservative, A Satire on Satirists, Alabiadas the Young Man *appeared in* Blackwoods, *while a satire on Irish Catholic priests—called* Terry Hogan—*was accepted by a firm called J. Wertheimer & Co.*

Forster was of the company when he joined Landor and Wordsworth at the theatre to see Talfourd's Ion. Crabb Robinson was also present.

'We all of us met afterwards at Talfourd's house; but of the talk that might have made such a night memorable I regret that I

---

[1] Elwin, *Landor*, p. 291.

*recollect only one thing, impressed upon my memory by what followed
a little later, that when the absence of Southey was deplored in
connection with the domestic grief that sadly occupied him at the
time, there was an expression of feeling from both Wordsworth and
Landor of unrestrained and unaffected earnestness. When a very few
weeks had passed after this, it was not a little startling to receive*
A Satire on Satirists, *very evidently by Landor, in which
Wordsworth was handled sharply for alleged disrespect to Southey.'*

A Satire on Satirists *was published by Saunders & Otley. In it
Landor attacked Wordsworth for his lack of appreciation of Southey.
Robinson was very angry, and wrote:*

'*What matters is that he* [Wordsworth] *is insensible to the
astonishing powers of Voltaire or Goethe ? He is, after all,
Wordsworth. In all cases I care little what a man is* not; *I look to
what he* is. *And Wordsworth has written a hundred poems the least
excellent of which I would not sacrifice to give him that openness of
heart you require. Productive power acts by means of concentration.
With few exceptions those only love everything who, like me, can
themselves do nothing*'.[1]

*Among other events was a dinner party given by Mrs Kenyon, wife
of John Kenyon, whom Landor had first met in Florence in 1827.
Kenyon had written enough verse of sufficient merit to be accepted for
his literary pretentions, and his wealth and good nature won him
popularity as a host and patron of literary men. Stout and hearty, he
had the face of a Benedictine monk, and the joyous talk of a good
fellow !*[2]

*The guests at Mrs Kenyon's party included Elizabeth Barrett and
Miss Mitford; the latter hardly appealed to Landor as a species of
attractive feminine beauty. It was an exciting evening, however, for
Miss Barrett:*

'"*I never walked in the skies before; and perhaps never shall again,
when so many stars are out !*" Landor—"*in whose hands the ashes
of antiquity burn again—gave me two Greek epigrams he had
lately written . . . and talked brilliantly and prominently*", *till her
brother, a young man of unhappy manners,—*"*abused him for*

[1] Forster, *Landor,* p. 316.
[2] Elwin, *Landor,* p. 243.

ambitious *singularity and affectation"*. *Determined to be "not at all
disappointed in Wordsworth, although perhaps I should not have
singled him from the multitude as a great man"*, she remarked,
"a reserve *even in his countenance, which does not lighten as
Landor does" and comparing him with "Landor—the brilliant
Landor !"—she* felt *the difference between great genius and
eminent talent.'*[1]

Pericles and Aspasia *was published in March 1836. It is one of his
most brilliant works. Colvin wrote that he thought 'it has the misfortune of being weighted with disquisitions too learned for the general
reader', an argument no longer tenable. Contemporary critics have
singled out this brilliant and succint work as an introduction to Landor
at his Hellenic best. Landor himself said, 'I had no books to consult. The
characters, thoughts, and actions, are all fictious. Pericles was somewhat less amiable, Aspasia somewhat less virtuous, Alciabides somewhat less sensitive; but here I could represent him so, being young, and
before his character was displayed'.*

*The work is cast in the form of an 'Imaginary Conversation', giving
the general reader, as usual, no background information. Aspasia has
arrived in Athens from her native Miletus. The work ends with the
death of Pericles in the third year of the Peloponnesian War. She
relates the development of her romance with Pericles and the incidents
of her life in a series of letters to her friend Cleone. This is one of
Landor's most joyous works—a masterpiece of wit, beauty and pure
Landor prose. A book that we are frequently forced to drop, in order to
surrender ourselves to the visions and memories, soft or sad, which its
words awaken and cause to pass through the mind.*

[1] Elwin, *Landor*, p. 288.

From *Pericles and Aspasia*[1]
1836

PERICLES. We may be introduced to Power by Humanity, and at first may love her less for her own sake than for Humanity's, but by degrees we become so accustomed to her as to be quite uneasy without her.

*　*　*

ASPASIA. Three affections of the soul predominate; Love, Religion, and Power. The first two are often united; the other stands widely apart from them, and neither is admitted nor seeks admittance to their society.

*　*　*

PERICLES. Ridicule often parries resentment, but resentment never yet parried ridicule.

*　*　*

CLEONE. Tears, O Aspasia, do not dwell long upon the cheeks of youth. Rain drops easily from the bud, rests on the bosom of the maturer flower, and breaks down that only which hath lived its day.

*　*　*

PERICLES. The man who is determined to keep others fast and firm, must have one end of the bond about his own breast, sleeping and waking.

*　*　*

CLEONE. The young mind should be nourished with simple and grateful food, and not too copious. It should be little exercised until its nerves and muscles show themselves, and even then rather for air

[1] In an endeavourment to show the varying aspects of this work, I have chosen brief excerpts in place of a consecutive episode.

than anything else. Study is the bane of boyhood, the paliment of youth, the indulgence of manhood, and the restorative of age.

*　　*　　*

CLEONE. I do believe, Aspasia, that studious men, who look so quiet, are the most restless men in existence.

*　　*　　*

ANAXAGORAS. Is it not in philosophy as in love? The more we have of it, and the less we talk about it, the better.

*　　*　　*

ASPASIA. The happiest of pillows is not that which Love first presses; it is that which Death has frowned on and past over.

*　　*　　*

CLEONE. The very beautiful rarely love at all. Those precious images are placed above the reach of the Passions; Time alone is permitted to efface them; Time the father of the Gods, and even *their* consumer.

*　　*　　*

CLEONE. Could Sappho be ignorant how infantinely inarticulate is early love? Could she be ignorant that shame and fear seize it unrelentingly by the throat, while hard-hearted impudence stands at ease, prompt at opportunity, and profuse in declarations! There is a gloom in deep love, as in deep water: there is a silence in it which suspends the foot, and the folded arms and the dejected head are the images it reflects. No voice shakes its surface: the Muses themselves approach it with a tardy and timid step, and with a low and tremulous and melancholy song.

*　　*　　*

ASPASIA. We are told by Herodotus that a boy in Persia is kept in the apartments of the women, and prohibited from seeing his father, until his fifth year. The reason is, he informs us, that if he dies before this age, his loss may give the parent no uneasiness. And such a custom he thinks commendable. Herodotus has no child, Cleone! If he had, far other would be his feelings and his judgement. Before that age, how many seeds are sown, which future years, and distant ones, mature successively! How much fondness, how much generosity, what hosts of other virtues, courage, constancy, patriotism, spring into the father's heart from the cradle of his child! And does never the fear come over him, that what is most precious to him upon earth is left in careless or perfidious, in unsafe or unworthy hands? Does it never occur to him that he loses in every one of these five years? What is there so affecting to the brave and virtuous man, as that which perpetually wants his help and cannot call for it? What is so different as the speaking and the mute? And hardly less so are unarticulate sounds, and sounds which he receives half-formed, and which he delights to modulate, and which he lays with infinite care and patience, not only on the tender attentive ear, but on the half-open lips, and on the eyes, and on the cheeks; as if they were all listeners. In every child there are many children; but coming forth year after year, each somewhat like and somewhat varying. When they are grown much older, the leaves (as it were) lose their pellucid green, the branches their graceful pliancy.

Is there any man so rich in happiness that he can afford to throw aside these first five years? Is there any man who can hope for another five so exuberant in unsating joy?

ASPASIA. Where on earth is there so much society as in a beloved child? He accompanies me in my walks, gazes into my eyes for what I am gathering from books, tells me more and better things than they do, and asks me often what neither I nor they can answer. When he is absent I am filled with reflections: when he is present, I have room for none beside what I receive from him. The charms of his childhood bring me back to the delights of mine, and I fancy I hear my own words in a sweeter voice. Will he (O how I tremble at the mute oracle of futurity!) Will he ever be as happy as I have been? Alas! and must he ever be as subject to fears and apprehensions? No; thanks to the Gods! never, never. He carries his father's heart within his breast: I see him already an orator and a leader, I try to teach him daily some of his father's looks and gestures, and I never smile but at his docility and gravity.

How his father will love him! The little thunderer! The winner of cities! the vanquisher of Cleones!

✳   ✳   ✳

CLEONE. (*writing to Aspasia at Athens*) Epimedea, it appears, has not corrupted very grossly your purity and simplicity in dress. Yet, remembering your observation on armlets, I cannot but commend your kindness and sufference in wearing her emeralds. Your opinion was firmly that we should be careful not to sub-divide our persons. The arm is composed of three parts: no one of them is too long. Now the armlet intersects that portion of it which must be considered as the most beautiful. In my idea of the matter, the sandal alone is susceptible of gems, after the zone has received the richest. The zone is necessary to our vesture, and encompasses the person, in every quarter of the humanized world, in one invariable manner. The hair, too, is divided by nature in the middle of the head. There is a cousinship between the hair and the flowers; and from this relation the poets have been called by the same name the leaves and it. They appear on the head as if they had been seeking one another. Our natural dress, very different from the dress of barbarous nations, is not the invention of the ignorant or the slave; but the sculptor, the painter and the poet, have studied how best to adorn the most beautiful object of their fancies and contemplations. The Indians, who believe that human pains and sufferings are pleasing to the deity, make incisions in their bodies, and insert into them unperishable colours. They also adorn the ears and noses and foreheads of their gods. These were the ancestors of the Egyptians; we chose handsomer and better-tempered ones for our worship, but retained the same decorations in our sculpture, and to a degree which the sobriety of the Egyptian had reduced and chastened. Hence we retain the only mark of barbarism which dishonours our natural dress, the use of earings. If our statues should all be broken by some convulsion of the earth, would it be believed by future ages that, in the country and age of Sophicles, the women tore holes in their ears to let rings into, as the more brutal of peasants do with the snouts of sows!

1837

'*Today is my birthday, and never on my birthday was I happy*', Landor
wrote to Lady Blessington on *30 January*.

> The day returns, my natal day,
>   Borne on the storm and pale with snow,
> And seems to ask me why I stay,
>   Stricken by Time and bowed by looe.
>
> Many were once the friends who came
>   To wish me joy; and there are some
> Who wish it now; but not the same;
>   They are whence friends can never come.
>
> Nor are they you my love watch'd o'er,
>   Cradled in innocence and sleep;
> You smile into my eyes no more,
>   Nor see the bitter tears they weep.

One wonders how deeply Landor felt at leaving his family in
Florence. One is inclined to think that he acted the stoic, constantly
adjusting himself to a new situation, and pre-occupying himself, firstly,
with his literary work, which, although he often declared that he would
write not one word more, he continued until his dying day; and,
secondly, being content that a pet dog always accompanied him. 'In
life and literature' wrote Colvin, 'Landor tended towards the suppression and control of emotion rather than towards its indulgence and
display . . . his ambition was to walk "with Epicurus on the right hand
and Epictetus on the left" . . .'[1]

Landor left Clifton in *1837* and went for a time to Llanbedr; he
then visited Lady Blessington in London and his sisters in Warwick.
Later he went to Torquay and joined Kenyon. He went also to see his
friend Armitage Brown at Plymouth. Moreover, he had heard that his
daughter Julia, who was nineteen, had fallen in love with her unstable
cousin, Edward Landor.

At an antiquarian book-shop in Bristol he bought a volume of
Blake and felt that Blake could have been Wordsworth's prototype,

[1] Colvin, *Landor*, p. 173.

*and 'wished they could have divided their madness between them'. He
read G. P. R. James's* Attila *and wrote to Lady Blessington:*

> 'I sat up all last night to read James's Attila, *not greatly to the
> benefit of my eyes or the credit of my prudence. But I never can
> leave off a book that interests me until I have gone thro' it. . . I
> have received more honour than Augustus, or Mecenas, or Louis
> Quatorze, or any other man living or dead, for to no one were
> ever inscribed two such works of imagination as the* Curse of
> Kehama *and* Attila'.

*On hearing from Crabb Robinson, who thanked him for Pericles, he
replied . . .*

> 'How much wiser are we with our own wisdom than with other
> people's! It fits us. . . Somebody told me that your illustrous friend
> Goethe hated dogs. God forgive him if he did. I never can believe
> it of him. They, too, are half-poets; they are dreamers. Do any
> other animals dream? For my part, as you know, I love them
> heartily. They are grateful, they are brave, they are communicative,
> and they never play at cards'.[1]

He went on to ask Robinson for a translation of Goethe's Iphigencia,
but he found it in Taylor's Specimens.

*In November Landor struck up one of his greatest friendships when
he met Colonel William Napier, whom he greatly admired and who
became one of his close friends.*

In December Landor published his Death of Clytemnestra *and* The
Madness of Orestes, Dramatic Scenes from the Pentalogia. *He
considered that his* Clytemnestra *was one of his finest pieces of writing.
Lastly came that considerable work,* The Pentameron. *Though he had
no financial success with it, his friends were unstinted in their welcome
and praise. 'I was at Talfourd's yesterday', wrote Kenyon, soon after
the volume appeared, 'and was condemned to listen on all sides to the
praises of your* Pentameron. *My friend Miss Barrett, too, says of it
that if it were not for the necessity of getting through a book, some of
the pages are too delicious to turn over.' Leigh Hunt reckoned it to be,
on the whole, Landor's masterpiece; and Julius Hare said that
literature had nowhere so delightful a picture of the friendship of two*

---

[1] Forster, *Landor*, vol. ii, p. 324.

supposed rivals, Goethe's actual intercourse with Schiller being the only thing to compare with it in beauty. To Crabb Robinson, also, who found it waiting for him on his return from Italy with Wordsworth in the autumn, it seemed as if no other of Landor's books had given him so great a pleasure; and the generality of the prose writing, by the side of it, seemed to him but as the murky fog of Little Knight Street during Michaelmas term compared to the pure atmosphere of Certaldo on such summer nights as he had spent between Fiesole and Florence.[1]

[1] Forster, *Landor*, vol. ii, p. 235.

Dramatic Scenes from the Pentalogia
1837

ESSEX AND BACON

Robert Devereux, Earl of Essex, was beheaded February 25, 1601.

ESSEX. I did believe, sir, I had helpt to raise
Many to wealth and station, some to fame,
And one to friendship.
    BACON.   You, my noble earl,
Have done it; and much more. We must lament
A power thus past (or rather thrown) away.
    ESSEX. Thou? thou lament it, Bacon?
    BACON.   To my soul.
    ESSEX. Why then, with energy beyond the pitch
Of brawling law, cry vengeance? when my fortune
Was pierced with every bolt from every hand,
Soon as the golden links were snapt asunder
Which those who rule the earth held round that bird
Who bore their lightnings and struck down their foes.
    BACON. My gracious lord! were always their commands
Well waited for?
    ESSEX.   Nay, by my troth, my zeal
Outflew them.
    BACON.   Your return was unadvised.
    ESSEX. Unwelcome: that is worse.
    BACON.   The worst of all
Was summoning to arms a loyal land,
Basking in peace and plenteousness.
    ESSEX.   How far
Extending this your basking? court indeed
And inns of law were warm enough; on those
The sun beats all the day, through all the year;
Everything there so still and orderly,

That he who sneezes in them is caught up
And cudgell'd for his pains.
  BACON.   Should he awake
Trumpets by sneezing, should he blow up banners,
'Twas well if only cudgels fell on him:
Our laws have sharper instruments, my lord!
  ESSEX. I know it; and I knew it ere I rose.
  BACON. O! had this never happened!
  ESSEX.   Then wouldst thou
Have lost some smiles, some parlyings, some tags
Of ermine, and, what more thou valuest
(As any wise man would) some little gold.
  BACON. Dross!
  ESSEX (*smiling*). Very true! . . . as men are dust and ashes.
  BACON. Such thoughts become all mortals; most of all
Those who have fallen under high displeasure,
Who have their God and Prince to reconcile,
And are about to change this brief vile life . . .
Nay, nay, my lord! your life may rest unchanged
For years to come, if you, upon your knees,
Humbly ask pardon . . .
  ESSEX (*fiercely*).   Pardon!
    (*After hesitation*). I will ask it . . .
  BACON. . . . Before the privy council, and the court
Especially assembled.
  ESSEX (*indignantly*). Not before
The best among them, were he quite alone,
No, by the soul of Essex! were he Raleigh . . .
The only great man there.
  BACON.   Are we so scorned?
  ESSEX. Bacon! I did not say the only wise one:
So, do not break thy ring, or loose the stone.
  BACON. My lord! my finger might have been uneasy
Without such notice from that once high peer
Erewhile the Earl of Essex . . . until treason
Leveled him lower than burgess or than churl.
  ESSEX. I will not say thou liest; for thy tongue
Lags far behind thy heart; thy strongest wit
May stretch and strain, but never make them yoke-mates.

BACON. This cork appliance, this hard breathing, served
While there was water under for support,
But cut a dismal figure in the mud.

ESSEX. To servile souls how abject seem the fallen!
Benchers and message-bearers stride o'er Essex!

BACON. Unmasted pinnace may row safely under
No high colossus, without pricking it.
But, sure, the valiant Earl is somewhat chafed . . .
Who could have thought it! . . . by a worm like me!

ESSEX. Begone! I have fairly weighed thee.

BACON (*alone*).   He weigh me!
No man is stout enough[1] to trim the balance,
Much less to throw the weight in . . .

                                   He weigh me!
Flaunting and brittle as a honeysuckle,
Sweet in the chamber, in the field blown down,
Ramping in vain to reach again its prop,
And crusht by the first footfall.

                              Arrogance
Stares, but sees badly . . . snatches with quick gripe
What seems within the reach, and, being infirm
Of stand, is overbalanced.

                        Shall I bear
Foul words upon me?

                     I have thrown them back
Manfully to the beard that wagged with them . . .
My courage is now safe beyond suspicion . . .
Myself can hardly doubt it after this . . .
Yet that audacious criminal dared spit
Reproaches! seldom are they bearable,
But, springing up from reason, sting like asps . . .
Not that the man has reason . . . he has none . . .

---

[1] Bacon little knew or suspected that there was then existing (the only one that ever did exist) his superior in intellectual power. Position gives magnitude. While the world was rolling above Shakespeare, he was seen imperfectly: when he rose above the world, it was discovered that he was greater than the world. The most honest of his contemporaries would scarcely have admitted this, even had they known it. But vast objects of remote altitude must be looked at a long while before they are ascertained. Ages are the telescope-tubes that must be lengthened out for Shakespeare; and generations of men serve but as single witnesses to his claims.—W. S. L.

For, what had I to do with it? I spoke . . .
And, when we are commanded, we must speak.
It was her Grace . . . and surely she knows best.
I may now wash my hands of him at last,
I have but done my duty . . . fall who may.

THE DEATH OF CLYMTENESTRA

Orestes and Electra.

ELECTRA. Pass on, my brother! she awaits the wretch,
Dishonorer, despoiler, murderer. . . .
None other name shall name him. . . . she awaits
As would a lover . . .
              Heavenly Gods! what poison
O'erflows my lips!
             Adultress! husband-slayer!
Strike her, the tigress!
             Think upon our father . . .
Give the sword scope . . . think what a man was he,
How fond of her! how kind to all about,
That he might gladden and teach *us* . . . how proud
Of thee, Orestes! tossing thee above
His joyous head and calling thee his crown.
Ah! boys remember not what melts our hearts
And marks them everymore!
             Bite not thy lip,
Nor tramp as an unsteddy colt the ground,
Nor stare against the wall, but think again
How better than all fathers was our father.
Go . . .
   ORESTES. Loose me, then! for this white hand, Electra,
Hath fastened upon mine with fiercer grasp
Than mine can grasp the sword.
ELECTRA.   Go, sweet Orestes!
I knew not I was holding thee . . . Avenge him!
(*Alone*). How he sprang from me!
             . . . Sure, he now has reacht
The room before the bath . . .
           The bath-door creaks!

... It hath creakt thus since he ... since thou, O father!
Ever since thou didst loosen its strong valves,
Either with all thy dying weight, or strength
Agonized with her stabs ...

                        What plunge was that?
Ah me.

        ... What groans are those?
    ORESTES (*returning*).   They sound through hell
Rejoicing the Eumenides.[1]

                    She slew
Our father; she made thee the scorn of slaves;
Me (son of him who ruled this land and more)
She made an outcast ...

                Would I had been so
For ever! ere such vengeance. ...
    ELECTRA.   O that Zeus
Had let thy arm fall sooner at thy side
Without those drops! list! they are audible ...
For they are many ... from the sword's point falling,
And down from the mid blade!

                Too rash Orestes!
Couldst thou not then have spared our wretched mother?
    ORESTES. The Gods could not.
    ELECTRA.   She was not theirs, Orestes!
    ORESTES. And didst not thou ...
    ELECTRA.   'Twas I, 'twas, I, who did it;
Of our unhappiest house the most unhappy!
Under this roof, by every God accurst,
There is no grief, there is no guilt, but mine.
    ORESTES. Electra! no!

             'Tis now my time to suffer ...
Mine be, with all its pangs, the righteous deed.

---

[1] An ancient scholiast has recorded that the name of Eumenides was given to these Goddesses after the expiation of Orestes. But Catullus (called the *learned* by his countrymen) represents Ariadne invoking them by this appellation long before the Trojan war. The verses are the most majestic in the Roman language.

Eumenides! quarum anguineis [quibus anguino] redimita capillis [capillo].
Frons expirantes præportat pectoris iras,
Huc, huc adventate! &c. [W. S. L.]

ORESTES. Heavy and murderous dreams, O my Electra,
Have dragged me from myself.

                               Is this Mycenai?
Are we . . . . . . are all who should be . . . . . . in our house?
Living? unhurt? our father here? our mother?
Why that deep gasp? for 'twas not sigh nor groan.
She then . . . . . . 'twas she who fell! when? how? beware!
No, no, speak out at once, that my full heart
May meet it, and may share with thee in all . . .
In all . . . but that one thing.

                           It was a dream.
We may share all.

                  They live: both live:

                                O say it!
ELECTRA. The Gods have placed them from us, and there rolls
Between us that dark river. . . . .

    ORESTES.   Blood! blood! blood!
I see it roll; I see the hand above it,
Imploring; I see *her*.

                    Hiss me not back
Ye snake-hair'd maids! I will look on; I will
Hear the words gurgle thro' that cursed stream,
And catch that hand . . . that hand . . . which slew my father!
It cannot be . . . . how could it slay my father?
Death to the slave who spoke it! . . . . slay my father!
It tost me up to him to earn a smile,
And was a smile then such a precious boon,
And royal state and proud affection nothing?
Ay, and thee too, Electra, she once taught
To take the sceptre from him at the door . . .
Not the bath-door, not the bath-door, mind that! . . .
And place it in the vestibule, against
The spear of Pallas, where it used to stand.
Where is it now? methinks I missed it there.
How we have trembled to be seen to move it!
Both looking up, lest that stern face should frown,
Which always gazed on Zeus right opposite.
Oh! could but one tear more fall from my eyes,
It would shake off those horrid visages,

And melt them into air.
                              I am not your's,
Fell Goddesses! A just and generous Power,
A bright-hair'd God, directed me.
                                    And thus
Abased is he whom such a God inspired!
                              (*After a pause.*)
Into whose kingdom went they? did they go
Together?

   ELECTRA. Oh! they were not long apart.

   ORESTES. I know why thou art pale; I know whose head
Thy flowerlike hands have garlanded; I know
For whom thou hast unbraided all thy love.
He well deserves it . . . . . he shall have it all.
Glory and love shall crown thee, my brave sister!

   ELECTRA. I am not she of Sparta. Let me live
(If live I must, Orestes!) not unnamed
Nor named too often. Speak no more of love,
Ill-omen'd and opprobrious in this house . . .
A mother should have had, a father had it,
O may a brother let it dwell with him,
Unchangeable, unquestioned, solitary,
Strengthened and hallowed in the depths of grief!
Gaze not so angrily . . . I dare not see thee,
I dare not look where comfort should be found.

   ORESTES. I dare and do behold them all day long,
And, were that face away so like my mother's,
I would advance and question and compel them . . .
They hear me, and they know it.

   ELECTRA.   Hear me too,
Ye mighty ones! to me invisible!
And spare him! spare him! for without the Gods
He wrought not what he wrought: And are not ye
Partakers of their counsels and their power?
O spare the son of him whom ye and they
Sent against Ilion, to perform your will
And bid the rulers of the earth be just.

   ORESTES. And dare they frighten thee too? frighten thee!
And bend thee into prayer?

                              Off, hateful eyes!
Look upon me, not her.
                              Ay, thus, 'tis well.
Cheer, cheer thee, my Electra!
                              I am strong,
Stronger than ever . . . steel, fire, adamant . . .
But cannot bear thy brow upon my neck,
Cannot bear these wild writhings, these loud sobs,
By all the Gods! I think thou art half-mad . . . . . .
I must away . . . . . . follow me not . . . . . . stand there!

From *High and Low Life in Italy*
1837-8

MR STIVERS TO THE PARROCO SPINELLA

If I had known what I was carrying to Leghorn with me I would
have turned back and taught you better. Ay, ay, Parson Spinella!
Argue in this manner, and I will answer for your readiness to *kiss*,
&c. &c. as you say you do. Now plague upon you! there is so
much craft in your parly that I cannot get the better of you, nor
master neither—I mean at the head nor the middle—but just before
you get to the dust and the devil, I am up to you.

You ask if *anything* can be removed as easily as raised? Cannot
money? I give up all the other things to you—the discontent,
the dust and the devil—and wish you joy of them. One word more.
You Tuscans who pride yourselves mightily on the elegance of your
expressions, and perhaps have reason on your side in many, might
afford a little improvement in one. You always say *Our Tuscany*, or
This our Tuscany. Now what in God's name have you to do with it?
You live in it merely by sufferance: you must not make an enquiry
about it as about an absent friend: you must *stand* when you are
ordered to *stand*, you must deliver up your money when you are
ordered to deliver up your money: you are first blindfolded and
then beaten. Parroco! Parroco! Tuscany is no more yours than my
grandmother's.

LANDOR

A passable girl here who has taken a whimsical sort of fancy for me, told me she knew I could do what I liked with my master. On my only nodding, which implied no such thing, but rather the contrary, she said she should be glad if I would lend her our carriage and horses for a day or two in the carnival. I did not like to disoblige her, though there was no reason on earth why I should oblige her, and I asked Mr Talboys what was to be done. Have I mentioned this gentleman to you? I think I have not: well then I will. My master, the great encourager, is the devil himself for picking up: he picked up a poet. I thought it hard, and more than flesh and blood could bear, that he should set down a poet at his own table, when I had lived with him two years, and stood behind it. True it is, master said, 'Stivers! a gentleman is coming to reside in the house; there may be a little more trouble, but I shall remember it at the end of the year.' I hope he will; he is much to be pitied, and half excused. He took to this poet, as people take sometimes to a dog, to keep others off. For here in Italy the poets are as troublesome as the flies, and pretty nearly as plentiful. At every inn as you alight, they bring you a *copy* of verses, as we Englishmen call it; but they Italians, who ought to call it so (for the same does for five hundred) call it by another name, *Epitalamio* or *Lode*, in which every prince is Tito, every green-grocer *Mecenate*. The light of these fire-flies darts high and low, over wet and dry, and, coming out of one insect, falls upon another. A certain Fantoni, who called himself Labindo, was father abbot to this order of Famelicans. He praised even Lord Cowper! What an appetite the poet must have had for dinner, and what a digestion must the peer have had for adulation! Well, Mr Talboys is not so much amiss. Although he is not very sociable with us he is not greatly more with master, but has good humour and a good word for all. This coin is very light, yet those who play with it always win more than those who stake down heavier. So that, although we ought to be displeased at his coming into the family without our being consulted, we are not upon bad terms with him. His qualifications as a poet are very questionable, for, when master, at first meeting, invited him to dinner, he declined it. This is not vastly in the spirit of poetry. I am, however, about to give you a specimen of what he can do in translation. He laughed

262

at my consulting him, and replied that the Signora Aurora Spinella
was something like a girl he remembered to have read of in an
ancient, and said he should be contented if he could resemble him
as much in poetry as I resembled him in manners. I told him I
would give I did not know what to get a touch of him. In the
evening, by way of quizzing me, he threw me the lines I am going
to write out. Here he has missed his cue: he shall never humble
me: he shall never make me say that our landau and horses are
master's and not mine. That was his drift. He is but shallowish,
like the rest of his tribe. I do believe he meant no harm; but, in
points of honour, I am tender as a gnat or a caterpillar.

Imitated from Catullus

> Varrus would take me t'other day
> To see a little girl he knew,
> Pretty and witty in her way,
> With impudence enough for two.

Here, my lady, I must stop awhile. There is no resemblance.
Aurora has just impudence enough for one, and I would fain keep
it all to myself: I know what to do with it.

To proceed.

> Scarce are we seated, ere she chatters,
> As city nymphs are wont to do,
> About all countries, men, and matters . . .
> 'And, pray, what has been done for *you*?'

> 'Bithynia, lady!' I replied,
> 'Is a good province for a pretor,
> For none (I promise you) beside,
> And least of all am I her debtor.'

> 'Sorry for that!' said she—'however
> You have brought with you, I dare say,
> Some litter-bearers; none so clever
> In any other part as they.'

> If I had told the truth I'd told her
> That I had no one, here or there,

Who could have mounted on his shoulder
　The leg of an old broken chair.

'Why, badly as my lot may fall,'
　Said I, ambitious to be grand,
'Eight or nine fellows, straight and tall,
　Are constantly at my command.'

'My dear Catullus! what good hap is
　Our meeting! lend me only eight—
I would be carried to Serapis
　To-morrow.'
　　　　　　　　　'Wait, fair lady! wait.'

I knew the number pretty well,
　There may be eight, I said, or nine.
I merely had forgot to tell
　That they are Anna's, and not mine.

It shows a mean spirit to take a hint: for my part I will not:
Aurora shall have her horses.

　　　　　　　　　　　　　I am, &c. &c. &c.

　　　　　　　　　　　　ROME, *Oct. 19.*

DEAR JACK,—Since I broke my leg and can ride no longer my
mistress has made me cook. I thought she was in joke when she
said, 'Isaac! you must dress our dinners, positively you must.
There is no eating all these apothecaries' shops: one cannot swallow
Ceylon upon Sumatra.' And indeed I myself was sated with clove
upon clove, nutmeg upon nutmeg, sugared chicken-claws, ducks'
necks trimmed with aniseed, raw ham yellower than saffron, to be
gulped only by the slipperiness of figs and to be diguised only by
the power of fenugreek; and oil enough at a single dinner to keep
in order our close carriage all the year. It would turn the stomach
of some among our squeamish gentlemen in England, if they saw,
as we do, the lamp emptied into the stew-pan, and the stew-pan
into the lamp. No debts are paid in Italy more regularly than
between these parties: whenever one is in want, the other is forth-
coming. Shew me the like in anything else since you have been

here. I replied to our good lady, 'Madam shall be served,'—the people's usual phrase, which I learned from the old cook, defunct, defunct I would say in his office; and the words had such an effect upon her appetite (for I cannot hope that my cookery produced it), she ate as if she could have eaten a stuffed stork out of the Museum. On Monday last a younker came over from Frascati with a couple of as fine cub foxes as ever you set your eyes upon, and asked for 'Signor the cook, if he or his adjutant major would condescend to honour him with an audience.' 'Yes, my honest lad!' said I, 'but what have you brought in that basket, beside the two foxes' heads?' He replied 'Dear signor, my dear, for the love of God! what would she wish that I should bring, unless it were the bust and whole persons of the same? which behold here!'

'Are they dead?' said I, for there was a gag in the mouth of each, and their eyes were open and red.

'Slain yesterday, after mass.'

'Well,' added I, 'and what am I to do with 'em?'

'As she desiderates,' he replied.

'Anything but skin them,' cried I. To which he answered that in his country nobody would eat a fox without skinning: that the skin was the privilege and *honorary* of the vendor, who had an egg at most honest houses for it, carried to them with the four pads; altho' some of the prelates in Rome kept a store of rotten ones, bought reasonably for the purpose, and sent them to their villas.

'And do you think,' said I, 'that my master and mistress, as good and great people as any in Rome without one exception...'

Would you believe it, Jack! the stripling had the boldness, though he never learned to box, to clap his hand before my mouth looking all the time as frightened as a cat caught in a dairy, and, crying out '*Zitto! Zitto! Signore Cuoco valentissimo!* always excepting our Holy Father, our Lady the Bambino, and Saint Romolo, my patron.' He then suddenly gave me a kiss upon both whiskers, told me to hope to be of courage, that he would pray for me, that it was a sin not of contumacy but of blindness, that there was a difference, though I could not know it nor he explain it—and then burst into tears. I was so taken by his tenderness of heart which after all does one more good than a tickle of the stiletto, that I bought his couple of cubs, though I told him I could not dress them. He said that if I was not sovereignly master of this intricate department in *nostralian* cookery, he would negotiate for me with His Signory, the egregious cook-major of His Eminence the Cardinal Opizoni, a high Purpurate; which cook-major, namely, the Signor Fabio Massimo Barnabà Cantagrillo, being a gallant man, would not demand at first for his kind offices more than a leg and loin, and at the close of the conference, after the pleasure of forming my acquaintance (the glory of his life) no more than a loin, together with liver and lights, and kidney, and heart, and a little of the blood to flavour certain dishes. The residue being well-seasoned with capers and marjoram and tarragon, a few cloves of garlic, the rind of a Seville orange or two, a flask of the white wine of Orvieto, a nut-meg, a pound of bacon cut into small squares, half a pound of sugar candy, half a pound of virgin oil, and garnished with snails and carrots alternately, was a dish that an Emperor might set before James the apostle of the Gentiles; nay, the angels themselves might have served it up to Saint Peter in prison.

'And faith! my friend,' said I, 'it would be likely to increase in quantity, like the loaves and fishes.'

'*Davvero!*' cried he—'*anche quello!*'

He took my money, counted it, kissed my hand, counted it again, sorted it, and seemed to be reckoning the amount both of the smaller coin and the greater; then he turned his back upon me and muttered some words to himself. I asked him if the money was not right; and why he mistrusted me so; and what he meant by putting the small coin in his pocket and holding the rest in hand. 'Sir!' said he, gravely and sorrowingly, 'I have been making a vow, (lest my heart should misgive me, for I am poor) to buy a wax-taper with this silver for the good of your soul, if any good can be done it; in order to expiate the things you said so unadvisedly. And now I entreat and implore you to believe,' cried he with energy as he fell upon his knees, 'that not only all the *milordi* in the world, but that likewise all the *Monsignori*, all the Purpurates and Eminences, tossed up together in a frittata, would not weigh the little finger of the Bambino. And then his dear sweet mother!' Here tears rolled down his cheeks—he sprang up, crying, 'Ca! Cospetto di Bacco!' and snapped his fingers, and ran out of the kitchen.

I related the history to my mistress, who was very far from being offended; 'but throw the stinking things away,' said she. My fellow servants murmured loudly when they understood the order, and begged they might dress the game for themselves, and while it was fresh and sweet. Cherubini ran to one of the fountains which he declared was the very best in Rome, not only to cure the migraine, but to extract the wild flavour from hares, woodcocks, partridges, and all other such animals, only by leaving them a night or two in it. But the rest, although they bowed to his superior lights on the subject, made an exception as to the duration of time, and said that hares indeed and woodcocks and partridges might require more soaking, but tender young foxes did not enter the gates every day, and that these two were *qualche cosa particolare.*

MR STIVERS TO MR HOMFRAY

DEAR ISAAC,—In spite of that confounded name of thine, thou art an honest fellow. And, now I remember, the name is not so bad a one neither. For I heard some learned English folks, at my master's, (a plain gentleman, like yourself) talk of one who was made a knight with it, in spite of his being a philosopher. And you too, my old lad, are a bit of a philosopher, as gentlemen are called who wear worsted stockings and dog-ear cravats. Well, I would not lose a friend by an imprudent action. I hate pressing and plaguing my friends. If you had wanted your money you would have taken it. I never should have said one syllable more about it, had you not told me that you were now the cook. Let Pitt be Pitt and Perceval be Perceval (aren't they dead tho?) neither of them could ever feather his nest like sensible men of your profession. An old master, an old mistress, full confidence, full larder, ready money, range of market, grocer, butcher, fishmonger—East and West Indies shrink, as the man in the play says, like a shrivelled scrole, before your blazing fire, blessed Isaac! You desired me, at parting, not to put myself to any inconvenience; and indeed I found not the least in slipping my hand again into my pockets, not to hurt your feelings. My mother used to say, 'That child always does as he's bid.' I forget whether she said it of me or my brother Ned. I am inclined to think it was of me; and I had always a great regard for my mother and cherish her memory. She died the other day in the hospital, poor woman, after lingering two or three years—or more, for what I know. I had not time to look in upon her before I left

London; and Lady C., in whose service I was then living, said that such sort of things were very distressing to both parties, and do good to neither. She said that if she could have seen me once more, (I mean my mother—and perhaps the other may say it too) she could have died happy. I dare say she thought so; but who knows whether she could? and I could not get up from cards in the evening—and leave my partner—and as for the daytime, I had only Sundays to be idle in. At all events, she is just as happy now as if she had seen me—and so am I. And if such sort of things are very distressing, I should have been very wrong to have thought about it, for my mother was distressed enough all her life. I wish you plenty of fun and foxes, and am, honest Isaac,

Your hearty Friend,
J. J. STIVERS.

P.S.—A few months ago I was appointed secretary to master— but upon my honour I am not much richer than I was before, which made me refer to you—you know what business, fearing that you might have heard more than the fact. In future be pleased to direct to me J. J. Stivers, Esq., Secretary to Milord Raikes, Esq., at Como, where our honest, rosy-faced Queen was. I am come the day after the fair. Non c'è rimedio! as master's tailor said, when master cut his bill sheer thro the middle, and asked him which half he chose should be paid.

*Landor now set to work on three plays. The fact that success for any
of his published works was as far away as ever never daunted him.
Two of these 'plays'—we place the word in quotes for Landor gave
them no more dramatic cohesion than he had* Count Julian, Andrea of
Hungary *and* Giovannia of Naples—*were to be published in 1839, the
third,* Fra Rupert, *in 1840. He was also engaged in enlarging his
'imaginary conversation' between Johnson and Tooke. Meanwhile, his
friend, Mrs Dashwood, suggested that he should collect together the
female conversationalists in his Imaginary Conversations. She proposed that the collection be called Landor's 'Female Characters
Illustrated', after the style of the popular Mrs Jameson's* Shakespeare's Female Characters. *He wrote to Lady Blessington on 4
March:*

'*I do not care a fig either for popularity or profit, for if ever I am
popular I shall never know anything about it; and if ever I get
money I shall neither spend nor save it! I have already more than
I want. But I really should like to make a pretty present of such a
volume as no other man living can write, embellished with writing
engravings. If you can manage this affair, I am confident you will'.*[1]

*He went to Gore House in May, and met Carlyle, whom he con-
sidered 'a vigorous thinker but a vile writer, worse than Bulwer'.
He also met Macaulay—'a clever clown—and Moore, too, whom I
had not seen till then'—Lord Northampton and Rogers. He was also
to meet Chorley, the foremost musical critic of his day, and Isaac
D'Israeli, who admired Landor and said of him, profoundly 'You will
be read hereafter. I know not whether you have written a century
too late or too early: too late, if the taste for literature has wholly
left us; too early, if the public mind has not yet responded to your
sympathies'.*[2]

Landor returned to Bath on 27 May, but soon after his return was

'*laid up a whole fortnight with a sprained ancle; a fool of a mason
dropt some mortar in Milsom Street; I sett my foot in it and twisted*

[1] Elwin, *Landor*, p. 317.
[2] Elwin, *Landor*, p. 319.

*my foot almost round . . . on Sunday after tea I began a drama on
Giovanna di Napoli (God defend us from the horrid sound, Joan of
Naples !), and before I rose from my bed on Monday morning, I had
written above a hundred and seventy verses as good as any I ever
wrote in my life excepting my Death of Clytemnestra'.*[1]

The play is a continuation of Andrea of Hungary, *and the trilogy
was completed with* Fra Rupert, *published in 1840. Andrea, who is
married to Giovannia, becomes greatly influenced by his worldly wife,
for he has been brought up under the influence of monks. He is now
jealously regarded by Fra Rupert, who contrives his death, and
Giovanna is unjustly accused of the murder. But in the second play she
is acquitted by Rienzi, while in the third play Rupert is discovered as
the murderer. Giovanna is to Italy what Mary Stuart is to Scotland,
and different judgements of her will always exist. Boccaccio praised her
qualities, while Petrarch compared her and her husband to two lambs in
the midst of wolves.*

*Any profits from these plays Landor wished to be given to the Grace
Darling Fund. Forster sent Landor his congratulations on 3 November
and was astonished to hear that he had written the second play in eight
days. There were, however, the usual difficulties in finding a publisher.
Saintsbury wrote:*

'The three pieces, which together extend to a hundred and forty large
pages, are much more than 'imaginary conversation in metric'; they
form, in fact, a historical novel, thrown into a conversational
dramatic form with all the redundancies of the novel as they may
seem from the dramatic point of view. Sometimes, the treatment
approaches more nearly to the fashion of an actable play scene;
sometimes, to that of a chapter of Scott or Dumas turned into verse
and put in action instead of narration. And this hybrid character
is maintained, almost continuously, in the pieces that follow: more
than a dozen in number, tho' always shorter, and sometimes much
shorter, than the Neapolitan set. Landor at last discovers the source
of that interest which he had failed to attain in Gebir and Count
Julian'.[2]

---

[1] *Idem,* p. 320.
[2] Saintsbury, G., *C.H.E.L.,* vol. xii, p. 212.

Two Dramatic Scenes
1838

[1]
ANNE BOLEYN AND THE CONSTABLE

Anne Boleyn. Sir William Kingston. Constable of the Tower.

ANNE BOLEYN. Is your liege ill, sir, that you look so anxious?
CONSTABLE OF THE TOWER. Madam!
ANNE.   I would not ask what you may wish
To keep a secret from me; but indeed
This right, I think, is left me . . . I would know
If my poor husband is quite well to-day.
    CONSTABLE. Pardon me, gracious lady! what can prompt
To this inquiry?
    ANNE.   I have now *my* secret.
    CONSTABLE. I must report all questions, sayings, doings,
Movements, and looks of yours. His Highness may
Be ruffled at this eagerness to ask
About his health.
    ANNE.   I am used to ask about it.
Beside, he may remember . . .
    CONSTABLE.   For your Highness
Gladly will I remind our sovran Lord
Of any promise.
    ANNE.   Oh, no! do not that!
It would incense him: he made only one,
And Heaven alone that heard him must remind him!
Last night, I do suspect, but am not sure,
He scarcely was what kings and husbands should be.
A little wine has great effect upon
Warm hearts (and Henry's heart *was* very warm)
And upon strong resentments . . . I do fear
He has those too . . . But all his friends must love him.
He may have past (poor Henry!) a bad night,
Thinking upon his hasty resolution.

CONSTABLE. Lady! I grieve to tell you, worse than that ...
Far worse!
ANNE. Oh, mercy, then! the child! the child!
Why not have told me of all this before?
What boots it to have been a guiltless wife,
When I, who should have thought the first about it,
Am an ill mother? Not to think of thee,
My darling! my Elizabeth! whose cradle
Rocks in my ear and almost crazes me.
Is she safe? Tell me, tell me, is she living?
CONSTABLE. Safe, lady, and asleep in rosy health,
And radiant (if there yet be light enough
To shew it on her face) with pleasant dreams,
Such as young angels come on earth to play with.
ANNE. Were I but sure that I could dream of her
As I, until last autumn, oft have done,
Joyously, blithely, only waking up
Afraid of having hurt her by my arms
Too wildly in my rapture thrown around her,
I would lay down my weary head, and sleep,
Although the pillow be a little strange,
Nor like a bridal or a childbed pillow.
CONSTABLE. Oh, spare those words!
ANNE.   Why spare them? when I feel
Departure from this world would never be
Departure from its joys: the joys of heaven
Would mingle with them scarcely with fresh sweetness.
CONSTABLE (*falling on his knees*). My queen!
ANNE.   Arise, sir constable!
CONSTABLE.   My queen!
Heaven's joys lie close before you.
ANNE.   And you weep?
Few days, I know, are left me; they will melt
All into one, all pure, all peaceable ...
No starts from slumber into bitter tears,
No struggles with sick hopes and wild desires,
No cruel father cutting down the tree
To crush the child that sits upon its boughs
And looks abroad ... too tender for suspicion,

Too happy even for hope, maker of happiness.
I could weep too, nor sinfully, at this.
　　Thou knowest, O my God! thou surely knowest
'Tis no repining at thy call or will.
　　　　(Constable, *on his knees, presents the Writ of Execution*.)
I can do nothing now . . . take back that writing,
And tell them so, poor souls! Say to the widow
I grieve, and can *but* grieve for her; persuade her
That children, although fatherless, are blessings;
And teach those little ones, if e'er you see them,
They are not half so badly off as some.
Fold up the paper . . . put it quite aside . . .
I am no queen; I have no almoner . . .
Ah, now I weep indeed! Put, put it by.
Many . . . I grieve (yet, *should* I grieve?) to think it,
Many will often say, when I am gone,
They once had a young queen to pity them.
Nay, though I mention'd I had nought to give,
Yet dash not on your head, nor grapple so
With those ungentle hands, while I am here,
A helpless widow's innocent petition.
Smoothe it; return it with all courtesy:
Smoothe it, I say again: frame some kind words
And see they find their place, then tender it.
What! in this manner gentlemen of birth
Present us papers? turn they thus away,
Putting their palms between their eyes and us?
Sir! I was queen . . . and you were kind unto me
When I was queen no longer . . . why so changed?
Give it . . . but what is now my signature?
Ignorant are you, or incredulous,
That not a clasp is left me? not a stone
The vilest; not chalcedony; not agate.
Promise her all my dresses, when . . . no, no . . .
I am grown superstitious; they might bring
Misfortune on her, having been Anne Boleyn's.
　　CONSTABLE. Lady! I wish this scroll could suffocate
My voice. One order I must disobey,
To place it in your hand and mark you read it.

I lay it at your feet, craving your pardon
And God's, my lady!
    ANNE.   Rise up; give it me;
I know it ere I read it, but I read it
Because it is the king's, whom I have sworn
To love and to obey.
    CONSTABLE (*aside*). Her mind's distraught!
Alas, she smiles!
    ANNE.   The worst hath long been over:
Henry loves courage; he will love my child
For this; although I want more than I have;
And yet how merciful at last is Heaven
To give me but thus much for her sweet sake.

[II]

SCENE IN EPPING FOREST
[May 19, 1536.]

HENRY, *Courtiers, Hounds, &c.*
    HENRY. Northumberland! pray tell me, if thou canst,
Who is that young one in the green and gold?
Dost thou not see her? hast thou left both eyes
Upon the bushes?
    NORTHUMBERLAND. There are many, sir,
In the same livery.
    HENRY.   *Her* I mean; her yonder
On the iron-gray with yellow round her ears.
Impudent wench! she turns away her cheek!
    NORTHUMBERLAND.   (*after inquiring.*)
The Lady Katharine Parr, an' please your Highness.
    HENRY. Faith! she *doth* please me. What a sap is rising
In that young bud! how supple! yet how solid!
What palpable perfection! ay, Lord Arundel!
    ARUNDEL. A bloom well worthy of a monarch's bower,
Where only one more lovely smiles beside him.
    HENRY. Though spring is stirring, yet give me the summer . . .
I can wait yet . . . though, some day, not far off,
I would confer with her at Hampton-Court . . .
Merely to ask her how she likes the chase:

We shall not have another all this season:
The stag alone can help us on in May:
To-morrow is the twentieth.

                              Hark! the knell
From Paul's! . . . the Tower-gun, too!

                                        I am right enough!
                                   (*Claps his hands.*)
I am a widower!   [*Again claps his hands.*
                        By this hour to-morrow
Sunny Jane Seymour's long and laughing eyes
Shall light me to our chamber.

                              Lords! prick on!
The merry hounds are chiding! To the chase
To-day! our coronation for to-morrow.

The year 1839 began with the harassments of the publication of the two plays. Landor had given them to Forster, who was chief reader to Bentley. Forster submitted the plays to that firm, but publication was delayed owing to Bentley's dispute with Dickens and Forster, resulting Dickens's withdrawal from the editorship of Bentleys Miscellany.[1] *It was Landor who suffered most over this quarrel for, although he was correcting some of the proofs as early as January, the plays were not reviewed before September. Moreover, Bentley made no effort to advertise them. He wrote to Rose Paynter[2] in March:*

'At last I am able to send you a little book. . .[3] If you attempt to read it before you set out again, I shall begin to think you guilty of curiosity—the only bad thing I can ever be induced to think of your sex. O ! that cruel chapter in Genesis which will not allow us, as good Christians, to disbelieve or doubt it ! But let us hope that it is wearing out in the world, for I have heard nothing about it lately. . . . I have exempted her [Giovanna] from the levities of her court and of her age, that due honour might be done to her; while I thought it requisite for that court and that age, that nearly all the other personages should partake in them. I merge my own gravity in the well of truth. . . .

'Believe me (indeed you will easily), it is a horrible thing to have many literary friends. They are apt to fancy that, however your time may be occupied, you must at all events have enough to read what they send you. Alas ! alas ! There are few who have time enough to read even all the very good books that have been written, old and new; and who can neglect the good for the bad without compunction and remorse ? . . . In regard to small authors, restless for celebrity, and wriggling on their level walks like worms exposed to the sunshine, I have scarcely ever seen one of these poor creatures who did not at one time excite my smiles, and at another my pity. . . . When years have sorted your mind with observation, you will

---

[1] Elwin, *Landor*, p. 323.
[2] In 1846 Rose Paynter married Sir Charles Bruce Grave-Sawle.
[3] *Andrea of Hungary* and *Govannia of Naples*.

continue to prefer Goldsmith to Bulwer, Miss Edgeworth to Lady Morgan. .'

Landor arrived at Gore House on 2 January 1840, and that evening Henry Reeve[1] called. He recorded: 'There is something of perpetual youth in his age: and he has that clear spirit of thought in him which shines like the eye of some large bird in the twilight'. He saw a good deal of Forster, and together they visited R. H. Horne, the author of The Death of Marlowe *which Landor had liked so much. He gave Horne a copy of* A Satire on Satirists. *He also met Dickens, and the two enjoyed each other's company, despite the fact that Dickens was only twenty eight and Landor sixty five. Moreover, Dickens was already the tremendously successful author of* The Pickwick Papers *and* Nicholas Nickleby, *which must have rankled a little. After Landor had returned to Bath, Dickens arrived at the York House Hotel, then one of the largest hotels in Bath. He was accompanied by Maclise and they immediately called on Landor and had dinner at his lodgings. Behind his lodgings was a small shop and it is there, it is said,* The Old Curiosity Shop *took fire. Writing to his wife the next day Dickens said: 'Indeed I was not bored—for which I am very thankful and devout this morning'.[2] Dickens was subsequently to give a memorable portrait of Landor in* Bleak House—*calling him Boythorn.*

On 15 March Landor received a copy of Browning's new book with a dedicated inscription. Landor wrote to Forster: 'You were right as to Browning. He has sent me some admirable things. I only wish he would atticize a little. Few of the Athenians had such a quarry on their property, but they constructed better roads for the conveyance of the material'.[3] Five years later he wrote to Forster: 'I have written to Browning; a great poet, a very great poet indeed, as the world will have to agree with us in thinking'.[4]

Crabb Robinson followed hot on the heels of Dickens, and they called on Sarah Burney. They discussed Landor's children, whom he was expecting, and he told Robinson that it was Julia he so much wished to see. It would appear that his sons were awaited in April, but they

---

[1] Reeve, Henry. Sometime editor Edinburgh Review and The Greville Memoirs.
[2] Dexter, *Mr & Mrs Charles Dickens*, 1935, p. 89.
[3] Forster, *Landor*, vol. ii, p. 424.
[4] *Idem*, p. 425.

*caught measles and their arrival was postponed till June. So Landor
went to Warwick to meet them. He wrote to Rose Paynter:*

> 'Arnold says he cannot stay beyond two months in England, since it
> grieves him to leave his mother for a long time. I cannot blame him
> nor argue with him on that point. It shows an affectionate heart
> which I am pleased at finding, although I may grieve in secret that
> it (he?) does not lean a little more toward me. I shall ask him only
> one favour; which is that he will allow me to show him Bath . . .'.[1]

*But he was doomed to disappointment; the boys set out from Fiesole and
arrived at Bologna, where Walter again fell ill—presumably from the
effects of measles. The younger son wrote and regretted that they were
unable to see him, but Arnold wrote and told him that he had decided
he would never come to England without his mother.*

*In August Landor decided to go to Torquay and Exmouth, where
the Paynters arrived. Returning to Bath for a short while, he then went
to Llandbedr to see his friend Joseph Atblet, returning via Cheltenham
to visit another old friend, Anthony Rosenhagen, 'a retired civil servant
who had retired after a promising career after Waterloo because of
failing eyesight. He was married to his second wife, a sister of Fleetwood Parkhurst, whom Landor remembered as a little girl'.[2]*

*Writing to Forster in December 1840, Landor said: 'My body, and
my mind more especially, requires strong exercise. I cannot walk
through the snow and slop . . . lately, from the want of sun and all
things cheerful, my saddened and wearied mind has often roosted on the
acacias and cypresses I planted.[3] The year ended with the third play of
the trilogy* Fra Rupert, *being published.*

*At last Landor heard from his son Walter that he intended to come
to see his father. He also met, for the first time, his brother-in-law
Colonel Stopford, who had married his wife's sister Laura, and to
whom he had dedicated the first volume of his* Imaginary Conversations.

> 'A more gentlemanly or more noble-minded man I never conversed
> with. His wife was overjoyed at our meeting, talked to me of
> Llanthony, and of the walk I took her over the hills, and of the
> grouse we started. Presently came in the Minister of Caraccas and

---

[1] Wheeler, *Private Letters*, p. 56.
[2] Super, *Landor*, p. 321.
[3] Elwin, *Landor*, p. 339.

*General Millar, who took over the command of the armies of
Colombia on the retirement of Bolivar . . . Neither of these men
think highly of Bolivar as a soldier; both of them like all his family,
and were pleased with the gracefulness of his manner. And now
appeared my niece Teresita.*[1] *She struck me as being very like dear
Julia, rather less beautiful, but more intellectual.'*

The Blessingtons took Landor regularly to the opera. He wrote to
Rose Paynter:

[*Gore House*] 'Saturday Morning [*May 8, 1841*][2] '. . . *We went this
evening to the German Opera.*[3] *Never was music so excellent. The
pieces were* A Night in Grenada *and* Fidelio. *Madame Schodel*[4]
*sings divinely, and her acting is only inferior to Pasta's. Grisi never
quite satisfied me excepting in* Norma. *There nobody can surpass her.
I have seen enough of viragos in real life—they no longer can
interest or even amuse me. Both D'Orsay and Lord Pembroke were
enchanted with Madame Schodel, and Lady B[lessington] and Miss
Power, both good judges, and the latter a fine composer, were
breathless. Tonight we go to the Italian Opera. At dinner nobody
but Lord Pembroke. Yesterday I missed seeing Mademoiselle Rachel,
who had just left Mrs Stopford, but I found there Miss Strickland,
authoress of the* Queens of England—*and went to find my old
acquaintance, Miss Porter,*[5] *and my new one, Miss Poulter.*[6]
Afterwards I went to Kenyon's. He and Bezzi[7] *were out, but Bezzi
saw me in Regent's Park and overtook me. I hope to see them this
morning, but I find I am too late for my passport, which I cannot
have before Monday. As the steamer sails on Sunday I shall go
without one.*

---

[1] She was subsequently to marry Lord Charles Beauclerk.
[2] Wheeler, ed. *Private Letters*, p. 67.
[3] 7 May 1841. German opera: Theatre Royal, Drury Lane, *A Night in Grenada*
by Conradin Kreutzer, to conclude with Beethoven's grand opera of *Fidelio*.
[4] She was also acclaimed on 12 May when she appeared in Spontini's *La Vestale*.
[5] Jane Porter (1776–1850), the novelist who had remarkable popularity with *The
Scottish Chiefs* (1831).
[6] Miss Poulter published, in 1841, *Imagination, with Other Poems*.
[7] Signor Bezzi was an accomplished Italian gentleman, a great friend of Mr John
Kenyon's. It was he discovered the portrait of Dante on the whitewashed tower
of the Bargello in Florence.

I left behind me only one thing, but the most important of all, the little key of my carpet bag in which my dress coat, &c., were packed up. I was forced to cut it open, and how to manage with it or without it is a puzzle. Lady B[lessington] and my other friends here wish me to stay until after Monday, when Mlle. Rachel[1] acts. I had heard that she is plain. Miss Stopford tells me she is quite the reverse, and that her manner is charming. This morning I shall know if the Ministers resign.[2] If they do, I shall call on Lord Normanby.[3] I will never pay a visit to a man in office. Some of my friends have left their cards on me—but I really heve never been at home, and on the opera nights nobody is received here. Walter has written to me from Leghorn, where all my family have been for the benefit of sea bathing, and will remain the whole of May . . .

Believe me, Dear Mrs Paynter,
Sincerely and affectionately yours,
W. S. Landor.

Shortly after this letter was written, Landor met his son Walter in Paris. In a further rhymed letter to Rose Paynter, he told her that his son was as thin as a lath; and that he met the historian Mignet. Thiers he described as looking like 'a mangy rat'. Colmache, Talleyrand's Private Secretary, introduced him to Alexandre Auguste Ledru-Rollin, one of the leading barristers in France, and while in his library he met the celebrated detective Vidocq. Of Chateaubriand he said he seemed 'like a small bottle of sugar and water fit only to catch flies.' He also met Madame Récamier, and Byron's mistress Countess Guiccioli. Father and son were in Paris for nine weeks before arriving in England. Walter visited his maternal grandmother and aunts at Richmond, while Landor stayed at Forster's Chambers at Lincolns Inn Fields. Though Walter did not accompany his father to some of the famous breakfasts, Landor did not impede him in any way from going to see any relatives. In August they were both visitors to Landor's sister Elizabeth.

In September he wrote to Rose Paynter:

[1] 'I went to see Mdlle. Rachel make her *début* last night which she did in Hermione.' – *Greville Memoirs*, 11 May 1841.
[2] They did. And Sir Robert Peel was invited to form a ministry, but declined to accept office, on the Queen's refusing to admit proposed changes of the ladies of the bedchamber. So Lord Melbourne took office again.
[3] Secretary of State for the Colonies in Lord Melbourne's administration.

'*You know that my hatred of politics is unfeigned—you also know that the dearest of my friends are Conservatives. Neither party can ever be of the slightest use or advantage to me; and I was not very highly pleased when I was desired and invited to ask for something. If the change of Minister[1] is beneficial to any of your connections I shall by no means regret it, for I am confident that the present men will bring about what the others failed to accomplish. The Duke of Wellington is the only man of either party in whom I can discern the semblance of greatness. The rest are clever scene-shifters and expert prompters, nothing more...*'[2]

On 14 October, he wrote to her again, from Bath:

'*Walter has left me grieved and solitary, but by permitting his return I have a better chance of seeing the rest. Poor dear Julia thought that Walter might succeed in bringing me back to Italy with him. I soon found out that anxious as he was to come to me, he came in character as an ambassador. This is one thing in the world in which my sweet Julia could not prevail with me. To stand firm on some occasions requires more power and more energy than any active effort, and wrenches both the mind and body more. I think my strength and spirits are rather the worse for this resistance, and long walks are ineffectual in bringing me back sleep and appetite. I shall soon, however, be more reconciled to the absence of my sweet-tempered boy, who is much improved by his residence in England, and the last shades of gloom will have disappeared before you return. I have been to visit your flowers—they are doing well, and the roses I planted seemed glad to see me.*'[3]

The following year (1842) his eldest son Arnold visited him, though he went through much anxiety before he arrived, on account of a train blowing up on 8 May between Paris and Versailles. Some fifty people were killed, and Landor had thought his son might have been on that train. 'I dreamt,' *he wrote to Rose Paynter,* 'on the morning of the sixth of May that he was dead. It is said that every man has some superstition. I have none, absolutely none. But I have always felt beforehand a fainter or stronger intimation of coming evils—in such a*

---

[1] Peel became Prime Minister in September.
[2] Wheeler, *Private Letters*, p. 82.
[3] *Idem*, pp. 88–89.

manner as to leave me the power of obviating them.'[1] *That day he refused to leave his house. But he received a letter from Arnold on the 17th intimating that he was leaving Florence on the 7th, and hoped to be with his father on the 21st.*

Landor was at Gore House in June. At the first great dinner party he met again his old friend Lord Pembroke, together with the Duc de Guiche. He also heard Rossini's Stabat Mater *for the first time at the Prince's Theatre. Mario and Staudigl were singing and Landor thought very highly of the last-named. We also get his account of a visit to the Royal Academy.*

All his life Landor was a collector of pictures, and the walls of his Florentine apartments were lined with them. Comments on Landor's taste in art were frequently made, for, as in all things, his opinions were direct and dogmatic as well as erratic. Writing to Rose Paynter on his visit to the Royal Academy, he commented:

> *'Three pictures struck me particularly. A scene in Hamlet—the play scene by Maclise.*[2] *The Queen is most admirable, but Hamlet is vulgar and too old. In reality he could not be twenty. All the accessories are admirable. There is another piece containing only Ophelia.*[3] *She is sitting under a withered tree, her feet naked, and hanging over the water in which she was so soon to die. The flowers are going down the stream. She has thrown in almost the last of them. Her countenance is mild and melancholy, and very beautiful. Even in the position of her feet there is pathos.*
> *'Landseer has several pictures all worthy of his skill and genius. One of them is equal in execution and invention to any work of the English School. He calls it the Sanctuary.'*[4]

It was in this year that Landor wrote his long and detailed essay on Catullus for Forster who had become editor of the Foreign Quarterly Review. *This essay was followed in October by* The Idylls of Theocritus. *The concluding summary on Catullus is included here and shows Landor in his most cantankerous mood. Carlyle, whom Landor quite obviously did not care for in the least, received equally opinionated treatment (not without some cause if he had read the final paragraphs*

---

[1] Wheeler, *Private Letters*, p. 94.
[2] Daniel Maclise, R.A.
[3] Ophelia by R. Redgrave, R.A.
[4] Wheeler, *Private Letters*, p. 100.

of his essay): 'he had fallen into an extravagant method of stating his opinions, which made any serious acceptance of them altogether impossible.'

Later critics, too, have decried Landor's essays on Catullus, and Super records:

'*A more thoroughly disorganized work never fell from his pen; it was a hodgepodge of miscellaneous notes, some written as long ago as his correspondence with Parr while he was at Oxford, it ranged through the bucolics of Virgil, medieval and modern Latinists, and* Paradise Regained (*fading into his essay materials later expanded on the Imaginary Conversation between Southey and Landor*). . .'

From *The Poems of Catullus*
1842

In selecting a poet for examination, it is usual either to extol him to the skies, or to tear him to pieces and trample on him. Editors in general do the former: critics on editors more usually the latter. But one poet is not to be raised by casting another under him. Catullus is made no richer by an attempt to transfer to him what belongs to Horace, nor Horace by what belongs to Catullus. Catullus has greatly more than he; but he also has much; and let him keep it. We are not at liberty to indulge in forwardness and caprice, snatching a decoration from one and tossing it over to another. We will now sum up what we have collected from the mass of materials which has been brought before us, laying down some general rules and observations.

There are four things requisite to constitute might, majesty, and dominion, in a poet: these are creativeness, constructiveness, the sublime, the pathetic. A poet of the first order must have formed, or taken to himself and modified, some great subject. He must be creative and constructive. Creativeness may work upon old materials: a new world may spring from an old one. Shakespeare found Hamlet and Ophelia; he found Othello and Desdemona: nevertheless he, the only universal poet, carried this, and all the other qualifications, far beyond the reach of competitors. He was creative and constructive, he was sublime and pathetic, and he has also in his humanity condescended to the familiar and the comic. There is nothing less pleasant than the smile of Milton; but at one time Momus, at another the Graces, hang upon the neck of Shakespeare. Poets whose subjects do not restrict them, and whose ordinary gait displays no indication of either greave or buskin, if they want the facetious and humorous, and are not creative, nor sublime, nor pathetic, must be ranked by sound judges in the secondary order, and not among the foremost even there.

Cowper, and Byron, and Southey, with much and deep tenderness, are richly humorous. Wordsworth, grave, elevated, observant, and philosophical, is equidistant from humour and from passion. Always contemplative, never creative, he delights the sedentary and tranquillizes the excited. No tear ever fell, no smile ever glanced, on his pages. With him you are beyond the danger of any turbulent emotion, as terror, or valour, or magnanimity, or generosity. Nothing is there about him like Burns's *Scots wha ha'e wi' Wallace bled*, or Campbell's *Battles of Copenhagen and Hohenlinden*, or those exquisite works which, in Hemans, rise up like golden spires among broader but lower structures, *Ivan* and *Casabianca*. Byron, often impressive and powerful, never reaches the heroic and the pathetic of these two poems: and he wants the freshness and healthiness we admire in Burns. But an indomitable fire of poetry, the more vivid for the gloom about it, bursts through the crusts and crevices of an unsound and hollow mind. He never chatters and chilliness, nor falls overstrained into languor; nor do metaphysics ever muddy his impetuous and precipitate stream. It spreads its ravishes in some places, but it is limpid and sparkling everywhere. If no story is well told by him, no character well delineated, if all resemble one another by their beards and Turkish dresses, there is however the first and the second and the third requisite of eloquence, whether in prose or poetry, vigour. But no *large* poem of our days is so animated, or so truly of the heroic cast, as *Marmion*. Southey's *Roderick* has less nerve and animation: but what other living poet has attempted, or shown the ability, to erect a structure so symmetrical and so stately? It is not enough to heap description on description, to cast reflection over reflection: there must be development of character in the development of story; there must be action, there must be passion; the end and the means must alike be great.

The poet whom we mentioned last is more studious of classical models than the others, especially in his *Inscriptions*. Interest is always excited by him, enthusiasm not always. If his elegant prose and harmonious verse are insufficient to excite it, turn to his virtues, to his manliness in defence of truth, to the ardour and constancy of his friendships, to his distinterestedness, to his generosity, to his rejection of title and office, and consequently of wealth and influence. He has laboured to raise up merit in whatever path of literature he found it; and poetry in particular has never had so intelligent, so impartial, and so merciful a judge. Alas! it is the will of God to deprive him of those faculties which he exercised with such discretion, such meekness, and such humanity.

We digress; not too far, but too long: we must return to the ancients, and more especially to the author whose volume lies open before us.

There is little of the creative, little of the constructive, in him: that is, he has conceived no new varieties of character; he has built up no edifice in the intellectual world; but he always is shrewd and brilliant; he often is pathetic; and he sometimes is sublime. Without the sublime, we have said before, there can be no poet of the first order: but the pathetic may exist in the secondary, for tears are more easily drawn forth than souls are raised. So easily are they on some occasions, that the poetical power needs scarcely be brought into action; while on others the pathetic is the very summit of sublimity. We have an example of it in the *Ariadne* of Catullus: we have another in the *Priam* of Homer. All the heroes and gods, debating and fighting, vanish before the father of Hector in the tent of Achilles, and before the storm of conflicting passions his sorrows and prayers excite. But neither in the spirited and energetic Catullus, nor in the masculine and scornful and stern Lucretius, no, nor in Homer, is there anything so impassioned, and therefore so sublime, as the last hour of Dido in the *Æneid*. Admirably as two Greek poets have represented the tenderness, the anguish, the terrific wrath and vengeance of Medea, all the works they ever wrote contain not the poetry which Virgil has condensed into about a hundred verses: omitting, as we must, those which drop like icicles from the rigid lips of Æneas; and also the similes which, here as everywhere, sadly interfere with passion. In this place Virgil fought his battle of Actium, which left him poetical supremacy in the Roman world, whatever mutinies and conspiracies may have arisen against him in Germany or elsewhere.

The *Ariadne* of Catullus has greatly the advantage over the *Medea* of Apollonius: for what man is much interested by such a termagant? We have no sympathies with a woman whose potency is superhuman. In general, it may be apprehended, we like women little the better for excelling us even moderately in our own acquirements and capacities. But what energy springs from her weaknesses! what poetry is the fruit of her passions! once perhaps in a thousand years bursting forth with imperishable splendour on its golden bough. If there are fine things in the *Argonautics* of Apollonius, there are finer still in those of Catullus. In relation to Virgil, he stands as Correggio in relation to Raffael: a richer colourist, a less accurate draughtsman; less capable of executing grand designs, more exquisite in the working-out of smaller. Virgil is depreciated by the arrogance of self-sufficient poets, nurtured on coarse fare, and dizzy with home-brewed flattery. Others, who have studied more attentively the ancient models, are abler to show his relative station, and readier to venerate his powers. Although we find him incapable of contriving, and more incapable of executing, so magnificent a work as the *Iliad*, yet there are places in his compared with which the grandest in that grand poem lose much of their elevation. Never was there such a whirlwind of passions as Virgil raised on those African shores, amid those rising citadels and departing sails. When the vigorous verses of Lucretius are extolled, no true poet, no sane critic, will assent that the seven or eight examples of the best are equivalent to this one: even in force of expression, here he falls short of Virgil.

When we drink a large draught of refreshing beverage, it is only a small portion that affects the palate. In reading the best poetry, moved and excited as we may be, we can take in no more than a part of it. Passages of equal beauty are unable to raise enthusiasm. Let a work in poetry or prose, indicating the highest power of genius, be discoursed on; probably no two persons in a large company will recite the same portion as having struck them the most forcibly. But when several passages are pointed out and read emphatically, each listener will to a certain extent doubt a little his own judgment in this one particular, and hate you heartily for shaking it. Poets ought never to be vext, discomposed, or disappointed, when the better is overlookt, and the inferior is commended. Much may be assigned to the observer's point of vision being more on a level with the object. And this reflection also will console the artist, when really bad ones are called more simple and natural, while in fact they are only more ordinary and common. In a palace we must look to the elevation and proportions; whereas a low grotto may assume any form and almost any deformity. Rudeness is here no blemish; a shell reversed is no false ornament; moss and fern may be stuck with the root outward; a crystal may sparkle at the top or at the bottom; dry sticks and fragmentary petrifactions find everywhere their proper place; and loose soil and plashy water show just what nature delights in. Ladies and gentlemen who at first were about to turn back, take one another by the hand, duck their heads, enter it together, and exclaim, 'What a charming grotto!'

In poetry, as in architecture, the Rustic Order is proper only for the lower story.

They who have listened, patiently and supinely, to the catarrhal songsters of goose-grazed commons will be loth and ill-fitted to mount up with Catullus to the highest steeps in the forests of Ida, and will shudder at the music of the Corybantes in the temple of the Great Mother of the Gods.

1843

On 21 March, at eight in the morning, Landor's closest friend of thirty-four years, Southey, the man who championed Gebir, *died. Landor wrote to Forster:*

'Southey's death is announced to me this morning. My reverence for his purity of soul, my grateful estimation of his affection towards me, are not to be expressed in words. But it would grieve me to think that any other man should have testified to the world regret at losing him, before I had done it.'

In the Examiner *of 25 March, there appeared:*[1]

> Not the last struggles of the Sun
> Precipitated from his golden throne
> Hold darkling mortals in sublime suspense,
> But the calm exod of a man
> Nearer, tho' high above, who ran
> The race we run, when Heaven recalls him hence.
> Thus, O thou pure of earthly taint!
> Thus, O my Southey! poet, sage, and saint.
> Thou, after saddest silent art removed.
> What voice in anguish can we raise?
> Thee would we, need we, dare we, praise?
> God now does that . . . the God thy whole heart loved.

Southey's widow, his second wife Caroline Bowles, to whom he had been married only four years (his first wife, to whom he had been devoted, having died insane) was left badly off. Landor, in his typically kind way, had immediately written to Monckton Milnes suggesting a state pension, but the proposal was rejected by the Government.

Landor was now at work upon a collected edition of his works and on an essay on Petrarch. He also heard that his daughter, Julia, was coming to England, and this event naturally delighted him. She was accompanied by her brother Walter, and they arrived in Bath in May. He celebrated the event by publishing the following poem in Blackwood's Magazine:

---

[1] Forster, *Landor*, vol. ii, p. 405.

By that dejected city, Arno runs,
Where Ugolino claspt his famisht sons.
There wert thou born, my Julia ! there thine eyes
Return'd as bright a blue to vernal skies.
And thence, my little wanderer ! when the Spring
Advanced, thee too, the hours on silent wing
Brought, while anemones were quivering round
And pointed tulips pierced the purple ground,
Where stood fair Florence: there thy voice first blest
My ear, and sank like balm into my breast.
For many griefs had wounded it, and more
Thy little hands could lighten were in store.
But why revert to griefs ? Thy sculptured brow
Dispels from mine its darkest cloud even now.
What then the bliss to see again thy face,
And all that Rumour has announced of grace !
I urge, with fevered breast, the four-month day,
O ! I could sleep to wake again in May.

Fortunately, he was not disappointed in Julia, and she did her best to win the affection of her father. They went everywhere together, visiting many people, including his sister Elizabeth. In his letters to Rose Paynter he relates his doings. In August he took Julia to a regatta: 'I thought my dear Julia might be amused by it, but she understood as little of the matter and enjoyed it as little as myself.'[1] Yet the regatta at Plymouth they went to the following month pleased them, though they were all glad to return to Bath.

That month he had contributed to The Examiner *an article on 'Greece and King Otho'. It was natural that Landor, with his republican ideals should have interested himself on this question.[2]*

Julia and Walter left in October, promising to return within six months. Meanwhile, Landor had become 'a cripple' with rheumatism. 'Perhaps a gallop round Doncaster Race Course would do me good, but I doubt my elasticity in springing to the saddle. I thought old age a fable until now. I now find it a serious and sad calamity'.[3]

On 5 December he went out to hear music at Mrs Yeate's, 'whose

[1] Wheeler, *Private Letters*, p. 115.
[2] A revolution had broken out in Greece, and King Otho promised his people a democratic constitution.
[3] Wheeler, *Private Letters*, p. 121.

pretty daughter played admirably. Now be cautious never to enter a wheel *chair in damp weather. It was by doing so that I caught as severe a cold and fever as ever befell me. Bread and butter pudding, Selzer water and strawberry jam have been my only sustenance'* he *wrote to Rose Paynter.[1] In this year he contributed one of his most famous 'Imaginary Conversations' to Lady Blessington's* Book of Beauty, *that between Aesop and Rhodopè. A second conversation appeared the following year.*

[1] *Idem,* p. 125.

To Charles Dickens

[*The Examiner*, 21 September]

Go then to Italy; but mind
To leave the pale low France behind;
Pass through that country, nor ascend
The Rhine, nor over Tyrol wend:
Thus all at once shall rise more grand
the glories of the ancient land.
   Dickens! how often, when the air
Breath'd genially, I've thought me there,
And rais'd to heaven my thankful eyes
To see three spans of deep blue skies.
   In Genoa now I hear a stir,
A shout . . . *Here comes the Minister!*
Yes, thou art he, although not sent
By cabinet or parliament:
Yes, thou art he. Since Milton's youth
Bloom'd in the Eden of the South,
Spirit so pure and lofty none
Hath heavenly Genius from his throne
Deputed on the banks of Thames
To speak his voice and urge his claims.
Let every nation know from thee
How less than lovely Italy
Is the whole world beside; let all
Into their grateful breasts recall
How Prospero and Miranda dwelt
In Italy: the griefs that melt
The stoniest heart, each sacred tear
One lachrymatory gathered here;
All Desdemona's, all that fell
In playful Juliet's bridal cell
   Ah! could my steps in life's decline
Accompany or follow thine!
But my own vines are not for me

To prune, or from afar to see.
I miss the tales I used to tell
With cordial Hare[1] and joyous Gell,[2]
And that good old Archbishop[3] whose
Cool library, at evening's close
(Soon as from Ischia swept the gale
And heav'd and left the dark'ning sail),
Its lofty portal open'd wide
To me, and very few beside:
Yet large his kindness. Still the poor
Flock round Taranto's palace door,
And find no other to replace
The noblest of a noble race.
Amid our converse you would see
Each with white cat upon his knee,
And flattering that grand company:
For Persian kings might proudly own
Such glorious cats to share the throne.
   Write me few letters: I'm content
With what for all the world is meant;
Write then for all: but, since my breast
Is far more faithful than the rest,
Never shall any other share
With little Nelly nestling there.

From *Imaginary Conversations*

1853
(first published in *The Book of Beauty*, 1844)

ÆSOP AND RHODOPÈ

Egypt, between 620 and 560 B.C.

ÆSOP. Albeit thou approachest me without any sign of derision, let me tell thee before thou advancest a step nearer, that I deem

---

[1] Francis Hare, died in 1842.
[2] Sir William Gell, died in 1836.
[3] Guisseppe Capèce-Latro, Archbishop of Tarentum, died in 1836.

thee more hard-hearted than the most petulant of those other young persons, who are pointing and sneering from the door-way.

RHODOPÈ. Let them continue to point and sneer at me: they are happy; so am I; but are you? Think me hard-hearted, O good Phrygian! but graciously give me the reason for thinking it; other wise I may be unable to correct a fault too long overlooked by me, or to deprecate a grave infliction of the Gods.

ÆSOP. I thought thee so, my little maiden, because thou camest toward me without the least manifestation of curiosity.

RHODOPÈ. Is the absence of curiosity a defect?

ÆSOP. None whatever.

RHODOPÈ. Are we blamable in concealing it if we have it?

ÆSOP. Surely not. But it is feminine; and where none of it comes forward, we may suspect that other feminine appurtenances, such as sympathy for example, are deficient. Curiosity slips in among you before the passions are awake: curiosity comforts your earliest cries; curiosity intercepts your latest. For which reason Dædalus, who not only sculptured but painted admirably, repre- sents her in the vestibule of the Cretan labyrinth as a Goddess.

RHODOPÈ. What was she like?

ÆSOP. There now! Like? Why, like Rhodopè.

RHODOPÈ. You said I have nothing of the kind.

ÆSOP. I soon discovered my mistake in this, and more than this, and not altogether to thy disadvantage.

RHODOPÈ. I am glad to hear it.

ÆSOP. Art thou? I will tell thee then how she was depicted: for I remember no author who has related it. Her lips were half-open; her hair flew loosely behind her, designating that she was in haste; it was more disordered, and it was darker, than the hair of Hope is represented, and somewhat less glossy. Her cheeks had a very fresh colour, and her eyes looked into every eye that fell upon them; by her motion she seemed to be on her way into the labyrinth.

RHODOPÈ. O how I wish I could see such a picture!

ÆSOP. I do now.

RHODOPÈ. Where? where? Troublesome man! Are you always so mischievous? but your smile is not ill-natured. I can not help thinking that the smiles of men are pleasanter and sweeter than of women; unless of the women who are rather old and decrepit, who seem to want help, and who perhaps are thinking that we girls are now the very images of what *they* were formerly. But girls never look at me so charmingly as you do, nor smile with such benignity; and yet, O Phrygian, there are several of them who really are much handsomer.

ÆSOP. Indeed? Is that so clear?

RHODOPÈ. Perhaps in the sight of the Gods they may not be, who see all things as they are. But some of them appear to me to be very beautiful.

ÆSOP. Which are those?

RHODOPÈ. The very girls who think me the ugliest of them all. How strange!

ÆSOP. That they should think thee so?

RHODOPÈ. No, no: but that nearly all the most beautiful should be of this opinion; and the others should often come to look at me, apparently with delight, over each other's shoulder or under each other's arm, clinging to their girdle or holding by their sleeve and hanging a little back, as if there were something about me unsafe. They seem fearful regarding me; for there are many venomous things in this country, of which we have none at home.

ÆSOP. And some which we find all over the world. But thou art too talkative.

RHODOPÈ. Now indeed you correct me with great justice, and with great gentleness. I know not why I am so pleased to talk with you. But what you say to me is different from what others say: the thoughts, the words, the voice, the look, all different. And yet reproof is but little pleasant, especially to those who are unused to it.

ÆSOP. Why didst thou not spring forward and stare at me, having heard as the rest had done, that I am unwillingly a slave, and indeed not over-willingly a deformed one?

RHODOPÈ. I would rather that neither of these misfortunes had befallen you.

ÆSOP. And yet within the year thou wilt rejoice that they have.

RHODOPÈ. If you truly thought so, you would not continue to look at me with such serenity. Tell me why you say it.

ÆSOP. Because by that time thou wilt prefer me to the handsomest slave about the house.

RHODOPÈ. For shame! vain creature!

ÆSOP. By the provision of the Gods, the under-sized and distorted are usually so. The cork of vanity buoys up their chins above all swimmers on the tide of life. But, Rhodopè, my vanity has not yet begun.

RHODOPÈ. How do you know that my name is Rhodopè?

ÆSOP. Were I malicious I would inform thee, and turn against thee the tables on the score of vanity.

RHODOPÈ. What can you mean?

ÆSOP. I mean to render thee happy in life, and glorious long after. Thou shalt be sought by the powerful, thou shalt be celebrated by the witty, and thou shalt be beloved by the generous and the wise. Xanthus may adorn the sacrifice, but the Immortal shall receive it from the altar.

RHODOPÈ. I am but fourteen years old, and Xanthus is married. Surely he would not rather love me than one to whose habits and endearments he has been accustomed for twenty years.

ÆSOP. It seems wonderful: but such things do happen.

RHODOPÈ. Not among us Thracians. I have seen in my childhood men older than Xanthus, who, against all remonstrances and many struggles, have fondled and kissed, before near relatives, wives of the same age, proud of exhibiting the honorable love they bore toward them: yet in the very next room, the very same day, scarcely would they press to their bosoms while you could (rather slowly) count twenty, nor kiss for half the time, beautiful young maidens, who, casting down their eyes, never stirred, and only said *'Don't! Don't!'*

ÆSOP. What a rigid morality is the Thracian! How courageous the elderly! and how enduring the youthful!

RHODOPÈ. Here in Egypt we are nearer to strange creatures; to men without heads, to others who ride on dragons.

ÆSOP. Stop there, little Rhodopè! In all countries we live among strange creatures. However, there are none such in the world as thou hast been told of since thou camest hither.

RHODOPÈ. Oh yes there are. You must not begin by shaking my belief, and by making me know less than others of my age. They all talk of them: nay, some creatures not by any means prettier, are worshipped here as deities: I have seen them with my own eyes. I wonder that you above all others should deny the existence of prodigies.

ÆSOP. Why dost thou wonder at it particularly in me?

RHODOPÈ. Because when you were brought hither yesterday, and when several of my fellow-maidens came around you, questioning you about the manners and customs of your country, you began to tell them stories of beasts who spoke, and spoke reasonably.

ÆSOP. They are almost the only people of my acquaintance who do.

RHODOPÈ. And you call them by the name of *people?*

ÆSOP. For want of a nobler and a better. Didst thou hear related what I had been saying?

RHODOPÈ. Yes, every word, and perhaps more.

ÆSOP. Certainly more; for my audience was of females. But canst thou repeat any portion of the narrative?

RHODOPÈ. They began by asking you whether all the men in Phrygia were like yourself.

ÆSOP. Art thou quite certain that this was the real expression they used? Come: no blushes. Do not turn round.

RHODOPÈ. It had entirely that meaning.

ÆSOP. Did they not inquire if all Phrygians were such horrible monsters as the one before them?

RHODOPÈ. O heaven and earth! this man is surely omniscient. Kind guest! do not hurt them for it. Deign to repeat to me, if it is not too troublesome, what you said about the talking beasts.

ÆSOP. The innocent girls asked me many questions, or rather half-questions; for never was one finished before another from the same or from a different quarter was begun.

RHODOPÈ. This is uncivil: I would never have interrupted you.

ÆSOP. Pray tell me why all that courtesy.

RHODOPÈ. For fear of losing a little of what you were about to say, or of receiving it somewhat changed. We never say the same thing in the same manner when we have been interrupted. Beside, there are many who are displeased at it; and if you had been, it would have shamed and vexed me.

ÆSOP. Art thou vexed so easily?

RHODOPÈ. When I am ashamed I am. I shall be jealous if you are kinder to the others than to me, and if you refuse to tell me the story you told them yesterday.

ÆSOP. I have never yet made anyone jealous; and I will not begin to try my talent on little Rhodopè.

They asked me who governs Phrygia at present. I replied that the Phrygians had just placed themselves under the dominion of a sleek and quiet animal, half-fox, half-ass, named Alopiconos.[1] At one time he seems fox almost entirely; at another, almost entirely ass.

RHODOPÈ. And can he speak?

ÆSOP. Few better.

RHODOPÈ. Are the Phrygians contented with him?

ÆSOP. They who raised him to power and authority rub their hands rapturously: nevertheless, I have heard several of the principal ones, in the very act of doing it, breathe out from closed teeth, '*The cursed fox!*' and others, '*The cursed ass!*'

RHODOPÈ. What has he done?

ÆSOP. He has made the nation the happiest in the world, they tell us.

RHODOPÈ. How?

ÆSOP. By imposing a heavy tax on the necessaries of life, and thus making it quite independent.

RHODOPÈ. O Æsop! I am ignorant of politics, as of everything else. We Thracians are near Phrygia: our kings, I believe, have not conquered it: what others have?

ÆSOP. None: but the independence which Alopiconos has conferred upon it, is conferred by hindering the corn of other lands, more fertile and less populous, from entering it, until so many of the inhabitants have died of famine and disease, that there will be imported just enough for the remainder.

RHODOPÈ. Holy Jupiter! protect my country! and keep for ever its asses and its foxes wider apart!

Tell me more. You know many things that have happened in the world. Beside the strange choice you just related, what is the most memorable thing that has occurred in Phrygia since the Trojan war?

ÆSOP. An event more memorable preceded it; but nothing since will appear to thee so extraordinary.

RHODOPÈ. Then tell me only that.

ÆSOP. It will interest thee less, but the effect is more durable than of the other. Soon after the dethronement of Saturn, with certain preliminary ceremonies, by his eldest son Jupiter, who thus became the legitimate king of Gods and men, the lower parts of nature on our earth were likewise much affected. At this season the

---

[1] 'Alopiconos': probably a reference to Lord Liverpool; Premier in 1815, when the duty to be levied on all corn imported into the country at less than 84s. the quarter was made prohibitive.

water in all the rivers of Phrygia was running low, but quietly, so that the bottom was visible in many places, and grew tepid and warm and even hot in some. At last it became agitated and excited: and loud bubbles rose up from it, audible to the ears of Jupiter, declaring that it had an indefeasible right to exercise its voice on all occasions, and of rising to the surface at all seasons. Jupiter, who was ever much given to hilarity, laughed at this; but the louder he laughed, the louder bubbled the mud, beseeching him to thunder and lighten and rain in torrents, and to sweep away dams and dykes and mills and bridges and roads, and moreover all houses in all parts of the country that were not built of mud. Thunder rolled in every quarter of the heavens: the lions and panthers were frightened and growled horribly: the foxes, who are seldom at fault, began to fear for the farm-yards; and were seen with vertical tails, three of which, if put together, would be little stouter than a child's whip for whipping-tops, so thoroughly soaked were they and draggled in the mire: not an animal in the forest could lick itself dry: their tongues ached with attempting it. But the mud gained its cause, and rose above the river-sides. At first it was elated by success; but it had floated in its extravagance no long time before a panic seized it, at hearing out of the clouds the fatal word *teleutaion,* which signifies *final.* It panted and breathed hard; and, at the moment of exhausting the last remnant of its strength, again it prayed to Jupiter, in a formulary of words which certain borderers of the principal stream suggested, imploring him that it might stop and subside. It did so. The borderers enriched their fields with it, carting it off, tossing it about, and breaking it into powder. But the streams were too dirty for decent men to bathe in them; and scarcely a fountain in all Phrygia had as much pure water, at its very source, as thou couldst carry on thy head in an earthen jar. For several years afterward there were pestilential exhalations, and drought and scarcity, throughout the country.

RHODOPÈ. This is indeed a memorable event; and yet I never heard of it before.

ÆSOP. Dost thou like my histories?

RHODOPÈ. Very much indeed.

ÆSOP. Both of them?

RHODOPÈ. Equally.

ÆSOP. Then, Rhodopè, thou art worthier of instruction than

anyone I know. I never found an auditor, until the present, who approved of each; one or other of the two was sure to be defective in style or ingenuity: it showed an ignorance of the times or of mankind: it proved only that the narrator was a person of contracted views, and that nothing pleased him.

RHODOPÈ. How could you have hindered, with as many hands as Gyas, and twenty thongs in each, the fox and ass from uniting? or how could you prevail on Jupiter to keep the mud from bubbling? I have prayed to him for many things more reasonable, and he has never done a single one of them; except the last, perhaps.

ÆSOP. What was it?

RHODOPÈ. That he would bestow on me power and understanding to comfort the poor slave from Phrygia.

ÆSOP. On what art thou reflecting?

RHODOPÈ. I do not know. Is reflection that which will not lie quiet on the mind, and which makes us ask ourselves questions we can not answer?

ÆSOP. Wisdom is but that shadow which we call reflection; dark always, more or less, but usually the most so where there is the most light around it.

RHODOPÈ. I think I begin to comprehend you; but beware lest anyone else should. Men will hate you for it, and may hurt you; for they will never bear the wax to be melted in the ear, as your words possess the faculty of doing.

ÆSOP. They may hurt me, but I shall have rendered them a service first.

RHODOPÈ. O Æsop! if you think so, you must soon begin to instruct me how I may assist you, first in performing the service, and then in averting the danger: for I think you will be less liable to harm if I am with you.

ÆSOP. Proud child!

RHODOPÈ. Not yet; I may be then.

ÆSOP. We must converse about other subjects.

RHODOPÈ. On what rather?

ÆSOP. I was accused by thee of attempting to unsettle thy belief in prodigies and portents.

RHODOPÈ. Teach me what is right and proper in regard to them, and in regard to the gods of this country who send them.

ÆSOP. We will either let them alone, or worship them as our

masters do. But thou mayst be quite sure, O Rhodopè, that if there were any men without heads, or any who ride upon dragons, they would have been worshipped as deities long ago.

RHODOPÈ. Ay; now you talk reasonably: so they would: at least I think so: I mean only in this country. In Thrace we do not think so unworthily of the gods: we are too afraid of Cerberus for that.

ÆSOP. Speak lower; or thou wilt raise ill blood between him and Anubis. His three heads could hardly lap milk when Anubis with only one could crack the thickest bone.

RHODOPÈ. Indeed! how proud you must be to have acquired such knowledge.

ÆSOP. If is the knowledge which men most value, as being the most profitable to them; but I possess little of it.

RHODOPÈ. What then will you teach me?

ÆSOP. I will teach thee, O Rhodopè, how to hold Love by both wings, and how to make a constant companion of an ungrateful guest.

RHODOPÈ. I think I am already able to manage so little a creature.

ÆSOP. He hath managed greater creatures than Rhodopè.

RHODOPÈ. They had no scissors to clip his pinions, and they did not slap him soon enough on the back of the hand. I have often wished to see him; but I never have seen him yet.

ÆSOP. Nor anything like?

RHODOPÈ. I have touched his statue; and once I stroked it down, all over; very nearly. He seemed to smile at me the more for it, until I was ashamed. I was then a little girl: it was long ago: a year at least.

ÆSOP. Art thou sure it was such a long while since?

RHODOPÈ. How troublesome! Yes! I never told anybody but you: and I never would have told you, unless I had been certain that you would find it out by yourself, as you did what those false foolish girls said concerning you. I am sorry to call them by such names, for I am confident that on other things and persons they never speak maliciously or untruly.

ÆSOP. No about thee?

RHODOPÈ. They think me ugly and conceited, because they do not look at me long enough to find out their mistake. I know I am not ugly, and I believe I am not conceited: so I should be silly if I were offended, or thought ill of them in return. But do you yourself always speak the truth, even when you know it? The story of the mud, I plainly see, is a mythos. Yet, after all, it is difficult to believe, and you have scarcely been able to persuade me, that the beasts in any country talk and reason, or ever did.

ÆSOP. Wherever they do, they do one thing more than men do.

RHODOPÈ. You perplex me exceedingly: but I would not disquiet you at present with more questions. Let me pause and consider a little, if you please. I begin to suspect that, as gods formerly did, you have been turning men into beasts, and beasts into men. But, Æsop, you should never say the thing that is untrue.

ÆSOP. We say and do and look no other all our lives.

RHODOPÈ. Do we never know better?

ÆSOP. Yes; when we cease to please, and to wish it; when death is settling the features, and the cerements are ready to render them unchangeable.

RHODOPÈ. Alas! alas!

ÆSOP. Breathe, Rhodopè, breathe again those painless sighs: they belong to thy vernal season. May thy summer of life be calm, thy autumn calmer, and thy winter never come.

RHODOPÈ. I must die then earlier.

ÆSOP. Laodameia died; Helen died; Leda, the beloved of Jupiter, went before. It is better to repose in the earth betimes than to sit up late; better, than to cling pertinaciously to what we feel crumbling under us, and to protract an inevitable fall. We may enjoy the present while we are insensible of infirmity and decay: but the present, like a note in music, is nothing but as it appertains to what is past and what is to come. There are no fields of amaranth on this side of the grave: there are no voices, O Rhodopè, that are not soon mute, however tuneful: there is no name, with whatever emphasis of passionate love repeated, of which the echo is not faint at last.

RHODOPÈ. O Æsop! let me rest my head on yours: it throbs and pains me.

ÆSOP. What are these ideas to thee?

RHODOPÈ. Sad, sorrowful.

ÆSOP. Harrows that break the soil, preparing it for wisdom. Many flowers must perish ere a grain of corn be ripened. And now remove thy head: the cheek is cool enough after its little shower of tears.

RHODOPÈ. How impatient you are of the least pressure?

ÆSOP. There is nothing so difficult to support imperturbably as the head of a lovely girl, except her grief. Again upon mine! forgetful one! Raise it, remove it, I say. Why wert thou reluctant? why wert thou disobedient? Nay, look not so. It is I (and thou shalt know it) who should look reproachfully.

RHODOPÈ. Reproachfully? did I? I was only wishing you would love me better, that I might come and see you often.

ÆSOP. Come often and see me, if thou wilt; but expect no love from me.

RHODOPÈ. Yet how gently and gracefully you have spoken and acted, all the time we have been together. You have rendered the most abstruse things intelligible, without once grasping my hand, or putting your fingers among my curls.

ÆSOP. I should have feared to encounter the displeasure of two persons if I had.

RHODOPÈ. And well you might. They would scourge you, and scold me.

ÆSOP. That is not the worst.

RHODOPÈ. The stocks too, perhaps.

ÆSOP. All these are small matters to the slave.

RHODOPÈ. If they befell you, I would tear my hair and my cheeks, and put my knees under your ancles. Of whom should you have been afraid?

ÆSOP. Of Rhodopè and of Æsop. Modesty in man, O Rhodopè, is perhaps the rarest and most difficult of virtues: but intolerable pain is the pursuer of its infringement. Then follow days without content, nights without sleep, throughout a stormy season, a season of impetuous deluge which no fertility succeeds.

RHODOPÈ. My mother often told me to learn modesty, when I was at play among the boys.

ÆSOP. Modesty in girls is not an acquirement, but a gift of nature: and it costs as much trouble and pain in the possessor to eradicate, as the fullest and firmest lock of hair would do.

RHODOPÈ. Never shall I be induced to believe that men at all value it in themselves, or much in us, although from idleness or from rancour they would take it away from us whenever they can.

ÆSOP. And very few of you are pertinacious: if you run after them, as you often do, it is not to get it back.

RHODOPÈ. I would never run after anyone, not even you: I would only ask you, again and again, to love me.

ÆSOP. Expect no love from me. I will impart to thee all my wisdom, such as it is; but girls like our folly best. Thou shalt never get a particle of mine from me.

RHODOPÈ. Is love foolish?

ÆSOP. At thy age and at mine. I do not love thee: if I did, I would the more forbid thee ever to love *me*.

RHODOPÈ. Strange man!

ÆSOP. Strange indeed. When a traveller is about to wander on a desert, it is strange to lead him away from it; strange to point out to him the verdant path he should pursue, where the tamarisk and lentisk and acacia wave overhead, where the reseda is cool and tender to the foot that presses it, and where a thousand colours sparkle in the sunshine, on fountains incessantly gushing forth.

RHODOPÈ. Xanthus has all these; and I could be amid them in a moment.

ÆSOP. Why art not thou?

RHODOPÈ. I know not exactly. Another day perhaps. I am afraid of snakes this morning. Beside, I think it may be sultry out of doors. Does not the wind blow from Libya?

ÆSOP. It blows as it did yesterday and when I came over, fresh across the Ægean, and from Thrace. Thou mayst venture into the morning air.

RHODOPÈ. No hours are so adapted to study as those of the morning. But will you teach me? I shall so love you if you will.

ÆSOP. If thou wilt *not* love me, I will teach thee.

RHODOPÈ. Unreasonable man!

ÆSOP. Art thou aware what those mischievous little hands are doing?

RHODOPÈ. They are tearing off the golden hem from the bottom of my robe; but it is stiff and difficult to detach.

ÆSOP. Why tear it off?

RHODOPÈ. To buy your freedom. Do you spring up, and turn away, and cover your face from me?

ÆSOP. My freedom! Go, Rhodopè! Rhodopè! This, of all things, I shall never owe to thee.

RHODOPÈ. Proud man! and you tell me to go! do you? do you? Answer me at least. Must I? and so soon?

ÆSOP. Child! begone!

RHODOPÈ. O Æsop, you are already more my master than Xanthus is. I will run and tell him so; and I will implore of him, upon my knees, never to impose on *you* a command so hard to obey.

1845

In early November Landor received a copy from Browning of the latter's Dramatic Romances and Lyrics. *In the* Morning Chronicle *a few days later there appeared the following poem:*

TO ROBERT BROWNING

There is delight in singing, tho' none hear
Beside the singer: and there is delight
In praising, tho' the praiser sit alone
And see the prais'd far off him, far above,
Shakespeare is not our poet, but the world's,
Therefore on him no speech! and brief for thee,
Browning! Since Chaucer was alive and hale,
No man hath walkt along our roads with step
So active, so inquiring eye, or tongue
So varied in discourse. But warmer climes
Give brighter plumage, stronger wing: the breeze
Of Alpine highths thou playest with, borne on
Beyond Sorrento and Amalfi, where
The Siren waits thee, singing song for song.

When Browning's Luria *and* A Soul's Tragedy *were published, the dedication was as follows:*

I dedicate
these last attempts for the present at dramatic poetry
To a Great Dramatic Poet;
'wishing what I write may be read by his light':
—if a phrase originally addressed, being not the least worthy
of his contemporaries,
to Shakespeare,
may be applied here, by one whose sole privilege
is in a greatful admiration
to Walter Savage Landor

On 17 February 1846, Rose Paynter married. This was a sad blow to Landor and added to his loneliness. Her husband was Sir Charles Bruce Graves-Sawle. Landor sent Rose the following lines:

306

To A Bride

A still, serene, soft day; enough of sun
To wrethe the cottage smoke like pine-tree snow,
Whither than those white flowers the bride-maids wore;
Upon the silent boughs the lissom air
Rested; and, only when it went, they moved,
Nor more than under the linnet springing off.
Such was the wedding-morn: the joyous Year
Lept over March and April up to May.
Regent of rising and of ebbing hearts,
Thyself borne on in cool serenity,
All heaven around and bending over thee,
All earth below and watchful of thy course!
Well hast thou chosen, after long demur
To aspirations from more realms than one.
Peace be with those thou leavest! peace with thee!
Is that enough to wish thee? not enough,
But very much: for Love himself feels pain,
While brighter plumage shoots, to shed last Year's;
And one at home (how dear that one!) recalls
Thy name, and thou recallest one at home.
Yet turn not back thine eyes; the hour of tears
Is over; nor believe thou that Romance
Closest against pure Faith her rich domain.
Shall only blossoms flourish there? Arise,
Far-sighted bride! look forward! clear views
And higher hopes lie under calmer skies.
Fortune in vain call'd out to thee; in vain
Rays from high regions darted; Wit pour'd out
His sparkling treasures; Wisdom laid his crown
Of richer jewels at thy reckless feet.
Well hast thou chosen. I repeat the words,
Adding as true ones, not untold before,
That incense must have fire for its ascent,
Else 'tis inert and cannot reach the idol.
Youth is the sole equivalent of youth.
Enjoy it while it lasts; and last it will:
Love can prolong it in despite of Years.

1846

In May the two volumes of Landor's Collected Works were published. They were printed by Bradbury and Evans, published by Edward Moxon and dedicated to Forster and Julius Hare.[1] That month Landor arrived at Gore House and on the 31st he dined at Forster's chambers. Macready called after dinner and enjoyed much talk on Milton, Shakespeare, Virgil, Horace, Homer, etc. Before returning to Bath, he went to stay with Lord Nugent,[2] and upon his return home he wrote to Rose Graves-Sawle:

'Last evening, when I attempted to open my writing desk,[3] I found it quite unpracticable. I do not believe the people of the house are capable of any kind of dishonesty, but it appears that my landlady was afraid of leaving it in my room, and took it into hers. So it got shaken and a good deal injured. She is unwell, and wrote me a note telling me that her nerves will never be right again while she has charge of such precious things in her house, and that (at my convenience) she hopes I will resign her lodgings. On this, I went instantly and engaged rooms at No. 2 in this Square, where I go the first of September. I hate to move, and I never can hope to live again in any Square. This grieves me. It is now eight years within a month that I have resided in St James's. I have a cat-like attachment to places. Talking of cats I must not forget to mention a couple of dormice given to me by Mrs Ravenshaw,[4] playful pets and dear delights to me. . .'[5]

[1] They were extremely unattractive volumes printed in double columns in small type and with no editorial matter.
[2] George Grenville, Lord Nugent, author of *Lands, Classical and Lay*.
[3] Given to him on his 70th birthday by his sister.
[4] Mrs Landor's sister, the wife of an Indian civilian.
[5] Wheeler, *Private Letters*, p. 155.

Verses from the *Collected Works*
1846

TO A CYCLAMEN

I come to visit thee again,
My little flowerless cyclamen!
To touch the hands, almost to press,
That cheer'd thee in thy loneliness.
What could those lovely sisters find,
Of thee in form, of me in mind,
What is there in us rich or rare,
To make us worth a moment's care?
Unworthy to be so carest.
We are but wither'd leaves at best.

LOVE IS LIKE AN ECHO

Love is like Echo in the land of Tell,
Who answers best the indweller of her bowers,
Silent to other voices (idly loud
Or wildly violent) letting them arouse
Eagle or carn'd brute, but never her.

IS IT NO DREAM

Is it no dream that I am he
  Whom one awake all night
Rose ere the earliest birds to see,
  And met by dawn's red light;

Who, when the wintry lamps were spent
  And all was drear and dark,
Against the rugged pear-tree leant
  While ice crackt off the bark;

Who little heeded sleet and blast,
  But much the falling snow;
Those in few hours would sure be past,
  His traces *that* might show;

Between those knees, unseen, unheard,
  The honest mastiff came,
Nor fear'd he; no, nor was he fear'd:
  Tell me, am I the same?

O come! the same dull stars we'll see,
  The same o'er-clouded moon.
O come! and tell me am I he?
  O tell me, tell me soon.

The Prayer of Orestes
1846

ORESTES. O king Apollo! god Apollo! god
Powerful to smite and powerful to preserve!
If there is blood upon me, as there seems,
Purify that black stain (thou only canst)
With every rill that bubbles from these caves
Audibly; and come willing to the work.
No; 'tis not they; 'tis blood; 'tis blood again
That bubbles in my ear, that shakes the shades
Of thy dark groves, and lets in hateful gleams,
Bringing me . . . what dread sight! what sounds abhorr'd!
What screams! They are my mother's: 'tis her eye
That through the snakes of those three furies glares,
And makes them hold their peace that she may speak.
Has thy voice bidden them all forth? There slink
Some that would hide away, but must turn back,
And others like blue lightnings bound along
From rock to rock; and many hiss at me
As they draw nearer. Earth, fire, water, all
Abominate the deed the Gods commanded!
Alas! I came to pray, not to complain;
And lo! my speech is impious as my deed!
                                    PRIESTESS OF APOLLO.
  Take refuge here amid our Delphian shades,
      O troubled breast!
  Here the most pious of Mycenai's maids
      Shall watch thy rest
  And wave the cooling laurel o'er thy brow,
      Nor insect swarm
  Shall ever break thy slumbers, nor shalt thou
      Start at the alarm
  Of boys infesting (as they do) the street
      With mocking songs,
  Stopping and importuning all they meet,

311

And heaping wrongs
Upon thy diadem'd and sacred head,
  Worse than when base
Œgisthus (shudder not!) his toils outspread
  Around thy race.
Altho' even in this fane the fitful blast
  Thou may'st hear roar,
Thy name among our highest rocks shall last
  For evermore.
ORESTES. A calm comes over me: life brings it not
With any of its tides: my end is near.
O Priestess of the purifying God
Receive her![1] and when she hath closed mine eyes,
Do thou (weep not, my father's child!) close hers.

---

[1] Pointing to his sister.

1847

In the first few months of this year Landor had been seriously ill. On 24 April he wrote to his friend Rosenhagen:

'For five and forty years I have never been seriously ill before this winter. The whole month of December I kept my room, and the greater part of the time my bed. Age has now come upon me: Years only had come upon me before. A year ago I could walk seven or eight miles without fatigue; at present I am tired after walking only two or three. But what a blessing is this discovery of inhaling ether ... we may die without pain—or even lose our teeth, which is a far more important thing. The last of mine was drawn was broken three times before it came out. It was the third of my martyrdoms ... I read nothing but novels. Monte Cristo is what I am reading now—and a wonderful work it is. I fear I shall be obliged to go to London in the beginning of May, and it cannot be until the end of July that I may promise myself the real happiness of visiting you.'[1]

In May he went to Gore House, where he saw Macready act and furthered his acquaintance. He afterwards heard Jenny Lind. 'The acting was infinitely beyond any I conceived to be possible. One night when she performed in the Somnambula, I had the good fortune to occupy a front seat in the Russian Minister's box just over the stage. Sometimes Jenny Lind came within four paces of me.' he wrote to Rose Graves-Sawle.[2] He later accompanied Julius Hare to Hurstmonceux, which he greatly enjoyed. 'He [Julius Hare] has married a sweet-tempered and intelligent wife who appears not only to reverence but to love him, which is better.' From Hurstmonceux Landor returned to Bath, and by July he received advance copies of his next work Poemata et Inscriptiones. *He was angry over printing errors which appeared. 'Truth is,' he wrote Forster, 'that unless I read with rapidity I lose my grasp of the subject. It is curious that the word* uetávoia, *which is chiefly used for* repentance, *is primitively* after-thought; *and the Italian painters call a correction a* pentemento.'[3] *Many scholars received the work from Landor and acclaimed it, but, of course, it did not sell.*

[1] Elwin, *Landor*, p. 375.
[2] Wheeler, *Private Letters*, p. 161.
[3] Forster, *Landor*, vol. ii, pp. 454–5.

The year ended with his publication of The Hellenics.

'*The massive individuality of Landor's mind was accompanied by a many-sided power of historical sympathy, which made him at home not in one only but in several, and those the most dissimilar, ages of the past. The strenuous gravity and heroic independence of Puritan England had entered into his imaginative being, as well as the contented grace and harmonious self-possession of ancient Hellas. But of all things he was perhaps the most of a Greek at heart. His freedom from any tincture of mysticism, his love of unconfused shapes and outlines, his easy dismissal of the unfathomable and the unknown, and steady concentration of the mind upon the purely human facts of existence, its natural sorrows and natural consolations, all helped him to find in the life of ancient Greece a dream without alloy, and in her songs and her philosophies a beauty and wisdom without shortcoming.*'[1]

[1] Colvin, *Landor*, p. 191.

The Death of Artemidora
1847

'Artemidora! Gods invisible,
While thou art lying faint along the couch,
Have tied the sandal to thy slender feet
And stand beside thee, ready to convey
Thy weary steps where other rivers flow.
Refreshing shades will waft thy weariness
Away, and voices like thy own come near
And nearer, and solicit an embrace.'
    Artemidora sigh'd, and would have prest
The hand now pressing hers, but was too weak.
Iris stood over her dark hair unseen
While thus Elpenor spake. He lookt into
Eyes that had given light and life erewhile
To those above them, but now dim with tears
And wakefulness. Again he spake of joy
Eternal. At that word, that sad word, *joy,*
Faithful and fond her bosom heav'd once more:
Her head fell back: and now a loud deep sob
Swell'd thro' the darken'd chamber; 'twas not hers.

This year was also notable for Landor's first meeting a remarkable young woman, then twenty-five years of age, when he was seventy-three. She was to have a considerable effect upon him during the remaining years in Bath. She was Eliza Lynn, who subsequently became Mrs Lynn Linton, an outstanding novelist, journalist and critic of her own sex. She was born in a Cumberland vicarage, in the parish of Crosthwaite near Keswick, where she had something of a Bronte-like upbringing, her mother having died a few months after her birth. Her father, the Reverend James Lynn, however, gave way to her pleadings to study in London. She found lodgings in Mr Chapman's famous establishment. Eliza took herself to the British Museum in order to study early Egyptian history for a historical novel which she wished to write and which was subsequently published under the title of Azeth the Egyptian (1846). *Her second novel attracted the attention of Landor. This was* Amymone (*1848*), *set in the age of Pericles. He praised the book. She was to write a further twenty-nine books, though none of these were historical novels. She was tall, with a beautiful complexion, and possessed fine eyes, though she was short-sighted and had to wear spectacles. As a young woman she was an advanced thinker, but years later became an opponent of female emancipation, especially where clothes were concerned.*

Her first meeting with Landor was, of course, in Bath. She wrote:

'*Long before this I had learnt his* Imaginary Conversations *by heart and was his enthusiastic admirer, without knowing whether the author was dead or alive, or where he lived, or, in fact, anything about him. I was visiting Dr Brabant*[1] *in Bath, and we were at Mr Empson's 'old curiosity shop', when we saw what seemed a noble-looking old man, badly dressed in shabby snuff-coloured clothes, a dirty old blue necktie, unstarched cotton shirt—with a front more like a nightgown than a shirt—and 'knubbly' apple-pie boots. But underneath the rusty old hat-brim gleamed a pair of quiet and penetrating grey-blue eyes; the voice was sweet and masterly; the manner that of a man of rare distinction. Dr Brabant spoke to him, and his sister, Miss Hughes, whispered to me, 'That is Mr Landor'. I was taken by surprise. Here stood in the flesh one of my great spiritual masters; one of my most revered intellectual guides. I remember how the blood came into my face as I dashed up to him with both hands held out, and said, 'Mr Landor? oh! is this Mr Landor?' as if he had been a god suddenly revealed. And I remember the amused smile with which he took both my hands in his, and said, 'And who is this little girl, I wonder?' From that hour we were friends: and I thank God I can say truthfully, that never for one hour, one moment, afterwards were we anything else. For twelve long, dear years, we were father and daughter. We never called each other anything else. He never signed himself to me, or wrote to me, as anything else; and in the last sad clouded days of his life, had not the circumstances of my own life been so changed as to render it impossible, I would have gone with him to Italy, and I would not have left him again while he lived. But if the circumstances*

[1] Dr Brabant was, according to Mrs Lynn Linton, the original of Casaubon in *Middlemarch*. This is interesting in view of the fact that Casaubon has generally been identified with Mark Pattison.

of my life had not been so changed, and I had still been able to visit him, and make his lodgings his home, as in olden times, he would never have needed to have gone back to Italy. Of this I am sorrowfully convinced. I could have kept him from the pain and misery that overtook him.'

Eliza Lynn used to stay with him in Bath for many weeks at a time, sometimes once and sometimes twice in the year. She made it her duty to go daily to his house, punctually at twelve o'clock, and sit or walk with him till two, when he dined. She also dined with him regularly twice a week, when he always took care to give her some favourite dish, 'and especially to have a bottle of his famous Malmsey Madeira on the table.' She was with him on the famous occasion when his favourite yapping dog Pomero got lost:

'We had gone out for a walk to Lansdowne Crescent, for the sake of the view thence—one of his favourite points—and when we came back, Pomero, who had accompanied us for a short time, and had then turned as we supposed to go home, was not to be found. I shall never forget the padrone's mingled rage and despair. He would not eat any dinner, and I remember how that it was a dinner of turbot and stewed hare, which he himself had seasoned and prepared with wine, etc., in the little sitting-room; for he was a good cook in that way, and to that extent. And both of these were favourite dishes with him. But he would not eat, and sat in his high-backed chair, which was not an easy one, or stamped about the room in a state of stormy sorrow, like nothing I had ever seen before, though I saw more than one like tempest afterwards. Now he was sure the dog was murdered, and he should never see him again; some scoundrel had murdered him out of spite and cruelty, or to make a few pounds by him stuffed, and there was no use in thinking more about him; then he would go out and scour all Bath for him; then he would offer rewards—wild rewards—a hundred pounds—his whole fortune—if any one would bring him back alive; after which he would give way to his grief and indignation again, and by way of turning the knife in his wound would detail every circumstance of the dog's being kidnapped, struck, pelted with stones, and tortured in some stable or cellar, and finally killed outright, as if he had been present at the scene. But in a short time, after the whole city had been put into an uproar, and several worthy people made exceedingly unhappy, the *little fellow was brought back as pert and vociferous as ever; and yelped out* mea culpa *on his master's knee, in between the mingled scolding and caressing with which he was received.*'[1]

[1] Layard. Life of Mrs Lynn Linton, p. 67.

The Last of Ulysses
Published in *Hellenics* 1847

Argument

[*Being made aware that Ulysses was coming home and moved by
jealousy of Minerva, Venus would see Penelope married to some one of
the suitors. She ordains that he who first meets Penelope shall be
overcome by love and be loved in his turn. Ulysses is that man. He
departs for Argiripa where Diomed is King.*]

Sing we the last of that man's days who tore
From Troy its safeguard, not against the will
Of Pallas; Pallas brought him safely home.
   Be with us, daughter of Mnemosyne!
Thou who, altho' thou visitest the abyss
Of Etna, where Enceladus is bound,
Tempestuous giant, mad with impotence,
And darest walk by Styx and Phlegethon,
Nor dreadest, bolt in hand, the Thunderer,
Yet from Sorrento gazest with delight
On waves so softly valuble. To these
I also turn: I seek that shore alone
Where stiffens on high rocks the hoary moss,
Too close and hard for idle child to strip
Or singing-bird to twine round slender nest.
When mute the trumpet of Misenus, mute
The Sybil's cave, when o'er Parthenope
Crumbles the bust and scarce her name remains,
Thou holdest up the deeds of glorious men
And followest their funerals with song.
Tell us then in what region sank to rest
Ulysses; say, what did he, suffered he,
When he departed homeward from these shores?
   Ogygia's secret, Circe's festive, bower,
Faithless to hospitality, we leave,

And harp that Phœbus scorns, and woof unseen
Of Pallas, tho' its shuttle be of gold:
Better by far to mark how pure and firm
Connubial bonds in life and death are blest.
 Jove pitied him who, after toils which man
Had never undergone, was guided now
By Pallas: he decreed in recompense
Penelope not only should retain
Her love and duty, but her youth and charms.
Many the marvels his eventful life
Had witnest; this more marvelous than all
Was unobserved; not through ingratitude;
But such he ever thought her; such she seem'd
In grace and beauty at all after-times
As when he left her to depart for Troy,
Or when he led her, with the fife before,
Under the garlands of her father's gate.
That which the God now gave her seem'd her due,
Her property; he never fear'd that age
Or fate could alter beauty such as hers.
He who sees all things saw the hero's mind.
The crowd of suitors own'd the miracle;
And now the wretched men began to fear
Who rioted so loosely in the house.
How late their piety! how scant their shame!
How rapidly death's wide and downward road
Opens before them! opens, yet unseen.
 Indignant that Penelope had borne
So long their importunities and threats,
And that Ulysses had in vain escaped
Calypso's wiles and Circe's bristling caves,
In vain had brought the archer back to Troy
With arrows poison'd in the hydra's blood,
The Sire to Venus 'Highth of wickedness!
Those suitors, once so patient, now abstain
Not even from the choicest of the herd,
Fatten'd, at his return, for us above:
Nor these alone the wretches would consume,
But their fierce lust burns fiercer from delay.

I doubt not . . . beauty often counsels ill . . .
If hope, if pleasure, give a brighter glow,
Or any deity her charms increase . . .
I doubt not . . . I fear greatly . . . that, subdued
By ardent prayers she lend a patient ear.
The more I dread it lest Minerva's ire
Again be kindled: therefor I abstain,
As thou dost wisely, daughter, from offence.
Within twelve days 'tis destin'd he returns
For whom thou, Venus, hast thro' wars and waves
Preserv'd the flame so vivid. Fate decrees
(What I could wish Fate never had decreed)
That the last comer carry off the prize,
Meeting her earliest on the twelfth day's morn.
A crowd of lovers shakes the faith of few,
He shakes it who stands back and waits his hour.
I hope she may not meet the better man
Than her Ulysses: if she should so meet
That better man, I would not he prevail.'

    Venus has listened to this wily speech
Fearing lest strong commands might follow it,
But when her father added nothing more
She fancied she could over-reach the wise
And potent, and make Pallas feel her might.

    No hesitation: thro' the air she flies,
She stands before Penelope asleep,
And thus, without awakening her.

                      'The first
In the twelfth morn who meets thee, shall be held
By thee in love unbroken, and subdue
Whatever enemy advances near.'

    Close to the bed she goes, and there she stops,
Admiring her own gifts: then to herself,
'If Paris had beheld thee . . . but just then
Thy husband took thee from the Spartan land . . .
I was wrong then . . . I am much wiser now . . .
But, had he seen thee, he, his house, his realm,
Had stil been safe; no guest betraid, no wrath,
By armure ript from heroes drag'd thro' dust,

By temples sunk in ashes, by the wounds
Of Gods, and even their bloodshed, unappeas'd.'
Gazing once more ere vanishing, she said
'How beautiful! how modest!'

                          When that morn
Advances, she repents the doom it brings,
And fears him angry whom she little fear'd
So gracious: now she wishes she may fail
In what she most desired: she blames her power
Of eloquence, to which Minerva's self
Must yield a victory greater than the last.
What should she do? alas! what had she done?
Unduteous wishes she would now unwish.
Upon no land is rest for her; no land
Can hide, not all Idalia shade her guilt,
Nor clouds of incense from a hundred shrines.
To heaven, where only there is peace, she flies,
Pity of Jove and pardon to implore.
With placid brow he heard his daughter plead.
Turning her eyes decorous from his face,
Distantly first she stood, then cast herself
Before his knees: he rais'd her and spake thus:
'Did not thy hand, my daughter, which of late
Covered with cloud Anchises' son, and led
To Africa, lead him whom thou hast blest,
Ulysses? for already hath he past
His city-gate, unknown, and hath approacht
The queen, a welcome unexpected guest.
See what your efforts, in a single day,
Applied with such discretion, can achieve!
Yea, I have granted . . . if indeed thy power
Hath any need of mine . . . that lasting love
Unite the brave and constant: but within
Thy rule this lies, when Juno hath approved.
Seldom with Juno art thou so agreed,
And seldom hast thou sanction'd so her bonds.
Behold what feats conjointly ye perform!
I too, by somewhat, slightly may assist.
Ulysses in the vigour of his youth

(Rejoice with me) shall flourish, and shall crush
All enemies he finds beneath his roof:
Moreover (and in this with me rejoice)
Beneath a calmer sky his day shall close.'
Astonisht at these words the Goddess wept
Thro' very shame, and hated Pallas more.

    Ah! we must now away from gentle Gods,
The Muse forbidding us to look behind
Or tarry longer. I would not decline
To sing of shipwrecks, wanderings, battles fought
By one against so many, thro' the love
He bore his wife, fought under her defence
Who shatters with her ægis arms unchaste:
For neither song hath fail'd me nor the blast
Of trumpet. Harder is the task, and skill
Greater, to take from age its weariness,
To give slow years fresh movement, and bear up
Sorrows when friends and household Gods are far.

*Landor followed the revolutionary movements of 1848 with close
interest. The abdication of Louis-Philippe was commemorated in an
'Imaginary Conversation' which was published in the* Examiner *for
March of that year, between Thiers and Lamartine. He also discussed
the leadership of Kossuth and declared that Poland must have complete independence. He now published at his own expense* The Italics
of Walter Savage Landor, *and this was followed—after Ferdinand II
of Sicily bombarded Messina and earned himself the title of King
Bomba—by a shilling pamphlet,* Imaginary Conversation of King
Carlo-Alberto and the Duchess Belgioioso, or The Affairs and
Prospects of Italy. *When Rose Graves-Sawle recommended Lamartine's* Histoire des Girondins, *his mind was full of what was happening
in France on the collapse of Louis-Philippe and his government; he
went rushing down to Bath library for the Lamartine volumes, only to
find they did not have them. In rage, he cancelled his subscription.
Lady Blessington told him that Louis Napoleon had set out for Paris,
and having read the* Italics *remarked that his 'honest indignation had
been ignited'. She told Forster 'It is comforting to see that his genius is
not tamed by time.'*[1]

*From now on, death was to take its toll of former friends. On 9
January Joseph Ablett died. 'Ablett' he had written on 25 April 1848
to his sister Elizabeth, 'is the kindest and most generous man in
existence, and particularly attached to me.' He was a wealthy man,
deeply interested in art. It was he who paid for and persuaded Landor
to sit for his bust by John Gibson.*

*In August he visited the Graves-Sawles at Restormel, where he
greatly enjoyed his stay, and saw for the first time their little daughter
Rose—his 'third' Rose. They visited the flower show and called on Sir
Joseph and Lady Graves-Sawle. The only trouble was that Landor
left his guide book and gold spectacles in Exeter. This gave him cause
to write a magnificent letter to one James Jerwood, a barrister.*

> *'Permit me, Sir to recall to your memory your insulting language
> and violent demeanour of yesterday; and to regret that I have no
> friend at Exeter who could express to you my sentiments, instead of*

[1] Super, *Landor*, p. 380.

this letter.—I had just taken refuge from the rain under your
verandah, when I heard the following words, uttered with a coarseness
and vehemence I never heard before from any well-dressed man on
any occasion. 'What do you want here? Be off with you.' Until I
heard the latter phrase spoken close to me, I did not imagine or
suspect that it was addressed to me. On my asking you, with perfect
composure, whether it was so, you answered in the affirmative, and
still more offensively. I then, with the same calmness, reminded you
that such language was not usually applied to a gentleman. You
expressed a doubt whether I am one. I gave you all the benefit of
this doubt, knowing that only a gentleman can judge of one correctly.
'But I thought my manner, my language, and my tone, were
unexceptionable, and (what you are more capable of appreciating) my
dress. It is that in which, during last week, I had visited several of
the first families in Cornwall, Sir W. Molesworth, Sir J. Sawle,
Mr Roberts, and others, in whose society you will never be admitted,
unless (to their sorrow) professionally. After much injurious and
insolent language from you, I informed you that even the lowest of
men are treated by gentlemen with decency. If you inquire, you will
find it to be the case. But in your terms and utterance there was
what Cicero calls subrancidum nescio quid. The curate of your parish
will explain this to you. Barristers in general carry a change of
tongue about them, altho some of them do not put on a clean one so
often as we could wish—The statement of your behaviour will be
forwarded to the Editor of the Examiner, *and others; so that it will*
come under the inspection of those appointed you to your office. What
they may think and decide on it, I know not; but I know full well
what the older Whigs would—such as Lds Rockingham, Chatham
and Shelburne. Every gentleman was of their order, *and they*
protected it. Perhaps there may be some even now, some few men in
power, who will question whether he is competent to decide on cases
of equity, who commits an injustice, and adds insolence of language
and demeanour to it. Of the language there can be little to doubt;
and I perceive no more in questioning the injustice of treating with
indignity an unoffending stranger.—I caused no obstruction: I stood
several feet from the doorway, and with my back toward it. On my
expostulating, you not only repeated the same insolence of expression,
but you advanced in a menacing and outrageous attitude. There is
no great bravery in thus insulting a man of seventy three, without a

cane or whip in his hand: but the man of seventy three has not yet forgotten, in case of necessity and in a proper time, and place, to repell a ruffian and to spurn a coward.

I have the honour to be &c.

Walter Savage Landor.'

One must venture to observe that Landor probably looked like a tramp since he never bought himself new clothes and cared not what he looked like! His mention of Whig aristocrats is typical.

*Mrs Ablett, the widow of his friend Joseph Ablett, became involved in litigation over her late husband's estate and asked Landor if he would come and testify. Of course Landor took up the cause. Not only did he visit her at Llanbedr, but with his usual vigour and impetuosity he published a pamphlet on the dispute at his own expense—A State-*ment of Occurrences at Llanbedr.

In April 1849 he fell ill and was looked after by 'Ianthe's' grand-daughter Luisina and Eliza Lynn. In July, after a long and close friendship, Lady Blessington died, thus depriving him of staying at Gore House when he went to London. In that same month his brother Charles's death occurred. 'Little did I think,' he wrote to Rose Graves-Sawle, 'my brother Charles would have died before me. He seemed to have life enough in him for fifty men and fifty years. He was the finest man and almost the most spirited I ever knew. To lose so early, a companion as Charles, and so kind a friend as poor Lady Blessington within so short a space of time bore heavily on my spirits'.[1]

In March Landor had left the house in St James's Square[2] and moved to Rivers Street.

January 30, 1850, was Landor's seventy-fifth birthday. Eliza Lynn was staying with him.

'At breakfast he would not touch his food until he had "scrawled off" a quatrain, one of the most beautiful he wrote:

> *"I strove with none, for none was worth my strife:*
> *Nature I loved, and, next to Nature, Art:*
> *I warm'd both hands before the fire of Life;*
> *It sinks; and I am ready to depart."*

[1] Wheeler, *Private Letters*, p. 176.
[2] A rather forlorn house now.

*"There," he said, as he flung the pages to me across the table, "I
could not sleep last night, so I wrote this. How do you like it?"
I remember the tears coming into my eyes when I said how beautiful
and patriotic I thought it. He smiled in his sweet, half-sad way—not
that boisterous laugh which was like the bursting fourth of a volcano,
but the quiet and gentle smile, which was perhaps his truer self and
his greatest charm. "There is one little girl, at all events, who
would be sorry," he said, and then changed the conversation.'*[1]

*Dickens and Forster now came regularly to Bath. Eliza Lynn met
them at dinner.*

'I find Dickens charming, and Forster pompous, heavy and ungenial.[2]
*Dickens was bright and gay and winsome, and while treating
Mr Landor with respect of a younger man for an elder, allowed his
wit to play about him, bright and harmless as summer lightning. He
included me, then quite a beginner in literature, and shy by
termperament, and made me feel at home with him; but Forster
was saturnine and cynical. He was the "harbitary gent" of the
cabman's rank, and one of the most jealous of men. Dickens and
Landor were his property—pocket-boroughs in a way—and he
resented the introduction of a third person and stranger.'*[3]

*In May, Landor went to London and dined on the seventh with
Crabb Robinson and Kenyon. He also saw Forster in his chambers at
Lincoln's Inn Fields, but the year 1850 brought change to the habits
and character of Forster and Dickens. Both were yet on the verge of
forty, but the energetic activities of their lives rendered each much
older than his years.*[4] *James Spedding had rooms in the same building
and one night Tennyson was there. Forster arranged for Landor to
meet him, while another visitor, W. J. Fox, M.P. 'having fallen down
in leaving the building and broken his arm, was brought into Forster's
dining room "white from pain". Tennyson recalled to his son and
biographer how "Old Landor went on eloquently discoursing of
Catullus and other Latin poets as if nothing had happened", which
seemed rather hard, but was perhaps better than utter silence.'*[5]

[1] Lynn Linton, *My Literary Life*, pp. 53–54. 1899.
[2] There was little liking between them, and it was finally ruptured when Mrs
Linton read Forster's *Life of Landor* and found that she was barely mentioned.
[3] Lynn Linton, *My Literary Life*, pp. 55–56.
[4] Elwin, *Victorian Wallflowers*, p. 197.
[5] Elwin, *Landor*, p. 396.

Landor paid public tribute in Fraser's Magazine *to Southey. In July he was visited by Carlyle.*

'*Landor was in his house, in a fine quiet street like a New Town Edinburgh one, waiting for me, attended by a nice Bologna dog. Dinner not far from ready; his apartments all hung around with queer old Italian pictures; the very doors had pictures on them. Dinner was elaborately simple. The brave Landor forced me talk to far too much, and we did very near a bottle of claret, besides two glasses of sherry; far too much liquor and excitement for a poor fellow like me. However, he was really stirring company: a proud, irascible, trenchant, yet generous, veracious, and very dignified old man; quite a ducal or royal man in the temper of him; reminded me something of old Sterling, except that for the Irish blarney you must substitute a fund of Welsh choler. He left me to go smoking along the streets about ten at night, he himself retiring then, having walked me through the Crescent, Park, etc. in the dusk before.*'[1]

[1] Elwin: Landor p. 396.

To the Reverend Charles Cuthbert Southey[1]

ON HIS FATHER'S CHARACTER AND
PUBLIC SERVICES

(*Fraser's Magazine*, 1850)

It is not because I enjoyed your father's friendship, my dear sir, that I am now about to send you my testimony to his worth. Indeed that very friendship, and the frequent expression of it in his letters for more than forty years, have made me hesitate too long before the public.

Never in the course of my existence have I known a man so excellent on so many points. What he was as a son, is now remembered by few; what he was as a husband and a father, shows it more clearly than the best memory could represent it. The purity of his youth, the integrity of his manhood, the soundness of his judgment, and the tenderness of his heart, they alone who have been blest with the same qualities can appreciate. And who are they? Many with one, some with more than one, nobody with all of them in the like degree. So there are several who possess one quality of his poetry; none who possess the whole variety.

For poetry there must be invention, energy, truth of conception, wealth of words, and purity of diction. His were indeed all these, excepting one; and that one often came when called for; I mean energy. This is the chief characteristic and highest merit of Byron; it is also Scott's, and perhaps more than equally. Shelley is not deficient in it; nor is Keats, whose heart and soul is sheer poetry, overflowing from its fermentation. Wordsworth is as meditative and thoughtful as your father, but less philosophical; his intellect was less amply stored; his heart was narrower. He knew the fields better than men, and ordinary men better than extraordinary. He is second to your father alone, of all poets, ancient or modern, in local description. The practice of the ancients has inculcated the belief that scenery should be rare and scanty in heroic poetry. Even

---

[1] Charles Cuthbert Southey was Southey's eighth and last child. He was born in February 1819. He had not possessed the brilliance of his brother Herbert, but he was a sound scholar who entered Queens College Oxford and edited his father's *Life and Correspondence*.

those among them who introduce us into pastoral life are sparing of it. Little is there in Theocritus, hardly a glimpse in Moschus or Bion: but Virgil has more and better of (what is called) *description*, in his *Æneid* than in his *Eclogues* or *Georgics*. The other epic poets, whatever the age or country, are little worth noticing, with the single and sole exception of Apollonius. I do not call *epic* that which is written in a *lyric* meter, nor indeed in any species of rhyme. For, the cap and bells should never surmount the helmet and breast-plate. To the epic not only a certain spirit but also a certain form is requisite, and not only in the main body, but likewise in the minute *Paradise Lost* a divine poem is in every sense of the word to call it rightly. I am inclined to think there is more of beautiful and appro-priate scenery in *Roderic* alone, than the whole range of poetry, in all its lands, contains. Whatever may be the feeling of others in regard to it, I find it a relief from sanguinary actions and conflicting passions, to rest a while beyond, but within sight. However, the poet ought not at any time to grow cool and inactive in the field of battle, nor retire often, nor long.

The warmest admirers of Wordsworth are nevertheless so haunted by antiquity, that there are few among them, I believe, who would venture to call him, what I have no hesitation in doing, the superior both of Virgil and of Theocritus in description. And description, let it be remembered, is not his only nor his highest excellence. Before I come to look into his defects, I am ready to assert that he has written a greater number of good sonnets than all the other sonneteers in Europe put together: yet sometimes in these compositions, as in many others of the smaller, he is expletive and diffuse; which Southey never is. Rural and humble life has brought him occasionally to a comparison with Crabbe. They who in their metaphors are fond of applying the physical to the moral, might say perhaps that Wordsworth now and then labors under a diarrhœa; Crabbe under a constipation; each without the slightest symptom of fever or excitement. Immeasurably above Crabbe, and widely different, less graphic, less concise, less anatomical, he would come nearer to Cowper, had he Cowper's humor. This, which Words-worth totally wanted, your father had abundantly. Certainly the commentator who extolled him for *universality*, intended no irony, altho it seems one. He wanted not only universality, but variety, in which none of our later poets is comparable to Southey. His humor is gentle and delicate, yet exuberant. If in the composition of Wordsworth there had been this one ingredient, he would be a Cowper in solution, with a crust of prose at the bottom, and innumerable flakes and bee-wings floating up and down loosely and languidly. Much of the poetry lately, and perhaps even stil, in estimation, reminds me of plashy and stagnant water, with here and there the broad flat leaves of its fair but scentless lily on the surface, showing at once a want of depth and of movement. I would never say this openly, either to the censurers or favorers of such as it may appear to concern. For it is inhumane to encourage enmities and dislikes, and scarcely less so to diminish an innocent pleasure in good creatures incapable of a higher. I would not persuade, if I could, those who are enraptured with a morrice-dancer and a blind fiddler, that their raptures ought to be reserved for a Grisi and a Beethoven, and that if they are very happy they are very wrong. The higher kinds of poetry, of painture, and of sculpture, can never be duly estimated by the majority even of the intellectual. The marbles of the Parthenon and the Odes of Pindar bring many false worshippers, few sincere. Cultivation will do much in the produce of the nobler arts, but there are only a few spots into which this cultivation can be carried. Of what use is the plough, or the harrow, or the seed itself, if the soil is sterile and the climate uncongenial?

Remarks have been frequently and justly made, on the absurdity of classing in the same category the three celebrated poets who resided contemporaneously, and in fellowship, near the Lakes. There is no resemblance between any two of them in the features and character of their poetry. Southey could grasp great subjects, and completely master them; Coleridge never attempted it; Wordsworth attempted it, and failed. He has left behind him no poem, no series or collection of his, requiring and manifesting so great and diversified powers as are exhibited in *Marmion,* or *The Lady of the Lake,* in *Roderic,* or *Thalaba,* or *Kehama.* His *Excursion* is a vast congeries of small independent poems, several very pleasing. Breaking up this unwieldy vessel, he might have constructed but of its material several eclogues; craft drawing little water.

Coleridge left unfinished, year after year, until his death, the promising *Christabel.* Before he fell exhausted from it, he had done enough to prove that he could write good poetry, not enough to prove that he could ever be a great poet. He ran with spirit and velocity a short distance, then dropt. Excelling no less in prose than in poetry, he raised expectations which were suddenly over-clouded and blank, undertook what he was conscious he never should perform, and declared he was busily employed in what he had only dreamt of. Never was love more imaginary than his love of truth. Not only did he never embrace her, never bow down to her and worship her, but he never looked her earnestly in the face. Possessing the most extraordinary powers of mind, his unsteddiness gave him the appearance of weakness. Few critics were more acute, more sensitive, more comprehensive; but, like other men, what he could say most eloquently he said most willingly; and he would rather give or detract with a large full grasp, than weigh deliberately.

What a difference there is between the characters of Coleridge and of Southey! Coleridge was fond of indulging in a soft malignity, while all the energy of Southey lay in his benevolence. Southey had long and continuous trains of thought; Coleridge was unable to hold together, in poetry or prose, as much as might be contained in half a dozen pages. Southey often walkt upon tenacious clay; Coleridge on deep and sparkling shingle. Southey valued truth above all things; Coleridge prized the copy far more highly than the original, and would rather see it reflected in the glass than right before him. He was giddy by the plethora of power, and after a few paces he was constrained to stop. He wanted not time to finish the finest of his poems, the *Christabel*, but the means he wanted. I think more highly of his *Ancient Mariner* than Southey did; but there are several poems of Shelley, Keats, and Wordsworth, incomparably better. Here I speak of poets who write no longer; I might speak it as justly of quite as many who are moving in the same path among us every day. Several of these have struck as deep a root, but in none of them are there such wide ramifications. Coleridge would have written a restless and rambling history; part very rich and part very ragged, its holes stuffed up with metaphysics and disquisition, without a man's face to be seen throughout: Southey has shown us he could do more than any other Englishman had done in this department, until Napier came and won from him the Peninsula.

Conscience with Southey stood on the other side of Enthusiasm. What he saw, he said; what he found, he laid open. He alone seems to have been aware that criticism, to be complete, must be both analytical and synthetic. Every work should be measured by some standard. It is only by such exposition and comparison of two, more or less similar in the prominent points, that correctness of arbitriment can be attained. All men are critics; all men judge the written or unwritten words of others. It is not in works of imagination, as you would think the most likely for it, but it is chiefly in criticism that writers at the present day are discursive and erratic. Among our regular bands of critics there is almost as much and as ill-placed animosity on one side, and enthusiasm on the other, as there is among the vulgar voters at parliamentary elections, and they who differ from them are pelted as heartily. In the performance of the ancient drama there were those who modulated with the pipe the language of the actor. No such instrument is found in the wardrobe of our critics, to temper their animosity or to direct their enthusiasm. Your father carried it with him wherever he sat in judgment; because he knew that his sentence would be recorded, and not only there. Oblivion is the refuge of the unjust; but their confidence is vain in the security of that sanctuary. The most idle and ignorant hold arguments on literary merit. Usually, the commencement is, '*I think with you, but,*' &c., or '*I do not think with you.*' The first begins with a false position; and there is probably one, and more than one, on each side. The second would be quite correct if it ended at the word *think;* for there are few who can do it, and fewer who will. The kindlier tell us that no human work is perfect. This is untrue: many poetical works are; many of Horace, more of Catullus, stil more of Lafontaine; if indeed fable may be admitted as poetry by coming in its garb and equipage. Surely there are some of Moore's songs, and several of Barry Cornwall's, absolutely perfect: surely there are also a few small pieces in the italian and french. I wonder, on a renewed investigation, to find so few among the Greeks. But the fluency of the language carried them too frequently on the shallows; and even in the graver and more sententious the current is greater than the depth. The Ilissus is sometimes a sandbank. In the elegant and graceful arrow there is often not only much feather and little barb, but the barb wants weight to carry it with steddiness and velocity to the mark. Milton and Cowper were the first and last among us who breathed without oppression on the serene and cloudless hights where the Muses were born and educated. Each was at times a truant from his school; but even the lower of the two, in his *Task,* has done what extremely few of his preceptors could do. Alas! his attic honey was at last turned sour by the leaven of fanaticism. I wish he and Goldsmith, and your father, could call to order some adventurous members of our poetical yacht-club, who are hoisting a great deal of canvas on a slender mast, and 'unknown regions dare explore' without compass, plummet, or anchor. Nobody was readier than Southey to acknowledge that, in his capacity of laureate, he had written some indifferent poetry; but it was better than his predecessor's or successor's on similar occasions. Personages whom he was expected to commemorate lookt the smaller for the elevation of their position, and their naturally coarse materials crumbled under the master's hand. Against these frail memorials we may safely place his *Inscriptions*, and challenge all nations to confront them. We are brought by these before us to the mournful contemplation of his own great merits lying unnoticed; to the indignant recollection of the many benefices, since his departure, and since you were admitted into holy orders, bestowed by chancellors and bishops on clergymen undistinguished in literature or virtue.[1] And there has often been a powerful call where there has been a powerful canvasser. The father puts on the colors of the candidate; and the candidate, if successful, throws a scarf and a lambskin over the shoulder of the son. Meanwhile, the son of that great and almost universal genius, who, above all others, was virtually, truly, and emphatically, and not by a vain title, Defender of the Faith, defender far more strenuous and more potent than any prelatical baron since the Reformation; who has upheld more efficiently, because more uprightly, the assaulted and endangered constitution of the realm than any party-man within the walls of the Parliament-house; who declined the baronetcy which was offered to him and the seat to which he was elected; he leaves an only son, ill-provided for, with a family to support. Different, far different, was *his* conduct in regard to those whom the desire of fame led away from the road to fortune. He patronized a greater number of intellectual and virtuous young men, and more warmly, more effectually, than all the powerful. I am not quite certain that poets in general are the best deserving of patronage: he however could and did sympathise with them, visit them in their affliction, and touch their unsoundness tenderly.

---

[1] Subsequent to the date of this letter a living was bestowed on Cuthbert Southey by Lord Chancellor Truro.—W. S. L.

REVEREND CHARLES CUTHBERT SOUTHEY

Invidiousness seems to be the hereditary ophthalmia of our unfortunate family; he tended many labouring under the disease, and never was infected. Several of those in office, I am credibly informed, have entered the fields of literature; rather for its haymaking, I presume, than for its cultivation. Whatever might have been the disadvantages to your father from their competition, will, I hope, be unvisited upon you. On the contrary, having seen him safe in the earth, probably they will not grudge a little gold-leaf for the letters on his gravestone, now you have been able to raise it out of the materials he has left behind. We may expect it reasonably; for a brighter day already is dawning. After a quarter of a million spent in the enlargement of royal palaces and the accommodation of royal horses; after a whole million laid out under Westminster Bridge; after an incalculable sum devoted to another Tower of Babel, for as many tongues to wag in; the Queen's Majesty has found munificent advisers, recommending that the entire of *twenty-five pounds annually* shall be granted to the representative of that officer who spent the last years of his life, and life itself, in doing more for England's commerce than Alexander and the Ptolemies did for the world's. He quelled the terrors of the desert, and drew England and India close together.

In February 1851 Landor published Popery, British and Foreign *as a pamphlet costing eighteen pence. In it he again stressed the need for Church reform.*

This was followed by a series of ten Letters to Cardinal Wiseman, *which were also contributions towards Church reform and showed that Landor had lost little of his fire and taste for argument about Church affairs. In 1849 Pius IX had appointed Cardinal Wiseman Archbishop of Westminster, and a papal bull announced the appointment of catholic bishops. The Cardinal, in a pastoral letter, stirred up the dormant 'no popery' feelings of the population by declaring 'Catholic England has been restored to its orbit in the ecclesiastical firmament from which its light had long vanquished.' The Cardinal's statement caused demonstrations, and instead of burning the tradition 'guy' on 5 November, the Pope and Wiseman were targets for popular hatred. Apart from these controversial issues—for Landor had consistently written on the Catholic problem—he wrote* Five Scenes *around the tragedy of Beatrice Cenci, which were published in* Fraser's Magazine. *He also contributed to Leigh Hunt's short-lived* Journal *a series of verses entitled* Poemetti.

With the opening of the Great Exhibition at the Crystal Palace, he wrote a letter to the editor of The Examiner *entitled 'What to do with the Crystal Palace. He suggested that*

> '*A grant by Parliament to Mr Paxton of the site of the building for life, with the unfettered disposal of the building during that period, would, I venture to suggest, be a proceeding on the part of Parliament and the Commissioners which would meet with the applause of the Nation. That Mr Paxton would devise uses for the building, which would meet with public approbation, I should have the fullest confidence. I take the liberty this notion to your judgement.*'

Landor contended that London offered the worst specimens of architecture of any country.

> '*My first hope is, that Parliament will among the hundreds of acts wch it passes in one session and rescinds in the following, will be wise enough to cancel its vote in regard to this noble edifice. Light as*

it is, it is constructed of such materials that it may out last the most ponderous building in the whole metropolis. And, what can be said of no other on earth, tens of thousands may enjoy it daily in the most ungenial months of the year, repairing health and prolonging life, and blessing the beneficence that raised it. The wealthy, no doubt, will contribute the rarest and most beautiful plants to its embelishment. The grant is the only one worthy of the Architect's acceptance, who has already received the highest honour in the friendship of the Duke of Devonshire.'[1]

He also contributed an 'Imaginary Conversation' between Nicholas and Nesselrode *to* The Examiner, *a commentary on Palmerston's policy towards the Czar. And when Kossuth came to England he printed a pamphlet on Kossuth's* Voyage to America, *which was distributed at a meeting held in Birmingham shortly before Kossuth sailed in November.*[2]

Finally, in December, he published his poem Tyrannicide, *a three-penny leaflet for the benefit of Hungarians in America.*

He was not without personal grief at this time. In July his beloved 'Ianthé' died at Versailles after sixteen hours' illness.

'This most afflicting intelligence was sent me by her son William, who was with her at the last hour. She will be brought over to the family vault in County Meath, of her first husband, Swift, great-great grandson of the uncle of the Dean of St Patrick. I hoped she might have seen my grave. Hers I shall never see, but my thoughts will visit it often. Though other friends have died in other days (why cannot I help running into verse?), One grave there is where memory sinks and stays.'[3]

Landor was at his best with her, Forster recorded.

1852–53

This year was notable in as much as Bleak House *appeared in parts in March, and Crabb Robinson remarked—[Landor's] fierce lines, tenderness of heart, and exaggerations in all his judgements described with great truth and force.'[4]*

[1] *The Examiner*, 28 June 1851.
[2] Elwin, *Landor*, p. 401.
[3] Forster, *Landor*, vol. 2, p. 483.
[4] Crabb Robinson: vol. ii, p. 717.

In the summer of that year Landor went to see *Julius Hare* at Hurstmonceaux, where he charmed his host and his hostess. He then returned to Kenyon, whom he had visited before going to Hurstmonceaux. He also visited Warwick to see his sister. There he heard the news of D'Orsay's death.

Two important books were published in 1853. In April the collected Imaginary Conversations of Greeks and Romans *appeared. It included four new 'Conversations' as well as all the previous texts. This work he dedicated to Charles Dickens. In November appeared* Last Fruit Off an Old Tree, *a volume of some 532 pages containing a selection of his works since the two-volume collected edition of 1846. It included eighteen 'Imaginary Conversations'. This was dedicated to the Marchese di Azeglio, an Italian patriot opposed to the Papacy. Landor also wrote a Preface to the volume in which he reiterated his dislike of Pius IX, the Czar Nicholas, King Louis Philippe and Louis Napoleon.*

As for completely new work, he wrote an 'Imaginary Conversation' between the Archbishop of Florence and Francesco Madiai, who had, even at that time, been imprisoned for heresy. The Papacy pamphlet as well as the Letters to Cardinal Wiseman, the five Scenes from Beatrice Cenci, the three Essays on Cattulus, Theocritus and Petrarca, all appeared in The Examiner, while toward the end of the year he wrote a number of letters to The Examiner on Czarist aggression.

The Royal Academy exhibited his portrait by Boxall: '[It] is considered to be a very good likeness,' he told Rosenhagen.

On 15 August he paid his last visit to Warwick to see his sister Elizabeth, for he was beginning to find travelling tiring. He told Forster that if he came to London and saw three men he knew, two of them would likely be scoundrels, and that

> 'I too often think at night of what I had been seeing in the morning, poor mothers, half-starved children, and girls habitually called unfortunate by people who drop the word as lightly as if it had no meaning in it. Little do they think that they are speaking of fallen angels; the real ones, not the angels of mythology and fable. So many heart-aches always leave me one.'

To The Princess Belgioioso

1853

Right in my path what goddess stands?
Whose is that voice? *whence* those commands?
I see thy stately step again,
Thine eyes, the founts of joy and pain,
Daughter of the Triulzi! those
But now on Lario's lake arose,
Shedding fresh blessings, purer light . . .
And hast thou left the Alpine hight,
The yellow vale, grey-budding vine
Whom guardian maple's nets entwine,
The villa where from open sash
We heard columnar fountains dash,
While candid Gods unmoved above
Soften and quietly reprove
Such restlessness, and citron's bloom
Waves from clear gem its warm perfume.
No loitering here: we must obey,
Where the loud trumpet points the way,
Where new-born men Ausonia calls,
And standards shine from mouldering walls
O'er dark Albunea's woods, and o'er
Where graceful Tibur's temples soar.
Cornelia's race lives yet; nor drown'd
In the drear gulph is Clelia; found
Again is Arria's dagger; now
Who bears it? Belgioioso, thou.
Light on the wounded rests a hand
Kings may no kiss, much less command;
Nor shrinkest thou to hear the shrill
Cry thro' gnasht teeth, nor (oozing stil)
To staunch the dense dark blood. At feats
Like these the prowling thief retreats.

Untrue to Italy, to all,
Untruest to himself, the Gaul!
The splayfoot of our British Muse
Wags woefully in wooden shoes;
Nor will the Graces bind their zone
Round panting bosom overgrown;
But thou shalt never feel the wrong
Of bruises from a barbarous tongue:
No, nor shall ditty dull and weak
Raise wrath or blushes to thy cheek;
Nor shall these wreaths which now adorn
Thy brow, drop off thee, dead ere morn.
When wars and kingly frauds are past,
With Justice side by side, the last
Sad stain of blood (O blessed day!)
Egeria's lymph shall wash away.

From *Last Fruit*
1853

LADY HAMILTON

Long have the Syrens left their sunny coast,
The Muse's voice, heard later, soon was lost:
Of all the Graces one remains alone,
Gods call her Emma; mortals, Hamilton.

THE DEATH OF MADAME ROLAND

Genius and Virtue! dismal was the dearth
  Ye saw throughout all France when ye lookt down,
In the wide waste of blood-besprinkled earth,
  There was but one great soul, and that had flown.

1854

The year began grimly. It was very cold and severe snowfalls kept Landor indoors; furthermore, he learned that his friend for many years, Miss Caldwell, sister to Lady Belmore, had died. Far worse, he heard that his dearly beloved sister Elizabeth was seriously ill with bronchitis. He was prepared to set off to see her, but his brother Henry persuaded him not to do so. She died in February. A month later he wrote of her:

> *Sharp crocus wakes the froward year:*
> *In their old haunts birds reappear;*
> *From yonder elm, yet black with rain,*
> *The cushat looks deep down for grain*
> *Thrown on the gravel-walk; here comes*
> *The redbreast to the sill for crumbs.*
> *Fly off! fly off! I can not wait*
> *To welcome ye, as she of late.*
> *The earliest of my friends is gone.*
> *Alas! almost my only one!*
> *The few as dear, long wafted o'er,*
> *Await me on a sunnier shore.*

Elizabeth left bequests which benefitted Walter's sons. By the middle of March Landor had recovered his spirits, and went out riding with a young lady who was staying with his friends.[1]

Landor received many letters from America. When T. W. Parsons in 1854 in Boston published a volume entitled Epistle to Walter Savage Landor, Poems, *Landor returned the compliment by producing a shilling pamphlet* Letters of an American mainly on Russia and Revolution, *which treated a great number of subjects.*

Landor was always greatly concerned about foreign affairs. Much had been happening which was to lead to the Crimean War. For during the last ten years the Ottoman Empire had been fast decaying despite the efforts of one of our greatest ambassadors, Stratford Canning, 1st Viscount Stratford de Redcliffe.[2] *It was in 1833, after giving up politics for some years, that Palmerston persuaded Canning to accept*

[1] Super, *Landor*, p. 420.
[2] 1786–1880.

the post of Ambassador to Nicholas I. Nicholas refused to accept him, considering Canning knew too much of Russian affairs, so he was posted again to Constantinople. As early as 1809 Canning had believed that Turkey was 'rotten at the heart; the seat of corruption is in the government itself.'[1] Despite the defeat of the Janissaries in 1832, Canning fought to back the power of the far-seeing Raschid, but there was no solidity in Turkish rule—corruption and indifference was destroying the empire and Raschid lost heart.[2] In 1852 Canning left Turkey. Meanwhile the Czar was much concerned at the deterioration of affairs in the Ottoman Empire as well as the improvement of Anglo-French affairs, and in June 1844 he arrived, unannounced, in this country. He made his views plain that if the Ottoman Empire collapsed, France would seize her opportunities. Lord Aberdeen played the game of assuring the Czar that England agreed, though he had no intention of undermining the French entente. Meanwhile, Napoleon, in order to secure the Catholic vote in France restored the temporal rights of the Popes in Rome. By 1852 France had acquired keys to the holy places in the Middle East, and in December the President of the French was declared the Emperor Napoleon III. In Great Britain Lord Derby resigned and Lord Aberdeen formed a ministry of Whigs and Peelites.

Landor's fears of Czarist 'oppression' were becoming a reality. Russia had now concerned herself over the Christians in the Turkish Empire, and Prince Menschikoff was sent to the Sublime Porte on a special mission. Menschikoff was a hasty and intemperate man, and when his demands became known Palmerston wanted 'a bold firm course, based on right . . . the policy and practice of the Russian Government has always been to push forward its encroachments as fast and as far as the apathy or want of firmness of other Governments would allow it to go, but always to stop and retire when it was met with decided resistance . . .[3]

Napoleon did not want war and promised support. On 13 June 1853 the British Fleet reached Besika Bay, while in July Russian troops passed Pruth and entered Moldavia. Canning advised the Sultan 'to send a special mission to Russia'. But it was all to no avail. In October Turkey declared war against Russia and defeated the Russians at

[1] S. Lane-Poole, *Life of Stratford Canning*, vol. i, p. 51.
[2] Woodward, *The Age of Reform*, p. 252.
[3] Temperley: *England and the Near East*, vol. i, p. 337.

Oltenitza. On 30 November, the Turkish Fleet was destroyed by the Russians in the harbour of Sinope. It was at this stage of the proceedings that Landor pinned his faith on Louis Napoleon, about whom he had considerable reservations. Nonetheless, he hated the Russians more.

From *Letters to an American*
1854

Thou hast, Napoleon, seiz'd on power: one-half
Of thoughtful men condemns thee, one applauds:
Unite them, for thou canst; let Western Rome
And Eastern spring to life again by thee.
Wave tomorous cousel off; distrust the speech
Anile, of statesmen who from earliest days
Have bowed to every despot, strong or weak.
Audacity, the necromancer's wand,
Can make them follow silent and submiss;
Or, like some muttered spell from lips accurst,
Can hold them fast and motionless in chains.
Fools! ignorant that wrong engenders wrong,
And that inaction is Death's stepping-stone,
Rais'd on the manly breast that beats no more.
We Britons have resigned our heritage,
Our ancient privilege to help opprest
And struggling nations. In my soul's dark depths
I grieve, with great tumultuous, that swells o'er,
And forces from my breast one last appeal,
And must it, O Napoleon, be to thee?
It must be! none hath courage, none hath strength,
To crush the snow-colossus, to stamp down
In to his native sands that shapeless bulk,
But thou alone. Rise then Napoleon,
To greatness he who went before thee might
(Had Honor led him onward) have attained.
If Poland's voice had reacht his frozen ear,
The nations of the earth had repossest
Their birthright: give it thou: give back what he
Held out, and then withdrew. No Scythian snows

A LETTER TO NAPOLEON

Impede thy path, no bodies of the slain,
League after league, upright as cetinels,
On either hand against the roadside ice,
But palms alone, and acclamation loud,
At which the war-horse in mid triumph rears.

In May Edward Fitzgerald found Landor looking so strong that he might rival old Rogers in age.[1] *In the autumn Landor was reading De Quincey and planning to write upon Florence Nightingale and the troops in the Crimea. He wrote to Forster of Eliza Lynn's selfless life and the difficulties she had surmounted. To a Kossuth charity he sent £5 which he could ill-afford, and wrote to Forster: 'In the twentieth year of the British Republic, some old man may recount tales of you and me. He will not be a very old man, if public affairs are managed another year as they have been this last.'*[2]

1855–56

Among the many persons Landor knew throughout his long life, William Napier was one of his closest friends. Napier was the younger brother of Sir Charles James Napier, the conqueror of Sind. He, too, achieved distinction and was appointed Governor of Guernsey in 1836. 'You do not know Landor,' said Sir William Napier to a friend offended by Landor's intemperate assaults on King Bomba or by some other favourite aversion.

> *'In matters of that sort he is reckless in expression only. What is savage in his speech does not spring from anything savage in his nature. Those wild cries of his at seeing his fellow-creatures overridden by injustice and tyranny are but the sign of an honest human feeling and a deep compassion. He has the lion-heart that springs forward to tear the wrongdoer, and the chained lion's roar of fury when he finds that he cannot reach him. Yet, if he saw tyrannicide lifting the knife, I am well convinced he would rather himself receive the blow than let it fall on the man it was aimed at.'*[3]

They both hated oppression and Landor thought William the most felicitous of historians.

Landor visited London for the last time in 1855. Forster took rooms in an hotel in Sydenham as he wanted to see Paxton's palace, and Sir Joseph Paxton set the fountains playing in his honour. He dined at Clapham Park, where the Napiers were then living. Writing to Lady Sawle in July, he said:

[1] Super, *Landor*, p. 421.
[2] Super, *Landor*, p. 422.
[3] Forster, *Landor*, vol. ii, p. 434.

'*I found my old friend in better health than I expected. He had never seen the Crystal Palace. Lame as he is, he came over the following day with Lady Napier, and we went together over the whole of it. And only fancy, the great fountains were set playing for me! The beautiful N. showed me her little girl, who was very amiable with me, as little girls always were: I mean very little ones. I was obliged to declare to Lady Napier that if she spoilt her grand-child, I would never make her a proposal. I spent some hours too with Kossuth, who would not dine with me and Forster because he had to receive a deputation quite unexpected; and by no means the smallest part of my pleasure was the introduction to me, the following day, of Mr Lytton. None of the younger poets of the present day breathes so high a spirit of poetry. Of what impressed me most in the palace itself I should tell you that I saw the statue of Satan by ——, and the wonderful picture of Cimabue and Giotto by ——. Alas! alas! every name flies off my memory when I would seize it. Leighton, I should have said, is the painter: the sculptor is Lough.*'[1]

Later he wrote Rose Graves-Sawle that Forster had told him he had proposed to write his biography.

'*I hope he is in no hurry. I am in none. I have never known more than two* great *men, although many good ones—Napier and Kossuth. I have only seen and once conversed with Kosciusko. Of Louis Bonaparte I will say nothing. He is the greatest and most powerful of living potentates—but a scoundrel like the rest.*'[2]

Landor had lost another close friend, for on 23 January, Julius Hare died. The Archdeacon had been ill when Landor last visited him at Hurstmonceaux, and he had left there with the feeling that they would not meet again. They had, on that occasion, talked about an old mulberry-tree in the garden at Warwick. Julius had said that the ancient Gods had each his favourite plant, and Hare had tried to explain why he considered that the mulberry should be Landor's favourite tree.

> *Of yore in Babylon the mulberry*
> *Changed colour at fond lovers' musery;*
> *In England, to her noblest poets dear,*

---

[1] Forster, *Landor*, vol. ii, p. 478.
[2] Wheeler, *Private Letters*, pp. 195–6.

It keeps the records of glad friendship here.
Twas Shakespeare's, Milton's, now 'tis Landor's tree;
Precious to those who love the gifted thee.[1]

In January 1856, in his eighty-first year, Landor published Antony and Octavious, Scenes for a Study, *as well as his* Letter to Emerson, *while in April* Fraser's Magazine *published two new 'Imaginary Conversations'*—Alfieri and Metastasio *and* Menander and Epicurus. *Many new poems*—Peace, Poet and May, To the Americans from an American. *In* The Examiner *there appeared* On General Count Leiningen, Cousin of Queen Victoria, Murdered at Arad by the Emperor of Austria, Oct 6 '49.
Landor wrote to Forster:

'*I have enjoyed better health this winter, such as it has been, than in almost any other since I left my paradise in Italy. Strength alone fails me in the corporeal, and memory in the mental. I remember what I would forget, and I forget what I would remember. I have nothing to do now but to look in the fire, and see it burn down, as I myself have done. Solitude was always dear to me; and at present more than ever; once a playful friend, and now a quiet mouse. Scarcely a soul of my old acquaintance is left in Bath. All have departed; the most part to that country where there neither are nor ever will be railroads. I must perforce remain where I am . . .*'

On 1 January he did not fail to send Rose her birthday greetings:

> *I was not young when first I met*
> *That graceful mien, that placid brow:*
> *Ah! twice ten years have past, and yet*
> *Near these I am not older now.*
>
> *Happy how many have been made*
> *Who gazed upon your sunny smile!*
> *I sate as happy in the shade*
> *To hear the voice that could beguile*
>
> *My sorrow for whate'er I left*
> *In bright Ausonia, land of song,*
> *And felt my breast not quite bereft*
> *Of those home joys cast down so long.*

[1] Forster, *Landor*, vol. ii, p. 457.

What pleasure Landor derived from the peace treaty signed on 30 March between Russia and Turkey, England, France and Sardinia, must have been completely overwhelmed by the death of his dog Pomero, whom he had had for the twelve years he had lived at Bath. It was a pugnacious Pomeranian, but he had adored it; indeed he loved dogs and despised people who feared them. 'When a dog flies at you, reason with it, remember how well-behaved the Molossian dogs were when Ulysses sat down in the midst of them as equal.'

He had written, in 1844, to Forster when he was in Warwick:

> *'Daily I think of Bath and Pomero. I fancy him lying on the narrow window-sill, and watching the good people go to church. He has not made up his mind between the Anglican and Roman Catholic; but I hope he will continue in the faith of his forefathers, if it will make him happier.'*[1]

Forster had been dazzled with the dog: 'the eager brightness of his eye and the feathery whiteness of his coat.' On another occasion Landor wrote to Forster:

> *'Pomero was on my knee when your letter came. He is now looking out of the window; a sad male gossip, as I often tell him. I dare not take him with me to London. He would most certainly be stolen, and I would rather lose Ispley or Llanthony. The people of the house love him like a child, and declare he is as sensible as a Christian. He not only is as sensible, but much more Christian than some of those who have lately brought strife and contention into the church. Everybody knows him, high and low, and he makes me quite a celebrity.'*[2]

The year ended with Landor being ill and the publication of his letter to Emerson on having read his English Traits. *The American poet and essayist had been born in Boston in 1803, the son of a Unitarian minister, and educated at Harvard. He was ordained in 1829 and became pastor of the Boston Second Church. He married Ellen Tucker, who died in 1831, whereupon Emerson had resigned and in the following year made the first of his three protracted visits to Europe. He first met Landor in Florence through the American sculptor Horatio Greenough. Emerson considered Landor*

[1] Forster, *Landor*, vol. ii, p. 426.
[2] Forster, *Landor*, vol. ii, p. 427.

LANDOR

'One of the foremost of that small class who make good in the nineteenth century the claims of pure literature. In these busy days of avarice and ambition, when there is so little disposition to profound thought or to any but the most superficial intellectual entertainment, a faithful scholar, receiving from past ages the treasures of wit, and enlarging them by his own love, is a friend and consoler of mankind. . . Whoever writes for the love of truth and beauty and not with ulterior ends belongs to a sacred class, among whom there are few men of the present age who have a better claim to be numbered than Mr Landor. Wherever genius or taste has existed, wherever freedom and justice, which he values as the element in which genius may work, are threatened, his interest is sure to be commanded. His love of beauty is passionate, and betrays itself in all petulant and contemptuous expression. But beyond his delight in genius and his love of individual and civil liberty, Mr Landor has a perception that is much more rare—the appreciation of character. This is the more remarkable considered with his intense nationality, for he is buttoned in English broadcloth to the chin . . . Such merits make Mr Landor's position in the republic of letters one of great mark and dignity. He exercises with a grandeur of spirit the office of writer, and carries it with an air of old and unquestionable nobility. His acquaintance with the English tongue is unsurpassed. He is a master of condensation and suppression, and that in no vulgar way. He knows the wide difference between compression and an obscure elliptical style. Dense writer as he is, he has yet ample room and choice of phrase, and often even a gamesome mood between his valid words. There is no inadequacy or disagreeable contraction in one of his sentences, any more than in a human face, where in a square space of a few inches is found room for every possible variety of expression . . . Of many of Mr Landor's sentences we are fain to remember what was said of those of Socrates, that they are cubes, which will stand firm place them how or where you will.'[1]

The last month of the year was clouded with loneliness and illness, including a severe bout of bronchitis.

[1] Forster, *Landor*, vol. ii, pp. 81–82.

Walter Savage Landor to Emerson
1856

MY DEAR SIR,—Your *English Traits* have given me great pleasure; and they would have done so even if I had been treated by you with less favour. The short conversations we held at my Tuscan Villa were insufficient for an estimate of my character and opinions. A few of these, and only a few, of the least important, I may have modified since. Let me run briefly over them as I find them stated in your pages. Twenty-three years have not obliterated from my memory the traces of your visit, in company with that intelligent man and glorious sculptor, who was delegated to erect a statue in your capital to the tutelary genius of America. I share with him my enthusiastic love of ancient art; but I am no *exclusive*, as you seem to hint I am. In my hall at Fiesole there are two busts, if you remember, by two artists very unlike the ancients, and equally unlike each other; Donatello and Fiamingo; surveying them at a distance is the sorrowful countenance of Germanicus. Sculpture at the present day flourishes more than it ever did since the age of Pericles; and America is not cast into the shade by Europe. I do prefer Giovanni da Bologna to Michael Angelo, who indeed in his conceptions is sublime, but often incorrect, and sometimes extravagant, both in sculpture and painting. I confess I have no relish for his prodigious *giblet pie* in the Capella Sistina, known throughout the world as his *Last Judgement*. Grand in architecture, he was no ordinary poet, no lukewarm patriot. Deplorable, that the inheritor of his house and name is so vile as sycophant, that even the blast of Michael's trumpet could not rouse his abject soul.

I am an admirer of Pietro Perugino, and more than an admirer of Raffaelle; but I could never rank the Madonna della Seggiola among the higher of his works; I see no divinity in the child, and no such purity in the Virgin as he often expressed in her. I have given my opinion as freely on the *Transfiguration*. The cartoons are his noblest works: they place him as high as is Correggio in the Dome of Parma: nothing has been, or is likely to be, higher.

Among my *cloud of pictures* you did not observe a little Masaccio

351

(one of his two easel-pictures) representing Saint Jerome. The idea of it is truer than Domenichino's.

The last of the Medici Grandukes, Giovanni Gaston, sent to the vicinity of Parma and Correggio an old Florentine, who was reputed to be an excellent judge of painting. He returned with several small pieces on canvas, which the painters at that time in Florence turned into ridicule, and which were immediately thrown into the Palazzo Vecchio. About a quarter of a century ago, the chambers of this Palazzo were cleared of their lumber, and I met in the Via degli Archibugieri a tailor who had two small canvases under his arms, and two others in his hands. He had given a few paoli for each; I offered him as many francesconi. He thought me a madman; an opinion which I also heard expressed as I sat under the shade of a vast old fig tree, while about twenty labourers were extirpating three or four acres of vines and olives, in order to make somewhat like a meadow before my windows. *The words were 'Matti sono tutti gli Inglesi, ma questo poi'* . . . followed by a shrug and an aposiopesis. I acquired two more *cerotti*, as they had been called, painted by the same master; three I have at Bath, and three remain at my villa in Tuscany. Mr. George Wallis, who accompanied Soult in that Marshal's *Eclectic Review* of the Spanish Galleries, pronounced them to be Correggios. What is remarkable, one is a landscape. It would indeed be strange if he, who painted better than any before or since, should have produced no greater number of works than are attributed to him by Mengs. I have seen several of which I entertain no doubt. Raffaelle is copied more easily; so perhaps is Titian, if not Giorgione. On this subject the least fallible authority is Morris More, who however could not save our National Gallery from devastation.

Curious as I was in collecting specimens of the earlier painters, I do not prefer them to the works either of their nearer successors or to those of the present day. My Domenichino, about which I doubted, has been authenticated by M. Cosveldt; my Raffaelle by M. Dennistoune, who was wrong only in believing it had been called a portrait of the painter. It is in fact the portrait of the only son of that Doni whose wife's is in the Tribuna at Florence. He died in boyhood; and the picture was long retained in his mother's family, the Strozzi, and thrown into a bedchamber of the domestics as a piece of *robaccia* and *anticaglia*.

We will now walk a little way out of the Gallery. Let me say, before we go farther, that I do not think 'the Greek historians the only good ones.' Davila, Machiavelli, Voltaire, Michelet, have afforded me much instruction and much delight. Gibbon is worthy of a name among the most enlightened and eloquent of the ancients. I find no fault in his language; on the contrary, I find the most exact propriety. The grave, and somewhat austere, becomes the historian of the Roman Republic; the grand, and somewhat gorgeous, finds its proper place in the palace of Byzantium. Am I indifferent to the merits of our own historians? indifferent to the merits of him who balanced with equal hand Wellington and Napoleon? No; I glory in my countryman and friend. Is it certain that I am indiscriminating in my judgement on Charron? Never have I compared him with Montaigne; but there is much of wisdom, and, what is remarkable in the earlier French authors, much of sincerity in him.

I am sorry to have '*pestered you with Southey*,' and to have excited the inquiry, '*Who is Southey?*' I will answer the question. Southey is the poet who has written the most imaginative poem of any in our own times, English or Continental; such is *The Curse of Kehama*. Southey is the proseman who has written the purest prose; Southey is the critic the most cordial and the least invidious. Show me another, of any note, without captiousness, without arrogance, and without malignity.

> *Slow rises worth by poverty deprest.*

But Southey raised it.

Certainly you could not make me praise Mackintosh. What is there eminently to praise in him? Are there not twenty men and women at the present hour who excell him in style and genius? His reading was extensive: he had much capacity, less comprehensiveness and concentration. I know not who may be the 'others of your recent friends' whom you could not excite me to applaud. I am more addicted to praise than censure. We English are generally as fierce partisans in literary as in parliamentary elections, and we cheer or jostle a candidate of whom we know nothing. I always kept clear of both quarters. I have votes in three counties, I believe I have in four, and never gave one. I would rather buy than solicit or canvass, but preferably neither. Nor am I less abstinent in the turbulent contest for literary honors. Among the many authors you have conversed with in England, did you find above a couple who spoke not ill of nearly all the rest? Even the most liberal of them, they who concede the most, subtract at last the greater part of what they have conceded, together with somewhat beside. And this is done, forsooth, out of fairness, truthfulness, etc.!

> The nearest the kennel are the most disposed to spash the polished boot.

I never envied any man anything but waltzing, for which I would have given all the little talents I had acquired. I dared not attempt to learn it; for, although I was active and my ear was accurate, I felt certain I should have been unsuccessful. Even the shameless (and I am not among those) have somewhat of shame in one part or other; and here lay mine.

We now come to Carlyle, of whom you tell us 'he worships a man that will manifest any truth to him.' Would he have the patience for the truth to be manifested? or would he accept it then? Certainly the face of truth is very lovely, and we take especial care that it shall never lose its charms by familiarity. He declares that *'Landor's principle is mere rebellion.'*

Quite the contrary is apparent and prominent in many of my writings. I always was a Conservative; but I would eradicate any species of evil, political, moral, or religious, as soon as it springs up, with no reference to the blockheads who cry out *'What would you substitute in its place?'* When I pluck up a dock or a thistle, do I ask any such question? I have said plainly, more than once, and in many quarters, that I would not alter or greatly modify the English Constitution. I denounced at the time of its enactment the fallacy of the Reform Bill. And here I beg pardon for the word *fallacy,* instead of *humbug,* which entered into our phraseology with two other sister graces, *sham* and *pluck.* I applaud the admission of new peers; and I think it well that a large body of them should be hereditary. But it is worse than mere popery that we should be encumbered by a costly and heavy bench of Cardinals, under the title of Bishops, and that their revenues should exceed those in the Roman States. I would send a beadel after every Bishop who left his diocese, without the call of his Sovran the head of the Church, for some peculiar and urgent purpose relating to it solely. I would surround the throne with splendour and magnificence, and grant as large a sum as a thousand pounds weekly for it, with two palaces; no land but what should be rented. The highest of the nobility would be proud of service under it, without the pay of menials. I approve the expansion of our peerage; but never let its members, adscititious or older, think themselves the only nobility; else peradventure some of them may be reminded that there are among us men whose ancestors stood in high places, and who did good service to the country, when theirs were cooped up within borough-walls, or called on duty from the field as serfs and villains.

Democracy, such as yours in America, is my abhorrence. Republicanism far from it; but there are few nations capable of receiving, fewer of retaining, this pure and efficient form. Democracy is lax and disjointed; and whatever is loose wears out the machine. The nations on the Ebro, and the mountaineers of Biscay, enjoyed it substantially for century after century. Holland, Ragusa, Genoa, Venice, were deprived of it by that *Holy Alliance* whose influence is now withering the Continent, and changing the features of England. We are losing our tensity of sinew; we are germanizing into a flabby and effete indifference. It appears to me that the worst calamity the world has ever undergone, is the prostration of Venice at the feet of Austria. The oldest and truest nobility in the world was swept away by Napoleon. How happily were the Venetian States governed for a thousand years, by the brave and circumspect gentlemen of the island city! All who did not conspire against its security were secure. Look at the palaces they erected! Look at the Arts they cultivated! Look, on the other side, at the damp and decaying walls; enter; and there behold such countenances as you will never see elsewhere. These are not among the creatures whom God will permit any Deluge to sweep away. Heretofore, a better race of beings has uniformly succeeded to a viler though a vaster; and it will be so again.

Rise, Manin! rise, Garibaldi! rise, Mazzini! Compose your petty differences, quell your discordances, and stand united! Strike, and spare not; strike high. '*Miles, faciem feri,*' cried the wisest and most valiant of the Roman race.

I have enjoyed the conversation of Carlyle within the room where I am writing. It appeared at that time less evidently than now that his energy goes far beyond his discretion. Perverseness is often mistaken for strength, and obstinacy for consistency. There is only one thing in which he resembles other writers, namely, in saying that which he can say best, and with most point. You tell us, 'he does not read Plato.' Perhaps there may be a sufficient reason for it.

Resolved to find out what there is in this remarkable philosopher, I went daily for several weeks into the Magliabechian library at Florence, and thus refreshing my neglected Greek, I continued the reading of his works in the original from beginning to end. The result of this reading may be found in several of the *Imaginary Conversations*. That one of them between Lord Chesterfield and Lord Chatham contains observations on the cacophony of some sentences; and many more could have been added quite as exceptionable. Even Attic honey hath its impurities.

'He (Carlyle) took despairing or satirical views of literature at this moment.'

I am little fond of satire, and less addicted to despair. It seems to me that never in this country was there a greater number of good writers than now; and some are excellent. Our epic is the novel or romance. I dare not praise the seven or eight of both sexes who have written these admirably; if I do, the *ignavum fuci pecus* would settle on me. All are glad to hear the censure, few the praise, of those who labor in the same vineyard.

We are now at Rydal Mount.

Wordsworth's bite is less fervid than Carlyle's: it comes with more saliva about it, and with a hoarser expectoration. 'Lucretius he esteems a far *higher* poet than Virgil.'

The more fool he! 'not in his system, which is nothing, but in his power of illustration.'

Does a power of illustration imply the *high* poet? It is in his system (which, according to Wordsworth, *is nothing*), that the power of Lucretius consists. Where then is its use? But what has Virgil in his *Eclogues*, in his *Georgics*, or in his *Æneid*, requiring illustration? Lucretius does indeed well illustrate his subject; and few even in prose among the philosophers have written so intelligibly; but the quantity of his poetry does not much exceed three hundred lines in the whole: one of the noblest specimens of it is a scornful expostulation against the fear of death. Robert Smith, brother of Sidney, wrote in the style of Lucretius such Latin poetry as is fairly worth all the rest in that language since the banishment of Ovid. Even Lucretius himself nowhere hath exhibited such a continuation of manly thought and of lofty harmony.

We must now descend to Wordsworth once again.

He often gave an opinion on authors which he never had read, and on some which he could not read. Plato, for instance. He speaks contemptuously of the Scotch. The first time I ever met him, and the only time I ever conversed with him longer than a few minutes, he spoke contemptuously of Scott, and violently of Byron. He chattered about them incoherently and indiscriminately. In reality, Scott had singularly the power of imagination and of construction: Byron little of either; but this is what Wordsworth neither said nor knew. His censure was hardened froth. I praised a line of Scott's on the dog of a traveller lost in the snow (if I remember) on Skiddaw. He said it was the only good one in the poem, and began instantly to recite a whole one of his own upon the same subject. This induced me afterwards to write as follows on a fly-leaf in Scott's poems,

> Ye who have lungs to mount the Muse's hill,
> Here slake your thirst aside their liveliest rill:
> Asthmatic Wordsworth, Byron piping-hot,
> Leave in the rear, and march with manly Scott.

I was thought unfriendly to Scott for one of the friendliest things I ever did toward an author. Having noted all the faults of grammar and expression in two or three of his volumes, I calculated that the number of them, in all, must amount to above a thousand. Mr. Lockhart, who married his daughter, was indignant at this, and announced at the same time (to prove how very wrong I was) that they were corrected in the next edition.

Poor Scott! he bowed his high intellect and abased the illustrious rank conferred on him by the unanimous acclaim of nations, before a prince who was the approbrium of his country for enduring so quietly and contentedly his Neronianism.

Scott's reading was extensive, but chiefly within the range of Great Britain and France; Wordsworth's lay, almost entirely, between the near grammar school and Rydal Mount. He would not have scorned, although he might have reviled, the Scotch authors, if he ever had read Archibald Bower, or Hume, or Smollett, or

Adam Smith; he would have indeed hated Burns; he would never have forgiven Beattie that incomparable stanza,

> O how canst thou renounce the boundless store
> Of charms that Nature to her votary yields,
> The warbling woodlands, the resounding shore,
> The pomp of groves and garniture of fields,
> All that the genial ray of morning gilds,
> And all that echoes to the song of even,
> All that the mountain's sheltering bosom shields,
> And all the dread magnificence of heaven;
> O how canst thou renounce and hope to be forgiven?

Nor would he have endured that song of Burns, more animated than the odes of Pindar,

> Scots wha hae wi' Wallace bled.

He would have been horrified at the Doric-Scotch of 'wha hae'; yet what wool in the mouth were *have* and *with*! Gerald Massey too must have fared ill with him; and the gentle and graceful Tennyson's dress-shoes might have stood in danger of being trodden on by the wooden. Wordsworth's walk was in lowlands of poetry, where the wooden shoe is commodious. The vigorous and animated ascend their high battle-field neither in that not in the slipper, but press on, and breathe hard, εὐκνημῖδες.

When Hazlitt was in Tuscany he often called on me, and once asked me whether I had ever seen Wordsworth. I answered in the negative, and expressed a wish to know something of his appearance.

'Sir,' said Hazlitt, 'have you ever seen a horse?' 'Assuredly.' 'Then, Sir, you have seen Wordsworth.'

When I met him some years after at a friend's on the lake of Waswater, I found him extremely civil. There was *equinity* in the lower part of his face: in the upper was much of the contemplative, and no little of the calculating. This induced me, when, at a breakfast where many were present, he said he 'would not give five shillings for all Southey's poetry,' to tell a friend of his that he might safely make such an investment of his money and throw all his own in. Perhaps I was too ill-humoured, but my spirit rose against his ingratitude toward the man who first, and with incessant

effort and great difficulty, brought him into notice. He ought to
have approached his poetical benefactor as he did the

illustrious peer,
With high respect and gratitude sincere.

Southey would have been more pleased by the friendliness of the
sentiment than by the intensity of the poetry in which it is expressed; for Southey was the most equitable, the most candid, the most
indulgent of mankind. I was unacquainted with him for many years
after he had commended in the *Critical Review,* my early poem,
Gebir. In the letters now edited by Mr. Water, I find that in the
Whitehaven Journal there was inserted a criticism, in which, on the
strength of this poem, I am compared and preferred to Goethe. I
am not too much elated. Neither in my youthful days nor in any
other have I thrown upon the world such trash as 'Werther' and
'Wilhelm Meister,' nor flavoured my poetry with the corrugated
spicery of metaphysics. Nor could he have written in a lifetime any
twenty, in a hundred or thereabout, of my *Imaginary Conversations.*
My poetry I throw to the Scotch terriers growling at my feet. Fifty
pages of Shelley contain more of pure poetry than a hundred of
Goethe, who spent the better part of his time in contriving a puzzle,
and in spinning out a yarn for a labyrinth. How different in features,
both personal and poetical, are Goethe and Wordsworth! In the
countenance of Goethe there was something of the elevated and
august; less of it in his poetry: Wordsworth's physiognomy was
entirely rural. With a rambling pen he wrote admirable paragraphs
in his longer poems, and sonnets worthy of Milton: for example,

'Two voices are there,' etc.

which is far above the highest pitch of Goethe. But his unbraced
and unbuttoned impudence in presence of our grand historians,
Gibbon and Napier, must be reprehended and scouted. Of Gibbon
I have delivered my opinion; of Napier too, on whom I shall add
nothing more at present than that he superseded the Duke, who
intended to write the history of his campaign, and who (his
nephew Capt. William Wellesley tells me) has left behind him
'Memoirs'.

I never *glorified* Chesterfield; yet he surely is among the best of
our writers in regard to style, and appears to have formed Horace

Walpole's and Sterne's, a style purely English. His Letters were placed by Beresford, Archbishop of Tuan, in the hands of his daughters. This I remember to have been stated to me by his son. A polished courtier and a virtuous prelate knew their value; and perhaps the neglect of them at the present day is one reason why a gentleman is almost as rare as a man of genius.

I am not conscious that I underrate Burke: never have I placed any of his parliamentary contemporaries in the same rank with him. His language is brilliant, but not always elegant; which induced me once to attribute to him the *Letters of Junius*. I am now more inclined to General Lee as author. Lord Nugent, an inquisitive and intelligent reader, told me he never could 'worm out the secret' from his uncle Mr. Thomas Grenville, who, he believed, knew it. Surely it is hardly worth the 'trouble' of a single hour's research. We have better things weekly in the *Examiner* and daily in the *Times*.

I do not 'undervalue Socrates.' Being the cleverest of the Sophists, he turned the fraternity into ridicule: he eluded the grasp of his antagonist by anointing with the oil of quibble all that was tangible and prominent. To compare his philosophy (if indeed you can catch it) with the philosophy of Epicurus and Epictetus, whose systems meet, is insanity.

I do not 'despise entomology.' I am ignorant of it; as indeed I am of almost all science.

I love also flowers and plants; but I know less about them than is known by a beetle or a butterfly.

I must have been misunderstood, or have been culpably inattentive, if I said 'I knew not Herschell even by name.' The father's I knew well, pernicious madman who tore America from England, and who rubbed his hands when the despatches announced to him the battle of Bunker's Hill, in which he told his equerry that his soldiers had '*got well peppered.*' Probably I had not then received in Italy the admirable writings of the great Herschell's greater son.

Phocion, who excites as much of pity as of admiration, was excellent as a commander and as an orator, but was deficient and faulty as a politician. No Athenian had, for so long a period, rendered to his country so many and such great services. He should have died a short time earlier; he should have entered the temple with Demosthenes. On the whole, I greatly prefer this last consistent man, although he could not save his country like Epaminondas and like Washington.

I make no complaint of what is stated in the following page, that 'Landor is strangely under-valued in England.' I have heard it before, but I never have taken the trouble to ascertain it. Here I find that I am 'savagely attacked in the Reviews.' Nothing more likely; I never see them; my acquaintances lie in a different and far distant quarter. Some honors have, however, been conferred on me in the literary world. Southey dedicated to me his *Kehama;* James his *Attila*: he and Dickens invited me to be god-father to their sons. Moreover, I think as many have offered me the flatteries of verse as ever were offered to any but Louis the Fourteenth.

P. 19. I think oftener with Alfieri than with any other writer, and quite agree with him that 'Italy and England are the only countries worth living in.' The only time I ever saw Alfieri was just before he left this country for ever. I accompanied my Italian master, Parachinetti, to a bookseller's, to order the Works of Alfieri and Metastasio, and was enthusiastic, as most young men were, about the French Revolution. 'Sir,' said Alfieri, 'you are a very young man; you are yet to learn that nothing good ever came out of France, or ever will. The ferocious monsters are about to devour one another; and they can do nothing better. They have always been the curse of Italy; yet we too have fools among us who trust them.'

Such were the expressions of the most classical and animated poet existing in the present or past century, of him who could at once be a true patriot and a true gentleman. There was nothing of the ruffianly in his vigour; nothing of the vulgar in his resentment; he could scorn without a scoff; he could deride without a grimace. Had he been living in these latter days, his bitterness would have overflowed, not on France alone, nor Austria in addition, the two beasts that have torn Italy in pieces, and are growling over her bones; but more, and more justly, on those constitutional governments which, by abetting, have aided them in their aggressions and incursions. We English are the most censurable of all. Forbear, in pity forbear to say, what I am afraid is too true, that we are a litter of blind lickspittles, waiting to be thrown with a stone about the neck into the next horsepond. Will historians be credited, some centuries hence, when they relate what our countrymen in the present have done against the progress of freedom throughout Europe? The ministers of England have signed that *Holy Alliance* which delivered every free State to the domination of arbitrary and irresponsible despots. The ministers of England have entered more recently into treaties with usurpers and assassins. And now, forsooth, it is called *assassination* to remove from the earth an assassin; the assassin of thousands; an outlaw, the subverter of his country's, and even of his own, laws. The valiant and the wise of old thought differently. Even now there are some, and they not devoid of intellect, who are of opinion that the removal of an evil at the least possible cost is best. They would not expose an army when one brave man could do the thing effectually: they would not impoverish a nation, nor maim and decimate the strong supports, nor leave destitute and desolate the fathers of its families, rather than strike a single blow which would sound the hour of their deliverance and security.

Impressed by these sentiments, which never have varied a tittle in the long course of my existence, I openly avowed that I had reserved insurance money, to a small extent, in favour of the first tyrannicide. My words are circulated in America and on our continent, and well received and widely echoed. I regret that here in England are some professing to be the friends of liberty and justice, who stand forward as shields and bucklers to the enemies of both. Surely wit and wisdom might be better employed. Permit me to repeat my words, written in a letter to Mr White.

'Sir, I have only one hundred pounds of ready money, and am never likely to have at my disposal as much in future. Of this I transmit five to you, toward the acquisition of the ten thousand muskets to be given, in accordance with your manifesto, "to the first Italian province which shall rise." The remaining ninety-five I reserve for the family of the first patriot who asserts by action the dignity of tyrannicide. Abject men have cried out against me for my commendation of this ancient virtue, the highest of which a man is capable, and now the most important and urgent.

'Is it not an absurdity to remind us that usurpers will rise up afresh? Do not all transgressors? But must we therefore lay aside the terrors of chastisement, or give a ticket-of-leave to the most atrocious criminals? Shall one enslave millions? Shall laws be subverted, and we then be told that we act against them, or without their sanction, when none are left us, and we lay prostrate the subverter? Three or four blows, instantly and simultaneously given, may save the world many years of warfare, of discord, and of degradation. It is everywhere unsafe to rob a citizen; shall it be anywhere safe to rob a people? Impelled unconsciously by a hand invisible, the hand of eternal justice, even the priest teaches the schoolboy the glory that always hath accompanied the tyrannicide. At the recital, he strikes the desk with his ferule, and the boy springs up at once into the man.'

Such are the sentiments I last avowed on reading how a brave man, with his two inoffensive children, were murdered by the usurper of the Hungarian crown, the abolitionist of Hungarian laws, and the persecutor and hangman of Hungarian patriots. Bearing these cruelties in memory, and seeing many more such daily before his eyes, let any true Englishman read the narrative of Colonel Türr, and then ask his own heart whether the atrocities there detailed can fail to excite the execration of every honourable man, and the chastisement of the perpetrator. There was a time, and I should be sorry to think it ended with Sydney, when the man who upheld the dignity of his fellow man, and who would strike down a felon in feathers and bedizened with stars and crosses, experienced far other treatment than contumely and buffoonery. Poerio and Kossuth and Türr, it seems to me, are greatly more deserving of our sympathy than their oppressors; yet these oppressors, being Potentates, we connive at them and coax them, and at last say, '*Now, pray! pray! don't! our own people will get angry with us, and force us into demonstrations.*' Meanwhile, it is only in set speeches to gain popularity, that a few of the ministry, and other members of parliament, warm up again a stale side-dish of pity for the exiled and imprisoned.

We once taught other nations; may other nations soon teach *us!* There is no great man in existence; shall it be said there is no brave one? The Crimea contradicts this, even to the face of our commanders. In the *Athenæum* you will find a paragraph, well worthy of notice, on the best of these.

While our readers were admiring the modesty which led the 'heroes of Kan' to ignore all merits *except their own*, a letter was on its way from the Bosphorus, and has been this week printed in the

Times, from General Kmety, in which the aged soldier addresses Sir W. F. Williams, in a tone of calm remonstrance worthy of his fame, on the historical suppression under which he, in common with others, is made to labor. Injustice of this sort, however, works its own cure. We hear with satisfaction that a subscription is being raised in the name of General Guyon, with a view to present that distinguished officer with a sword of honour.

The sword of honour was the sword he carried; the other may be laid across his coffin. The valiant and virtuous Guyon is no more. It is now a year since I read a letter from the most affectionate of wives, announcing that his heart was broken. Even her love could no longer support it. What then must be the weight of grief under which it at last was crushed! But he had fought against Austria; and Austria is German; German is England too. We may now expect that Orsini be demanded from us, and delivered up to the perjured Apostolic Majesty. No intercession was made by our Court for the cousin of our Queen; he had committed the heinous crime of asserting the cause of freedom.

And we are now called sticklers for assassination, who by one sweep of the arm would deliver a nation from its oppressor, and hurl down the tower that overhangs the dungeon! It was the lictor who carried the axe; he was no assassin; he bore before the magistrate the symbol of unity and of law. Only one man worthy of notice reprehends me. Ah Manin! Manin! when he of ebullient blood sits down again after exertion, he is apt to take cold so as to keep his room.

No one is more averse than I am to interference with other governments; but it is our duty to insist on the observance of the treaties they have made with us. Let the people of each be their own defenders and avengers. I must repeat what already is declared in several of my writings, that I have no fondness for innovation. Whatever is changed should rest, if possible, on what has been tried. Edifices are corroded and crumble first in their exterior and ornamental parts, leaving the foundation, if ever solid, the more solid the longer it hath stood. Far as our English Constitution is from absolute perfection, farther is it from that region of earthquakes where chance and change are causing by their indomitable fire incessant eruptions and oscillations. Certain it is, however, that we shall not rest where we are; but uncertain is it whether, when Enceladus hath shaken his shoulder and turned his side, we shall then rest long.

Accept this memorial, which your name will render of less brief duration, of the esteem in which you are held by

WALTER LANDOR.

P.S.—If you have not received our *Morning Advertiser*, you will ask for it, and will read with indignation the conduct of Lord Clarendon toward Colonel Türr. It was hoped that the family of Villiers had left its earlier titles in abeyance. Here is evidence of the contrary.

1857

Instead of Landor's last years being blessed with glory and comfort, they were shrouded in 'Lear-like' tragedy, culminating in his having to flee from Bath. The first of these disasters was an action brought by the Reverend Morris Yescombe against John Webb Roche and his mother-in-law for abducting Louise Koch, a governess, from the plaintiff's employ. Yescombe was a native of Cornwall, who had married a recently widowed woman who was the wife of the Honourable George William Massy, second son of the third Lord Massy. She continued to use the title of 'Honourable' to which she was, of course, in no way entitled. Landor was called as a witness because he had published statements in the Bath Express *when the case was* sub judice. *What was particularly galling were the statements made by Saunders Roche's counsel, who, in his summing up, referred to Landor as 'a poor, miserable old man whom no one could respect more than he did, having read his* Imaginary Conversations *and other works . . . but it was a miserable exhibition to bring the poor old man into the box to talk the twaddle he had.'*[1]

The danger of these and subsequent proceedings was that Mrs Yescombe was an unreliable woman, and Augustus Hare's prediction that she would be the ruin of Landor was to prove correct. She had 'protected' a girl of sixteen, called Geraldine Hooper, whom she alleged was ill-treated by her parents and whom she introduced to Landor, who was to shower gifts upon her. He went so far as to sell sixty-five of his best paintings, the proceeds from which he undoubtedly intended to give her. The matter took on a dramatic and serious nature when Mrs Yescombe arrived at Landor's to get two of his poems which she had set to music by a local music publisher. It was estimated that the cost would be some £17 or £18 to publish them. Landor did not demur and paid the publisher. A little later Geraldine Hooper returned to him alone and told him that he had underpaid the publisher, who was demanding a further £8. Landor was suspicious and assumed that it was Mrs Yescombe who really wanted the money and had sent this 'innocent' young girl to collect it. There had been previous rumours of Mrs Yescombe's petty pilfering. Subsequently Geraldine was told to ask Landor to return a locket she had given him, as well as an album of his

[1] Elwin, *Landor*, p. 418.

*verses which he had previously presented to her and borrowed back.
Whereupon, Landor wrote the girl's mother, returning the locket but
revealing at the same time the stories of ill-treatment to which the girl
had been subjected according to Mrs Yescombe. As a result, the girl
was sent away by Mrs Hooper to her uncle in Cheltenham. It later
became known that Geraldine had run up debts all over the town and
the father had been forced to disclaim them.*

*Landor, on receiving anonymous letters, was soon became caught up
in his usual impetuous anger and rushed into print with a pamphlet*
Walter Savage Landor and the Honourable Mrs Yescombe. *There
were no delays in printing this highly controversial document. Of
course, the Yescombe's consulted their solicitor, who informed Landor
that if he would retract and apologise, they would not go to court. But
Landor replied with yet another pamphlet,* Mr Landor Threatened,
*and this led to the case being brought before the Courts in August.
Luckily, Forster arrived in Bath in July and apparently heard of the
mischief for the first time. He insisted that Landor should sign a
retraction. Forster recorded:*

> '*I quitted the place with a sorrowful misgiving that the last illness of
> the old man, while it had left him subject to the same transitory
> storms of frantic passion, had permanently also weakened him,
> mentally yet more than bodily; and that, even when anger was no
> longer present to overcloud his intellect, there had ceased to be
> really available to his use such a faculty of discrimination between
> right and wrong, or such a saving consciousness of evil from good, as
> is necessary to constitute a responsible human being. He had not now
> even memory enough to recollect what he was writing from day to
> day: and while the power of giving keen and clear expression to
> every passing mood of bitterness remained to him, his reason had too
> far deserted him to leave it other than a fatal gift. He could apply
> no gauge or measure to what he was bent on either doing or saying;
> he seemed no longer to have the ability to see anything not palpably
> before him; and of the effect of any given thing on his own or
> another's reputation, he was become wholly powerless to judge.*'[1]

*Withal, Landor made a sane enough Will on 22 May, appointing his
brother Henry as executor. The amounts he had to leave were pathetically small but he remembered everybody except his wife.*

[1] Forster, *Landor*, vol. ii, p. 549.

Landor was now occupied in rounding up unpublished poems for a book which he finally decided to call Dry Sticks, Fagoted by Walter Savage Landor. *Published in 1858, it was a volume which met with Forster's strong disapproval:*

> 'He grieved to do anything in the teeth of my advice, he said: but, if he did not publish the poems, others would. He had for the time persuaded himself that he had really no other motive: yet I could not but suspect that another, quite unconsciously to himself, lurked behind; and that he thought he might thus find excuse for occasional covert allusion to occurrences which the result of my interference had bound him, not indeed by express agreement on my part (as erroneously supposed at the time), but by honourable understanding on his, no longer to notice openly.'[1]

There were ugly rumours of another libel action, but in March, Landor suffered a seizure, and for a while it was thought that he would not survive. His physique, however, must have been tremendous, for he recovered.

On 14 January Felice Orsini and three associates had attempted to assassinate Louis Napoleon, on the premise that he had once been a sworn member of the Carbonari and that the penalty of breaking that oath was death. The bomb missed the mark. As some of Orsini's conspirators were English, relations between England and France became strained. 'Miserable Orsini!' wrote Landor to Forster. 'He sat with me two years ago at the table on which I am now writing. Dreadful work!'

Louis Napoleon did not meet Cavour (at Plombières) until July when it was arranged to expel the Austrians from Italy and to form an Italian Kingdom. Landor had met Louis Napoleon in 1839 at Gore House, and they apparently enjoyed each other's company, though subsequently Louis Napoleon was a suspect character to Landor. Landor had attacked Napoleon for his anti-Italian views on the revolutionaries. Landor's views on a united Italy had been very clearly expressed, especially in his letter to Emerson, 'Rise, Marini! rise Garibaldi! rise Mazzini! . . . Strike and spare not . . .' etc.[2] Two years before this incident Orsini had been Landor's guest, and when Dr Simon Bernard was arrested in England as Orsini's accomplice, a letter

[1] Forster, *Landor*, vol. ii, p. 550.
[2] See *Letter to Emerson*, p. xxx.

*of Landor's was read offering to 'help the family of a patriot who com-
mitted tyrannicide.'*[1] *Landor thereupon wrote to* The Times *on 17
March denying that he had countenanced Orsini's attempt.*

*Landor's intemperate outbursts spurred the Yescombes into action
again, and a writ for libel was served on him. Landor's solicitors,
Taylor and Williams, told him that if there was an adverse verdict it
could bankrupt him for years, and advised him that he should hand
everything over to his niece Kitty, and fly the country. On receiving this
information, Landor decided to see Forster in London. He sent him a
telegram to that effect.*

*'Some friends of mine were dining with me,' records Forster,
'among them Mr Dickens, who, on the arrival of the old man too
fatigued by his journey to be able to join the dinner-table, left the
room to see him; and from another friend, the Rev. Mr Elwin, who
was also one of the party, I received very lately a letter reminding me
of what occurred. "I thought that Landor would talk over with him
the unpleasant crisis; and I shall never forget my amazement when
Dickens came back into the room laughing, and said that he found
him very jovial, and that his whole conversation was upon the
character of Catullus, Tibullus, and other Latin poets." He crossed
to France four days later, on the morning of the 15th of July; and
I never saw him again.'*[2]

1858

Landor wrote to Lady Graves-Sawle from Boulogne on 23 July 1858:

'Dear Rose,
*'In leaving England for ever, the heaviest of my sorrows is that
I shall never see you again. I shall retain in my inmost heart the
greatful memory of your kindness and compassion. How is it possible
that I could ever forget the comfort you gave me when circumstances
made it impossible for me to remain in Italy. How often have I
listened to a voice sweeter if possible in conversing with me than in
singing at my request. Well do you remember the interest I took at
all times in your welfare. The most affectionate of an affectionate*

[1] Elwin, *Landor*, p. 428.
[2] Forster, *Landor*, vol. ii, p. 556.

*family could not more heartily rejoice in your happiness. I regret my
misfortune in the impossibility of my seeing Francis, and helping him
a little way over the horns of Latin and Greek. It might have
caused me some vexation to part with my pictures. But my legal
friends tell me that it is necessary . . . I am going to Genoa in another
fortnight. May God continue to you every earthly blessing, for you
deserve them all. Think sometimes of your faithful old friend.'*[1]

The case came up on 23 August before Baron Channell and a jury,
the Yescombes suing Landor on three counts for libel and on another
for breach of agreement. The jury found for the plaintiffs and damages
were assessed at a thousand pounds—£750 for the three libels and £250
for the breach of agreement. The press sided with the self-righteous
Yescombes; it was typical of the age. There were exceptions, however,
and one of the most important was Mrs Lynn Linton. True, she was
admirer, friend and devotee, but she was equally outspoken, and nobody
could deflect her from expressing her disapproval. She had married the
Socialist engraver, W. J. Linton, on 24 March. Alas, the marriage was
doomed to failure, and Landor had written her:

'I have been waiting very anxiously for the letter I received this
morning. Tell me, without loss of a single day, to what address I may
send the shabby trifle you at last have permitted me to offer on your
marriage. God grant it may be as happy as I believe it will be.
Everybody speaks highly of Mr Linton. If he should become as rich
as Rothschild or Lord Westminster, you must encourage him not to
desert his noble art in "three or four years". I was amused at your
expression, "He works wickedly". You believe you are original, you
are only classical. Virgil steps before you with his labor improbus.
Do not be fastidious about furniture. Oh had you seen Ipsley Court!
The chairs were Charles the Second's time—the beds about Queen
Anne's. You would have believed them made expressly for a spaniel
and her family, a favourite and fat one, unable to jump up higher
than eighteen inches. But what a width! I expect the whole furniture
of eleven or twelve rooms was sold for somewhat less than £100!
excepting one Chinese cabinet and one marble table. The mirrors may
have been large enough to reflect the whole of the face—they were
only in the bedrooms, eight or nine of them. Some had been gilt,*

---

[1] Wheeler, *Private Letters*, p. 220.

but mine was not. I confess I like really old furniture, even if it is faked. Ever your affectionate Father.'[1]

At Boulogne *Kitty* Landor handed Landor over to the care of his son *Walter*, who assured him that he would receive a welcome home, and that his daughter *Julia* would meet him in Genoa. But none of his arrangements went according to plan, and there was to be no cosy family re-union. That Landor's wife would welcome him with open arms was hardly to be expected. Indeed, Landor soon became his cantankerous self. Because Lord *Normanby* had not welcomed him as he saw fit, he wrote him with the imperiousness of a *Queen Elizabeth.*

'We are both of us old men, my Lord, and are verging on decreptitude and imbecility, else my note might be more energetic. Do not imagine I am unobservant of distinctions. For by the favor of a minister are *Marquis of Normanby*, I by the grace of God am
Walter Savage Landor.'[2]

Forster observed

'that he was irritable, difficult to manage, intemperate of tongue, subject to all kinds of suspicions, fancies, and mistakes; that even when treated most considerately he was often unjust, but when met by any kind of violence, was apt to be driven wild with rage; that, in a word, choleric as he had always been, he was now becoming very old,—is not I fear to be doubted.'[3]

Shortly before Christmas *1858* he left the villa for lodgings. Thrice during those ten months he left Fiesole; thrice he was brought back.

[1] Layard, *Life of Mrs Lynn Linton*, p. 113.
[2] Elwin, *Landor*, p. 435.
[3] Forster, *Landor*, vol. ii, p. 561.

From *Poems of 1858*

CREDO

I do believe a drop of water
May save us from the fire herea'ter.
I do believe a crumb of bread,
O'er which the priest his prayer hath said,
May be the richest flesh and blood . . .
I would believe too, if I could,
Pius's word is worth a crumb
Or drop; but here awe strikes me dumb.

LOUIS NAPOLEON

Bees on imperial mantle Louis bears,
And the same emblem thro' his court appears,
They buz about the hall, they mount the chamber,
The Empress washes them in liquid amber.
They lull the people with their humming wings,
Few taste their honey, many feel their stings.
Yet England's praise hath Louis justly won
In sheltering valiant Guyon's homeless son.

DEDICATION OF AN ANCIENT IDYL TO ROSE
Published in *Dry Sticks*, *1858*
Europa Carried Off

Friend of my age! to thee belong
The plaintive and the playful song,
And every charm unites in thee
Of wisdom, wit, and modesty;
Taught hast thou been from early youth
To tread the unswerving path of truth,
And guided to trip lightly o'er

DEDICATION OF AN ANCIENT IDYLL

The amaranth fields of ancient lore,
Turn thou not hastily aside
From her who stems the Asian tide,
For shores henceforth to bear her name ...
Thine, thine shall be a better fame;
Lands yet more distant shall it reach
Than yonder Hellespontic beach
Or where the bravest blood now flows
Before perfidious Delhi, Rose!
From boyhood have I loved old times
And loitered under warmer climes.
I never dream such dreams as there ...
Voices how sweet, and forms how fair!
The Nymphs and Graces there I find,
The Muses too, and thee behind,
All chiding thee, all asking why
Thou whom they cherish art so shy;
They will not listen when I say,
Thou hast some dearer ones than they.
'Ungrateful!' cry they, 'can it be?
We have no dearer one than she.'

THE ANCIENT IDYL
Europa and her Mother

MOTHER. Daughter! why roamest thou again so late
Along the damp and solitary shore?
EUROPA. I know not. I am tired of distaf, woof,
Everything.
MOTHER.   Yet thou culledst flowers all morn,
And idledst in the woods, mocking shrill birds,
Or clapping hands at limping hares, who stampt
Angrily, and scour'd off.
EUROPE.   I am grown tired
Of hares and birds. O mother! had you seen
That lovely creature! It was not a cow,
And, if it was an ox,[1] it was unlike

---

[1] Bulls are never at large in those countries; Europa could not have seen one. W.S.L.

373

My father's oxen with the hair rubb'd off
Their necks.
    MOTHER.   A cow it was.
    EUROPA.   Cow it might be . . .
And yet . . . and yet . . . I saw no calf, no font
Of milk: I wish I had; how pleasant 'twere
To draw it and to drink!
    MOTHER.   Europa! child!
Have we no maiden for such offices?
No whistling boy? Kings' daughters may cull flowers,
To place them on the altar of the Gods
And wear them at their festivals. Who knows
But some one of these very Gods may deign
To wooe thee? maidens they have wooed less fair.
    EUROPA. The Gods are very gracious: some of them
Not very constant.
    MOTHER.   Hugh!
    EUROPA.   Nay, Zeus himself
Hath wandered, and deluded more than one.

1859

Landor would not allow the Yescombe affair to die, and he wrote to Mrs Lynn Linton to know whether she could induce her husband to undertake the publication of a pamphlet of his Defence.[1] *He may well have conveniently forgotten that both she and Forster had gone down on their knees to him not to publish anything further about the case 'or speak on the matter to anybody, lest he was led into doing so by some indiscreet tatlers, who knew both parties and doubtless carried sayings of one to the other.'[2] But on this matter neither the Republican Linton nor his wife would handle this 'free-hand' material, which he wanted advertised with the following sentence appended: 'I know not whether the husband infected the wife, or the wife the husband, with the virulent and incurable postules of mendacity, or whether the distemper is in the blood of both, breaking out in all quarters and at all seasons.'*

Landor then approached G. J. Holyoake, a Chartist, and disciple of Robert Owen. Wrote Holyoake:[3]

> 'I had Landor's manuscript copied in my own house, so that no printer should by chance see the original manuscript in the office. My brother Austen, whom in all these things I could trust as I could trust myself, set up and printed with his own hands Landor's defence, so that none save he and I ever saw the pamphlet until the post delivered copies at their destination. A reward of £200 was offered for the discovery of the printer without result. Twelve years later, Landor being dead, I told Lord Houghton I was the printer of his "defence" but until this day I have mentioned it to no one else.'

It was the Yescombes who had offered a reward of £200 but, as Holyoake records, they were unable to discover the printer. So they instituted proceedings to set aside the deed transferring Landor's annuity, and the Court of Chancery granted an injunction against payment of rents from the estate until the damages and costs were paid. When Landor heard this he tried to stab himself.[4]

---

[1] *Mr Landor's Remarks on a Suit preferred against him at the Summer Assizes, in Taunton 1858, illustrating the Appendix to his Hellenics.*

[2] Layard, *Life of Mrs Lynn Linton*, p. 116.

[3] Holyoake, *Sixty Years of an Agitator's Life*, 1892, vol. ii.

[4] Elwin, *Landor*, p. 437.

In July, Landor left Fiesole, having had further rows with his family. By good fortune, he met Robert Browning, then living at Casa Guidi, who gave him shelter. Mrs Landor handed over a few personal things after having received a letter from Browning to do so.

Landor did not wish to become an encumbrance to Browning, and remembering that the American sculptor William Wetmore Story had stayed with him in Bath, he wrote him telling him he would like to see him. Story and his wife then asked Landor to stay with them at Siena. Browning took Landor to the Storys, who 'felt as if he were really Lear come back again'. There Landor was happy, and the Storys too enjoyed his stay. Meantime the Brownings moved to Siena, and on 6 August Landor took a cottage near the Browning's villa. He wrote to Forster,

> *'You will have heard that I am now in a cottage near Siena, which I owe to Browning, the kind friend who found it for me, whom I had seen only three or four times in my life. Yet who made me the voluntary offer of what money I wanted, and who insists on my managing my affairs here, and paying for my lodgings and sustenance. Never was such generosity and such solicitude as this incomparable man has shown on my behalf.'[1]*

Forster records that from then on until the day of Landor's death, he handed over to Browning two hundred pounds every year by quarterly payments, to which an additional sum of fifty pounds was held always in reserve for special wants.

Landor's last home was in Florence: No 2671 Via Nunziatina where he had a suite of rooms on the first floor. In this year, 1859, a new edition of his Hellenics *was published which was dedicated to his old friend Sir William Napier who died in February 1860. When it appeared it was edited in a slovenly manner, and Landor angrily blamed Forster for delays and carelessness. On 29 November, Landor, always fighting for the unification of Italy, wrote* The Times *his letter on 'Garibaldi and the Italians', and, the following month, on 'The State of Italy'.*

1860–64

Again Landor seemed to be in full possession of his wits. He began the New Year of 1860 by writing to Eliza Lynn Linton, whose marriage

[1] Forster, *Landor*, vol. ii, p. 562.

had failed utterly. She who ought to have found a 'Robert Browning'
was to find that her artist-husband was a dedicated republican unable
to continue to live in a well-conducted household. He cared not whether
his children ran wild and uncontrolled and he had no time for the
society of friends which his wife enjoyed, with the result that his wife's
income dwindled fast. This rather Christ-like figure soon disillusioned
the once dashing and by no means unattractive, gay and highly
intellectual Eliza.

Landor, whom she greatly missed, wrote her from his new address in
Florence:

'*My dear daughter. A Sunday can never be more properly employed*
than on on expression of thanks for a kind action. Three days have
nearly elapsed since I received your letter and yesterday I was
devising the means of paying you for the photographs, though your
delicacy would not allow you to tell me what they cost. I must not
lose a single hour in putting the money in the hands of a correspondent
of him whose shop I have dealings for wine and chocolate, one
Townley, desiring him to be expeditious. I intend to send two fine
pictures, a Salvator and a Bronzino, for sale in London. Philips
I hear, is the best auctioneer for this purpose. Tell me where his
residence is. Many good judges have thought the one which is
attributed to Bronzini is really by Michael Angelo. It represents the
Last Judgement—it is six feet long and four high. It was a present
from Cardinal Pacca to Bishop Baynes. The condition is perfect.
I think there is scarcely a finer picture in existence. I think I will
also add a picture of Carracci representing Christ and St Peter on
the coast of Galilee. This has no frame. It was in a very fine one,
sold to a dealer from Leghorn and sent by him to England. It is
as long as the above but not so high by a foot. Its value is much less.
Our winter here has been more foggy and frosty than any one I
remember in Bath during the twenty-five years I spent there.
Yesterday the rain ran in torrents.

'*I know not what money the pictures will produce. Whatever it*
may be, you shall have one half of it. This you must not hesitate to
accept, because it may serve to buy a few books and playthings for
the children.

'*Do not tire yourself by writing a long letter for this tedious one*
of mine. Ever your affectionate father, with kind regards to your

*husband and children. Tell the auctioneers to place all the money in
your hands. You may send me my share.'*[1]

*In June 1860 he told her he was reading Shakespeare's plays for the
third time, but that for his other works twice was sufficient. Later he
announced to her that he had finished his 'last' work. Everything he
had written had been his 'last work'. He 'would never write a line again,'
he said.* But he was busily adding to his 'Imaginary Conversations' with
Savonarola and the Prior of San Marco, *the proceeds from the sale of
which were to be given to the relief of Garibaldi's soldiers. It is a matter
of astonishment to think how little Landor had schooled himself to live
on after his worldly finances had disappeared. It is true he looked like
a tramp and he ate little, and he certainly never drank much.
In July he wrote Eliza Lynn Linton:*

'. . . *Thanks and thanks again for the capital work which contains
my letters to Kossuth and Garibaldi. I hope this vigorous publication
will enjoy the long life it promises. Am I mistaken in my suspicion
that I trace my own dear daughter's hand in it? The article which
relates to the genius and powers of women is hardly fair. You know
my estimate of your writings, and not only for their purity of style
but for their vigorous intellect.*[2] *What does the author think of
Madame de Staël and Mrs Stowe? The last book I have been
reading I have read a second time; it is* The Minister's Wooing.[3]
*It should have left off at the marriage of the young lovers, but no
man alive has given the world a novel so excellent. It is generally
thought that the ancients were less complimentary to women of
genius than the moderns. The poetry of Sappho and some others was
extolled by them. The two odes of the tawny Lesbian are quoted by
Longinus and admirably translated, "Blest as the immortal gods
is he", etc. Mrs Hemans has written much better poetry, and more
kinds than one, but especially in her "Casa Bianca" [sic] and
"Ivan".*[4] *I doubt whether any short pieces in one language are*

[1] Layard, *Life of Mrs Lynn Linton*, p. 119.
[2] Up to that time Mrs Lynn Linton had only published her first novel *Azeth,
the Egyptian* (1846), *Amymone* (1848), which Landor had praised, and *Realities*
(1851). All her major work was yet to come.
[3] By Mrs Stowe (1859).
[4] Modern criticism mostly praises *The Forest Sanctuary* (1826) otherwise her
poetry has been forgotten.

*comparable to these, excepting Campbell's "Hohenlinden" and
"Battle of the Baltic."*[1]

'*Some years ago I turned over the whole of Brunck's Greek
Anthologia and was vext at finding so little of thought or imagination.
I refreshed myself by a draught of the Anapos, and roving with
Theocritus among the fresh flowers of Enna. The Greeks never
overload, but too often drive dull oxen yoked to an empty crate.
Anacreon has composed one exquisite song fairly worth all the
Anthologia.
'The rest are mostly inferior. An older man than old Anacreon
may be expected to write worse; on the other side I will give you a
proof, with my blessing to all you love.*'[2]

*Life took on a new interest when Story gave him a dog which he
named Giallo. It became as great favourite as Pomero, and soon
Landor became known to the Florentines as* il vecchio con quel bel
canino. *He too, out of the slender pittance he had, was buying bad
pictures.*

*With no Eliza Lynn to understand and help him, and having
quarrelled now with Forster over the delay of the new edition of his
Hellenics, Landor met Kate Field, Anthony Trollope's great friend,
for in October Trollope had arrived in Italy.*

*Kate Field at this time was a girl of twenty, the daughter of Joseph
M. Field, an actor, of some importance, and a friend of Edgar Allan Poe.*

'*A precocious child, she grew into a schoolgirl of unusual intelligence.
Provoking a somewhat overheated affection from a younger sister
of her mother's, who had married a rich man and lived in Boston,
Kate was introduced during her impressionable 'teens into the
literary and artistic society that her adoring aunt collected round her.
That from such beginnings she should have developed first into a
Schwärmerin for all the arts, then into a blue-stocking, and
finally into a champion of woman's rights, was well-nigh inevitable.
Her achievement lay in the retention—despite her somewhat grim
preoccupations—of an allurement and freshness which impressed
all and enslaved not a few of those who made her acquaintance.*'[3]

---

[1] Thomas Campbell (1777–1844). Such sentiments are not nearly as 'far-fetched'
as those appertaining to Dorothea Hemans.
[2] Layard, *Life of Mrs Lynn Linton*, p. 120.
[3] Sadleir, *Trollope, A Commentary*, p. 219.

LANDOR

Kate Field had left the United States in January 1859 to study music and art in Rome and Florence, and she was much fêted by the Brownings whom she met just in time, for Elizabeth died on 29 June 1861, and Browning departed for England that August.

Kate Field leaves us a vivid picture of Landor: he was almost toothless, partially deaf, and his appearance much changed from the drawing made by William Wetmore Story in Siena in July 1859, when he was still clean-shaven. Now he wore a snow-white beard, which made him look like a lion. And he could on occasions behave like one, with Garibaldi as his hero.

Landor's eldest son continued to behave with studied insolence and meanness. Withal, during that year Landor published in The Athenaeum on 2 March 1861 an article relating to the Pope's temporal power and the occupation of Rome by French troops. The following week that paper published an 'Imaginary Conversation' between Virgil and Horace on the Road to Brundusium with Augustus and Mecaenas. On 20 April there appeared 'Fashions in Spelling,' and a long 'Imaginary Conversation' between Milton and Marvel; and on 12 October another between Machiavelli and Guicciardini.

On 30 July Landor had written to Browning:

'As you leave Florence tomorrow or the next day, it is improbable that we shall ever meet again. You correspond occasionally with my brother Henry and Mr Forster. You will add greatly to your many acts of kindness if you will desire Mr Forster, to whom I gave at his request all the letters of many years addrest to me, that he will take the trouble to look among them for one from my son Arnold. There are few from him; but this one contains a promise to pay, after his mother's death, to his brothers and sisters an annuity of £150 each, being about two-thirds of her jointure. He now refuses to do it, altho' I gave him everything. And could have disposed of nearly £40,000. £150 a year is quite as much as they can ever want, in addition to what they have.

'My daughter has already more than she deserves. If I could venture to ask my brother to take any more trouble about my affairs, it would be that he write a line of remonstrance to Arnold on his ingratitude and dishonesty. Mr Forster, I trust, will consign to you his letter, by which his brothers may legally claim the £150 *annuity—I remain, ever Sincerely Yours, W. S. Landor.'*[1]

Browning settled at St Enogat near Dinard, and here Landor again wrote to him:

'The second time I visited France, I travelled alone thro' Brittany, leaving my carriage at St Malo, and passing from St Servan to Dinan. In the passage-boat up the beautiful little river I found the sisters of Chateaubriand.

'Dinan, Rennes and Tours are the three places I would rather reside in than any on the north of the Alps.

'It gives me pleasure to feel sure that Robert enjoys his country rides. I rode thro' a great part of Brittany, and grieved at the devastation made both by republicans and Chouans. I hope to see you here again before I make my last expedition—that upon men's shoulders. Ever affectionately yours. W. S. Landor.'[2]

Landor had always wanted to be buried at Widcombe and had made arrangements with the authorities. In November he had written Browning to this effect. His friend Sandford, who was living at Bath, paid the bill of ten pounds five shillings for digging and bricking the grave, and for four months Landor worried over the means of repayment.[3] *On 23 November 1861 he wrote to Browning:*

'Your letter, like all your letters, is considerate and kind. Assure my brother that I will do nothing at any time contrary to his wishes. What I wrote him about the avoidance of expense to him was suggested by what I conceived to be a sense of duty to him. At no time have I for a moment felt an inclination to remove from my present quarters, being perfectly content with wife and husband equally.[4] Whatever I have expended beyond the necessaries of life, since the eight pounds two years ago for the repurchase of those pictures which my son Arnold sold, came out of ten pounds sent to me by the Editor of The Examiner, who made a visit last week. In regard to clothes it is now about four years since I have spent beyond twenty-four shillings, and not five shillings more will ever be required.

[1] Minchin, H. C., *Last Days, Letters & Conversations*, 1934, pp. 132–3.
[2] Minchin, *Last Days, Letters & Conversations*, 1934, pp. 134–5.
[3] Elwin, *Landor*, p. 450.
[4] The Brownings' former maid, Wilson, who had married an Italian Romagnoli.

'I am suffering from rheumatism and sciatica and am unable to mount a carriage even with help. My grave is being made at Widcombe, where the good clergyman, now leaving the place, reserved a place I pointed out fixt upon sixty years ago by a lady who loved me to her last hour. Tears spring out at the memory of her,[1] so adieu.—Ever most affectionately yours W. S. Landor.'[2]

Undaunted, Landor continued to write a new book which he called Sweepings from Under the Study Table. *It was not, however, published until 1863, when it was brought out by T. C. Newby of 30 Welbeck Street, Cavendish Square, London. Newby was mainly a publisher of fiction and was completely unsuited for such a book. It is amazing, at this late date, with the reputation Landor possessed, that he was still forced to rely on small publishers, and that not one of the great established houses would have been proud to have added his name to their list for prestige despite small sales. Furthermore, Landor never asked for large sums of money. He made and received mere pittances. This, his last book, was an astonishing compilation. It ran to no less than 348 pages and contained a tremendous variety of verse, both serious and gay, as well as a collection of poems in Latin. Of course, Newby failed to sell the work properly, and it was remaindered, though it was later reissued by another firm of publishers called Morgan and Hebron.[3] Landor also wrote his last letter to* The Times *upon The Kingdom of Italy; a second 'Imaginary Conversation' between Milton and Marvel, and an Epitaph to be placed on the grave of G. P. R. James, who had died in 1860 and was buried in Venice.*

In January 1862 he had written to Browning about his grave in Widcombe churchyard, of his painful cough which prevented him sleeping at nights, and of the sciatica which 'so affected me that I find it painful to bend over my writing-table.' He added that he had been confined to his room for nearly three months.

He still received visitors. One of them was Seymour Kirkup, the American painter who had arrived in Florence in 1816 and lived in that

---

[1] 'Ianthé', Sophia Jane Swift, later Countess de Molandé, who had died at Versailles in 1851. Landor had written at that time to Forster that he hoped she would have seen his grave.

[2] Minchin, *Last Days, Letters & Conversations*, 1934, pp. 138-9.

[3] *See* Wise and Wheeler, *Bibliography of Landor*, p. 194.

city till he died aged ninety-two; others were the Countess Baldelli and her two little daughters. He also continued to write regularly to Browning about his grave, asking him to pay ten pounds to his brother Henry. He gave away, one by one, his pictures and belongings before death overtook him and his sons seized everything.

Affairs in Italy gave him cause to worry, for in August Garibaldi was defeated and captured at Aspromonte by the Sardinian forces. Victor Emmanuel was soon to be King of a United Italy. By the end of the year he was writing to Browning:

'*It grieves me to hear that my good brother Henry is so afflicted. He is eight or nine years younger than me, and he has had no such calamities as I have. His eyesight, I fear, is irrecoverable. My son Walter has been repaid by some pictures for the ten pounds he advanced for my grave. Your letter has induced me to rest my bones in Florence, where my two sons, Walter and Charles, will defray the expense of my funeral. I shall leave pretty nearly things enough to repay them, for my express orders are that only the small common stone covers my body, with this inscription—*

Walter Savage Landor
born January 30, 1775
died   1862

My imprudent will must be burnt. My school-books and a few others I leave to your Robert. My sons know this . . .'

Landor wrote his last letter to Rose Graves-Sawle on her birthday, 19 January 1863, and in the spring he was cheered by the arrival in Florence of Edward Twistleton, the brother of Lord Saye and Sele, and a friend of Browning's. He took back to England the corrected proof of Heroic Idyls, *and persuaded Landor to forget his quarrel with Forster.*

'*He found me, I will not say on my last legs, but really and truly on no legs at all. These last three days I have been extremely ill, totally deaf and almost insensible during two of them, half-deaf and just alive the third. But Mr Twisleton has tolerated my half-deafness, and has nearly cured the other half. How refreshing it is to find a well-bred man anywhere! And what rare good sense Mr Twisleton adds to good humour and fine scholarship!*'[1]

[1] Forster, *Landor*, vol. ii, p. 526.

LANDOR

On *14 December Landor broke the ice and wrote to Forster that someone was attempting to write his biography. This greatly upset him.*

In March 1864 young Algernon Swinburne called on him. Landor did not take to him and suspected he might have been the aspirant biographer, but

> 'Back at his hotel, Swinburne wrote a line of apology and explanation. . . . expressing (as far as was expressible) "my immense admiration and reverence in the plainest and sincerest way I could manage", and received in reply an invitation to come again. This time he found Landor "as alert, brilliant, and altogether delicious as I suppose others may have found him twenty years since."'[1]

On May Day (1864) he rang for Mrs Romagnoli at two in the morning, asking for windows to be thrown open, and for pen, ink, paper and the date. Having written a few lines of verse, he leaned back and said, 'I shall never write again. Put out the lights and draw the curtains.' Then he died.

He was buried in the English cemetery at Florence. His two sons were the only mourners. Thus passed one of the great men of letters of English literature after a long life of harassment, muddle, and many grievous mistakes. Unlike so many contemporaries he received no honours. His works were little read. And even now he has few of the readers he deserves, save for a small circle who honour his name as one of the brightest stars in the firmament of English literature.

[1] Elwin, *Landor*, p. 457.

Joan of Arc and her Judge
Published posthumously in *Letters, &c.,* 1897

JUDGE. After due hearing in our court supreme
Of temporal and spiritual lords,
Condemn'd art thou to perish at the stake
By fire, forerunner of the flames below.
Hearest thou? Art thou stunn'd? Art thou gone mad?
Witch! think not to escape and fly away,
As some the like of thee, 'tis said, have done.
   JOAN. The fire will aid my spirit to escape.
   JUDGE. Listen, ye lords. Her spirit! Hear ye that?
She owns, then, to have her Familiar.
And whither (*to* JOAN)—whither would the spirit, witch,
Bear thee?
   JOAN. To Him who gave it.
   JUDGE.   Lucifer?
   JOAN. I never heard the name until thus taught.
   JUDGE. He hath his imps.
   JOAN.   I see he hath.
   JUDGE.   My lords!
Why look ye round, and upward at the rafters?
Smile not, infernal hag! for such thou art,
Altho' made comely to beguile the weak,
By thy enchantments and accursed spells.
Knowest thou not how many brave men fell
Under thy sword, and daily?
   JOAN.   God knows best
How many fell—may their souls rest in peace!
We wanted not your land, why want ye ours?
France is our country, England yours; we hear
Her fields are fruitful: so were ours before
Invaders came and burnt our yellowing corn,
And slew the labouring oxen in the yoke,
And worried, in their pasture and their fold,
With thankless hounds, more sheep than were devour'd.

JUDGE. Thou wast a shepherdess. Were those sheep thine?
JOAN. Whatever is my country's is mine too—
At least to watch and guard; I claim no more.
Ye drove the flocks adrift, and we the wolves.
JUDGE. Thou shouldst have kept thy station in the field,
As ours do.
JOAN.   Nobles! have I not? Speak out.
In the field, too—the field ye shared with me—
The cause alone divided us.
JUDGE.   My lords!
Must we hear this from peasant girl, a witch?
Wolves we are call'd. (*To* JOAN). Do wolves, then, fight for glory?
JOAN. No; not so wicked, tho' by nature wild,
They seek their foods, and, finding it, they rest.
JUDGE. Sometimes the devil prompts to speak a truth
To cover lies, and to protect his brood.
But, *we* turn'd into wolves!—*we* Englishmen!
Tell us, thou knowing one, who knowest well—
Tell us, then, who are now the vanquishers.
JOAN. They who will be the vanquished, and right soon.
JUDGE. False prophets there have been, and thou art one,
And proud as he that sent thee here inspired.
Who ever saw thee bend before the high
And mighty men, the consecrate around—
They whom our Lord exalted, they who wear
The mitre on their brows?
JOAN.   One—one alone—
Hath seen me bend, and may he soon more nigh,
Unworthy as I am! I daily fall
Before the Man (for Man he would be call'd)
Who wore no mitre, but a crown of thorns
Wore he; upon his hands no jewel'd ring,
But in the centre of them iron nails,
Half-hidden by the swollen flesh they pierced.
JUDGE. Alert to play the pious here at last,
Thou scoffest Mother Church in these her sons,
Right reverend, worshipful, Beatitude's
Creation, Christ's and Peter's lawful heirs.
JOAN. *My* mother Church enforced no sacrifice

Of human blood; she never made flames drink it
Ere it boil over. Dear were all *her* sons,
Nor unforgiven were the most perverse.
    JUDGE. Seest thou not here thy hearers sit aghast?
    JOAN. Fear me not, nobles! Ye were never wan
In battle; ye were brave to meet the brave.
I come not now in helm or coat of mail,
But bound with cords, and helpless. God incline
Your hearts to worthier service!
    JUDGE.   Darest thou,
After such outrages on knight and baron,
To call on God, or name his holy name?
'Tis mockery.
    JOAN.   'Tis too often, not with me.
When first I heard his holy name I thought
He was my Father. I was taught to call
My Saviour so, and both my parents did
The like, at rising and at setting sun
And when they shared the oaten cake at noon.
    JUDGE. So thou wouldst babble like an infant still?
    JOAN. I would be silent, but ye bade me speak.
    JUDGE. Thou mayst yet pray—one hour is left for prayer.
Edify, then, the people in the street.
    JOAN. I never pray in crowds; our Saviour hears
When the heart speaks to him in solitude.
May we not imitate our blessed Lord,
Who went into the wilderness to pray?
    JUDGE. Who taught thee tales like this? They are forbidden.
Hast thou no supplication to the court?
    JOAN. I never sued in vain, and will not now.
    JUDGE. We have been patient; we have heard thee prate
A whole hour by the bell; we have endured
Impiety; we have borne worse affronts.
My lords, ye have been bantered long enough.
The sorceress would have turned us into wolves,
And hunt us down; she would be prophetess.
    JOAN. I am no sorceress, no prophetess;
But this, O man in ermine, I foretell:
Thou and those round thee shall ere long receive

Your due reward. England shall rue the day
She entered France—her empire totters.
                                    Pile,
Ye sentinels, who guard those hundred heads
Against a shepherdess in bonds—pile high
The faggots round the stake that stands upright,
And roll the barrel gently down the street,
Lest the pitch burst the hoops, and mess the way.
                              (*To the court.*)
Ye grant one hour; it shall be well employed.
I will implore the pardon of our God
For you. Already hath He heard my prayer
For the deliverers of their native land.

INDEX

INDEX

INDEX

INDEX